D0926823

Indexed in

E G L I 1992

This set of essays is concerned with the explanation of large-scale social change. Concentration is on the social stagnation characteristic of agrarian circumstances, the conditions for exit from that world and the varied social orders that inhabit, sometimes precariously, the modern world community. The distinguished contributors, from archaeology, anthropology, sociology, economic history and philosophy, have all been stimulated by the work of Ernest Gellner, and the essays are in dialogue with his view of our social condition.

# TRANSITION TO MODERNITY

# TRANSITION
# TO MODERNITY

*Essays on power, wealth and belief*

EDITED BY

## JOHN A. HALL

*McGill University*

AND

## I.C. JARVIE

*York University, Toronto*

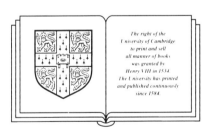

CAMBRIDGE UNIVERSITY PRESS

*Cambridge*
*New York   Port Chester*
*Melbourne   Sydney*

Published by the Press Syndicate of the University of Cambridge
The Pitt Building, Trumpington Street, Cambridge CB2 1RP
40 West 20th Street, New York, NY 10011–4211, USA
10 Stamford Road, Oakleigh, Victoria 3166, Australia

© Cambridge University Press 1992

First published 1992

Printed in Great Britain at the University Press, Cambridge

*A catalogue record for this book is available from the British Library*

*Library of Congress cataloguing in publication data*

Transition to Modernity / edited by
John A. Hall and I.C. Jarvie
p.   cm.
Includes indexes.
ISBN 0-521-38202-5 (hardback)
1. Social change. 2. Gellner, Ernest. I. Gellner, Ernest. II. Hall, John A., 1949–   .
III. Jarvie, I. C. (Ian Charles), 1937–   .
HM101.P658   1992
303.4—dc20
90-28305 CIP

ISBN 0 521 382025 hardback

GO

*For*
*Ernest Gellner*

# Contents

PART III MODERNITY AND ITS DISCONTENTS

# Illustrations

# List of contributors

JOSEPH AGASSI is Professor of Philosophy at Tel Aviv University and York University, Toronto

PERRY ANDERSON is Professor of History at the University of California, Berkeley

RONALD DORE is Professor of Sociology at the Massachusetts Institute of Technology

LOUIS DUMONT is Professor of Anthropology at the Ecole des Hautes Etudes en Sciences Sociales

JOHN DUNN is Professor of Political Theory at the University of Cambridge

JOHN A. HALL is Professor of Sociology at McGill University

I.C. JARVIE is Professor of Philosophy at York University, Toronto

A.M. KHAZANOV is Professor of Anthropology at the University of Wisconsin, Madison

ALAN MACFARLANE is a Fellow of King's College, Cambridge

MICHAEL MANN is Professor of Sociology at the University of California, Los Angeles

JOSE MERQUIOR, who died in 1991, was the Brazilian Ambassador to UNESCO

SIR KARL POPPER retired as Professor of Logic and Scientific Method, University of London, in 1972

GERARD RADNITZKY is University Professor Emeritus of Social Theory at the University of Trier

COLIN RENFREW is Disney Professor of Archaeology at the University of Cambridge

JOHN WATKINS retired as Professor of Philosophy, University of London, in 1989

E.A. WRIGLEY is a Senior Research Fellow of All Souls College, Oxford

# Introduction

> Power, belief, wealth: the questions about human society
> are clustered around these notions. They concern the
> manner in which a society controls its members; the
> manner in which it forms their thought, and in which their
> thinking sustains it; and the manner in which it keeps alive
> and uses its resources.

These are the opening sentences of Ernest Gellner's most technical and least known book: *Saints of the Atlas* (1969), his anthropological fieldwork report on the Berbers of the High Atlas. The tripartite division of the questions about society into those concerning power, belief and wealth correspond to the fields covered in PPE, the degree subject which Gellner read at Oxford. Yet his approach to all three notions is encapsulated in this short epigraph. It is to be noted that he puts the stress on *society*, not on cultures or individuals; that he writes of *ideas formed by society* rather than vice versa; and that he implies that *resources belong to a society*. He thus shows himself favourable to a sociological as opposed to a cultural or psychological approach to social phenomena; to an anti-idealist view in philosophy; and he envisions resources being deployed by societies rather than markets, classes or individuals.

Gellner's immense range is usually taken as simple diversity, forays into separate realms united only by his interest in them. A more demanding yet more fruitful way to comprehend his range is to see it as a single line of thought that unites problems and ideas around which the academy has put artificial disciplinary boundaries.

The grand and ambitious scale of Gellner's thought was not perhaps apparent at the beginning. His first published article, 'Maxims', appeared in the philosophical journal *Mind* in 1951. His most recent book at this writing, *Plough, Sword and Book* (1988) attempts to give an overall explanation of the entire sweep of human history. How did a trained analytical philosopher come to be a theorist of society and of history? The usual view treats the fact that Gellner has contributed to all the 'fields' he had studied for PPE as a personal quirk. Such a view is congenial to fellow academics, to whom the parallel structure of hermetic departments is a natural feature of their world. Those who dabble in several fields are oddities, no more. A less superficial view seeks the unity of Gellner's thought as it has evolved from within analytical ordinary language philosophy out towards an overall view of the history of mankind.

As a young philosopher fresh out of Oxford, Gellner voiced various doubts from within about analytic ordinary language philosophy in his articles of the nineteen fifties and in his best-selling book *Words and Things* (1959). With hindsight we see clearly that he was intrigued by what he has taught us to think of as the sociological aspects of Wittgenstein's views of language in general and concepts in particular, but that he was simultaneously repelled by the linguistic idealism that engulfed it and the failure of its adherents to attend to empirical research of any sort. In the notorious final chapter of the book, he asked whether there was significance to the fact that ordinary language philosophy was invented and perpetuated by a professoriate lacking scientific and mathematical education, and operating in a tutorial teaching system that placed a premium on verbal fluency and rhetorical skill. This was reflexive, since the question was Wittgensteinian, based as it is on the thesis, Wittgensteinian par excellence, that meaning is grounded in forms of life. Nevertheless, his asking the question enraged the Wittgensteinian professional philosophers just because it took seriously and applied to them the very idea that they were proposing: observation of social institutions and their daily practices are part of daily verbal practices. Given that these philosophers were engaged in verbal practices of sorts, he offered explanations for their verbal conduct, indeed for the rise of a philosophical school and its influence. They were enraged not only because they were given their own medicine and dissected with their own scalpel: they viewed language as ordinary when put to ordinary use, but they took their own use as rather extraordinary, as therapeutic, as bringing concepts back to where they belong. But where does the concept of bringing back belong to? And where do concepts belong to, and where do they all come from? His critique of ordinary language analytic philosophy was that in its systematic oversight of these questions its social ambience became not a real society inhabited by real people but a society of concepts, an idealistic ambience.

At the time of *Words and Things* Gellner was teaching in that hive of the social sciences the London School of Economics, a circumstance that may well have been fortuitous. The criticism of linguistic idealism which he pressed home owed much to Marx, Durkheim and Weber, who are usually taken as founding fathers of the social sciences. But Gellner showed in diverse studies that their interests were philosophical: it was their following the argument wherever it led that drew them into social theory. All of this did not receive the attention it deserved. It was easier, at a time when the social sciences had a very poor standing in the British academic hierarchy, to treat his arguments as *ad hominem*; that hierarchy was indignant over the corollary to his view, that he characterised established philosophers, if not the whole of the philosophical establishment, as disingenuous.

The sociology of intellectuals, why and how they thought as they did, has continued to preoccupy Gellner throughout his career. *Words and Things* and many subsequent essays offered his views of academic philosophers in Britain and America as a professional guild. Other groups of intellectuals that Gellner has written about include social scientists, especially anthropologists; the Soviet and East European intelligentsias, especially the social scientists among them; psychoanalysts and other psychologists. His works on Islam belong to this genre also: he has constantly focused on the interplay between strands of thought in Islam and the way they upset and alter social organisation. He has also made a special study of nationalism, which is a preoccupation of both intellectuals and ordinary citizens in the modern era, and he managed to characterise it in an intellectual manner that reflects a social situation. In order to be effective the ideas of nationalism had to be comprehensible by intellectual and simpleton alike. Indeed, Gellner's theory of nationalism could be described as the quest, socio-economically based, for a common intellectual denominator.

The sociology of intellectuals, is, however, sociology. Gellner began as a philosopher; the search for an underlying problem in his work might better zero in on a philosophical one. The dispute between realists and idealists is perhaps what underlies Gellner's interest in the sociology of intellectuals. Around what problem does this dispute centre? That is not easy to specify. Crudely, the problem can be put as, which comes first, human thought about the world or the material world? Put like that, today's common sense (of the scientific and industrial modern world) would see no contest: the material world came first. But let us replace the material world with the social. Do we think about how we want society to be and then alter it, or are we, as products of society, already thinking in terms and categories that derive from society? Common sense lends itself to no easy dismissal of this problem. In Marxist idiom this becomes the question, what are the determinations of consciousness?, in Gellner's own idiom these are the issues of *Thought and Change* (1964) and *Legitimation of Belief* (1975).

Where does Gellner stand on the issue? As an Enlightenment thinker he is plainly attracted to materialism rather than idealism. But he does not think society can be wholly reduced to or explained by material factors. Thought plays a role. What role? The answer is a three-part one. First there was the pre-modern world; second there was a transition; third there is the modern world. Gellner thinks that for much of human life on earth social organisation was prior to and dominant over thought. Then things changed and the scientific revolution became possible. After the scientific revolution, and within its parameters, some thought managed to transcend its social determinations and take on an independent power to shape the world. Gellner has put this rather vividly in his image of there being a Big Ditch between the modern world and its precursor. The aspect of the Ditch that interests him is the nature of the thought-systems on each side, the differing relationships they have to social organisation, and the mysterious means by which mankind crossed the Ditch.

Beyond the Ditch, in our human past, there were thought systems which were highly varied. Early Gellner treated this diversity as without cognitive interest because of the pervasive error in those thought systems. Thus in that pre-modern world it was the forms of social organisation that interested him, not the ideas. More recently, especially in *Plough, Sword and Book*, he has shown much greater awareness of the importance of intellectual developments within the agrarian era. The conditions necessary for the escape from 'the cosy social cocoon of early man' are connected to the social change brought about by surplus and by literacy. The manipulation of literacy by the clerisy – scripturalist religions – and the possibility, inherent in writing, of disembodied thought, make possible the emergence of scientific thought. His view of the decisive importance of the emergence of scientific thought has remained unchanged. In scientific thought we witness the birth of a new form of power, cognitive power, a development with immense social implications. Utterly new forms of social organisation become possible, totally new demands for the improvement of life-chances are realistic. But the comfortlessness of the world as scientific thought views it ensures that it must co-exist with a re-enchantment industry, a cognitive Disneyland.

The actual world today consists of a few societies in which modern scientific thought is dominant, even if not without challenge, and other societies in various phases of crossing the Ditch. Thus pre-modern social forms persist into this modern period, so the categories should not be taken as purely historical. Gellner has been very concerned with societies changing in the here and now in his writings on both the anthropology of the Islamic world and the politics of Eastern Europe. But beginning perhaps with his paper 'Our Current Sense of History' (1971), and culminating so far in his sweeping survey of human development *Plough, Sword and Book*, he has also looked at the transition to the modern world as a series of historical events.

In seeking to bring together a group of scholars who wish both to honour and to debate with Gellner, we have relied on the three-part problematic of the Ditch to organise the volume. The authors brought together in this book have tackled problems either on one side of the Ditch (Part I: The pre-modern world) or the other (Part III: Modernity and its discontents), or the travails of crossing the Ditch (Part II: Transitions to the modern world). We thus think to do justice to both the range and the most current formulations of Gellner's ideas.

In Part I, The pre-modern world, there are three papers which offer new ideas about the pre-modern condition. Colin

Renfrew tackles the major question of the spread of human beings across the globe as it is discernible in the pattern of linguistic dispersion. He attempts a major synthesis and explanation of the present evidence which, if accepted, would clarify the outlines of the prehistory of mankind. The proliferation of many forms of this major human innovation of language was of course essential groundwork for the possibility of thought on either side of the Ditch. A.M. Khazanov also attempts to synthesise and clarify current evidence, in this case about the movements and migrations of the nomads in the vast area of Central Asia. Gellner has held that the extraction of surplus gave incentive for brute force to commandeer and utilise that power. If this implies that in the absence of such predatory force there would be fairness and equality, account would now have to be taken of the powerful argument put forward by E.A. Wrigley, to the effect that poverty, rather than exploitation, was a structural feature of traditional societies.

In Part II, Transitions to the modern world, Sir Karl Popper and Alan Macfarlane offer further suggestions on factors affecting the transition, in the Mediterranean and the British Isles, respectively. Sir Karl Popper looks to a single invention, popular marketing of the proto-book, Macfarlane to a complex of circumstances unique to Britain. Nationalism often plays a major role in contemporary transitions to industrialisation, but Michael Mann connects its European form to geopolitical power politics. Reflecting on the historical factor of individualism, Ronald Dore raises the question of what kind of world we can expect from the new era of high technology industrialisation that, as in Japan, may owe little if anything to individualism.

In the third Part, Modernity and its discontents, the contributors cover the range of Gellner's thought, from its earliest manifestations to its most recent. Perry Anderson portrays Gellner's philosophy of the modern world as fundamentally Weberian in its problematic and its outlook. This is echoed by Joseph Agassi, who sees Gellner's secret charm as his attempt to synthesise rationalism with as much romanticism as logic permits, and his peculiarity in delineating the outcome only in stages. John Watkins urges against Gellner the universality of science by defending the idea that its methodology need have, indeed, no biasing presuppositions. I.C. Jarvie tries to show that Gellner's positivistic view of science prevents him from giving an account of how we get knowledge from experience. He claims that the philosophy that Gellner rejects, Popper's falsificationism, would permit him to conserve almost all the components of his system of thought and also to give a coherent account of how we get knowledge from experience.

The final five papers take up the politics of change in Europe, especially following on the collapse of the Soviet satellite régimes and the resultant questions about the viability of Marxist solutions to the discontents of modernity. Louis Dumont shows how the categories of Left and Right have evolved in France since the revolution, and how the meanings they have taken on there derive from particular circumstances. Cautious generalisation should only proceed from careful comparative work. John Dunn considers the staying power of the ideals and hope of socialism; Gerard Radnitzky challenges the basic understanding of society on which socialist thought rests. José Merquior and John A. Hall address themselves to the forms of social and geo-political organisation we may find in the modern world after the Cold War.

Our aim in assembling these essays was a volume which conformed to the spirit of Gellner's own approach to scholarship and inquiry: namely papers that would stimulate discussion not only of his ideas, but of the topics about which he has ideas. Thus, whether the authors agree with him or not, they have found his work worth engaging.

If the volume is a tribute to the range and fertility of his ideas, to the value of pushing inquiry into a single cluster of problems deeper and deeper, thus making contact with an ever-broadening range of cognate problems, our best hope as its editors is that Gellner in turn will find it fuels his project.

John A. Hall
I.C. Jarvie

PART I

*The pre-modern world*

CHAPTER 1

# World languages and human dispersals: a minimalist view

*Colin Renfrew*

Entia non sunt multiplicanda praeter necessitatem

William of Occam

'Don't be afraid to be wrong', Sir Mortimer Wheeler once wrote to me encouragingly. When one thinks of Ernest Gellner it is of intellectual audacity, tempered however with tough-mindedness and refreshing and often self-critical wit. He certainly lives up to Wheeler's maxim – which is not, for a moment, to suggest that he is indeed wrong with any frequency. To be asked to contribute to a Festschrift in his honour seemed to me a daunting task. But my initial faltering wish to contribute was strengthened when my reading in the rather hazy overlap area between the fields of archaeology and language brought me to glimpse the possibility of an emerging synthesis on a grand scale, important if right, – but not yet securely documented and therefore to be judged 'premature' among sound (conservative) academics[1]. If upheld it would offer a strikingly simple view of the origins of linguistic diversity, and one conforming satisfyingly with that stern injunction, the razor, of William of Occam. It is a pleasure, however, to offer this 'wild surmise' in admiration to a scholar who seeks to perceive the broad perspective and who will respond first to any originality, and only later gently point out the objections[2].

To do so is doubly appropriate, in view of Ernest Gellner's generous response to my book *Archaeology and Language*, itself not without critics. I well member a very agreeable evening with Ernest and Susan at 9 Clarendon Street, after a seminar where the distinguished Soviet (now Israeli) scholar A.M. Khazanov had been discussing ethnicity. Khazanov told me of the 'Nostratic hypothesis', of which I had only dimly heard at that time,

11

formulated by the late V.M. Illich-Svitych and by Khazanov's colleague Aron Dolgopolsky, in which a number of the language groups of Eurasia were seen as related. I went away – as so often after a visit to the Gellners – with some new ideas, new enthusiasm and some new references. The present contribution is offered in thanks for occasions such as that.

## A. CONVERGENT DISCIPLINES: THE EMERGING SYNTHESIS

The pattern of languages distributed upon the map of the world has hitherto seemed a very confusing one, and one which certainly defied any kind of rational historical explanation in terms of coherent processes of culture change. Of course, for the past two centuries there have been attempts to explain linguistic relationships in historical terms by recourse to archaeology. But they have all too often relied upon the assertion of long-range and rather unexpected migrations of tribes between areas unrelated by any plausible historical links. Over the past few years, however, there have been developments in the otherwise not traditionally related fields of palaeolithic studies, language classification, archaeological theory and molecular biology, which may for the first time all be leading in the same direction. It is possible now to indicate some areas of convergence and to suggest the outlines of what may be an emerging synthesis, as well as to pose some questions which remain to be answered.

The several, potentially converging strands are as follows:
1) The recognition that the fully-modern human species, *Homo sapiens sapiens*, seems to have emerged in Africa about 100,000 years ago, and that the human population of the world today is the result of the dispersal of this new species, and its replacement worldwide of earlier hominid forms. In Europe Neanderthal Man, *Homo sapiens neanderthalensis*, is on this view no longer seen as an ancestor of modern humans, an intermediate link in the evolutionary chain, but simply as an extinct branch. The extinction will have come about some 35,000 years ago in the face of the relatively rapid dispersal of modern humans. This view is now widely advocated, although there are influential dissenters who would argue for local transitions

from *Homo erectus* to *Homo sapiens sapiens* in areas additional to Africa, for instance in south-east Asia.[3]

2) With this view of the dispersal of modern humankind goes a reassessment of the capacities of earlier hominid forms. Lewis Binford has been one of the severest critics of those who have argued for the emergence of a range of human-like capacities, such as the ability to work in cooperative hunting groups, in the hominids of the Lower Palaeolithic period.[4] Many anthropologists today would argue that the capacity for speech, as we know it among all living groups, along with various social and intellectual abilities, not least the ability to manipulate symbols in a sophisticated way, is a property of *Homo sapiens sapiens*. Such abilities, it is argued, were largely lacking in earlier hominids.[5]

3) The classification of the world's languages has been greatly simplified as a result of recent work, notably by the American scholar Joseph Greenberg. The genetic classification, which he has himself proposed for the languages of Africa and the Americas allows the recognition of some twenty or so linguistic phyla, which encompass the entire range of the world's languages, apart from six or seven linguistic isolates (and a number of pidgins and creoles of patently recent origin).[6] This picture is at present a source of controversy among linguists, for Greenberg and his colleagues base their classification mainly upon multilateral lexical comparisons among contemporary languages without the demonstration of phonological changes according to explicit rules which are expected in an analysis along traditional Neogrammarian lines. But while the classification has proved controversial, it has, as Ruhlen points out in his global survey, at least for Africa, been almost universally followed.[7]

Over the past 25 years, in work still only little known in the west, Soviet linguists have themselves been undertaking large-scale classifications, and linking language families into macro-families.[8] The long-recognised Hamito-Semitic group, for instance, is now widely seen as part of a larger entity termed Afro-Asiatic.[9] Rather more ambitious is the proposal that this and Indo-European, along with the Uralic, Altaic, Dravidian and Kartvelian (South Caucasian) languages, should all be linked within a larger, more embracing 'Nostratic' phylum.[10]

The term 'Nostratic' was originally proposed by Pedersen in 1903.[11] This Soviet work is not yet well known in the west, let alone widely accepted, but there is a striking convergence here between the approach of Greenberg and his followers and that of the Soviet group and others.[12]

4) Prehistoric archaeologists have recently shown renewed interest in the relationship between their discipline and historical linguistics, an interdisciplinary area which since the 1930s had not been a very active one.[13] There is a renewed expectation abroad that methods may be found to bring the archaeological data and the linguistic data into more effective relationship without the excess of sometimes gratuitous migrations so often used in this field in the past.

5) Developments in molecular biology are now allowing biochemists to make much more precise determinations of genetic affinity between living populations. Until the past ten or fifteen years such comparisons were generally based upon rather gross phenetic data, involving cranial measurements or dentition or the like. Subsequently, through blood group studies, it became possible to study gene frequencies within living population groups, with promising results.[14] In very recent years, however, through the use of both nuclear DNA and mitochondrial DNA from the blood of living individuals, it has been possible to make more precise genetic comparisons between individuals.[15] Moreover the possibility exists of applying some of these techniques to the preserved remains of long-dead individuals recovered from archaeological deposits.[16] This field is a fast growing one.

To bring these different approaches into effective and fruitful relationship is no easy matter. To the linguistic data, for instance, it is almost impossible to assign a date without making very wide-reaching assumptions of the kind which gave the methods of glottochronology such a bad name in their early years.[17] The genetic data are, of course, informative about human descent, but the extent to which this is relevant to linguistic ancestry remains to be decided: obviously language replacement can and does occur in some areas accompanied only by minimal genetic changes within the human population. And the procedures for relating linguistic and archaeological data remain to be fully worked out and agreed. But already attempts at a synthesis between disciplines are being made: for instance between human genetics and linguistics.[18] It may not be too early, therefore, to speculate about the kind of grand synthesis which may yet emerge.

## B. CHOOSING SOME MINIMALIST PRINCIPLES

The territory between historical linguistics and prehistoric archaeology has in general been rather an undisciplined one. There is no agreed and coherent framework for bringing the two disciplines into a fruitful relationship. In this section I should like to touch on some of the areas where some measure of agreement would be useful.

### *1. Use of models for changes in language and material culture*

I have argued elsewhere that only by using models that relate social and demographic changes, on the one hand, to language change, and on the other to changes in material culture, can we hope to make systematic progress. In other words some theoretical discussion is necessary.[19] The suggestion was made that a given language comes to be spoken in a given territory as a result of the combination of four major processes:[20]

(i)  *Initial colonisation* of a hitherto unoccupied territory by an incoming human population with its own language or languages.

(ii)  *Divergence*, when through processes of isolation and linguistic drift, existing languages and dialects increasingly differ through time. Divergence is often represented by tree diagrams.

(ii)  *Convergence*, where through social contacts of various kinds linguistic innovations come to be shared over a considerable area, often represented by the mapping of isoglosses. (The wave model is relevant here, as are loanwords and Sprachbund effects.)

(iv)  *Language Replacement*, whereby the existing language in the territory is replaced by another incoming language.

It is possible, furthermore, to suggest a number of distinct and coherent models within the language replacement category:

(a)  *Subsistence/demography model*, where large numbers of

people speaking the new language move into the territory. They do not conquer by force of arms but are able to settle because they are possessed of a subsistence adaptation which either occupies a different ecological niche from that of the earlier population, or is significantly more effective and productive within the same niche through the possession of some technological advantage.

(b) *Élite dominance*, where an incoming, minority élite is able, usually by military means, to seize control of the levers of power within the territory. This implies that the incoming group will have some centralised organisation (that is, a stratified or highly ranked structure), and often that the group conquered will have some ranking also.

(c) *System collapse*, where the collapse of a highly centralised (state) society leads to instability on its perimeter and to significant local movements of people and of power. Such was the position in the late days of the Roman Empire and their aftermath, the so-called 'migration period'. Here again the pre-existence of a stratified or state society is a precondition.

(d) *Lingua franca*, where a trading language (pidgin) develops within the territory as the result of intense trading or other activity by outsiders. The pidgin is usually a simplified version of the outsider language, and a creole may develop, spoken by many of the inhabitants as their natal tongue.

No doubt other such models can be devised, and these re-defined, but without an explicit theoretical basis of this kind it is difficult to see how such phenomena can be coherently discussed.

### 2. Parsimony in human dispersal

The phenomenon of initial dispersal is a well-established one in biogeography. Indeed one appropriate model for the spatial advance of humans into a territory not otherwise populated (by humans) is precisely the 'wave of advance' model which has also been used for the dispersal of a farming population (with its potential for high population density) into a region previously only populated by hunter-gatherers at low density.[21]

Once there is a hunter-gatherer population within a given territory, however, it is not to be expected that a second dispersal is likely to be effective, unless the new population is possessed of some cultural device or adaptation which gives it a competitive advantage – precisely the subsistence/demography model for language replacement discussed above.

Of course it should be noted, as Zvelebil and Zvelebil have stressed, that an innovation or adaptation in the field of subsistence can be transmitted by acculturation, without any transfer of population whatever.[22] In such cases the genetic composition of the population would remain unaltered. So too might the language, despite the significant subsistence change. But it is also possible that the language of hunter-gatherers may indeed change when they adopt farming: this would be a different model of language replacement from those outlined above, one already indicated by Ehret.[23]

The important question arises, in this connection, as to the nature of the human dispersals out of Africa following the emergence there of *Homo sapiens sapiens*, if for the sake of argument we agree to assume here the 'monogenesis' hypothesis for modern humankind, noted earlier. Are we to think in terms of one wave, or several successive waves, of members of the new species leaving Africa? Certainly there is evidence in Israel, from the Qafzeh Cave, for the presence there of anatomically modern humans around 90,000 years ago.[24]

The principle of parsimony invoked here suggests that we should prefer one wave to several, unless we can see clearly how – that is, by what ecological factors – second and successive 'waves' might be propagated. Such waves would, presumably, lead to instances of language replacement. In egalitarian societies the phenomena of élite dominance, system collapse and (perhaps) lingua franca are not usually found. We should therefore expect some argument in the subsistence/demography sphere, or an altogether different model of linguistic emulation. Until such arguments are formulated, it may be preferable to think of one major episode of the adaptive radiation of our species from Africa.

### 3. Parsimony with extraneous entities

Clearly language replacement sometimes occurs. When it does, the new language, by definition almost, has an origin outside the territory of the language which is replaced. The point of the principle tentatively suggested here is that, wherever possible, we should avoid introducing specific and ready-formed languages from an external source unless we have some other evidence for their existence there.[25] This implies, among other things, that we are not usually speaking of the transfer of a language from A to B, but rather of the extension of the territory where it is spoken at A to include B. (Here I am not speaking of the phenomena of élite dominance and systems collapse, where this observation need not be correct.)

To choose a specific example, it seems lacking in parsimony to speak, in the case of Greece, of 'the coming of the Greeks', if that implies the existence of some external and well-defined homeland where the Greek language supposedly formed. We may well envisage the coming to Greece of persons speaking a Proto-Indo-European language, from which Greek later developed through divergence and other processes. But the notion of a separate and well-defined Greek homeland is better avoided unless there is some independent evidence for it. The same point applies to the Indo-Pacific languages of Papua New Guinea. Some scholars suggest the influx into New Guinea of populations speaking a series of Papuan or Proto-Papuan languages.[26] It seems to me preferable where possible to assume the arrival of an earlier and more generalised language, from which Papuan would develop, probably within New Guinea itself. Of course during the human dispersals in question there will have been dialectal variations and other divergence phenomena. But the 'billiard ball' model of pre-formed language units bouncing round the linguistic map is best avoided.[27]

### 4. Questions of time depth

The question of time depth seems one of the most difficult in the entire field of historical linguistics. In cases of divergence of two or more languages from a common ancestor, it is obviously desirable to be able to reach some sort of estimate of the effective date of divergence. Many linguists condemn the findings of glottochronology, yet at the same time almost all will claim some 'feel' for the order-of-magnitude scale of time involved.

Yet it is clear that many factors can affect rate of change, including literacy, nature of centralised organisation and administration, hunter-gatherer versus farming economy, sedentary versus mobile existence, and so on.[28]

Moreover some formulations of glottochronology offer different rates for lexical replacement depending upon the *meanings* of individual words.[29] This is related to the 'dregs effect' cited by Greenberg, where some terms persisted more readily than others.[30]

I have no solution to offer here: this simply seems an area where a coherent body of theory is needed and is at present lacking.

## 5. *Questions of spatial and demographic scale*

A further topic where some body of guiding theory is needed is in the scale of language units. It should be possible to predict, under a given set of circumstances, roughly how large in both spatial and population terms the language community will be. Of course we can see that within the modern nation state there will often be a single language but, as Gellner has shown, this kind of ethnicity is of relatively recent origin.[31]

But in non-state societies, there are clearly regularities to be observed. The long-standing agricultural/horticultural communities of Papua New Guinea have an astonishing multiplicity of languages: there are some 700 languages in a land mass of 200,000 square miles. By contrast the hunter-gatherer languages of Australia are estimated at 250 in a land-mass of 3 million square miles (although a number may have become extinct since colonial contact without being recorded).

The dynamics of social interaction in the Australian case have been analysed, notably by Birdsell, along with some of their linguistic correlates.[32] It is clear that hunter-gatherers need themselves to exploit much larger areas than agricultural communities within the normal range of their activities. It is also the case that in years of hardship they are more dependent upon their neighbours, so that mutual intelligibility is adaptively useful in a way which is not necessarily the case in food-producing communities. These are issues which need to be further developed before we can use some general anthropology of language to guide us in our historical reconstructions.

## 6. The need to understand refuge effects

In a number of cases we can identify language isolates (for example Basque, Burushaski, Sumerian) or language groups (for example North Caucasian, Kartvelian) which may plausibly be interpreted as survivors representing possibly larger groups of speakers who have suffered partial language replacement by some other tongue. These isolates and small groups seem to survive for a long period where related languages have long been extinct.

In some cases the geographical location offers some clue as to how survival may have occurred. The relatively remote mountain locations of the speakers of some of the Caucasian languages is a case in point, and the relative remoteness of the area where Basque is now spoken is a comparable case. But it would be interesting to understand precisely how it is that such 'refuges' do indeed survive.[33]

## 7. The need for linguistic adequacy of explanation

The foregoing has so over-simplified the notion of language and of language group as to give the patently erroneous impression that internal relationships within the language family can be ignored. Evidently this is not the case. It follows that a good historical explanation will not only satisfy some of the principles outlined above. It must also lead to further insights at a detailed level into the relationships, phonological, morphological and grammatical as well as lexical, between the languages within the group. It is on this point that Greenberg has been most severely taken to task by his critics: his taxonomic classifications do not lead, or at least have not yet led, to a more detailed understanding of the evolution of phonology and grammatical structure in each case.[34] The same reproach has quite justifiably been made of my own hypothetical explanation for the distribution of the Indo-European language.[35] While the explanation may carry some conviction at a general level, it has not yet proved helpful in understanding specific linguistic features which unite or divide specific pairs of languages or sub-groups of languages within the family. But a good explanation must be expected to do this. Of course there is work involved, which will have to be undertaken by competent linguists, to see how relationships can be recognised which harmonise with the new historical explanation. But if it were to prove impossible to recognise such relationships, then it must be conceded that the explanation cannot be regarded as entirely satisfactory.

### C. THE PROBLEM

Seventeen language phyla are listed by Ruhlen into which the vast majority of the world's 5,000 languages may be classified.[36] The problem is to offer some reasonably coherent historical explanation for this linguistic distribution, and to do so following reasonable and simple principles of the kind outlined in the last section.

The language phyla proposed by Ruhlen are the following:
1. Khoisan
2. Niger-Kordofanian
3. Nilo-Saharan
4. Afro-Asiatic
5. Caucasian
6. Indo-European (Ruhlen used the term 'Indo-Hittite')
7. Uralic-Yukaghir
8. Altaic
9. Chukchi-Kamchatkan
10. Eskimo-Aleut
11. Elamo-Dravidian
12. Sino-Tibetan
13. Austric, including
    I    Miao-Yao
    II   Austroasiatic
    III  Austro-Tai, comprising
        A. Daic
        B. Austronesian

14. Indo-Pacific
15. Australian
16. Na-Dene
17. Amerind
18. Language isolates (Basque, Burushaski, Ket, Nahali)

The pidgin and creole languages and the invented languages listed by Ruhlen will not be considered here, since they may all be taken to be of relatively recent origin, correlating with the European colonial expansion from the fifteenth century AD. It is doubtful if any long-lasting creole languages came into existence before the formation of major imperial powers. I am indebted to Claude Boisson for pointing out that Greenberg's Indo-Pacific phylum is viewed as controversial by many linguists (but within it the Trans-New Guinea phylum is considered safer), and that Ket is not strictly an isolate, forming part of the Yeniseian family.

My aim, then, is to give some explanatory account of this distribution using the sort of simplifying models briefly discussed above. The simplest model of all would, of course, be no more than that of the dispersal of our species from the region in which it originally developed, followed by the increasing linguistic divergence of those populations which had become geographically isolated from each other. But it would appear that other processes have also been at work serving to disrupt the relatively simple mosaic pattern of languages which might emerge as a result of a long phase of divergence after initial dispersal.

I shall propose that the explanation in terms of subsistence/demography offered in the Indo-European case can be applied by analogy to several of the phyla here.[37] In such cases the model operates in terms of the dispersal of a farming economy.

There is certainly in addition one case (that of the Altaic languages) which may perhaps best be explained in terms of élite dominance.

A remaining group of linguistic phyla is found along the northern periphery of Europe, Asia and America. These languages may be tackled in terms of a rather late series of initial colonisations of these northern lands.

The language groups which remain, when the effect of the

three preceding have been taken into account, can best be considered in terms of the early, primary dispersal of humankind out of Africa.

It should clearly be understood that in each case nearly all the factors and models earlier indicated may operate to some extent together. For instance in the Amerind case, while the overall pattern may (obviously enough) be explained in terms of initial colonisation, there are other factors at work. Within the Amerind phylum the subsequent distribution of languages following initial dispersal will have been radically influenced by the operation of subsistence/demography processes, and we should expect to be able to trace within these the effects of plant and animal domestication. Moreover in this as in other areas there will also be significant (and mainly later) élite dominance effects. The intention here is to try to indicate the main first-order variables only. In every individual case the specific history will be a more complicated one with its own particularities.

These can only be hypothetical proposals at the moment. But they have the merit, as we shall see, of offering a relatively simple account in historical terms for the distribution of languages of the world, in broad harmony with the principles outlined above. They also find some support from the genetic data to be discussed below.

It should, however, be clearly understood that the identification of the problem, as outlined here, and hence the validity of any proposed solution to it, is very much dependent upon the classification, indicated above, of the world's languages into some seventeen phyla or superfamilies or macro-families. It was noted earlier that such a division into large aggregate linguistic units in this way has not been without its critics. Recently Professor Anna Morpurgo Davies has written:

Over the years we have developed and tested the method which we use to demonstrate linguistic kinship. This obviously starts by comparing words but then goes further and makes use of regular phonological correspondence and, if possible, of morphological comparison. On the other hand, if we take as an example of how super-families are established the latest book by J. Greenberg about the languages of America, we discover that there the methodology is very different. Greenberg does not rely on phonological or morphological correspondences, but on what he calls 'multilateral comparison', i.e. on lexical similarities studied in a number of languages at the same time. He jettisons the standard techniques not because they lead to wrong conclusions but because they do not allow him to go beyond the standard families. Yet we do not know whether super-families established in this way have the same properties as the families established with the standard comparative method. If they do not, there is a serious risk that the whole concept of super-family is vacuous. At the moment it is not clear to me whether this is so or not so.[38]

This statement very clearly sets out the reservations that many linguists feel about the super-families of Greenberg and Ruhlen. Rather similar criticisms have been made for the 'Nostratic' superfamily intensively studied in recent years by a number of Soviet linguists. In what follows the classification of Ruhlen will be used without further *caveat*, as if it were well established. Clearly, however, that is not yet the case, and the hypothetical and tentative nature of any conclusions based upon the macrofamily classification should be recognised.

In what follows, I shall proceed in a sort of modified reverse order, discussing first some of the more recent replacement processes, whose consequences are relatively obvious. These include both the agriculturally-based dispersals of the past 10,000 years (Section D) and the still more recent episodes of élite dominance (Section E). Then I shall turn to the patterns and regularities that are left upon the map when we have dealt with these: most of them are the product of episodes of initial colonisation. Again, the more readily explained are those of more recent date – in late Pleistocene and Holocene times (Section F). Their explication (if such it be) leaves upon the map the very much older residuum of the earlier dispersals of Pleistocene times (Section G). The story is, I think, more intelligible when set out in this order, which is, in effect, the reverse of the supposed sequence of events.

### D. AGRICULTURAL DISPERSALS

It is here proposed that one of the most significant processes determining the modern distribution of the world's languages was that of 'agricultural dispersal'. This is an instance of the subsistence/demography model of linguistic replacement discussed above. In each case it postulates that the language, or

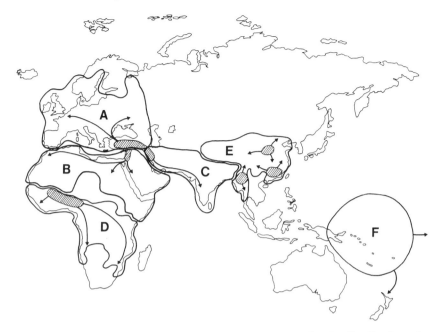

Map 1. Agricultural dispersals are proposed to account for the distribution of
the following macrofamilies: A: Indo-European; B: Afroasiatic; C: Elamo-
Dravidian; D: Niger-Kordofanian; E: Sino-Tibetan; F: Austronesian.

more often the proto-language, which we are considering was
brought into the area now occupied by populations speaking
tongues descended from that proto-language, by persons
whose relatively small-scale and local movements may be
explained in terms of the model. It postulates also that there
ensued the significant linguistic consequences which the model
predicts (see Map 1).

The same model, which has already been applied in some
detail to account for the Indo-European language distribution,
may be applied to that of the Afro-Asiatic and the Elamo-
Dravidian languages, and with modifications to the Niger-
Kordofanian and perhaps the Sino-Tibetan languages as well.
The relationship between agricultural and linguistic dispersals
has been well expressed by Cavalli-Sforza.[39] The same author
has independently made proposals, to which my own are
closely similar, for the Indo-European, Afro-Asiatic and

Dravidian languages.[40] It may be applied, with one very significant modification, to the distribution of the Austronesian languages also, as many scholars have indicated.[41] But this is a special case of agricultural dispersal, for here the population was in many cases entering environments hitherto not populated by humans: this was then a case of initial dispersal and not of language replacement.

*Indo-European*

In a recent book it was proposed that the basic mechanism for the dispersal of the proto-Indo-European language was a language replacement on the subsistence/demography model activated by the inception of farming in Central Anatolia and its subsequent spread following a 'wave of advance' model.[42] Some critics, notably Zvelebil and Zvelebil, have argued that insufficient weight was paid to the pre-existing (non-Indo-European speaking) population of Europe, and that some of these groups adopted farming, thus undergoing population increase and retaining their original language.[43] I had foreseen this point for the Basque and possibly the Etruscan and Iberian languages, but it may well apply to others also, as the Zvelebils suggest. They accept, however, that the process for the proto-Indo-European spread for the Balkans and Central Europe was much as proposed. This proposal had been made primarily on archaeological grounds.

It was encouraging, therefore, to learn that the distinguished Soviet (now Israeli) linguist Aron Dolgopolski had reached a comparable conclusion on linguistic grounds:

On the basis of the linguistic evidence . . . we conclude that the habitat of proto-Indo-European should be sought in Anatolia, while that of Late proto-Indo-European (ancestral to all the Indo-European languages except Hittite-Luwian) is most likely to have been somewhere in the Balkan peninsula.[44]

It is proposed moreover that Indo-European speech first reached the Russian steppe lands as farming economy and proto-Indo-European speech spread up from Greece into the Balkans and east to the Ukraine. The development of an agro-pastoral economy, based in part upon the domestic horse, initiated a second demography/subsistence dispersal across the steppe lands of Central Asia from the third millennium BC. In this way Indo-European speech may have reached north India and Pakistan as early as 3000 BC, and penetrated as far east as Sinkiang, where the Tocharian languages are documented from a rather later date.

This early pastoral phase did not yet involve mounted warfare on any scale, which developed towards the end of the second millennium BC. Nor should this early phase be regarded as an episode of élite dominance, although the later exploits of nomad horseman warriors are another matter, and may well be an instance of that model.

Anatolia, however, only represents one of the lobes of the area in which the basic western Asian pattern of farming (based mainly on wheat and barley, sheep and goats) was developed with the domestication of local wild species. Comparable processes were certainly going on in the Levant, and in the foothills of the Zagros Mountains (that is, along the 'hilly flanks of the fertile crescent').[45] It seems appropriate to suggest that comparable dispersals of the other local mesolithic-turned-neolithic populations would have occurred, with analogous linguistic consequences.

Of course we do not know what languages were spoken in these two areas, any more than we know for Central Anatolia: we are dealing here with hypothetical matters of inference.

*Afro-Asiatic*
Given the modern distribution of Semitic languages over the area in question, which belong to the larger Afro-Asiatic family, it seems appropriate to suggest that these first farmers of the Levant and their mesolithic predecessors (including the Natufian culture) were speaking a proto-Afro-Asiatic language, and that the spread of mixed farming based largely on cereals, sheep and goats to north Africa took this proto-Afro-Asiatic language with it, from which the modern Berber and Chadic languages would have developed. The dispersal of these farming components would have taken dialects ancestral to the Omotic and Cushitic languages southwards.[46] It may be that proto-Semitic continued to develop within the Levant and Syria area, since both Eblaite and Akkadian (early Semitic languages) are there attested early, the former around 2400 BC. (The original farming dispersal would, however, have taken place

very much earlier, around 7000 BC.) Other dialects of early
Semitic ancestral to Arabic may have subsequently developed in
Arabia. The dispersal of Arabic through north Africa was of
course a later episode which may be regarded as partly one of
élite dominance.

This outline is, of course, absurdly sketchy and the origins of
agriculture are not to be described in terms of dispersal alone.
But it offers a hypothesis for the primary mechanism. Moreover,
as Claude Boisson has pointed out to me, analogous conclusions
have independently been reached by Militarev and Shnirelman,
who write, 'In the Levant the population deriving from the
Mesolithic Natufian culture could well give rise to the
subsistence/demography replacements associated with the dispersal of the Afro-Asiatic languages.[47] The full picture will have
been very much more complex, and no doubt additional factors
are relevant, especially for the Omotic and Cushitic languages.

*Elamo-Dravidian*
Analogous arguments may be offered for the Elamo-Dravidian
languages. Elamite is attested from around 2000 BC in what is
now Khuzistan in southern Iran. The Dravidian languages are
today located mainly in southern India and Sri Lanka, with an
enclave (Brahui) in Pakistan. The languages of north India and
Pakistan are, as we have seen, Indo-European and may ultimately be due to the development of an agro-pastoral economy
on the Russian steppes from the fourth millennium BC
onwards.

Since some of those speaking Dravidian languages in India are
(or were) hunter-gatherers, a straightforward explanation in
terms of farming dispersal may be oversimplified. Yet McAlpin
has plausibly demonstrated the familial relationship between
Elamite and the Dravidian languages.[48] So therefore it may
seem reasonable to propose a version of the farming/language
hypothesis in this case also. But today many of the speakers of
the Dravidian languages depend less on the food crops of north
India and Pakistan, which are very much those of western Asia,
than on a different complex, including rice, so that there are
problems here. Dravidian is included by Soviet scholars in the
Nostratic family, but not by Greenberg in his Eurasiatic phylum.

It should be noted that Sumerian is known to have been

spoken in southern Mesopotamia before 3000 BC, but does not appear to have undergone any widespread dispersal. As a tentative suggestion I would propose that the very early (late Upper Palaeolithic) Sumerian-speakers were already exploiting the marshes at the mouths of the Tigris and Euphrates rivers, and did not initially take up agriculture in the seventh or sixth millennia BC when their neighbours to the north did so.

*Niger-Kordofanian (specifically the Bantu languages)*
It is now widely, although certainly not universally, accepted that the very wide dispersal of the Bantu languages originated in western Africa. The hypothesis that this was also a dispersal of what we would here regard as the subsistence/demography type has been argued in detail.[49]

If we accept this view for the Bantu dispersal, there remains a major band of the remaining Niger-Kordofanian languages in west and central Africa south of the Sahara. In the main they are now spoken by agriculturalists and pastoralists, but they are here regarded as the descendants of the earlier hunter-gatherer populations in approximately these areas.

*Austronesian languages (within the larger Austric phylum)*
For Polynesia the spread of farming/horticulture has been very well documented.[50] For these islands it was, of course, also an initial colonisation, not a language replacement. But the case is appropriately considered here since it was certainly also an agricultural dispersal.

For the islands of Melanesia and Micronesia the case is more complicated. The matter has been well discussed by Bellwood in the wider context of the Austric languages,[51] and whatever the position for the other tongues in the Austric group, the case for the islands seems clear enough in outline.

*Sino-Tibetan*
represents the other major language phylum, where the scale of the linguistic unity and a consideration of the prehistory suggests a farming dispersal. Taking the Chinese language (or languages) first, the considerable uniformity within the group is striking. The long-term ethnic and cultural unity of much of China is well known. Moreover this is a case where an initial

farming dispersal will have been reinforced by élite dominance effects during the later centuries of centralised control.

There appear to be two foci for farming origins in China. The first, dependent largely upon wheat and millet, centres upon the Yellow River valley, where the early neolithic Pan p'o culture may be traced down, through a possibly unbroken continuity to the dynastic (i.e. Shang) times circa 1600 BC. The writing of the Shang period is already recognisably of the Chinese language.

The second focus is on the coast in Chekiang province, where early rice cultivation (circa 5000 BC) is reliably documented from the site of Hemudu.[52] Rice may prove to have been domesticated also in other areas of south-east Asia, and this is clearly of importance for the Austric languages other than Austronesian. They are further discussed below.

At the moment one may be inclined to see the homeland area of the Proto-Chinese language as in Shensi province.[53] The early dispersal of Tibetan to the south may well have been part of this process. Processes of élite dominance, perhaps at the time of the Chou, Ch'in and Han dynasties, may have played an important role. However this may not give sufficient weight to the cultivation of rice, already discussed, and that is a matter for further consideration.

It should be noted that the Soviet linguist S.A. Starostin has posited a still broader linguistic group, Sino-Caucasian, encompassing North Caucasian (including Hurrian-Urartian and possibly Hattic), Yeniseian (including Ket) and Sino-Tibetan.[54] Recently, as Claude Boisson informs me, S. Nikolaev has suggested that Sino-Caucasian may be related to the American phylum Na-Dene, forming Dene-Caucasian. But while a relationship between Sino-Tibetan and Na-Dene might be readily enough explicable in historico-geographical terms, that between Sino-Tibetan and North Caucasian seems more problematic (as indeed does Starostin's recently hypothesised relationship between Nostratic and Sino-Caucasian).

### E. DISPERSAL BY ÉLITE DOMINANCE: THE ALTAIC GROUP

It has been suggested earlier that élite dominance as a mechanism of language dispersal may have been a process of rather late date, certainly not before the bronze age in the western Old World, circa 3000 BC. Of course it will have played a role in the later prehistory of many areas, as has already been suggested for China. (It may be noted also that the spread of the (Indo-European) languages of the European colonial powers from the fifteenth century AD may be regarded as largely a matter of élite dominance, although the subsistence/demography model played a role in areas of low population density.)

It seems appropriate to suggest that élite dominance, based upon mounted warfare, practised by nomad pastoralists, was responsible for the very widespread distribution of the Altaic languages. Certainly this seems appropriate for the Turkic languages, and the Mongolian languages whose speakers are known to have been effective mounted warriors from the early second millennium AD. There are indications from Chinese written sources that these warriors were active as much as a millennium earlier. Indeed it may confidently be suggested that in much of the area where Turkic languages are now spoken, there was formerly an Indo-European language. The extinct Tocharian languages in Sinkiang would be one indicator of this.

In trying to fix an original focus for the Altaic languages we should probably be looking for a source of fighting on horseback.

One complicating factor is that the Japanese and Korean languages (and Ainu) are now considered to belong to the Altaic family by some authors.[55] Farming may not have come to Japan much earlier than 3000 BC, but this was rice farming. Moreover recent discussions of Japanese prehistory lay stress upon local continuities.[56] More research will be needed to find cultural correlates for the possible displacement by early Altaic (or proto-Nostratic) speakers of the earlier languages associated with Upper Palaeolithic and then Jomon Japan.

The inclusion of the Altaic languages within the 'Nostratic' macrofamily by Soviet scholars (and by Greenberg in his Eurasiatic phylum) poses a problem here. For this might lead one to seek an area of origin for them rather closer to the regions already discussed for Indo-European, Afro-Asiatic and Elamo-Dravidian, and indeed Kartvelian, that is, closer to the fertile crescent. On this approach one might consider Turkmenia, with its early farming focus. But Russian scholars point also to the Kelteminar culture of Central Asia, and the matter is hardly clear. That this language family underwent a rather later dispersal than most of those which we have been discussing does, however, seem plausible. It is one case where the role of mounted warrior horsemen may indeed have been crucially significant.

## F. INITIAL COLONISATION BY HUNTER-GATHERERS IN LATE PLEISTOCENE AND HOLOCENE TIMES

When one considers the map of world language families, taking note of those large territorial expanses which, on the arguments above, owe their extension to farming dispersals, a further series of language groups catches the eye. They are all at the north of the map, near or beyond the margin of the region where farming is at present climatically practicable. For the same reason, they are near or beyond the margin of possible settlement by hunter-gatherers during Pleistocene times. These groups are thus, speaking generally, composed of hunter-gatherers adapted to survival in cold climates. It may be proposed that they owe their present location to human dispersals taking place over the past 10,000 years.

*The Uralic-Yukaghir*
family is represented by a number of language groups (notably Finnic, Ugric and Samoyed) located mainly beyond the northern margins of early European agriculture. The Hungarian language, part of the Ugric family, represents an exception: its distribution is the result of an episode of élite dominance associated with the arrival of the Magyars in the eighth century AD. This was brought about by mounted warriors, very much in the manner of the Huns and Mongols of the Altaic group discussed in the last section. It is to be assumed that the Magyars took up mounted nomad pastoralism during the time of its development by Altaic-speaking groups.

Within the North Finnic family, the Saami (or Lapps) are prominent, depending largely upon reindeer herding. The other members of this group are in the main also dependent upon rather specialised adaptations of this kind which allowed them to colonise this northern area.[57] They clearly did so from the steppe lands further to the south, but from which part of this very broad band it is at present difficult to say. It should be noted that Uralic is classed by Illich-Svitych as part of his Nostratic superfamily, and by Greenberg within his Eurasiatic one. If we follow the view advanced here that the origin of the communality of the other main Nostratic languages derives from a common origin in or near western Asia, then we may imagine an early distribution of proto-Uralic to the north and perhaps the north-west of the Caucasus.

*The Eskimo-Aleut*
languages, mainly in northern Alaska and Canada and in Greenland, are spoken by groups whose culture represents a special adaptation to arctic conditions. There is general agreement that it is an adaptation of relatively recent origin. On the linguistic side it is appropriate to quote Greenberg:

Eskimo itself is divided into Yuit and Inuit, with a sharp boundary between the two on the west coast of Alaska. Everything north and east of Unalakleet is Inuit, extending through Alaska and Canada to Greenland. The other branch, Yuit, consists of Siberian Eskimo, Central Alaskan Eskimo, and Pacific Coast Alaskan Eskimo. One form of Siberian Eskimo, Sirenik, is so different from the rest of Eskimo, that it may form a separate branch, distinct from both Inuit and Yuit. If this hypothesis is correct, there is a possibility that Proto-Eskimo was spoken on the western side of the Bering Strait. However the geographical location of Aleut rather suggests southwestern Alaska as the ancestral homeland, with Siberian Eskimo a reverse movement, perhaps, earliest in the case of the speakers of Sirenik.[58]

The Thule culture around 1000 AD is often equated with the early Eskimo-speaking communities.[59] The material culture correlates for an ancestral proto-Eskimo-Aleutian language are at present less clear: Laughlin has suggested the Anagula culture of the eastern Aleutian islands, dated around 8500 BC.[60] It should be noted that Greenberg places Eskimo-Aleut within his wider Eurasiatic macrofamily.

*The Na-Dene*
languages form, along with Eskimo-Aleut and Amerind, the third major language group of the Americas identified by

Greenberg.[61] It comprises three languages of the Pacific north-west (Haida, Tlingit and Eyak) together with the Athabaskan family. The Athabaskan group (which includes the Navajo-Apache languages) has perhaps the appearance of a later dispersal from the north-western area, where the other speakers are located.

If Greenberg's tripartite division be accepted, the Amerind languages represent a much earlier dispersal to the Americas – presumably over the Bering Strait area, and probably at a time when there was a land-bridge.

The Na-Dene languages would represent a subsequent adaptation to a Tundra environment. In this area the 'single dispersal per area' rule for hunter-gatherers (see Principle 2 above) must be considered modified by the severe climatic changes in the circumpolar regions which could render areas hitherto hospitable quite uninhabitable to specific adaptations. West has offered a hypothetical population curve for central Beringia (that is, the east Siberia–west Alaska area).[62] He suggests a population crash of reindeer, possibly around 12,000 BC. Had the Beringia area been occupied by a proto-Na-Dene-speaking population around this time, the crash might well have led that population to move south into its present territories in America. The later Eskimo-Aleut colonisation of part of the same Beringia area (the eastern part) would then represent a fresh, 'initial' colonisation of a territory at the time unoccupied. The archaeological culture in question would be the Palaeo-Arctic culture of the Late Pleistocene.

It should be noted that the Na-Dene languages are not thought by Greenberg to be related to the Eskimo-Aleut or the Chukotian languages (which form components of his 'Eurasiatic' macrofamily). He inclines rather to the hypothesis first advanced by Edward Sapir of a relationship with the Sino-Tibetan languages (see also above).[63]

*The Chukchi-Kamchatkan*

or 'Palaeosiberian' languages, or rather their speakers, occupy the Chukchi and Kamchatkan peninsulas in north-eastern Siberia, to the west of the Bering Sea. The cultural adaptation is related to that of the Eskimo, and a fairly close relationship between this group, the Eskimo-Aleut languages and Gilyak is widely accepted.[64] Greenberg has all three as separate families within his larger 'Eurasiatic' macro-family (although Soviet scholars do not include them within the Nostratic phylum).

It is likely, then, that the origin of the Chukchi-Kamchatkan language distribution is not unlike that of the Eskimo-Aleut. Both may be the consequence of expansive dispersals, as a result of climatic amelioration, into territories formerly occupied (but then abandoned) by proto-Na-Dene-speaking Palaeo-Arctic groups. Chard has drawn attention to an early neolithic in this area from around 5000 BC, suggesting that in later phases the regional and local differentiation observed may correspond to some ethnic differentiation.[65] 'Perhaps we may see in this an original, roughly homogeneous Arctic Mongoloid population, differentiating through time into separate linguistic and genetic groupings, with the Eskimo at one extreme and the Kamchadal at the other.[66]

Beyond this it is at present difficult to go. For it must be admitted that the archaeology of Beringia is not yet sufficiently well advanced to document with precision the three phases of occupation implied by the Greenberg three-wave hypothesis (Amerind; Na-Dene; Eskimo-Aleut), nor to distinguish clearly between the Siberian Eskimo and the Chukchi-speaking (or proto-Chukchi-speaking) inhabitants of neighbouring areas just one or two thousand years ago. But in any case the special nature of human adaptations to the tundra environment, and the specially crucial role of climatic variations in the circumpolar regions, are bound to play an important part in more detailed explanations.

### G. PLEISTOCENE DISPERSALS OF HUNTER-GATHERERS

The remaining language groups of the Ruhlen classification cannot readily be explained in terms of agricultural or of Holocene hunter-gatherer dispersals. They take us back to an earlier period, and perhaps to the original process of the adaptive radiation of our species out of Africa.

Here it is relevant to note that more than one underlying process may have been at work. The first would be, quite simply, dispersal, which in a homogeneous plain may also be

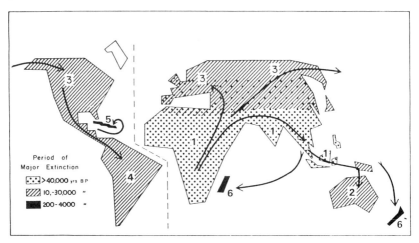

Map 2. Global extinction of large mammals, possibly caused by the initial
dispersal of *Homo sapiens sapiens* (after Martin[69]).

modelled by the 'wave of advance' – a model more familiar for
agricultural dispersal.[67] Given a modest tendency for mobility,
even a random-walk model will produce a gradual dispersal,
which may be more rapid if demographic effects are taken into
account.

There is, however, a second and potentially complicating
factor: the impact of the human population upon its environment. Where the activities of hunter-gatherers resulted in
significant depletion of resources, there was an additional
reason to move on. Paul Martin, in his discussion of the global
extinction of large mammals, offers a potential insight,
although his chronology now needs revision[68] (see Map 2).

The dispersal of the human species from Africa, first to the
Near East and then beyond, carried hunter-gatherer populations to the areas later to be occupied (as we have seen) by
speakers of the Afro-Asiatic, Indo-European and probably
Elamo-Dravidian languages. Next in line was south-east Asia.

*The Austric*

language group, already briefly mentioned in relation to the
late, agricultural dispersal of its Austronesian component,
represents the outcome of that dispersal to south-east Asia,
together with the superimposed palimpsest of later processes.

Some of the relevant issues have been discussed by Bellwood.[70] The ancestors of the Sino-Tibetan group, not yet widely distributed through their later agricultural dispersal, must go back to this time.

### The Indo-Pacific

languages of the Andaman Islands and of Papua New Guinea may be discussed in similar terms. It is now recognised that New Guinea has been occupied for well over 40,000 years. Plant domestication is likely to have occurred there locally, and the extreme 'balkanisation' of the linguistic map into small language communities will have followed this process. The linguistic divisions indicated by Wurm certainly point to further significant processes within this general outline which will be responsible for the patterning observed.[71] (One may note in passing that the assigning of the extinct Tasmanian language to this Indo-Pacific group, following Greenberg, looks geographically and historically very odd.[72] It would be surprising if his critics on this point were not justified. An early relationship with the Australian family would be more intelligible in spatial terms.)

### The Australian

family goes back to an initial colonisation at least 40,000 years ago.[73] Some 170 languages are known. It is today generally accepted that all the indigenous languages of the Australian continent, including the language of the western Torres Straits, but excluding Meriam (a Papuan language of the eastern Torres Straits) are genetically related.[74] The position of the Tasmanian languages is disputed.

Within the Australian phylum some 15 language groups are recognised, and some 15 further language isolates. It may be premature to attempt any hypothetical archaeological correlations.

### The Amerind

family represents the other major area of the globe reached during the process of Pleistocene dispersal. Greenberg's simplification of the linguistic classification of the Americas in this phylum, plus the two discussed earlier (Na-Dene and Eskimo-Aleut) makes an archaeologically plausible picture. The initial date of colonisation of the Americas is not yet clear. A date as early as 13,000 BC may be confidently accepted. The various indications of human activity which have been claimed already in South America around 37,000 BC suggest the possibility of a time depth not far short of that now well documented for Australia and Papua New Guinea.[75]

The Greenberg proposal that the native languages of the Americas, with the exception of those belonging to the Na-Dene and Eskimo-Aleut groups, be assigned to a single, all-embracing Amerind category, has already been severely criticised in many quarters.[76] But he and his collaborators have emphasised the convergence between the linguistic, dental and genetic evidence that can be taken to indicate three phases of human migration to the Americas via the Bering Strait land bridge. These would, it is claimed, correspond with the Amerind, Na-Dene and Eskimo-Aleut linguistic groups respectively.[77] Paradoxically the accumulating evidence of human activity in South America well before the end of the Pleistocene period may make this hypothesis more difficult to sustain.[78] But it remains a plausible one, and it harmonises with the perspective adopted here.

*The Khoisan*
languages of southern Africa, along with the Nilo-Saharan and the Niger-Kordofanian languages to the north, presumably represent the descendents of the original languages of Africa. (The agricultural dispersal of the Bantu subgroup of the Niger-Kordofanian languages was discussed earlier.)

On this view, the African component of the Afro-Asiatic languages (that is the Berber, Cushitic, Omotic and Ancient Egyptian languages) would represent a 'reflux' back to Africa following the domestication of plants and animals in the Near East. Such a view may do insufficient justice to the local farming adaptations seen in northern Africa, but at least it has the merits of explaining for us the underlying linguistic unity of this very large group.

On this view the 'indigenous' languages of Africa are represented essentially by these three groups (and we shall see below that there is some molecular genetic support for this view). Why there should be three major groupings rather than a single one is not immediately clear. Once the territory of emergence of *Homo sapiens sapiens* can be more clearly established, it may be possible to evaluate whether one group corresponds with the area of initial emergence, and the others to phases of dispersal.

Of course we should avoid an approach which regards one language group as more 'ancient' than another, simply because it is located in or near the area of initial human emergence. On the perspective followed here, all languages in themselves are of equal antiquity. Nor is any line of descent more 'direct' than another. It is the taxonomic and genetic affinities *between* languages which vary. So there is no reason to imagine that one group will show features more 'archaic' than another on the grounds of its territorial location or dispersal history.

*The Caucasian*
language group, the last remaining of the Ruhlen classification, is most conveniently considered in the next section, (although it may logically belong in this one).

## H. EURASIAN ISOLATES

The picture offered so far of the world language map is one of human dispersals from Africa, covering much of the world by 30,000 BC. They were, it is argued, supplemented by later dispersals in the circumpolar area and in Austronesia, mainly within Holocene times. Much of the world's language map is, however, constituted by those language groups, discussed in section E above, where a new subsistence basis, in most cases the inception of farming, was responsible for language replacement on a grand scale.

Beneath the record of these major expansions, most of them dating from the time range 7000 to 3000 BC, lie fragmentary indications of earlier languages, now imperfectly recorded, whose status and affinities are often not clear.

*The Caucasian*
language family or families represents the most obvious case of this phenomenon. It would have been perfectly possible to consider it in the last section, on an equal footing, for instance,

with the Indo-Pacific languages of Papua New Guinea. The Caucasian languages may have a comparable antiquity in the area in which they are now spoken. And they may owe their great diversity to comparable factors, if the inhabitants of the Caucasus either developed a farming technology from local plants and animals, or adopted that technology from neighbours to the south.

We should note at once that the classifications of Ruhlen and of Greenberg differ most seriously at this point.[79] Greenberg distinguishes between the North Caucasian and a Kartvelian (south Caucasian) language family. Ruhlen places both as sub-groups within a single Caucasian family. Only in one other case (the assimilation of Austroasiatic and Austro-Thai within an Austric phylum) does Ruhlen conflate major families separated by Greenberg (although Greenberg in his Eurasiatic group links as one unit five families separately listed by Ruhlen (Indo-European, Uralic-Yukaghir, Altaic, Chukotian and Eskimo-Aleut). Ruhlen concedes: 'it is possible that these two subfamilies, North and South Caucasian, do not constitute a valid genetic node'.[80] At any rate the marked differences between the two should be noted.

The classification of Kartvelian (South Caucasian) within the Nostratic macrofamily was noted earlier, as was the assignment of North Caucasian to the Sino-Caucasian macrofamily by Starostin, and the linkage of this in turn to Na-Dene by Nikolaev. From the perspective of these hypothetical macrofamilies, the Caucasian language groups would no longer be regarded as isolates. The separation between North Caucasian and South Caucasian would however be maintained.

In any case, the Caucasian families are now surrounded by languages (Indo-European, Semitic and Turkic) which owe their location largely to later processes. However I have suggested that the homelands for the proto-languages ancestral to Indo-European, for Afro-Asiatic, and for Elamo-Dravidian, were located nearby in Anatolia, in the Levant, and in the southern Zagros, respectively.

We have evidence for several other languages in these areas. The case of Sumerian was mentioned earlier. Hattic, a non-Indo-European language of Anatolia, may conceivably be related to proto-North Caucasian, as Ivanov has proposed.[81]

Moreover, Hurrian, an early language of east Anatolia and northern Iraq, may (along with the later Urartian) be related to the East Caucasian sub-group of the North Caucasian languages.[82] Such relationships would not be surprising in simple spatial terms in view of the proximity of all these areas.

We have plenty of candidates, then, for the palaeolithic languages of the Near East. Such, however, is not the case for south Asia, if we accept the view that the dispersal of Dravidian was a Holocene phenomenon. Burushaski and Nahali represent language isolates, existing as enclaves in what is now Indo-European-speaking India. On the view tentatively advanced here they would earlier have been isolates in a Dravidian speaking environment, and earlier still, languages of hunter-gatherers among other, now extinct languages which were replaced by the Dravidian dispersal. In like manner the Dravidian language Brahui would have been left as an isolate by the later Indo-European dispersal. These are, however, weak hypotheses in that they are not supported by any data beyond the framework of arguments advanced here.

Turning to Europe, it is relevant to ask what were the languages spoken here before the Indo-European dispersal. Basque, of course, represents the only living isolate. It is interesting to note that a relationship with the South Caucasian (Kartvelian) languages has been suggested by some authors.[83] Etruscan is the most important other isolate, whose non-Indo-European status is widely, but not universally accepted. Recently a case has been made for regarding it as an Eastern Caucasian language,[84] but of course pairwise comparisons have been made between Etruscan and many of the languages of the world.

Perhaps, however, we should not be dismissive of the possibility that, before the Indo-European dispersal, there was a relatively small number of language groups in Europe and in western Asia.[85] Potential relationships between the relict languages need not therefore occasion surprise.

The only remaining European language for which a non-Indo-European status is widely agreed is Iberian. But there are other possibilities, unfortunately none attested by very numerous inscriptions, including Sicel, Pictish, Rhaetian, Messapic and Illyrian, as Zvelebil and Zvelebil have recently reasserted in their discussion of Indo-European dispersals.[86]

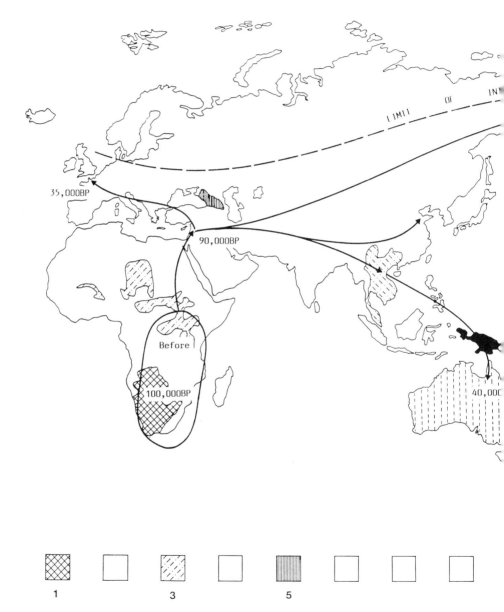

Map 3. Existing language macrofamilies which may be regarded as the product of initial colonisation during the Pleistocene by *Homo sapiens sapiens*. 1: Khoisan; 3: Nilo-Saharan; 5: Caucasian; 13: Austric (Daic and Austroasiatic); 14: Indo-Pacific; 15: Australian; 17: Amerind.

HUMAN

COLONISATION

?40,000 BP

|  |  |  |  | 13 | 14 | 15 |  | 17 |

Map 4. Modern world macrofamilies resulting from processes of initial
colonisation and agricultural dispersal. Key as for map 6.

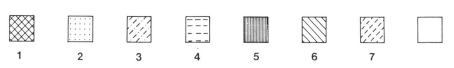

Map 5. Modern language macrofamilies whose distribution may be assigned
to processes of initial colonisation by hunter-gatherers in Late Pleistocene and
Holocene times (indicated north of the bold line). 7: Uralic-Yukaghir;
9: Chukchi-Kamchatkan; 10: Eskimo-Aleut; 16: Na-Dene.

Map 6. Modern world language macrofamilies following major élite
domination processes (for the distribution of Indo-European languages in
Iran and south Asia; and G: the Altaic macrofamily). These result, together
with the processes seen in maps 2 to 5, in the modern distribution of
macrofamilies of the world's languages.[1]

Key: 1: Khoisan; 2: Niger-Kordofanian; 3: Nilo-Saharan; 4: Afro-Asiatic;
5: Caucasian; 6: Indo-European; 7: Uralic-Yukaghir; 8: Altaic; 9: Chukchi-
Kamchatkan; 10: Eskimo-Aleut; 11: Elamo-Dravidian; 12: Sino-Tibetan;
13: Austric (Daic and Austroasiatic); 14: Indo-Pacific; 15: Australian;
16: Na-Dene; 17: Amerind

The hypothetical sequence proposed here for the dispersal of the world's language families is illustrated schematically in maps 3 to 6. (It should be noted that the maps show only those areas *currently* occupied by each language family, once the colonial effects of recent centuries are discounted.)

## I. THE GENETIC EVIDENCE

The sceptical reader may already have formed the view that the arguments offered so far (if such they can be called) amount to little more than a migrationist fantasy, proposing movements of language speakers not only thousands of years but tens of thousands of years before there is any written record whatever of the languages spoken in the world. To turn now to what used to be termed physical anthropology may conjure up an unhappy and anachronistic return to the racist delusions of an earlier era, when craniometric measurements were used to distinguish one human 'race' or 'folk' from another and supposedly to trace their wanderings upon the surface of the earth.

It is to be admitted that most of the major linguistic macrofamilies and their distributions have been discussed here in terms of population displacements – first in terms of initial population and then in terms of agricultural dispersal. But these were very slow processes, certainly not 'migrations' in the traditional sense of large-scale movements of people, 'folk movements', conceived on the model of the so-called Migration Period, and often based upon the mobility offered by the use of the horse. As discussed earlier, these would often amount to episodes of élite dominance, and would require an already highly structured social order. Nor have any distinctions in terms of 'race' been advanced here, and the term is not strictly relevant to the discussion in this section either.

Current research in the field of molecular genetics now offers the hope of testing some of the hypotheses that have been outlined here. For it is the case that both the model of initial colonisation and that of agricultural dispersal entailing language replacement carry implications in terms of human genetics. In the case of initial colonisation, there evidently must have existed an ancestral group from which later generations within the territories subsequently occupied were descended.

And in the case of language replacement by agricultural dispersal, the marked increase of population accompanying that agricultural dispersal may, on some models, favour the intrusive, agriculture-using group, and lead to the numerical (and linguistic) dominance of its members within the territories in question. Such would certainly be the implications of the wave of advance model. This situation would carry very significant genetic consequences.

On the other hand, were we to accept a model for language change based either upon 'seepage' – that is to say the gradual change in language without significant change in the human population – or upon élite dominance, which would have the same consequence, then the genetic effects would be very different. The indigenous group would remain numerically dominant from the genetic standpoint. Were we to be in the position of assessing reliably the genetic relationships of these early populations or of their descendents, it might well be possible to discriminate between the two cases, and to decide in favour of one or the other.

Recent advances in molecular genetics bring us close to that position. It is no longer necessary to measure phenotypic characteristics (that is to say ones which, while dependent upon genetic composition, do not reflect it directly) such as cranial dimensions. It is now beginning to be possible to approach the genotype directly, using methods of DNA sequencing. It is possible also, without going so far as to investigate the sequences of bases within a specific DNA molecule, to study characteristics which are very much more closely controlled by the genetic composition than are such phenomena as cranial measurements: much work of this kind has been done in the field of blood groups.

Traditionally, of course, statements about genetic origins have frequently been based upon metrical, and especially craniometrical characteristics, but such techniques are now being superseded by more sophisticated methods.[88] In a recent study, a careful statistical analysis of the dental characteristics of different human groups was used to make proposals about the origins of the American Indians, and indeed to link these with the tripartite linguistic classification (Amerind, Na-Dene, Eskimo-Aleut) reported above for the language of the Americas.[89] While the correlation between methods is undoubtedly of interest,

however, it seems likely that more specifically genetic
approaches will increasingly be used in the future.

Such approaches have already been put to ambitious use, and
linguistic inferences drawn, through the analysis of gene frequencies based upon classical genetic markers. Gene-frequency
data were utilised for human blood group antigens, enzymes
and proteins, and analysed statistically to compute genetic
distances.[90] It should clearly be understood that these 'classical'
markers do not depend upon analyses at the molecular level
where base-sequences of human DNA are examined. It should
also be noted that hitherto the analyses in question have been
undertaken upon samples from living individuals. What is
being measured is the 'genetic distance' between living individuals and between populations. In well-defined cases this may
give clear indications of their genetic affinities viewed in
historical terms, although it can itself, as a method, give no
direct chronological information. Coupled with simulation studies,[91] inferences about the origins of the populations in
question may be drawn. Cavalli-Sforza, Piazza, Menozzi and
Mountain have gone on to propose linguistic inferences.[92]
They identified the languages spoken by the individuals or
groups studied, and compared the broad linguistic groupings
advocated for them by Ruhlen with the genetic tree based on
the genetic distance computations.[93] They found a good correspondence between the genetic tree and the classification of
linguistic phyla. But I think it is fair to say that there are pitfalls
here, and that their article should be seen as a pioneering and
suggestive initiative, not yet as more than this. Comparable data
have also been studied by Harding and Sokal, who concluded
that, when the genetic distances are investigated, 'The resulting
classification largely reflects geographic propinquity rather
than linguistic origins'.[94] However this does not of itself necessarily call into question the value of the method: spatial autocor-
relation is to be anticipated with any long-standing spatial
patterns. It is certainly seen in the linguistic field.[95] Underlying
the spatial correlations there may well also be patterning
indicative of genetic origin.

At every point it has to be reasserted that there is no
necessary and ineluctable connection between genetic and
linguistic origins. The population of a territory can change

substantially without significant linguistic change, and, as we have seen, in some cases language replacement can indeed occur with very insignificant changes in population terms. But as stressed above, linguistic replacement based upon élite dominance is a social phenomenon: in the words of Diamond, 'Most such transfers probably depended on a degree of political organization that emerged in the past 5,000 years. Before that, the match between linguistic phyla and genetic clusters would have been undisturbed.'[96]

The most promising evidence for the future will surely come from studies at the molecular level, based upon DNA. Already there are indications that, in favourable cases, it will be possible to extract suitable samples from such ancient specimens as Egyptian mummies.[97] To be able to work with archaeological specimens directly is obviously the archaeologist's ideal. This will bring with it vastly improved possibilities for establishing genetic relationships, and for determining the origins, in terms of descent, of individual humans and of human groups. At present, however, most of the work has been with samples drawn from living individuals, and attention has focused upon very broad themes in the field of human origins.[98]

Human mitochondrial DNA has a structure derived exclusively from that of the mother, and thus allows inferences about the matriarchal descent line. The patriarchal line is open to study via the Y-chromosome which is passed on by the father.[99] Discussion has so far mainly focused upon inferences, drawn from the study of mitochondrial DNA, that the entire species *Homo sapiens sapiens*, as it exists today, is descended either from a single human female or from a small group, located in Africa in the Pleistocene period.[100] It has also been proposed that a relatively steady state of mutation may be assumed for mitochondrial DNA. It may be possible to calibrate this rate of mutation, knowing the approximate dates of separation of various descent lines in the early history of human populations (for example the initial colonisation of Australia or of theAmericas). A biological clock would then be available.[101] Of course the sceptic will see here an evident parallel with glottochronology, where rate of word loss might be compared with the mutation rate underlying the biological clock. However there is no good reason to assume that word loss in languages proceeds at a constant rate: it must be socially dependent. Mutation in mitochondrial DNA is presumably much less likely to be dependent upon human social factors.

Nuclear DNA has also been investigated by comparable techniques.[102] Already interesting results have been obtained that bear upon Polynesian origins.[103] Such results have not yet been applied to questions of linguistic origin. Once again it is relevant that the technique can supply information only about the genetic origins and affinities of the individuals and groups under study. Whether or not that bears upon linguistic questions is, as in the cases discussed earlier, a matter of inference. But certainly these techniques are eminently appropriate for studying not just the broad sweep of human evolution, but closer affinities also upon a more restricted time scale.

I believe that these techniques will, within a decade or two, completely revolutionise our understanding, not just of human origins in the broad phylogenetic sense, but of the origins and affinities of specific human populations. To make inferences about cultural or linguistic affinities will always be very much more difficult. Naturally the genetics tells us about genes, about human descent in the purely biological sense. Language, like culture, is, however, learnt, and the paths of transmission, as we have discussed earlier, need not follow the biological path of genetic descent. But the genetic evidence will be exceedingly useful for those cases when the two paths coincide. As noted earlier, initial colonisation and language displacement by agricultural dispersal are two of the most important of these.

## J. EXPLAINING WHAT?

Before concluding, it is perhaps worth asking afresh precisely what the foregoing arguments would achieve, even if they were indeed correct.

A critic could quite reasonably ask how one could ever form a balanced judgement as to whether or not the explanations offered are indeed valid. How might they be tested, and either refuted or supported? Evidently direct tests as to which languages were spoken at times situated deep in prehistory are difficult to conceive. But it is undoubtedly the case that the hypotheses offered, within the theoretical framework established, do carry implications (that is, make predictions) which may or may not prove well founded when set against the available data, or against the new data which will become available, for instance through progress with molecular biology. In that sense the explanation offered, while undoubtedly 'historical' (in proposing specific historical events in the past to account for present language distributions) is also 'scientific' in the Popperian sense of carrying testable implications: it is hypothetico-deductive.

I see two difficulties: one relating to the accompanying theoretical framework, the other to complexity. I will deal with complexity first. It is the function of models to simplify and make intelligible, so that despite the scepticism of some, it is no reproach to my explanations that they are simple, and offer simpler outcomes than are seen in reality among the data.[104] It is to be predicted that there were also all manner of subsidiary effects at work, and that the patterns of distribution of specific languages require them to be generated at a more detailed level by ancillary models, giving a finer structure than the broad distributions of the macrofamilies. But the dilemma, when we are concerned with testing the larger, primary models discussed here, is that one could always retreat, in the face of a non-correspondence between prediction and data, to some criticism of the ancillary model. Alternatively one could use a secondary model to 'save the phenomena' which the primary model had failed to predict.

The second difficulty concerns the theoretical framework within which one is working. This framework involves the assumption that there are indeed regularities in the workings of language change which one may seek to correlate with social change and hence make accessible to archaeological research.[105] This is an assumption which many linguists and probably most historical linguists would at present question.[106]

Moreover, for the hypotheses advanced here to win some degree of acceptance, there are certain broad objections which would have to be overcome. The most significant of these is that of time depth. As noted earlier, most historical linguists would argue that language change takes place very much more rapidly than has been allowed for here. They would, for instance, see common proto-Indo-European at a time prior to a postulated dispersal which they would situate at around 4000 BC rather than 8000 BC. They would doubt that any significant linguistic relationships whatever could be established between languages that became isolated from each other as much as 10,000 years ago. This is a difficulty, I think, even for Greenberg himself, if he were forced to accept that the dispersal process for the early American Indian languages would have separated the early speakers of proto-Amerind in North and South America perhaps as much as 30,000 years ago, as now seems likely.

If, however, we set aside for the moment these very weighty objections, it is pertinent to ask what problems have been answered by the suggested 'explanations' offered here and what obvious problems remain. Clearly the discussion here has been at the macrofamily level, and much further work would be needed in each region to work out local histories for specific languages. But it is of course the case that very often such detailed work has already been undertaken at the local level, and the immediate task would be to set this within the broader context outlined here.

In effect what has been proposed here is an explanation in terms of primary dispersals (that is, initial colonisation) modulated by subsequent agricultural dispersals and by episodes of élite dominance. This is not intended to call into question the operation of other models locally, including those resulting in the formation of creole languages which have recently been the subject of such productive study.[107] In this context it is interesting to ask what the language map of the world would look like, had the dominant process been simply that of initial colonisation followed by divergence. What would be the linguistic 'steady state' in a large territory which underwent initial colonisation, followed only by simple and standard processes of divergence and convergence (but without externally impelled agricultural dispersal or élite dominance) for a period of 1000 years, or 10,000 or 100,000 years? Clearly the answer is a different one when we are speaking of low-population-density hunter-gatherer communities, or of higher density communities, possibly with an agricultural subsistence base.

How big, in both territorial and population terms, are the language units involved? Presumably, after 100,000 years, geographically distant languages would show few or no affinities. Adjacently located languages, however, never having been completely isolated, would have diverged less. In addition they would have been more markedly subject to processes of convergence such as the acquisition of loanwords.[108] I would like to see dynamic linguistic models developed for such a situation. Presumably after some predictable length of time matters would reach some equilibrium, and any measure of affinity would settle down to a constant level, reflecting a continuing balance between convergence and divergence processes, rather than any discernible community of origin.

For the linguistic geography of the languages of hunter-gatherers, Australia presumably offers the most obvious 'laboratory'. Since detailed linguistic work among the Australian aborigines, with a few pioneering exceptions, has been undertaken only in the last 50 years, while many languages became either extinct or much reduced in territorial extent before that time, any language maps must be largely hypothetical. Dixon offers two maps which at least allow one to begin to think concretely in terms of scale.[109]

There are of course always problems of terminology, in deciding at what point what might be taken for different dialects of a language should be considered rather as different languages in their own right. Lexicostatisticians have attempted to use comparisons of word-lists (often using 100 words). Cognate scores of more than 70 per cent have been taken to indicate dialects of one language, cognate scores of the order of 50 to 70 per cent to indicate distinct languages which share membership of the same subgroup, scores of 25 to 50 per cent languages which share membership of the same group.[110] While such scores are crude, and when mechanistically applied can give misleading results, they do nonetheless suggest in outline the degree of mutual intelligibility which speakers of the same language may be expected to share.

The map of the relatively populous Australian south-east suggests that the language territories there might range in area from 5000 to 100,000 square kilometres. It has been estimated that at the time of contact the population of Australia may have been about 300,000, while the number of languages spoken may have been between 200 and 250, suggesting an average of around 1200 to 1500 speakers for each language.[111] Naturally, in desert regions, the territorial extent of a language would be very much greater in area.

Dixon, in his treatment of the Australian languages, emphasises the limitations of classifying languages into subgroups by means of vocabulary comparisons alone, and is scathing about the quality of lexicostatistical work which has in fact been undertaken in Australia.[112] He argues, moreover, that 'if two rather different languages come into contiguity, they will borrow back and forth until the proportion of common lexemes gradually rises, and eventually makes up about 50 per cent (in practice say 40–60 per cent) of each language's total vocabulary.[113] But a similar result is envisaged for closely related languages: 'If one tribe splits into two new tribes, each will taboo and replace words independently, and the percentage of common vocabulary will steadily drop until it reaches the 50 per cent 'equilibrium level".[114] He estimates 'some thousands of years' for two languages to reach the notional 50 per cent equilibrium level. But he makes no predictions as to the scale of the linguistic units (that is, the territorial extent of the languages) when the equilibrium point is reached. The scale is not quite the same as the extent of tribal units (i.e. tribes), since it is envisaged that several tribes may speak the same language, albeit with different dialects. (Blake's estimates suggest on average about three tribes per language.) It should be noted that on this terminology it would be altogether exceptional for one tribe's area to embrace several languages, while one language area can indeed include several tribes. Such discussion may be seen as almost tautological, however, when it is remembered that the definition of 'tribe' is often externally imposed and that linguistic data constitute a crucial factor when an anthropologist is determining where to set the notional boundaries of the tribal unit. I am not aware of any cross-cultural study that considers the dynamics of hunter-gatherer communication in geographical terms. Evidently factors of mobility will be important, as will those of population density. It is the case that many living or recent hunter-gatherer communities occupy what are now regarded as marginal lands, often desert

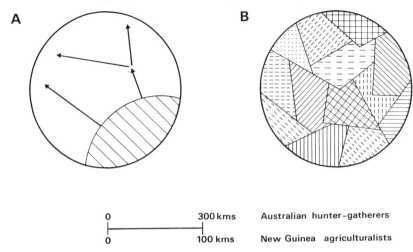

A    B

```
0                    300 kms    Australian hunter-gatherers
├──────────────────┤
0                    100 kms    New Guinea  agriculturalists
```

Figure 1 Unity versus mosaic: the contrasting patterns from (A) language replacement and (B) initial colonisation with subsequent processes for convergence and divergence. In B one may compare the different scales for the language map for hunter-gatherers and for the agriculturalists whose agricultural economy is indigenous, resulting in a mosaic of small language units. (The language units are for convenience separated by lines: this is not intended to suggest that they are discrete or bounded entities nor to deny the existence of intermediate dialects.)

or tundra, and only little evidence can remain for the linguistic geography of hunter-gatherer groups in areas which have proved agriculturally productive.

If Australia offers the paradigm case for languages of hunter-gatherers evolving in relative isolation after initial colonisation, the same has sometimes been claimed for New Guinea so far as horticultural or agricultural communities are concerned, since the indigenous development of agriculture seems increasingly well documented.[115] It is, however, not easy to find language maps for New Guinea which set out clearly the territorial extent of languages spoken (see Fig. 1).

Wurm estimates that there are some 700 Papuan languages, some with large speech communities approaching and even surpassing 100,000 in a few instances.[116] Many other languages, however, have as few as 100 speakers. It is tempting to imagine the New Guinea situation as a mosaic of horticultural communities, with ecological and geographical factors determining the scale of the tribal/linguistic units. The larger classifications into linguistic phyla that Wurm and his colleagues have undertaken serve to stress the great variety in the Papuan languages. This could be used in support of a long-term *in situ* evolution, without major episodes of élite dominance, or of agricultural dispersal. Once again no models appear to be available that would undertake to predict the size of speech communities, nor their real extent.

If we try to imagine, then, a world whose language distribution was the product of initial colonisation, followed by convergence and divergence effects, but without the effects of agricultural dispersal or of élite dominance, might we perhaps imagine the linguistic configuration of Australia generalised for those areas with a hunter-gatherer economy, and that of New Guinea for those with an indigenous agricultural economy?

It is against this background that several of the linguistic macrofamilies are seen to differ very markedly from each other in their distributions. It is towards the explanation of these differences that the present paper, in a preliminary way, has been dedicated.


K. CONCLUSIONS

I have tried to show how the linguistic, archaeological and genetic evidence may be brought together to suggest a mutually compatible history for human dispersals and their aftermath. The implications, for archaeology and for historical linguistics, would be significant if this emerging synthesis found some further confirmation.

Its importance should not, however, be exaggerated. For there is something ultimately very arbitrary about precisely which given language a given community may speak. The identity of that language is, as the foregoing makes clear, simply a matter of some historical circumstance, albeit an interesting one. There is absolutely no indication that any one language has an adaptive advantage over any other (although each proves itself appropriate in its concepts and vocabulary to the cultural context in which it developed). There is, I would argue, no cause for mysticism here. There is no necessary correlation for instance between one's language and one's belief system, although correlation is possible. This is one reason that I look with suspicion upon the concept of 'Indo-European religion', or 'Indo-European mythology' or comparable notions where an inherent linkage is claimed between a particular language family and the community's mode of thought.

The lines of linguistic descent suggested here do indeed have implications, and suggest avenues to explore, in relation to the evolution of cultural attributes other than speech. But the ease with which religions originating in Semitic-speaking lands have spread to Indo-European-speaking lands (for example Judaism, Christianity, Islam) or religions originating in Indo-European speaking areas have spread beyond (for example Buddhism) counsels against too close a linkage.

Many of the really interesting questions in the field of human cognitive abilities lie outside the area examined in this paper. That is, perhaps, one of its most important conclusions. For often it is only in solving a problem, or at least in proposing a solution, that one comes to realise that the problem itself is less significant than one had earlier supposed.

What I have said here has, then, only limited bearing upon such questions. It does not much illuminate that fascinating question of the actual emergence of human linguistic abilities as such. For they are here seen as linked with the emergence of our own species. This paper does not seek to achieve much in these respects. But it clears the decks. As such I hope it may prove an acceptable offering to its dedicatee.

## NOTES

1. The work on which this paper is based has benefited from the encouragement and advice of several colleagues, not least Ernest Gellner. I particularly wish to acknowledge the helpful correspondence of Professor Claude Boisson, who has opened new horizons for me with his bibliographic references and has offered valued observations on the present paper. It is appropriate that I acknowledge explicitly not only the relevance of earlier and recent work by Professor L.L. Cavalli-Sforza, but also the convergence in our thinking on the possible relationship between agricultural and language dispersals, well brought out in a recent paper, 'The basque population and ancient

migrations in Europe', *Munibe (Antroplogia y Arqueloqia)
Suplemento*, vol. 6, 1988 of which he kindly sent me a copy in
proof. Other recent and helpful correspondents have been
Peter Bellwood, Alvar Ellegard, Vitaly Sheveroshkin and Kamil
Zvelebil. Dr Chris Scarre kindly drew the figures.

2. E. Gellner, *Plough, Sword and Book: The Structure of Human
History*, London, 1988.

3. See respectively C.B. Stringer and P. Andrews, 'Genetic and
fossil evidence for the origin of modern humans', *Science*, vol.
239, 1988 and M.H. Wolpoff, 'Multiregional evolution: the
fossil alternative to Eden', in P. Mellars and C.B. Stringer, eds.,
*The Human Revolution, Behavioural and Biological Perspectives on
the Origins of Modern Humans*, volume 1, Edinburgh, 1989.

4. L.R. Binford, *Bones: Ancient Men and Modern Myths*, New York,
1981.

5. L.R. Binford, 'Human ancestors: changing view of their behaviour', *Journal of Anthropological Archaeology*, vol. 4, 1985.

6. J.H. Greenberg, *The Languages of Africa*, Bloomington, 1963 and
*Languages in the Americas*, Stanford, 1987.

7. M. Ruhlen, *A Guide to the World's Languages*, volume 1, Stanford,
1987.

8. M. Kaiser and V. Shevoroshkin, 'Nostratic', *Annual Review of
Anthropology*, vol. 17, 1988.

9. On the Hamito-Semitic group, see I.M. Diakonoff, *Hamito-Semitic
Languages*, Moscow, 1965 and *Afrasian Languages*, Moscow, 1988;
on the claim that the Hamito-Semitic group is part of a larger
Afro-Asiatic entity, see C.F. Voegelin and F.M. Voegelin, *Classification and Index of the World's Languages*, New York, 1977.

10. V.M. Illich-Svitych, *A Comparison of the Nostratic Languages*,
Moscow, volumes 1 and 2, 1976, volume 3, part one, 1984;
Kaiser and Shevoroshkin, 'Nostratic'; R. Bulatova, 'Illich-
Svitych: A biographical sketch', in V. Shevoroshkin, ed., *Recon-
structing Languages and Cultures*, Bochum, 1989.

11. H. Pedersen, *The Discovery of Language: Linguistic Science in the
Nineteenth Century*, Bloomington, 1972.

12. Ruhlen, *A Guide to the World's Languages*, p. 259.

13. P. Bellwood, 'A Hypothesis for Austronesian origins', *Asian
Perspectives* vol. 26, part 1, 1985; C. Renfrew, *Archaeology and
Language, the Puzzle of Indo-European Origins*, London and New
York, 1987; J. Terrell, *Prehistory in the Pacific Islands*, Cambridge,
1988; A. Sherratt and S. Sherratt, 'The archaeology of the
Indo-Europeans, an alternative view', *Antiquity*, vol. 62, 1988.

14. R. Harding and R. Sokal, 'Classification of the European language families by genetic distance', *Proceedings of the National
Academy of Sciences of the USA*, vol. 85, 1988.

15. A.C.S. Hill, B. Gentile, J.M. Bonnardot, J. Roux,

D.J. Weatherall and J.B. Clegg, 'Polynesian origins and affinities: globin gene variants in eastern Polynesia', *American Journal of Human Genetics*, vol. 40, 1987; R.L. Cann, M. Stoneking and A.C. Wilson, 'Mitochondrial DNA and human evolution', *Nature*, vol. 325, 1987.

16. S. Pääbo, 'Molecular cloning of Ancient Egyptian mummy DNA', *Nature*, vol. 314, 1985.

17. M. Swadesh, *The Origin and Diversification of Language*, London, 1972.

18. L.L. Cavalli-Sforza, A. Piazza, P. Menozzi and J. Mountain, 'Reconstruction of human evolution: bringing together genetic, archaeological and linguistic data', *Proceedings of the National Academy of Sciences of the USA*, vol. 85, 1988; S.J. Gould, 'Grimm's greatest tale', *Natural History*, number 2, 1989.

19. C. Renfrew, *Archaeology and Languages*; Sherratt and Sherratt, 'The archaeology of the Indo-Europeans'.

20. C. Renfrew, 'Models of change in language and archaeology', *Transactions of the Philological Society*, vol. 87, 1989.

21. A.J. Ammerman and L.L. Cavalli-Sforza, 'A population model for the diffusion of early farming in Europe', in C. Renfrew, ed., *The Explanation of Culture Change: Models in Prehistory*, London, 1973.

22. M. Zvelebil and K.V. Zvelebil, 'Agricultural transition and Indo-European dispersals', *Antiquity*, vol. 62, 1988.

23. C. Ehret, 'Language change and the material correlates of language and ethnic shift', *Antiquity*, vol. 62, 1988.

24. H.P. Schwarz, R. Grün, B. Vandermeersch, O. Bar-Yosef, H. Valladas and E. Tchernov, 'ESR dates for the hominid burial site of Qafzeh in Israel', *Journal of Human Evolution*, vol. 17, 1988.

25. E. Pulgram, 'Linguistic expansion and diversification', in E. Pulgram, ed., *Studies Presented to Joshua Whatmough on his Sixtieth Birthday*, 's-Gravenhage, 1957, p. 245.

26. S.A. Wurm, 'Linguistic prehistory in the New Guinea Area', *Journal of Human Evolution*, vol. 12, 1983.

27. Sherratt and Sherratt, 'The archaeology of the Indo-Europeans'.

28. J. Bengtson, 'On the fallacy of "diminishing returns" in long range lexical comparison', in Shevoroshkin, ed., *Reconstructing Languages and Cultures*.

29. J.B. Kruskal, I. Dyen and P. Black, 'The vocabulary method of reconstructing language trees: innovations and large-scale applications', in F.R. Hodson, D.G. Kendall and P. Tautu, eds, *Mathematics in the Archaeological and Historical Sciences*, Edinburgh, 1971.

30. Greenberg, *Language in the Americas*, p. 342.

31. E. Gellner, *Nations and Nationalism*, Oxford, 1983.
32. J. B. Birdsell, 'Some predictions for the Pleistocene based on equilibrium systems among recent hunter-gatherers', in R. Lee and I. Devore, eds, *Man the Hunter*, Chicago, 1968.
33. Cavalli-Sforza, 'The Basque population and ancient migrations in Europe'.
34. A. Morpurgo Davies, 'Comments on C. Renfrew, "Models of change in language and archaeology"', *Transactions of the Philological Society*, vol. 87, 1989.
35. R. Coleman, 'Review of C. Renfrew, *Archaeology and Language*', *Current Anthropology*, vol. 29, 1989, p. 451.
36. Ruhlen, *A Guide to the World's Languages*, p. 290.
37. Renfrew, *Archaeology and Language*.
38. Morpurgo Davies, 'Comments on C. Renfrew', p. 167.
39. L.L. Cavalli-Sforza, 'Cultural evolution and genetics', in F. Vogel and K. Sperling, eds, *Human Genetics*, Berlin, 1987 and 'Cultural transmission and adaptation', *Trends in Archaeology*, vol. 116, 1988.
40. Cavalli-Sforza, 'The Basque population and ancient migrations in Europe', p. 134, figure five.
41. P. Bellwood, 'The colonization of the Pacific, some current hypotheses', in A.V.S. Hill and S.W. Serjeantson, eds, *The Colonisation of the Pacific, A Genetic Trail*, Oxford, 1989 and 'The Austronesian dispersal and the origins of language families', unpublished paper.
42. Renfrew, *Archaeology and Language*.
43. Zvelebil and Zvelebil, 'Agricultural transition and Indo-European dispersals'.
44. A. Dolgopolski, 'The Indo-European homeland and lexical contacts of Proto-Indo-European with other languages', *Mediterranean Language Review*, vol. 3, 1987, p. 26.
45. D. Zohary, 'Domestication of the south-west Asian assemblage of cereals, pulses and flax', in D.R. Harriss and G.C. Hillman, eds., *Foraging and Farming*, London, 1989.
46. C. Renfrew, 'The prehistory of language: new light upon Indo-European origins', *Scientific American*, vol. 261, 1989, p. 90; Cavalli-Sforza, 'The Basque population and ancient migrations in Europe'.
47. A.Y. Militarev and V.A. Shnirelman, 'The problem of the Indo-European home and culture', in *12th International Congress of Anthropological and Ethnological Sciences, Zagreb, Yugoslavia, July 24–31 1988*, Moscow, 1988, p. 8.
48. D.W. McAlpin, *Proto-Elamo-Dravidian: The Evidence and its Implications*, Philadelphia, 1981. Cf. K. Zvelebil, 'Review of D.W. McAlpin, *Proto-Elamo-Dravidian: The Evidence and Its Implications*', *Journal of the American Oriental Society*, vol. 105, 1985.

49. D.W. Phillipson, 'The spread of the Bantu languages', *Scientific American*, vol. 236, 1977 and *African Archaeology*, Cambridge, 1985.

50. Terrell, *Prehistory in the Pacific Islands*; P.V. Kirch, 'Rethinking East Polynesian prehistory', *Journal of the Polynesian Society*, vol. 95, 1986; P.V. Kirch and R.C. Green, 'History, phylogeny and evolution in Polynesia', *Current Anthropology*, vol. 28, 1987.

51. P. Bellwood, *Prehistory of the Indo-Malaysian Archipelago*, New York, 1985; *The Polynesians*, London, 1987; and 'The Austronesian dispersal and the origins of language families'.

52. T.T. Chang, 'The origins and early cultures of the cereal grains and food legumes', in D.N. Keightley, ed., *The Origins of Chinese Civilisation*, Berkeley, 1983; R. Pearson, 'The Ch'ing-lien-kang culture and the Chinese neolithic', in Keightley, *The Origins of Chinese Civilisation*.

53. E.G. Pulleyblank, 'The Chinese and their neighbours in prehistoric and early historic times', in Keightley, *The Origins of Chinese Civilisation*.

54. V. Shevoroshkin, 'A symposium on the deep reconstruction of languages and cultures', in Shevoroshkin, ed., *Reconstructing Languages and Cultures*, p. 8.

55. Ruhlen, *A Guide to the World's Languages*, p. 294. Greenberg does not accept this position in *Language in the Americas*, p. 332.

56. G.L. Barnes, '*Jiehao, tonghao*: peer relations in East Asia' in C. Renfrew and J.F. Cherry, eds., *Peer Polity Interaction and Socio-Political Change*, Cambridge, 1986.

57. P.M. Dolukhanov, 'Natural environment and the Holocene settlement pattern in the north-western part of the USSR', *Fennoscandia Archaeologica*, vol. 3, 1986.

58. Greenberg, *Language in the Americas*, p. 333.

59. D.E. Dumond, *The Eskimos and the Aleuts*, London, 1987, pp. 133, 152.

60. W.S. Laughlin, *Aleuts: Survivors of the Bering Land*, New York, 1980.

61. Greenberg, *Language in the Americas*.

62. F.H. West, *The Archaeology of Beringia*, New York, 1981, p. 201.

63. E. Sapir, 'The similarity of Chinese and Indian language', *Science*, vol. 62, 1925.

64. Ruhlen, *A Guide to the World's Languages*, p. 136.

65. C.S. Chard, *Northeast Asia in Prehistory*, Madison, 1974, p. 101. Chard at this point is citing N.N. Dikov, 'The stone age of Kamchatka and the Chukchi peninsula in the light of new archaeological data', *Arctic Anthropology*, vol. 3, 1965.

66. Chard, *Northeast Asia in Prehistory*, p. 102.

67. A.J. Ammerman and L.L. Cavalli-Sforza, 'A population model for the diffusion of early farming in Europe'; 'The wave of

66     C O L I N   R E N F R E W

advance model for the spread of agriculture in Europe', in C. Renfrew and K.L. Cooke, eds, *Transformations, Mathematical Approaches to Culture Change*, New York, 1979, and *The Neolithic Transition and the Genetics of Populations in Europe*, Princeton, 1984.

68. P.S. Martin, 'The pattern and meaning of Holoarctic mammoth extinction', in D.M. Hopkins, J.V. Matthews, C.W. Schweger and S.B. Young, eds., *Paleoecology of Beringia*, New York, 1982.

69. This figure follows Martin, 'The pattern and meaning of Holoarctic mammoth extinction'.

70. Bellwood, *Prehistory of the Indo-Malaysian Archipelago* and 'A hypothesis for Austronesian origins'.

71. S.A. Wurm, *Papuan Languages of Oceania*, Tubingen, 1982 and 'Linguistic prehistory in the New Guinea area'.

72. J.H. Greenberg, 'The Indo-Pacific hypothesis', in T.A. Seboek, ed., *Linguistics in Oceania (Current Trends in Linguistics Volume 8)*, The Hague, 1971.

73. R. Jones, 'East of Wallace's line: issues and problems in the colonisation of the Australian continent', in Mellars and Stringer, eds, *The Human Revolution*.

74. Ruhlen, *A Guide to the World's Languages*, p. 188.

75. R.G. Bednarik, 'On the Pleistocene settlement of South America', *Antiquity*, vol. 63, 1989.

76. L. Campbell, 'Comment on J.H. Greenberg, C.G. Turner and S.L. Zegura, "The settlement of the Americas"', *Current Anthropology*, vol. 27, 1986.

77. J.H. Greenberg, C.G. Turner and S.L. Zegura, 'The settlement of the Americas: a comparison of the linguistic, dental and genetic evidence', *Current Anthropology*, vol. 27, 1986.

78. Bednarik, 'On the Pleistocene settlement of South America'.

79. Ruhlen, *A Guide to the World's Languages*; Greenberg, *The Languages of the Americas*.

80. Ruhlen, *A Guide to the World's Languages*, p. 71.

81. V.V. Ivanov, 'Ob otnosenii xattskogo jazyka k severozapadno-kavkazskim', *Drevn'aja Anatolija*, 1985.

82. I.M. Diakonoff and S.A. Starostin, *Hurro-urartian as an Eastern Caucasian Language*, Munich, 1986.

83. K. Bouda, 'Baskisch-kaukasisch', *Zeitschrift für Phonetik*, vol 2, 1948: R. Lafon, 'Basque et les langues kartveles', *Revue Internationale des Etudes Basques*, vol. 24, 1933 and 'Concordance morphologiques entre le basque et les langues caucasiques', *Word*, vols 7 and 8, 1952, quoted by Ruhlen, *A Guide to the World's Languages*, p. 75; K.H. Schmidt, 'The two ancient Iberias from the linguistic point of view', *Veleia*, vols 2–3, 1986.

84. V.E. Orel and S.A. Starostin, 'Etruscan as an Eastern Caucasian Language', Paper Presented to the First Interdisciplinary Symposium on Language and Prehistory, Ann Arbor, November 1988.

85. E. Polome, 'Indo-European and substrate languages in the west', in Shevoroshkin, ed., *Reconstructing Languages and Culture*. Boisson has argued for a Nostratic presence in Europe prior to early Indo-European.

86. Zvelebil and Zvelebil, 'Agricultural transition and Indo-European dispersal'.

87. Modern distribution is drawn from Ruhlen, *A Guide to the World's Languages*.

88. S. Vencl, 'The role of hunting-gathering populations in the transition to farming: a central European perspective', in M. Zvelebil, ed., *Hunters in Transition*, Cambridge, 1986.

89. Greenberg, Turner and Zegura, 'The settlement of the Americas'.

90. Cavalli-Sforza, Piazza, Menozzi and Mountain, 'Reconstruction of human evolution'. Cf. A. Sanchez-Mazas, L. Excoffier and A. Langaney, 'Measure and representation of the genetic similarity between populations by the percentage of isoactive genes', *Theoria*, vol. 2, 1987; and J.M. Diamond, 'Genes and the tower of Babel', *Nature*, vol. 336, 1988.

91. S. Rendine, A. Piazza and L.L. Cavalli-Sforza, 'Simulation and separation by principal components of multiple demic expansions in Europe', *The American Naturalist*, vol. 128, 1986.

92. Cavalli-Sforza, Piazza, Menozzi and Mountain, 'Reconstruction of human evolution'; see also L.L. Cavalli-Sforza, *The History and Geography of Human Genes*, Princeton (in press).

93. Ruhlen, *A Guide to the World's Languages*.

94. Harding and Sokal, 'Classification of the European language families by genetic distance', p. 9372.

95. J.J. Chew, 'The geographical context of change in linguistic structure', Paper Presented to the Fourteenth International Conference of Linguists, East Berlin, 1987.

96. Diamond, 'Genes and the tower of Babel', p. 622.

97. Pääbo, 'Molecular cloning of Ancient Egyptian mummy'.

98. S. Rouhani, 'Molecular genetics and the pattern of human evolution: plausible and implausible models', in Mellars and Stringer, eds., *The Human Revolution*.

99. G. Lucotte, 'Evidence for paternal ancestry of modern humans: evidence from a Y-chromosome specific sequence polymorphic DNA probe', in Mellars and Stringer, eds, *The Human Revolution*.

100. Cann, Stoneking and Wilson, 'Mitochondrial DNA and human evolution'; M. Stoneking and R.L. Cann, 'African origin of human mitochondrial DNA', in Mellars and Stringer, *The Human Revolution*; J.S. Jones and S. Rouhani, 'How small was the bottleneck?', *Nature*, vol. 319, 1986.

101. A.C. Wilson, H. Ochman and E.M. Prager, 'Molecular time scale for evolution', *Trends in Genetics* 3 (9), 241–7; A.C. Wilson,

M. Stoneking, R.L. Cann, E.M. Prager, S.D. Ferris, L.A. Wrischnik and R.G. Higushi, 'Mitochondrial clans and the age of our common mother', in F. Vogel and K. Sperling, eds, *Human Genetics*, Heidelberg, 1987.

102. J. Flint, A.V.S. Hill, D.K. Bowden, S.J. Oppenheimer, P.R. Sill, S.W. Serjeantson, J. Bana-Koiri, K. Bhatia, M.P. Alpers, A.J. Boyce, D.J. Weatherall and J.B. Clegg, 'High Frequencies of α-thalassaemia are the result of natural selection by malaria', *Nature*, vol. 321, 1986; J.S. Wainscot, A.V.S. Hill, S.L. Thein, J. Flint, J.C. Chapman, D.J. Weatherall, J.B. Clegg and D.R. Higgs, 'Geographic distribution of alpha- and beta-globin gene cluster polymorphisms', in Mellars and Stringer, eds, *The Human Revolution*.

103. Hill, Gentile, Bonnardot, Roux, Weatherall and Clegg, 'Polynesian origins and affinities: globin gene variants in eastern Polynesia'.

104. Coleman, 'Review of C. Renfrew'.

105. Renfrew, 'Models of change in language and archaeology'.

106. P.H. Matthews, *Do languages obey general laws?: an inaugural lecture delivered before the University of Cambridge on 17 November 1981*, Cambridge, 1982.

107. S.G. Thomason and T. Kaufman, *Language contact, creolization, and genetic linguistics*, Berkeley, 1988.

108. Chew, 'The geographical context of change in linguistic structure'.

109. R.M.W. Dixon, *The Languages of Australia*, Cambridge, 1980, pp. 241, 243.

110. Dixon, *The Languages of Australia*, p. 263.

111. B.J. Blake, *Australian Aboriginal Languages*, Sydney, 1981, p. 6.

112. Dixon, *The Languages of Australia*, p. 263. Cf. G.N. O'Grady, C.F. Voegelin and F.M. Voegelin, *Languages of the World: Indo-Pacific Fascule 6 (Anthropological Linguistics 8)*, 1966; G.N. O'Grady, 'Lexicographic research in aboriginal Australia', in T.A. Seboek, ed., *Linguistics in Oceania*; S.A. Wurm, 'Classifications of Australian languages including Tasmanian', in Seboek, ed., *Linguistics in Oceania*.

113. Dixon, *The Languages of Australia*, p. 254.

114. Dixon, *The Languages of Australia*, p. 254.

115. G. Golson, 'The origins and development of New Guinea agriculture', in Harriss and Hillman, eds, *Foraging and Farming*.

116. S.A. Wurm, 'The Papuan linguistic situation', in Seboek, *Linguistics in Oceania*.

# CHAPTER 2

# Nomads and oases in Central Asia

## A.M. Khazanov

The whole history of Central Asia may be, and must be, to a large extent conceived as interaction between sedentary population and pastoral nomads, particularly those migrating to and settling in the area. The aim of this paper is to demonstrate that oases were the focal points in this process, and that an influx of nomads into Central Asian oases strongly affected their ethnic composition and socio-political characteristics.

Central Asia comprises the area which is flanked in the north by the Aral Sea and the Kazakh steppes, in the south by the Kopet-Dagh and Hindu Kush, in the west by the Caspian Sea, and in the east by the Pamirs.

Central Asia and the northern parts of Inner Asia, along with several other regions, constitute the vast geographical zone of Eurasian steppes, semi-deserts and deserts which stretch from the Danube to North China. This temperate zone of Eurasia may be subdivided more or less neatly into areas favourable for irrigation agriculture and areas favourable for extensive pastoralism. Together these forms of economic activities were possible only on the banks of rivers and inland reservoirs, and also in mountain piedmonts and valleys. However, the regions of mixed economy were nothing more than small enclaves interspersed among wide territories occupied by nomads.[1]

In Central Asia proper, and in the steppes to the north, dry farming in the form of so-called bogar agriculture, and small-scale irrigation agriculture, were located mainly in mountain regions and in the foothills.[2] These forms of cultivation were usually combined with extensive pastoralism. Agriculture with irregular irrigation and kair agriculture were practised in the lower reaches of the rivers, particularly those with a variable annual flow.[3]

Widespread irrigation agriculture in Central Asia dates from the beginning of the first millennium BC. All Central Asian oases are artificial, man-made fertile spots surrounded by meagre soils and having no analogues in the natural environment. Some oases vanished for centuries, while new ones emerged. These changes, however, were of minor importance. Most oases were located in one and the same territory for millennia; only their borders and general configuration occasionally changed.

Some irrigation canals that were built many centuries ago are still in use, like the main Dargom canal in the Samarqand oasis, which dates to the turn of the Christian era, or the Salar canal in the Tashkent oasis constructed in the first century AD.[4] The main canals of the Merv oasis have an even more ancient origin.[5]

Some oases occupied narrow belts along shallow rivers, others occupied small territories in foothills, while still others stretched for miles and miles in the valleys and deltas of the Amu Daria, Zarafshan, Murghab and other rivers.[6]

It was in such large oases that agricultural life in Central Asia was for the most part concentrated, being characterised by a high density of population.

The oases were also centres of urban life in Central Asia. Such towns as Samarqand (ancient Maraqanda), Leninabad (ancient Alexandria Eschata, medieval Khodjend), Bukhara, Tashkent, Ura-Tube (ancient Kurushkada) and Mary (ancient and medieval Merv) were known from the first millennium BC; Margilan (Marginan), Andijan (Andukan), Shakhrisiabz (Kesh?) and many others were known from early medieval times.[7]

Already in pre-Islamic times towns in many oases of Central Asia had become market centres engaged in external trade and serving as transhipment points particularly on the Great Silk Route. They also handled the trade with nomads on the borders with the Steppe. In several historical periods some of these towns were of considerable size, with developed handicrafts. In the ninth to tenth centuries, and again from the seventeenth century even some rural settlements in the oases specialised in certain handicrafts, or in trade with neighbouring pastoralists.[8]

Moreover, irrigation agriculture in many oases (for example, in those of Bukhara, Farghana, Tashkent, Murghab and Tad-jen) was combined with herdsman husbandry and stable stock-breeding. This added much to the stability of the economy of these oases.

In ancient times, particularly in the first millennium BC, oases in Central Asia were smaller and occupied even less territory than in the Middle Ages; they were then nothing more than rare islands in an ocean of untilled lands. By the second half of the first millennium BC, irrigation canals of 10–15 kilometres in length were most typical. In his trek from the Oxus (Amu Daria) river to Maraqanda (Samarqand), Alexander the Great encountered not a single hamlet. Quintus Curtius asserted that in Soghd, as well as in Bactria, most of the territories were covered by uninhabited sands, and that those desolate regions were unsettled by man and did not yield any agricultural products because they lacked water. This is in striking contrast to al-Istakhri's glowing account of conditions in early medieval Soghd. Only by the last centuries BC, and especially from the first centuries AD, in the Kushan period, was the construction of large-scale irrigation networks begun in the southern areas of Central Asia. The main canals in this period were frequently 100 kilometres or more in length, and the Eski Angor canal that watered the Karshi oases reached 200 kilometres.[9]

This helped to increase the size of irrigated lands; however, it did not change the general situation drastically.[10] Thus, Khwarazm remained encircled by steppes on all sides; an eight-day journey separated it from the nearest Bukharan oasis and, according to al-Istakhri, between the two there was only pasture lands. A similar situation existed between Bukhara and Samarqand oases. Even now, when a journey from Bukhara to Samarqand takes only five to six hours by car, the highway in the main still crosses uncultivated steppes. This general environmental situation affected interrelations between nomads and sedentaries in several ways.

On the one hand, a joint utilisation of the same ecological zones by both nomads and agriculturalists, sometimes on a rotational seasonal basis, which is most characteristic for the Middle Eastern nomads, was much less common among the nomads of the Kazakh and Mongolian steppes remote from the main oases of Maveraunnahr.[11] Except for the Syr-Daria river, Semirechye, and the northern regions of Khwarazm, which served as a principal contact zone between the nomadic and sedentary worlds, the main cultivated territories in Central Asia were situated southwards, between the Amu Daria and Syr-Daria rivers, and beyond the limits of the regular migratory routes of the Dasht-i-Qipchaq nomads.

On the other hand, most of the Maveraunnahr steppes, semi-deserts and true deserts are unlike the barren waterless terrain of the Iranian Dasht-i-Lut and Dasht-i-Kavir. These could be utilised by nomads, and those migrating into them found themselves in immediate proximity to the cultivated zones because in some cases fingers of the surrounding deserts and steppes actually penetrate the oases (for example, in the Bukhara and Kashgha-Daria oases). In Khwarazm this phenomenon may be traced to ancient times.[12]

However, those nomads who, for various reasons, had migrated into Maveraunnahr, almost always faced a shortage of pastures. It is not accidental that from time to time the supply of pastoral products was insufficient in the area, and under favourable conditions their importation from the Dasht-i-Qipchaq steppe regions was very profitable.

On more than one occasion nomads tried to solve the problem by turning agricultural territories into pastures. Perhaps the best known example is Semirechye, where the Mongols, attracted by the rich pastures of the region, destroyed the sedentary life which had flourished in the previous period.[13]

However, this way of increasing grazing territory was possible only when nomads were stronger than sedentaries. And most importantly, it was not a long-term and complete solution to the problem. Thus, nomadic migrations into the area, whatever their reasons and causes, produced a tendency to sedentarise after a while. This tendency should be regarded as an adaptation not only to the new socio-political environment but to the natural environment as well.

For the late medieval period, two large groups may be singled out among those migrants into oases who continued semi-nomadic or semi-sedentary ways of life. The first group is represented by a large part of the Karakalpaks, some Turkmen, and Kazakhs of the Syr-Daria region, whose ways of life became more or less stable and constant. For the second, consisting of nomads who were settling in oases or on their fringes (some subdivisions of the Uzbeks and Kazakhs may be listed among them), such ways of life were only temporary stages on their path to complete sedentarisation.[14]

Even in the region of the Syr-Daria oases, a considerable part of the Kazakh people had had to turn to sedentary or semi-sedentary ways of life by the seventeenth century.[15] The sedentarisation of nomads proceeded more intensively in Maveraunnahr proper since, in contrast to the Kazakh steppes, pure pastoral nomadism there had few economic advantages in comparison to agriculture.

It is no wonder, then, that in Maveraunnahr pure nomads, that is those who did not practise cultivation even as a supplementary activity, were always outnumbered by semi-nomads. Moreover, the boundaries between pure nomadism and semi-nomadism, as well as between these and other forms of extensive pastoralism, were much less distinct and much easier to cross in Central Asia than they were, for example, in Arabia (and more particularly in the Sahara). Among the Turkmen there was a division between nomads (charva) and sedentary agriculturalists (chomur), but this division was neither clear-cut nor permanent. Often, the members of one and the same family practised different kinds of economic activities.[16]

Semi-nomads who inhabited the steppes, semi-deserts and deserts of Central Asia practised cultivation, and sometimes even irrigation agriculture by temporary water sources. However, when circumstances were favourable, both pure nomads and semi-nomads often migrated into the oases and sooner or later became peasants or, more willingly, land-owners.

Such processes had frequently occurred in Central Asia from antiquity. The last to follow this path were the nomadic Uzbeks after Shaybani Khan had taken Central Asia from the Tumurids. Thus, the insufficiency of livestock and pastures in the Khiva oasis compelled the Uzbeks to sedentarise. Less than a century after their appearance there they had mastered the skill of irrigation agriculture and even participated in canal building and in restoration of old canals.[17]

All in all the oases, being the centres of agricultural production and craftsmanship, at all times attracted nomads like a magnet. That by itself contributed much to an unstable and sometimes complex ethnic composition in the oases. And the periods when oases were under the sway of the nomads were simultaneously the most favourable for their settlement there.

The settling of nomads in the oases of Central Asia and the impact of this on the ethnic composition of the oases followed traditional, centuries-old patterns. When new groups of nomads arrived in the oases, they were usually opposed by all the inhabitants of the latter, notwithstanding the time and circumstances of their own settlement there.

However, the outright extermination of the oasis's population, or its complete displacement by invading or migrating nomads, cannot be considered a typical phenomenon of the past. When the newcomers settled in the oases, they had to split up. Only small segments and groups were able to settle together, and even they often lived interspersed or intermingled with other ethnic groups. On the other hand, migrations themselves inevitably brought together the nomads and the sedentaries, with the consequence of their economic and cultural differences gradually becoming obliterated. The newcomers to the oases adopted the material and, to a large extent, the domestic culture of the indigenous sedentary population.

At the beginning of the twentieth century Russian observers noted that the domestic life of the sedentarising Uzbeks did not differ at all from that of the earlier migrants or even the indigenous inhabitants of the oases.[18] Moreover, if one and the same nomadic group had settled in different oases characterised by local peculiarities in material culture, the new arrivals also adopted these peculiarities. That happened, for example, to the Iuz Uzbeks who settled in Farghana and in the oases along the Zarafshan river.[19]

Nomadic migrations and the following socio-political, economic and cultural coalescence of different ethnic groups in the same oases, as well as their coexistence within the same states, activated various ethnic processes. Above all, they facilitated changes of languages and linguistic assimilation. While it was the culture of the sedentary population of oases that gradually took the upper hand over the culture of nomadic settlers, the languages of the latter usually turned out to be stronger, at any rate in the Middle Ages.

However, different sides of all these processes were developing at different rates, and they did not always result in the emergence of new ethnicities, nor in a complete assimilation of the former ones. Periodic invasions and infiltrations complicated and often disrupted ethnic integration in the oases. Moreover, there was no constant and dominating ingredient in the Central Asian 'melting pot', and the mingling processes lasted there for centuries and often had some local and temporal peculiarities in various oases.

Apparently, such ethnic processes in the oases of Central Asia may be traced back to the period not later than the first millennium BC. However, the meagre sources at our disposal are insufficient to describe its ancient manifestations in meticulous detail. Moreover, one should remember that in ancient times there was no clearcut linguistic, ethnic and to some degree even cultural separation between oases inhabitants and nomads roaming in the surrounding steppes and deserts. Both the sedentaries and the nomads spoke the Iranian languages, and it is not impossible that sometimes they were even conscious of their ethnic kinship. Strabo asserted that the Khwarazmians were nothing more than a part of the Sakae and Massagetae;[20] he also noticed that the Soghdians and Bactrians differed little from the nomads in their way of life and their mores. This propinquity facilitated ethnic mingling when the ancient nomads migrated into the oases. It is true that already Avesta called down curses upon the Tura pastoralists, but differences in the way of life, not ethnic separatedness, underlay this vilification.

Up to the last centuries BC, large-scale nomadic migrations into the oases of Central Asia are not explicitly noted in the written sources, although there are archaeological data that allow us to assume such a possibility. The first nomadic conquerors of the agricultural regions of Central Asia were the Parnae, who seized Parthiena from the Seleucids and various peoples who destroyed the Graeco-Bactrian Kingdom. Among the latter the Kushans soon gained the upper hand. The next nomadic conquerors of the area were the Hephthalites. Apparently a part of these invaders soon became sedentarised in the oases and was assimilated by the indigenous population. Procopius stated that 'the Hephthalites did not live as nomads but had settled on fertile lands since olden times'.[21]

The great bulk of nomads in the Qaghanate of the Western Turks continued to roam in steppes remote from the oases of Central Asia. Nevertheless, little by little the Turks penetrated into the conquered sedentary countries. A part of them settled in the oases (Shash, Farghana), while others continued to adhere to pastoralism on their fringes.

Obviously, at that time, if not earlier, processes of ethnic mingling of the Turkic-speaking nomads with the Iranian-speaking oases population had already started, as well as the Turkisation of the latter.[22] These processes markedly accelerated in the eleventh to twelfth centuries, after the fall of the Samanid State. In the Qarakhanid period nomads were migrating into and settling in the agricultural areas of Central Asia, including Soghd, in considerably larger numbers than in the previous period.[23]

Although Firdawsi opposed Iran to Turan, that is the sedentaries to the nomads, as 'two elements, fire and water, which rage against each other', the Turkic practice of marrying women from other ethnic groups, which Atabinen has labelled 'xenogamy',[24] obviously played a certain role in the Turkisation of the sedentary population of the oases. The data of physical anthropology seem to support this conjecture. However, the dissemination of the Turkic language was facilitated even more by the fact that it had become a language of ruling élites and also served as a lingua franca, even though it did not reach the status of an official language in the Central Asian states.

A sedentarisation of the Oghuz and Qipchaq nomads in Khwarazm had resulted in the almost complete disappearance of the Iranian Khwarazmian language and its replacement with the Turkic language in the thirteenth century. Earlier, Mahmud Kashghari testified that in the eleventh century some people in Semirechye spoke both Turkic and Soghdian, while others spoke only Turkic; but even then there were no persons who knew only Soghdian. Evidently, it was in the eleventh century that the Turks for the first time began to use the name 'the Tadjiks (Taziks)' for the whole of the sedentary Muslim population of Central Asia and Iran, by that time still mainly Iranian-speaking even in Central Asia.[25] At the same time Maveraunnahr gradually began to be called by the new name –

'Turkestan'.[26] The famous saying of Mahmud Kashghari, 'There is no Turk without a Tadjik; there is no head without a hat', may serve as a proof of the intensity of the interrelations between the Turkic-speaking nomads, or former nomads, and the Iranian-speaking indigenous sedentary population.

Mongolian invasion into Central Asia and the migration of many new Mongolian and Turkic-speaking nomadic groups there (the former soon becoming Turkicised), as well as the conquest of Central Asia by the nomadic Uzbeks from Dasht-i-Qipchaq in the sixteenth century and the following migrations, contributed greatly to the further complication of the ethnic situation in the oases.

Beginning in the late medieval period, the ethnic history of many oases in Central Asia is characterised by their gradual Uzbekisation. As a rule, it was various Turkic-speaking groups that merged most quickly with the nomadic Uzbek incomers. By the end of the sixteenth century the whole population of the Khanate of Bukhara was divided into the Uzbeks, Turks and Tadjiks; a century later, only two, Uzbeks and Tadjiks, are in evidence. In the first part of the seventeenth century the Chaghatays had still been a separate ethnic group in the Khiva oasis, but later they were assimilated by the Uzbeks. On the other hand, the descendants of the older sedentary population from the Khwarazm times in Khiva itself firmly retained their peculiarities during the seventeenth to nineteenth centuries, although they had long ago shifted to the Turkic language.

The Uzbekisation of different Turkic-speaking groups on the territory of the modern Uzbek Soviet Socialist Republic was only more or less completed after the Bolshevik revolution, and the process can still be observed today. Even the Iranian-speaking Tadjiks, especially those of Farghana and Tashkent, having lost their mother tongue, merged with the Uzbeks.[27] Most of the inhabitants of Bukhara also called themselves Uzbeks, notwithstanding the fact that they spoke the Tadjik language and that even some former Turkic-speaking groups shifted to the Tadjik language after they had settled in the town.[28]

An assimilation of Tadjiks on the territory of Uzbekistan particularly intensified from the 1920s, as a result of a new political delimination of Central Asia and often under direct pressure from the Uzbek authorities. In the late twenties the Tadjiks of Bukhara acknowledged: 'In the past we were Tadjiks, but now we become Uzbeks'.[29] The same was admitted by the Tadjiks of Urgut in Samarqand province: 'We are Tadjiks, but our children will be Uzbeks'.[30]

Nevertheless, at the time of the Russian conquest of Central Asia, and even later, the population of most of its oases continued to be heterogeneous. The endogamy of small kinship or local groups separated and isolated from each other contributed to this situation. Sometimes even the populations of neighbouring villages (kishlaks) hardly associated with each other, particularly if these villages were located on different main canals.[31]

One particular factor that hindered ethnic integration and assimilation requires special mention. The social stratification in the oases of Central Asia was partly built on differences between the nomadic newcomers and the sedentary population; more often than not nomadic aristocracy, or its descendants, were at the apex of the social pyramid. This was a centuries-old characteristic. Thus, at the moment of the Russian conquest of Central Asia, different Uzbek tribes dominated in all three khanates.

The population of the main oases consisted then of three main elements. For the most part the direct descendants of the ancient sedentary Iranian-speaking population in Central Asia were called Tadjiks.[32] However, up to the first half of the twentieth century the term 'Tadjik' sometimes also had some economic and social connotations. In several oases, especially those located in the basins of the Zarafshan, Kashgha-Daria and Surkhan-Daria rivers, where the sedentary population lived in the neighbourhood of the semi-nomadic Uzbeks, this term was applied to any sedentaries, even the Uzbek-speaking ones. Thus, the old tradition continued there, according to which any Islamic population in Central Asia, Iran and sometimes even in several Caucasus regions, which had been sedentarised for a long period of time, was called the 'Tadjiks'.

The second important ethnic element in the oases of Central Asia was the Uzbeks. At first the term 'Uzbek' was associated with one of the Chingizid dynasties and its entourage, then with a short-lived state of Abul-Khair-Khan, and only finally with a special ethnicity. However even in the nineteenth century the term 'Uzbek' was mainly applied to the descendants of those nomads who migrated to Central Asia from the Dasht-i-Qipchaq steppes during the Shaybani Khan conquest and settled in the valleys of Zarafshan, Kashgha-Daria and Surkhan-Daria rivers and in the oases of Tashkent and Khiva.[33] Moreover, the term 'Uzbek' was mostly used when the Uzbeks as a whole were opposed to other ethnic or ethno-local groups, for example the Tadjiks, the Kazakhs, the Karakalpaks or the Sarts. Only in Khiva did this term become widespread as an ethnonym, and it is hardly accidental that in this oasis the large subdivisions of nomadic Uzbeks had sedentarised en masse, without fragmenting into small groups. In the oases of Farghana, Bukhara and Samarqand, the term 'Uzbek' was used much more rarely.[34]

By the beginning of the twentieth century, a considerable part of the Uzbeks of Dasht-i-Qipchaq origin had already become sedentary. Moreover, in such oases as Samarqand, Bukhara, Shakhrisiabz and Karshi, they constituted the majority of the rural population, partly due to assimilation of the indigenous population and previous migrants to the area.[35] However, many of the Uzbek groups there still retained some peculiarities of speech and some of the traits of their former nomadic culture.

The Uzbeks also kept their segmentary kinship-based organisation. This was characteristic of those who practised pastoralism, as well as new settlers in the oases. This organisation served as a criterion of social stratification, particularly in comparison with the organisation of residents of long standing, or indigenous inhabitants in the oases who lacked these characteristics.[36]

Thus, the Uzbeks of Dasht-i-Qipchaq origin were subdivided into distinct groups ('tribes'), each one united by fictitious genealogical ties. According to tradition, the Uzbeks were composed of 92 tribes. An individual thought of himself primarily as a Mangut, a Kyngrat or a Keneges; and only secondarily and in specific situations did he acknowledge that he was also an Uzbek. Their self-identification may be characterised as an hierarchical one. Not only different Uzbek tribes, but also clans and even sub-clans maintained their separatedness and often rivalry with each other.

As late as 1926, the head of the commission for the districting of Central Asia, I.P. Magidovich, complained:

In several localities of the Samarqand province, not to speak about Bukhara, a notion of Uzbek is almost absent. Instead, some small tribal denominations (the Kipchaq, the Naiman, etc.) exist. These groups are so detached from each other and often so hostile to each other that it is difficult for a time to compel them to work together within the same small administrative unit.[37]

Apart from the Tadjiks and the Uzbeks the third most numerous ethnic element in the oases of Zarafshan valley, Farghana, Tashkent, Khiva, and of the lower Syr-Daria river, was represented by the Sarts. The Sarts were either Turkicised descendants of the indigenous population, or descendants of Turkic migrants who had settled in oases long before the arrival of the Dasht-i-Qipchaq Uzbeks. They were similar to the Tadjiks in their economic activities and way of life. Both groups lacked kinship-based segmentary social organisation. Most of the Sarts spoke Uzbek, although they did not consider themselves even nominally to be Uzbeks. The name 'Uzbek' for them carried a negative nuance, 'the bumpkin', or 'the simpleton'.[38] On the other hand, the Sarts of different oases hardly conceived of themselves as a distinct people. They lacked a firm sense of ethnic identity; their group identity was anchored in locality and in a specific lifestyle. In some situations they designated themselves only by their place of settlement, for example, Tashkenlyk – the inhabitants of Tashkent.[39]

The descendants of the nomadic Uzbek conquerors in their turn often used the term 'Sart' as a pejorative applied to the descendants of the conquered sedentary population. They said: 'When we have a dinner with a Tadjik, or drink tea with him we call him a Tadjik, but when we quarrel with him we call him a Sart'.[40]

However, in the Tashkent oasis, in Farghana and in Khiva, the term Sart also served as a self-denomination of the local population here and lacked any derogatory connotation.[41]

Yet another ethnic element should be singled out, composed of those descendants of the nomads of Turkic and Mongol origin who migrated to Maveraunnahr before or during the Mongol conquests and who continued to maintain a semi-nomadic or semi-sedentary way of life, sometimes on the fringes of oases or in their vicinity, and sometimes in more remote places, in the steppes, piedmont valleys and foothills, and mountainous regions where only bogar agriculture was possible. In many cases they were driven to these regions by the Uzbeks who came to Central Asia from the Dasht-i-Qipchaq steppes. Their attitude towards these newcomers was in general rather negative and they preferred to maintain contacts not with the Uzbeks but with the Sarts and the Tadjiks.[42]

These people kept a segmentary kinship-based organisation and spoke the Uzbek language with insignificant dialectal differences. They also maintained some peculiarities in their material culture. Although many of these groups were assimilated by the Uzbeks during the sixteenth to nineteenth centuries, others considered themselves, and were considered by outsiders as separate from the Uzbek ethnic groups. They were often called 'the Turks' and the same name sometimes served as their self-denomination.[43] Their inability to secure territory for settlement in the oases was one of the main factors preventing their assimilation by the Uzbeks.

Ethnicities not only reveal themselves in oppositions, they may also result from oppositions. The native peasantries (dih-qans) of the isolated and scattered oases were too fragmented and insular to develop any national unity or common ethnic identity that was capable of transcending local particularism. Thus, nomadic migrations to the oases of Central Asia and their consequences, directly or indirectly, facilitated ethnic processes that sometimes transcended the particularism of individual oases, cut across their boundaries, and often embraced the population of different oases and even different states.

On the other hand these migrations had never resulted in the creation of ethnicities of the western type with clear self-consciousness and self-identification. The creation of the modern-type nations is a recent event in Central Asian history. To some extent it was not a spontaneous process but the result of deliberate Soviet policy of ethnic engineering. However, the relative ease with which this was accomplished supposes that some of the preconditions already existed in the pre-modern societies of Central Asia.

Such are my ideas about the ethnic situation in the oases of

Central Asia up to the time of the Bolshevik revolution. Now I shall move on to the socio-political aspects of interrelations between nomads and sedentaries in the area.

In my several works I have tried to demonstrate how contacts and interrelations with sedentaries, and especially conquests of the sedentary territories of Central Asia, influenced the socio-political organisation of the nomads.[44] Now I would like to dwell upon the reverse side of the problem and to address the question of what influence, if any, the nomadic invasions exerted upon the socio-political organisation of the oases.

The late archaeologist and historian of ancient Central Asia, M.M. Diakonov, claimed:

> Rivers unite. It is mountains that separate. All ancient regions of Central Asia are easily singled out along the river basins. Thus, Parthia occupied the basins of the upper Atrek and Gurghen rivers, Area, the valley of the Herirud – Tadjen river, Margiana – the valley of the Murghab river, Khwarazm – the basin of the lower Amu Daria, Bactria – the basin of the middle and upper Amu Daria (Piandz), Sogdiana – the basin of the Zarafshan and Kashgha-Daria rivers.[45]

However, the separation and isolation of oases, well known in other areas, was also a characteristic of the Central Asian ones. There it was partly favoured by the fact that the largest oases occupied different river basins, or, when on the same river, were remote from each other and, thus, did not compete for water sources.

Only one long-standing factor, the pressure of nomads, favoured a tendency toward amalgamation of the oases in Central Asia into a single state, although this only occasionally resulted in their unification.

Notwithstanding the almost constant danger from nomads, the states capable of overcoming the oases's separatism, and incorporating all or most of them, usually emerged outside Central Asia. Most often they were the states of the so-called conquest type, and as a rule they were of nomadic origins. The only exceptions were the states of the Samanids, and to a lesser degree those of the Khwarazm-Shahs and Timuruds. Besides, the emergence of all three was due to very specific historical circumstances in an area wider than Central Asia proper. These circumstances are too far remote from my topic to be discussed in the present paper.

The states based on one or several neighbouring oases were sometimes more stable. However, by no means were they always centralised, in spite of the fact that the maintenance of irrigation networks and the building of new canals usually demanded a certain degree of governmental management and participation.[46]

Thus, after the dissolution of the Kushan Empire, Transoxiana lacked political unity for many centuries. The Arabs found there only small oasis-states, sometimes united in loose federations.

However, the political instability of oasis-states (to which repeated nomadic incursions and conquests contributed to a large degree) was, on the other hand, accompanied by the relative stability of the social and economic relations prevailing there. At any rate from the eleventh century, political changes in Central Asia, such as the fall of some states and the emergence of others, changes in frontiers or in a composition of ruling classes, were more essential and fundamental than basic changes in social and economic relations.

Two main factors provide the explanation. The first is the great conservatism of social organisation in traditional societies based on irrigation agriculture, particularly on oasis-type irrigation. During the whole medieval period, irrigation, technology and agricultural implements in Central Asia underwent few improvements. Thus, in the Zarafshan basin the irrigation network has remained basically the same from pre-Arab times. During most of the medieval period the presence of peasant communities, together with landless tenant-peasants and metayers, was the characteristic feature of the oases. Members of these communities jointly participated in public works and jointly settled questions connected with irrigation and many other matters.

The social and economic organisation of the oases in Central Asia was not only more developed, but in some respects more stable than that of the nomads. It could be destroyed only in conjunction with its basic economic foundations, and such occurances were extremely rare and incomplete in practice. Moreover the organisation had a considerable capacity for regeneration, which made it even more difficult to change such an organisation in a fundamental way.

However, the nomads in no way aimed at such drastic changes in the social organisation of the oases, nor had they the necessary capabilities. After the conquest was completed, it was not in their interest, at least not for the ruling strata, to 'slay the hen that lays the golden egg'. What they were mostly interested in was to assert themselves as a new ruling class and to set about exploiting the conquered territories. The already existing mechanisms of social relations in oases served this aim quite adequately.

The devastating effects of nomadic invasions are often overestimated by many scholars, mostly historians, who are overly influenced by medieval authors from sedentary countries. It is true that the Mongolian invasion was extremely devastating but this was rather an exception to the rule. Many wars between sedentary states themselves, in Central Asia and in other areas, were more destructive than nomadic invasions such as the Saljuk, Qarakhanid, Khitan or Uzbek ones, which in the main only produced changes in the composition of the ruling classes.

The second factor concerns the repetitive character of nomadic invasions. Of course, no single one of these invasions, or its consequences was exactly like another. Every specific historical case is unique and unrepeatable. Nevertheless, for long historical periods, at any rate during a good part of the Middle Ages, the social systems of oases evolved mostly in circular repetitive patterns, and this was partly due to incursions and conquests by nomads.

Under the circumstances, nomadic invasions at the most only modified the already existing social systems in the oases, or promoted a development of certain elements of these systems. Thus, a number of peculiarities in land-ownership and land-tenure in the oases of Central Asia may be explained by the fact that the nomads, including the sedentarising ones, were modifying these institutions in accordance with their own traditions.

The institution of iqta-, the military 'fiefs' in the form of conditional land property with concomitant fiscal and sometimes broader immunity, may serve as a good example in this respect. In spite of all the disputes about the time of its appearance, lines of evolution and local peculiarities, one point seems to be evident. Under the Buyids and Samanids the iqta- of the type described above was still an exception; military troops at this time were simply paid a salary.[47] Only from the eleventh century, under the Saljuqs and Qarakhanids, was the iqta- practised on a large scale and only then did it become an instrument of dominance of the nomadic Turkic aristocracy over the peasantry in the conquered countries. Under the circumstances, the sedentary class of Iranian land aristocracy, especially the dihqans of Maveraunnahr, suffered much from this reform.[48]

It is no wonder that under the conditions of repetitive nomadic conquests of the Central Asian oases, the iqta- in its various forms tended to be revived again and again. Thus, the institution of tankha, the temporary and conditional grant in return for services to the state, was widely practised in the Khanate of Bukhara. The tankha granted not the lands them- selves, but only the right to collect land taxes. Therefore, it signified a return to the original forms of the iqta-.

The sources permit us to study in detail the social organisa- tion of the three states that had emerged on the ruins of the Shaybanid State and embraced most of the Central Asian oases. P.P. Ivanov concluded that the property relations existing in these states in the nineteenth century had already come into being in the sixteenth century.[49] Although it is difficult to prove with precision, I would hazard a conjecture that his conclusion may be extended to some other socio-economic institutions. Furthermore it may well be applied to more remote times. For example, the system of land division into state-owned, mulk (unconditionally privately-owned, without an obligation of service to the state) and waqf (belonging to the Moslem religious institutions) had existed already in the Samanid State.

A relatively poor development of estate hierarchy in Central Asia can in part also be explained by the influence of nomads. It may be argued that this was the characteristic of many other countries in the Muslim Orient. However, its causes are still not explained in any detail. It seems to me probable that in the Middle East this characteristic may also be partly due to the influences and traditions of the nomads.

The question about the peculiarities of the socio-political and economic relations in the medieval Muslim Middle East is still open for discussion. At this point, I do not wish to become involved in this prolonged debate and to discuss whether these relations may be characterised as feudal ones or not, although I am inclined to reject this claim. What I would like to stress is that these peculiarities did in fact exist and are conspicuous, if only we compare the Middle East with medieval Europe or China.

These peculiarities have been noticed and admitted by scholars of different schools of thought and different ideological allegiances. In the Soviet Union, L.B. Alaev recently stated:

Notwithstanding all differences between societies of the Near East, altogether they had conspicuous differences with societies of other large areas, such as China and India.[50]

Here, in the West, Ernest Gellner writes:

For all the indisputable diversity, the remarkable thing is the extent to which Muslim societies resemble each other. Their traditional political systems, for instance, are much more of one kind than those of pre-modern Christendom. At least in the bulk of Muslim societies, in the main Islamic block between Central Asia and the Atlantic shores of Africa, one has the feeling that the same and limited pack of cards has been dealt. The hands vary, but the pack is the same.[51]

Alaev, bound by the five-stage schema of societal development obligatory to Soviet scholars, characterises these societies as 'oriental feudal' and tries to demonstrate that differences between them and societies of medieval Europe were not fundamental.[52] He thinks that the peculiarities of the Near Eastern societies were connected with the more active role of the State in processes of redistribution.

Gellner explains peculiarities of the Muslim societies in terms of ecology and technique:

Muslim societies between the Hindu Kush and the Atlantic were characterised by the symbiosis of urban, literate, centrally governed, trade-oriented communities, with tribal ones. Tribes may be defined as rural communities which partly or totally escape control by central government, and within which the maintenance of order, such as it is, is left largely to the interplay of local groups, generally conceived in terms of kinship.

The central power does not possess adequate technical and organizational resources for the effective subjugation of the tribes; at the same time the general ecology of the tribes is such that they need urban markets and specialists, and remain in sustained contact with the towns ... This economic need is reinforced by what may be termed moral ecology: the tribesmen identify with a religion which, through literacy, ultimately must have an urban base. These factors lead to that characteristically violent symbiosis of tribe and urban-based government.[53]

To my mind, other factors should be also taken into consideration. In trying to examine and to explain the societies of the medieval Middle East we should take into account not only the influence of Islam, but also the structures typical of societies based on irrigation agriculture, especially in its oases variety and, last but not least, the nomadic impact and the regularities of interactions and interrelations between the sedentaries and the nomads in the area.

## NOTES

1. A.M. Khazanov, *Nomads and the Outside World*, Cambridge, 1984, pp. 44–5.
2. The bogars (from the Tadjik word 'bakhor' – spring time) are cultivated lands dependent upon the spring rains.
3. Kair agriculture is cultivation with no irrigation, in the river deltas, on moist, sandy and silt soils.
4. See respectively A.R. Mukhamedjanov, 'Vodosnabzhenie drevnego Samarkanda', in *Istoriia Samarkanda*, vol. 1, ed. I. Muminov, Tashkent, Institute of History and Archaeology, 1969, pp. 40–45, and Iu. F. Buriakov, *Istoricheskaia topografiia drevnikh gorodov Tashkentskogo oazisa*, Tashkent, 1975, pp. 184–190.
5. V.M. Masson, *Drevnezemledelcheskaia Kultura Margiany*, Moscow–Leningrad, 1959, pp. 67 ff.
6. M.P. Petrov, *Pustyni SSSR i ikh osvoenie*, Moscow, 1964, p. 66.
7. V.V. Barthold, *Zwolf Vorlesungen uber die Geschichte der Turken Mittelasiens*, Berlin, 1935, pp. 188–89; N.N. Negmatov, *Khodzhent i Usruchana v drevnosti i srednevekovie*, Moscow, 1968; B.A. Litvinsky, 'Drevnii sredneaziatskii gorod', in *Drevnii Vostok, Goroda i torgovlia*, Erevan, 1975, pp. 99–125, Isd-vo AN Armianskoi SSR; A.M. Belenitsky, N.B. Bentovich and O.G. Bolshakov, *Srednevekovyi gorod Srednei Azii*, Leningrad, 1973, pp. 3–14, 163–210.
8. O.A. Sukhareva and N.O. Torsunov, 'Iz istorii gorodskikh i selskikh poselenii Srednei Azii vtoroi poloviny XIX-nachala XX v.', in *Zhilishche narodov Srednei Azii i Kazakhstana*, Moscow: Nauka, 1982; pp. 34–5.
9. E.V. Zeimal, 'Politicheskaia istoriia drevnei Transoksiany po

numizmaticheskim dannym', in *Kultura Vostoka, Drevnost i rannee srednevekovie*, Leningrad: Avrora, 1978, pp. 201 ff; A.R. Mukhamedjanov, 'K istorii irrigatsii v kushanskuiu epokhu', in *Tsentralnaia Aziia v kushanskuiu epokhu*, vol. 2, Moscow: Nauka 1975, p. 279.

10. G.A. Koshelenko, ed., *Drevneishie gosudarstva Kavkaza i Srednei Azii*, Moscow, 1985, pp. 339–40.

11. F. Barth, *Nomads of South Persia*, Oslo, 1964.

12. B.I. Vainberg, 'Skotovodcheskie plemena v drevnem Khorezme', in *Kultura i iskusstvo drevnego Khorezma*, Moscow, 1981.

13. V.V. Barthold, 'Turkestan v epokhu mongolskogo nashestviia', in *Sochineniia*, vol. 1, Moscow, 1963, p. 538.

14. *Narody Srednei Azii i Kazakhstana*, vol. 2, Moscow: Izd-vo Akademii Nauk SSR, 1963, p. 68.

15. K.A. Pishchulina, 'Prisyrdarinskie goroda i ikh znachenie v istorii kazakhskikh khanstv v XV–XVII vekakh', in *Kazakhstan v XV–XVII vekakh*, Alma-Ata: Nauka, 1969.

16. *Narody Srednei Azii i Kazakhstana*, p. 49.

17. P.P. Ivanov, *Ocherki po istorii Srednei Asii (XVI–seredina XIX v.)*, Moscow, 1958, pp. 72, 149.

18. I.I. Geiger, *Turkestan*, Tashkent, 1909, p. 33.

19. S.P. Poliakov, *Istoricheskaia etnografiia Srednei Azii i Kazakhstana*, Moscow, 1980, p. 147.

20. Strabo, XI, 8, 8.

21. Procopius, *Wars*, I, 3

22. S.G. Kliashtorny, *Drevnetiurkskie runicheskie pamiatniki kak istochnik po istorii Srednei Azii*, Moscow, 1964, p. 174.

23. Barthold, 'Turkestan v epokhu mongolskogo nashestviia', p. 213.

24. R.S. Atabinen, *Les apports turcs dans le peuplement et la civilisation de l'Europe orientale*, Istanbul, 1952, p. 119.

25. On the term 'Tadjik' see Barthold, *Zwolf Vorlesungen*, p. 42, L. Krader, *Peoples of Central Asia*, Bloomington, 1966, p. 54 and B.G. Gafurov, *Tadjiki. Drevneishaia, drevniaia i srednevekovaia istoriia*, Moscow, 1972, pp. 375 ff.

26. *Narody Srednei Azii i Kazakhstana*, p. 531.

27. Ivanov, *Ocherki po istorii Srednei Asii*, pp. 72–3, 151.

28. O.A. Sukhareva, *K istorii gorodov Bukharskogo khanstva*, Tashkent, 1958, p. 79; Sukhareva and Torsunov, 'Iz istorii gorodskikh i selskikh poselenii Srednei Azii vtoroi poloviny XIX–nachala XX v.', p. 28.

29. O.A. Sukhareva, *Bukhara, XIX–nachalo XX v. (Posdnefeodalnyi gorod i ego naselenie*, Moscow, 1966, p. 122.

30. I.I. Zarubin, 'Spisok narodnostei Turkestanskogo kraia', *Trudy Komissii po izucheniiu plemennogo sostava Rossii i sopredelnykh stran*, Number 9, Leningrad, 1925, p. 7.

31. G.P. Vasilieva and B. Kh. Karmysheva, eds, *Etnograficheskie ocherki uzbekskogo selskogo naseleniia*, Moscow, 1969, p. 40.

32. *Narody Srednei Azii i Kazakhstana*, pp. 53, 170.
33. M. Vakhabov, *Formirovanie uzbekskoi sotsialisticheskoi natsii*, Tashkent, 1961, p. 19.
34. S.A. Tokarev, *Etnografiia narodov SSSR*, Moscow, 1958, p. 347.
35. Sukhareva, *K istorii gorodov Bukharskogo khanstva*, pp. 75, 119, 132; Vasilieva and Karmysheva, *Etnograficheskie ocherki uzbekskogo selskogo naseleniia*, pp. 20–21.
36. N.A. Kisliakov, *Patriarkhalno-feodalnye otnosheniia sredi osedlogo selskogo naseleniia Bukharskogo khanstva v kontse XIX–nachale XX veka*, Moscow, 1962.
37. I.P. Magidovich, 'Naselenie', in *Materialy po raionirovaniiu Srednei Azii*, vol. 1, Tashkent, 1926, part one, p. 2.
38. Vakhabov, *Formirovanie uzbekskoi sotsialisticheskoi natsii*, p. 198.
39. L. Kostenko, *Turkestankii Krai*, vol. 1, St Petersburg, 1888, p. 352.
40. Tokarev, *Etnografiia narodov SSSR*, p. 347.
41. A. Samoilovich, 'K voprosu o sartakh', *Zhivaia starina*, vol. 19, 1910, p. 269; S.S. Gubaeva, *Etnicheskii sostav naseleniia Fergany v kontse XIX–nachale XX v.*, Tashkent, 1983, pp. 47–48.
42. Vakhabov, *Formirovanie uzbekskoi sotsialisticheskoi natsii*, p. 75.
43. B. Kh. Karmysheva, 'Etnograficheskaia gruppa "tiurk" v sostave uzbekov', *Sovetskaia etnografiia*, no. 1, 1960.
44. A.M. Khazanov, *Sotsialnaia istoriia skifov*, Moscow, 1975; A.M. Khazanov, 'The Early State among the Eurasian Nomads', in H. Claessen and P. Skalnik, eds. *The Study of the State*, The Hague, 1981; Khazanov, *Nomads and the Outside World*.
45. M.M. Diakonov, 'Slozhenie klassovogo obshchestva v Severnoi Baktrii', *Sovetskaia arkheologiia*, vol. 19, 1954, p. 123.
46. The ancient symbolic custom was still preserved in Khiva in the nineteenth century. Before the yearly canal clearing a great ceremony took place, after which a khan himself started the work. On this matter, see Ia. G. Guliamov, *Istoriia Khorezma s drevneishikh vremen do nashikh dnei*, Moscow, 1957.
47. A.N. Lambton, 'Reflections on the Iqta', *Arabic and Islamic Studies in Honor of Hamilton A. Gibb*, G. Makdisi, ed., Leiden, 1965, pp. 346 ff.
48. Barthold, 'Turkestan v epokhu mongolskogo nashestviia', pp. 369–71.
49. Ivanov, *Ocherki po istorii Srednei Asii*, p. 131.
50. L.B. Alaev, ed., *Tipy obshchestvennykh otnoshenii na Vostoke v srednie veka*, Moscow, 1982, p. 24.
51. E. Gellner, *Muslim Society*, Cambridge, 1981, p. 99.
52. Alaev, *Tipy obshchestvennykh otnoshenii na Vostoke v srednie veka*, p. 58.
53. Gellner, *Muslim Society*, p. 100.

# CHAPTER 3

# Why poverty was inevitable in traditional societies

## E.A. Wrigley

That poverty was the lot of the large majority of people in all or almost all societies before the industrial revolution is widely recognised. Poverty is a general and rather abstract concept. Its reality was bitter and particular: a hungry child, apathetic from lack of food; a shivering family unable to buy fuel in a harsh winter; the irritation of parasites in dirty clothing and the accompanying sores and stench. The extent and severity of poverty in the past is difficult to express in quantitative terms for lack of relevant data in most cases, but that the poor were very numerous and that they suffered greatly at times in most societies is an assertion unlikely to be widely challenged. When St Matthew reports Jesus as saying, 'ye have the poor always with you', the context suggests that the remark was not controversial.[1]

In industrialised countries today poor people may still be found. Their poverty is, however, now taken to be problematic in a way that used not to be the case, because it is widely believed that the continued existence of poverty reflects not the intrinsic nature of the human condition but the failure of the social system or the political regime. The capacity to produce on a scale to provide acceptable minimum conditions for all patently exists, and it is therefore natural to argue that poverty can be overcome by an act of will, by a suitable piece of social engineering. Looking back from a vantage point in the late twentieth century, it may be tempting to suppose that the same was true of earlier times, that the misery of the masses could have been alleviated by deliberate policy or institutional change. The purpose of this essay is to examine the constraints common to all traditional societies which meant that the ambition to achieve a general escape from poverty belonged to the

realm of pipedreams rather than policy. My argument is
general and simplistic. It should not be taken as an assertion
that social structure and political forms had no bearing on the
incidence of poverty in traditional societies, but rather as
reflecting the conviction that any room for manoeuvre was
greatly circumscribed by certain features common to the economies of all such societies.

The hierarchy of human wants is well reflected in the employment structure and the allocation of hours of work in traditional societies. Food, clothing, shelter and fuel were the basic
necessities of life, the three last increasing in relative importance with increasing distance from the equator. Everywhere
food was the dominant concern, whether in the lives of
individuals or in the preoccupations of governments. The
dominance of the demand for food is clear from the fact that it
was common for 70–90 per cent of the total labour force to be
engaged in agriculture. Probably the proportion of all the
hours devoted to productive labour that was spent in farm
work was broadly similar.[2] In most traditional societies the bulk
of food output did not go through the market but was
consumed on the holding which produced it. Therefore little
can be learnt from estimates of the proportion of total market
demand spent on food, but the structure of the labour force is a
good proxy measure of the point at issue – how much of the
total productive effort of a society went into satisfying the
demand for the most basic of all necessities.

The three lesser necessities were also satisfied by the flow of
produce from the land. A productive agriculture meant comparatively abundant supplies of wool, cotton, flax and silk,
while the size of cattle herds determined whether leather for
footwear was scarce or readily available. The relative abundance or scarcity of such materials determined the cost of the
raw materials of clothing and thus standards of attire. Wood
was normally the prime fuel and often also the most important
material used in construction. Thus the degree of success
achieved in maximising the flow of produce from the land
governed how far man was able to meet not only his need for
food, but also his need for clothing, shelter and fuel.

Until basic needs are met, the demand for other material

goods or for services will remain minimal in the bulk of the population; or to express the same idea in different language, the income elasticity of demand for the necessities will remain close to unity as long as basic wants are only met inadequately.[3] If a half-starved family experiences a sudden rise in income, all the additional spending power may go towards alleviating the hunger from which its members suffer. If, therefore, a large proportion of the population lived in poverty, a modest improvement in their circumstances might cause very little change in the structure of employment or in the pattern of economic activity. Only a substantial rise in income could have produced significant structural change, and that in turn could only have arisen from a major change in output per head.

When the great majority of the work force labours on the land, a big rise in productivity must involve a big increase in individual output amongst those living and working on the land. An escape from poverty, therefore, must begin in this way. Without it there will be no significant demand for prod-ucts other than the four main necessities, and no major surge in employment off the land. An escape from poverty hinged upon the possibility of securing a major improvement in output per head in agriculture. This was the key. Why was it so hard to achieve?

One answer to this question which has influenced subsequent thinking powerfully was given by Adam Smith. At the very beginning of the *Wealth of nations* he suggested a paradigm for productivity growth in the parable of the pinmakers. Smith was anxious to illustrate the sensational increases in output per head that might be obtained even without major changes in production techniques if there were division of function. Specialisation could bring immense benefits. Ten pinmakers acting collaboratively could produce at least 240 times as many pins each as could have been made by one man working on his own.[4] Moreover there would be an improvement in quality as well as in quantity since a worker, relieved of the necessity of being a jack of all trades, could succeed in becoming the master of his particular specialism. An increase of productivity on this scale, even an increase one tenth as large, is so vast that it might seem that poverty must be easy to vanquish. Smith drew no such conclusion: indeed he was in general pessimistic about the future prospects for real incomes.[5] His pessimism sprang from several considerations, but one he mentioned almost immediately after telling the pinmaker parable.

Having described the pin manufactory, Smith initially emphasised the general relevance of his example.

In every other art and manufacture, the effects of the division of labour are similar to what they are in this very trifling one; though, in many of them, the labour can neither be so much subdivided, nor reduced to so great a simplicity of operation. The division of labour, however, so far as it can be introduced, occasions, in every art, a proportionable increase of the productive powers of labour.

The prospect seemed fair, but Smith then noted that farming formed an exception.

The nature of agriculture, indeed, does not admit of so many subdivisions of labour, nor of so complete a separation of one business from another, as manufactures ... The spinner is almost always a distinct person from the weaver; but the ploughman, the harrower, the sower of seed, and the reaper of the corn, are often the same.[6]

The most important means by which manpower productivity could be increased scarcely applied to agriculture, by far the largest industry.

A first obstacle to the radical improvement in living standards in traditional societies, therefore, stemmed from the fact that advances that might be available in much of the rest of the economy through specialisation were much harder to secure on the land. Had this been the only problem, however, poverty might still have proved a tractable issue, but other dragons lay in the path.

The most fiercesome dragon in the eyes of the classical economists who followed Adam Smith, such as Ricardo and Malthus, was the spectre of diminishing marginal returns.[7] Since nothing could be done to expand the land surface available for cultivation, it seemed inevitable that a rising demand for the products of the land, whether arising from an increasing population or from industrial growth with an associated increase in the demand for raw materials, must at some stage lead to the use of more marginal land, or to the more intensive cultivation of existing agricultural land, or to both. Even though some technical progress was to be expected, the difficulty could only be postponed and not circumvented. To squeeze increased production from the intensive or extensive margins must involve the use of more labour or capital, or more probably of both, to secure a unit increase in output. Declining returns to labour (and also, of course, to capital) must ensue.

This constituted a problem central to the entire economy and not just to the supply of food, for traditional societies were organic economies, economies in which animal and vegetable raw materials were used exclusively in almost all branches of material production. Spinners, weavers, tailors, shoemakers, millers, brewers, glovers, hatters, carpenters, coopers, bakers, butchers; these were the occupations in which most of those engaged in material production worked, apart from agriculture. In all of them the raw materials used were animal or vegetable in origin. Furthermore, even those industries which used mineral raw materials, such as metal-working, brickmaking or glassmaking, needed much energy in the form of heat to transform their raw materials, and this came largely from wood, leaving them also closely dependent on the productivity of the land and exposed to the risks associated with declining marginal returns.

This sketch of the reasons why the parable of the pin-makers did not serve to sustain hope of an escape from poverty in a traditional society is too stark. Even within the context of a Ricardian world there were important sources of improved agricultural productivity available in favourable circumstances. For example, while opportunities for specialisation of function among workers on a particular farm were limited, specialisation by farming region was capable of increasing productivity significantly by allowing each region to concentrate its production on the crops or pastoral products to which it was suited by geographical circumstances or by distance to market. There might also be gains from specialisation among workers on individual farms where the farm ceased to be a self-sufficient unit and was devoted instead to raising a more limited range of crops or animals. That large gains in output per head were possible even in a long-settled land and despite the problem of declining marginal returns is shown by English agricultural history, since in round terms output per head on English farms probably doubled between 1600 and 1800.[8]

The problem of endemic and ineluctable poverty in traditional societies, though heavily conditioned by the difficulty of increasing agricultural productivity, embraced a much wider range of issues. A second such issue will always be associated with the name of Robert Malthus. The argument associated with his name, expressed in its crudest form, is that adventitious improvements in living standards among the labouring poor will always prove short-lived because they will tend to cause mortality to fall and fertility to rise, thus increasing the rate of population growth, and the resultant additional supply of labour will soon force wages back towards some conventional minimum. The argument was not original to Malthus; for example, it can be found succinctly and starkly stated in the *Wealth of nations*.[9]

The argument attributed to Malthus usually fails to do justice to the nature and subtlety of his thinking. He asked to be granted two *postulata* – that food is necessary to support existence and that 'the passion between the sexes' is a constant.[10] He believed it to be safe to deduce from the former that population could not grow faster than the supply of food, and from the latter that the rate of growth of population, unless checked by an exterior, intervening force, was constant. Further, he considered that the rate at which the supply of food could be increased always tended to be lower than the rate at which population would grow if unhindered.[11] It followed, of course, that, except where there was a large stock of unsettled land, when for a time the output of food could keep pace with the rise in population, some checks must constantly be at work constraining the growth of population to keep it in step with the rise in food output. Interpreted in an extreme and mechanical way, this schema can lead to the assertion that populations are kept constantly close to a precipice over which some fraction will plunge from time to time because of a chance event, such as a run of poor harvests.

Malthus himself was not a Malthusian in this sense. Even in the first version of his *Essay*, published in 1798, he recognised and enumerated the complexity of the factors affecting the reactions between production and reproduction. Later, with the benefit of much wider reading, foreign travel and more reflection, he moved towards a position that was, perhaps paradoxically in view of the later use of the adjective 'Malthusian', more shaded and flexible than that of either Adam Smith or Ricardo. He distinguished between a 'European' case, representing one extreme, and the 'Chinese' case at the other. In all cases there was tension between production and reproduction, but in much of western Europe the accommodation between the two was secured chiefly by moderating fertility to avoid too rapid a rise in numbers, whereas in the 'Chinese' case savage bursts of mortality operated as the prime regulator.

The difference between the two was associated with the differences in marriage practice. Where marriage was early and universal, as in China, and fertility was therefore not responsive to economic circumstances, the potential rate of growth was high, and, since high population growth rates were unsustainable, mortality must also be high to offset the high fertility. Where celibacy was comparatively common, and marriage came later in life and was a moveable feast responsive to economic pressures, as in much of western Europe, the potential population growth rate was lower and, even though the economy might be slow growing, the prevailing mortality level could be comparatively modest. Living standards could be substantially higher in such circumstances.[12] The standard of living prevailing in a traditional society might therefore vary substantially from a 'worst case' in which many people lived on the margin of bare subsistence to a situation in which even the labouring poor were reasonably well-buffered against outright starvation and most families could secure the four main necessities of life and even aspire to modest comforts. Malthus's bitter opposition to the poor law of his day sprang from his belief that it was undermining some of the most important institutional constraints upon fertility, thereby provoking faster population growth, and so tending to ensure that the lot of the poor would deteriorate.[13] More generally, however, Malthus regarded the capitalist system as possessing features that were likely to inhibit poverty, while he believed the reverse to be true of the political systems prevailing in some extra-European areas, such as the Turkish Empire.[14]

Malthus's analysis, therefore, created a wide spectrum of possibilities. Nevertheless, the tension between production and reproduction was inescapable except in countries of recent settlement with large areas of unsettled land available. The rate at which production could be expanded was less than the rate at which population growth would occur if unchecked. The history of settlement in North America provided a salutary reminder of the truth of this observation. There a European stock, drawn largely from the British Isles, and closely similar in social, cultural and political character to the communities which the settlers had left behind, had doubled in number by natural increase alone in every quarter-century since the beginning of settlement, though their communities of origin on the eastern side of the Atlantic had grown far more slowly.

Malthus was less pessimistic than either Adam Smith or Ricardo about the necessary implications for living standards of the interplay between economic and demographic forces.[15] But even in his analysis the pressure of population was a prime reason for widespread poverty. He used an intriguing metaphor to make his view clear:

In an endeavour to raise the proportion of the quantity of provisions to the number of consumers in any country, our attention would naturally be first directed to the increasing of the absolute quantity of provisions; but finding that, as fast as we did this, the number of consumers more than kept pace with it, and that with all our exertions we were still as far as ever behind, we should be convinced, that our efforts directed in this way would never succeed. It would be setting the tortoise to catch the hare. Finding, therefore, that from the laws of nature we could not proportion the food to the population, our next attempt should naturally be, to proportion the population to the food. If we can persuade the hare to go to sleep, the tortoise may have some chance of overtaking her.[16]

All traditional societies faced the problem confronting the tortoise. Prudence and foresight might alleviate it; nothing could be found to justify the hope that it might be banished.

To the difficulties associated with declining marginal returns on the land, the elusiveness of gains from specialisation and the tensions arising from the expansive power of population, must be added a further reason why poverty was built into the nature of traditional societies. Even if none of the difficulties just enumerated were of serious consequence in a given traditional society, it would not follow that living standards would be high, or capable of being raised significantly. To secure a high level of output per head it was essential to command energy on a large scale. Producing a finished product fit for use or consumption always entailed the expenditure of energy. This was true of each stage in the process, from the primary stage of production onwards. Many of the most important operations of the agricultural year were heavily energy-intensive. Ploughing, manuring, scything, stooking, carting and winnowing all required the expenditure of much mechanical energy, as did almost all aspects of production from mines. Later in the production sequence the same held true in varying degrees. Either heat or mechanical energy was needed wherever a material was cut, twisted, bent, hammered, shaped, woven, smelted, boiled or baked; in short, when it was subjected to some form of physical or chemical change. And if the consumer was finally to benefit from the production process, the finished product had to be transported from the site at which it was produced to the market in which it was sold. This, too, meant the expenditure of energy.

Traditional economies, however, were grievously short of energy. This was true in a general and absolute sense. It is estimated, for example, that, although energy sweeps in from the sun in vast abundance even to a small northern land such as Britain, the proportion that could be tapped by man in traditional societies was tiny because photosynthesis only captures at best perhaps 0.5 per cent of the inflow of solar energy. Yet photosynthesis forms the base of the pyramid of vegetable and, further up the food chain, of animal life from which all useful mechanical and heat energy had to be derived in organic economies,[17] and which had in addition to provide almost all raw materials and food. Photosynthesis might notionally capture the energy equivalent of 20 million tons of coal over the land surface of Britain each year and convert it into vegetable matter. Of this relatively modest theoretical total (less than a fifteenth of the consumption of energy in Britain in the 1980s), only a limited amount could be harnessed to productive ends in practice.[18]

Extending the analysis from the general to the particular underlines the seriousness of the limitations on productivity imposed by energy constraints. Heat energy, for example, came principally from the burning of wood. Even if the whole of Britain had been forested wherever physically possible and the whole of the annual cut of timber had been devoted to combustion, the resulting quantity of heat energy would have fallen well short of the theoretically possible figure just quoted. But, since the same land had also to provide all the mechanical energy used by man, the operative maximum figure was far lower. The mechanical energy used in the productive process came in the main from human muscle, supplemented in some contexts by animal muscle. The wheat, barley and rye from which bread was made not only served to sustain life but also represented the fuel needed to 'drive' tools, instruments and machines.[19] Looms and saws were not driven by steam generated from coal or by electricity derived ultimately from nuclear fission, but by muscles fuelled by bread. Similarly, the grass grazed by livestock was not simply being turned into beef, pork or mutton, but was charging the muscles of oxen and horses to pull the plough or pump water from a mine. The many disparate material needs of traditional societies all entailed the exploitation of the land and therefore only a fraction of the land could be devoted to the production of heat or mechanical energy.

Empirical studies suggest that there is a close connection between productivity per head and the amount of energy per head consumed.[20] The implication of this relationship was gloomy so far as living standards in traditional economies were concerned. Many types of production are inescapably energy-intensive, and productivity must be low if energy is in short supply. For example, to cultivate the soil the sod must be turned, but it is heavy and often difficult to work. Where this task is performed by a man with a spade or some other digging tool, the total area that he and his family can cultivate may be so limited that it is a struggle to produce enough food and other raw materials to meet their needs, and there is little possibility of growing enough to maintain other families as well. This remains true even where there is no shortage of land, no evidence of population pressure, where no Ricardian or Malthusian devils lurk. But if this is the case, there is also by the same token little possibility of large-scale employment in manufacturing or of urban growth, since a man cannot be a specialist weaver unless he can obtain food from others, nor can town dwellers meet their own food needs. A more generous production horizon opens up where animal muscle can be used to supplement human effort. A ploughman with a horse can dwarf the achievement of a peasant with a spade. There is thus a sense in which the domestication of draught animals was a precondition for the existence of any considerable proportion of the population engaged in non-agricultural work.

The seriousness of any constraints associated with limited energy supplies varied with context. It was pronounced in many aspects of arable cultivation but less significant in pastoral activities. It was acute in, say, metal manufacture, but minimal in clockmaking. Its overall impact is hard to quantify. It is likely, however, that it was one of the most significant of all the influences that made an escape from poverty out of the question in traditional society. Equally, access to abundant and cheap supplies of energy was one of the key changes associated with the industrial revolution, arguably constituting the most important single factor enabling output per head to be raised steadily and substantially once the industrial revolution was in train.[21]

Faced with the combined pressures exerted by all the constraints that have now been briefly surveyed, any tendency towards increased output per head that might in time have rescued a population from poverty was foredoomed to lose momentum. Attempts to measure the standard of living are fraught with both empirical and theoretical problems even in modern economies. The same is true *a fortiori* for societies in the past. Reliable price and wage series seldom exist, and any study that attempts to cover centuries must run into difficulties from which studies of shorter periods are largely free. It would be quixotic to ignore the data that are available, however, on the grounds that they are less reliable than one might wish. The study with the longest time span is that carried out by Phelps Brown and Hopkins.[22] It strongly suggests that while real wages in England varied substantially between the thirteenth and eighteenth centuries, displaying wide secular fluctuations,[23] there was no long-term tendency for real wages to rise, no evidence that poverty was declining.

There may be technical reasons for wishing to question this conclusion,[24] but, such as it is, the PBH series provides no ammunition for those who might hope to discern an approaching end to poverty in the early modern period. Since in this period there were substantial changes in material technology; in the geographical scope of the trading economy focused on western Europe; in the institutions through which economic activity was carried on; and, in England, in the scale of urbanisation,[25] the apparent near-constancy in the real wage over the long run cannot be lightly ignored. It may be very difficult to pinpoint the particular constraints that were most powerful but their collective impact seems to have been as weighty even in the last decades of the traditional economy as they had been half a millennium earlier.

The classical economists, who were surveying the last decades of the traditional, organic economy in England, and who had, of course, no expectation that the basic structure of the economy would change, were united in their expectation that the period of growth that was visible over the two preceding centuries would prove difficult to sustain and that the station-ary state would supervene. Adam Smith set the tone both in expecting that this would occur and in supposing that the stationary state, though incorporating the most advanced com-mercial practices and technology, would be a bleak place both for labour and for capital.

In a country which had acquired that full complement of riches which the nature of its soil and climate, and its situation with respect to other countries, allowed it to acquire; which could, therefore, advance no further, and which was not going backwards, both the wages of labour and the profits of stock would probably be very low.[26]

Both the expectations of well-informed contemporaries and the fruits of modern empirical research, therefore, suggest that poverty had been an unchanging feature of the human condi-tion. Mercifully, subsequent events have shown that the expec-tations of the classical economists were ill-founded. To the degree that poverty is still to be found in industrialised coun-tries, this may more properly be regarded as evidence of the deficiencies of particular social and political arrangements, assumptions and institutions than as an affliction arising directly from the limited productive powers of society. There is now ample evidence that output can be induced to rise exponentially decade after decade at a greater pace than population growth, thus opening up the possibility of steadily rising real incomes. And, in any case, the inference that Malthus drew from one of his two postulates has proved wrong. The passion between the sexes may be as strong as ever, but that does not imply that population growth will continue, even though mortality before the end of the child-bearing period is now negligible. Few women now die before their fiftieth birthday, but few choose to bear many children either. Prosperity is regarded as more likely to reduce than to increase fertility, a development that would greatly have surprised social commentators in earlier years. A society may still wilfully or inadvertently fail to match resources to basic needs but there is no longer any difficulty in matching the sum total of production to the sum total of needs, or even to the total of needs plus comforts and many luxuries. Problems of the distribution of wealth may remain; problems of its production are much less oppressive.

One characteristic of economic growth in traditional societies deserves special emphasis when considering the prevalence of poverty. The process of growth itself tended to aggravate the underlying difficulties. If the statics of poverty were discouraging, its dynamics were even more so. Negative feedback tended to prevail both sectorally and within the economy as a whole. Economic models that assume linear relationships between the variables incorporated in the model fail to do justice to the reality of economic life in the past.

The basic problem was straightforward. In an organic economy growth necessarily entailed finding ways of making the land yield more abundantly than previously. This necessity followed directly from the fact that all food and almost all the raw materials of industry were vegetable or animal in constitution. A process of growth that did not increase the demand for food and raw materials is not easy to conceive. Even with a stationary population this was likely to be true. But normally economic growth was associated with a rise in population as

well. It was almost unanimously expected by contemporaries
that if individual prosperity improved there would be a fall in
mortality, or a rise in fertility (whether as a result of earlier and
more universal marriage or for other reasons), or both. If this
happened the intrinsic growth rate must rise. If population was
increasing, and *a fortiori* if real income per head was also rising,
the demand for food and raw materials was bound to grow.
Either output from agriculture and forestry rose in step with
the increased demand, or, if not, growth would decelerate,
output per head and real incomes would be likely to fall, and
the growth process would grind to a halt. Securing the required
increase in output, without at the same time suffering Ricardian penalties, must prove inordinately difficult.

Some relief from the problems of expansion was attainable.
The classical economists depicted growth as, in effect, a constant struggle between those elements in the economic system
where there could be increasing returns to scale, as in the case
of the pinmakers, and those where increasing returns were
always hard to secure and must eventually be replaced by their
opposite, as in the case of agriculture. Their understanding of
the process seems just. The extent and duration of any reprieve
from decreasing returns depended principally on the pace of
innovation, broadly understood to include changes of an organisational nature as well as changes in material technology.

In agriculture, for example, not only might the introduction
of new crops, of better breeds of cattle, of improved drainage,
or of more appropriate and sophisticated implements, increase
both total output and output per head, but so also might better
labour discipline, more effective cultivational techniques, more
complex crop rotations, specialisation of land use as a result of
creating a larger integrated market area, or more efficient
transport and marketing facilities. For decades, generations,
even centuries, such developments might preserve or even
enhance living standards in spite of more intensive use of land
and the steady growth in aggregate output, but eventually
further growth would entail a reduction in output per head
and therefore in living standards as more and more effort was
needed to secure a unit increase in production.

The malign effects of the presence of negative feedback in
the economy might be postponed but could not finally be

denied. Further aggregate growth was always possible but at some stage could only occur at the expense of output per head. The dynamics of growth in an organic economy were such that at some point further growth, in the sense of an increase in the aggregate output of the economy, might be expected to increase the prevalence and severity of poverty in the population.

The line of argument that I have pursued in this essay implies that poverty in traditional society could not have been overcome whatever the institutional forms of social and political life prevailing; that societies dependent upon the land, organic societies, were subject to physical restrictions that ensured this outcome. Not all traditional societies, however, were equally poor, nor was poverty equally widespread and acute in all of them. Social and political structures played a considerable part in determining how many were poor and how poor they were.

In some societies responsibility for the poor lay principally with their family and kin. In others the church played a prominent part in trying to help the victims of poverty. In yet others the secular authorities created an institutional structure designed to alleviate poverty, as in the case of the Tudor poor law and its subsequent modifications. Custom or the law in varying combinations provided rules by which the poor were judged. Some forms of poverty were taken to be less culpable than others. The poverty of a widow and her dependent children might evoke pity and be recognised as constituting a decisive claim upon the resources of others. The poverty of an able-bodied man who was out of work was much less certain to be seen as worthy of relief. His destitution might be no less real but he was much more likely to be seen as at fault and so disqualified from help.

Sometimes both the proportion of the population which enjoyed relief and the scale of the transfer payments involved were substantial. Under the English poor law, for example, help might be forthcoming both to cope with an abrupt, unpredictable crisis, such as the failure of a harvest, and to counter long-term difficulties, such as those associated with chronic sickness or increasing age. The cumulative weight of such provision might involve a significant tax burden.[27] Where the community was both tolerably prosperous and generous, starvation might be rare or non-existent, few needed to go barefoot, and fuel to heat the cooking pot might seldom be lacking. But the fact that careful provision could hold the worst ravages of poverty at arm's length should not be taken to imply that greater generosity would have put comforts as well as necessities within reach of the poor (that is, that the problem of poverty was a problem of maldistribution).

Marx excoriated capitalism because it exploited the bulk of the population who depended for their livelihood upon the sale of their labour for the exclusive benefit of the small and shrinking minority who owned capital. Huge new income flows and vast wealth were coming into being but only to enlarge the gulf between the fortunate few and the deprived multitudes. Marx's appreciation of the trends in income distribution was at fault, though it may have been hard to detect this at the time when he was writing *Capital*. But his analysis is not only a tribute to his sense of justice but also to his understanding of the depth of the transformation wrought by man's new ability to expand the productive powers of society in a manner without previous parallel. He was mistaken in thinking that the poor were not to share in the rising tide of income, but he was fully justified in believing that the means to overcome poverty were rapidly coming into being. He lived in the first age in which poverty had become problematic. If the capitalists had monopolised all income gain, no doubt the proletariat would have risen in revolt. Certainly it would have been hard to deny them any right to aspire to do so, since the gap between their poverty and the wealth of the few would have grown steadily greater. The scale of new wealth was becoming so great that its redistribution could solve the worst material ills of the poor. It was reasonable to suppose that an act of political will combined with some appropriate social engineering could abolish poverty, and could give to man whatever dignity can be conveyed by adequate food, fuel, housing, clothing and the like.

The mid nineteenth century, however, was the first age in which such a view was tenable. Before then there had been insufficient headroom for mankind to stand up free from poverty, whatever the political regime or institutional framework. It was not merely that existing income flows or accumulations of wealth however dispersed could not have matched the basic needs of the multitude, but that the obstacles that stood in the way of increasing income and wealth were first and foremost physical and biological, and not primarily social, political or economic. The doubts about the possibility of sustained growth and individual wellbeing reflected in the writings of the classical economists, and the further doubts associated with the limited availability of both heat and mechanical energy, were well founded in the world that existed before the industrial revolution. Between them they set bounds to the growth that could occur, and all had the frustrating characteristic that the very process of growth tended to make them act with steadily increasing severity. Success now meant failure later.

## NOTES

1. St Matthew, 26:11.
2. In other words, although many craftsmen laboured in the fields at times of greatest activity on the land, such as harvest time, it is also true that yeomen, husbandmen and labourers devoted a part of their time to building work, crude carpentry and rough handicrafts.
3. There is some fascinating material bearing on this issue, derived from Gregory King's estimates of the consumption patterns in social groups with differing income levels in R. Stone, 'Some seventeenth century econometrics: consumers' behaviour', *Revue Européenne des Sciences Sociales*, 26, 1988, pp. 19–41.
4. A. Smith, *An inquiry into the nature and causes of the wealth of nations*, ed. E. Cannan, 2 vols, orig. pub. 1904 (Chicago, 1976), I, p. 9.
5. E.A. Wrigley, *People, cities and wealth: the transformation of traditional society*, Oxford, 1987, pp. 30–4.
6. Smith, *Wealth of nations*, I, pp. 9, 10.
7. The classical statement of the principle may be found in D. Ricardo, 'On the principles of political economy and taxation' in *The works and correspondence of David Ricardo*, ed. P. Sraffa with the collaboration of M.H. Dobb, Cambridge, 1951, I, pp. 120–7. Similar ideas, however, may be found in T.R. Malthus, *An inquiry into the nature and progress of rent, and the principles by which it is regulated*, London, 1815.
8. Wrigley, *People, cities and wealth*, ch. 7, 'Urban growth and agricultural change: England and the continent in the early modern period', esp. pp. 164–74.

9. Smith, *Wealth of nations*, I, pp. 88–90.
10. T.R. Malthus, *An essay on the principle of population as it affects the future improvement of society with remarks on the speculations of Mr Godwin, M. Condorcet and other writers*, London, 1798, p.11.
11. Malthus, *Essay on population*, pp. 11–17.
12. For a simple graphical exposition of this point see E.A. Wrigley, *Continuity, chance and change: the character of the industrial revolution in England*, Cambridge, 1988, fig. 1.1, p. 21.
13. 'The poor laws of England tend to depress the general condition of the poor in these two ways. Their first obvious tendency is to increase population without increasing the food for its support. A poor man may marry with little or no prospect of being able to support a family without parish assistance. They may be said therefore in some measure to create the poor which they maintain.' (His second point is to do with workhouses.) Malthus, *Essay on population*, p. 83. It should be noted that Malthus was not at all opposed in principle to the transfer of income between rich and poor; rather the reverse: but he feared that it must prove futile. 'I should indeed think that the whole, or a much greater sum [than currently levied under the poor law], was well applied, if it merely relieved the comparatively few that would be in want, if there were no public provision for them, without the fatal and unavoidable consequence of continually increasing their number, and depressing the condition of those who were struggling to maintain themselves in independence. Were it possible to fix the number of the poor and to avoid the further depression of the independent labourer, I should be the first to propose that those who were actually in want should be most liberally relieved, and that they should receive it as a right, and not as a bounty.' T.R. Malthus, *Amendment of the poor laws*, London, 1807, pp. 12–13.
14. Malthus argued that in capitalist agriculture the interest of the farmer ensured that the product of the marginal worker could never be less than the conventional minimum wage, whereas in other systems this restriction did not apply (in an extreme case, the product of the *average* worker might fall to this level). T.R. Malthus, *An essay on the principle of population; or a view of its past and present effects on human happiness*, 2 vols, 6th edn, London, 1826, II, p. 154. Comments on the disadvantages of Turkish political institutions may be found in Malthus, *An essay on the principle of population; or a view of its past and present effects*, pp. 180–5.
15. Malthus held that there were what he termed 'oscillations' in the relationship between output and population which meant that living standards did not continue at an invariant level but moved up and down in sympathy. Whether or not any period of

improved living standards was consolidated or was succeeded by starker times depended on the particular circumstances of the society in question. 'From high real wages, or the power of commanding a large portion of the necessaries of life, two very different results may follow; one, that of a rapid increase of population, in which case the high wages are chiefly spent in the maintenance of large and frequent families; and the other, that of a decided improvement in the modes of subsistence, and the conveniences and comforts enjoyed, without a proportionate acceleration in the rate of increase.' T.R. Malthus, *Principles of political economy considered with a view to their practical application*, 2nd edn, London, 1836, p. 226. The bluntness of Adam Smith's view that the long term prospect for real wages was poor may be found, for example, in Smith, *Wealth of nations*, I, p. 98. Ricardo's judgement was closely similar.

16. Malthus, *An essay on the principle of population; or a view of its past and present effects*, II, pp. 290–1.
17. A definition of the concept of an organic economy will be found on p. 95 above.
18. Wrigley, *Continuity, chance and change*, p. 52, n. 46.
19. In round terms an intake of 1500 calories a day is needed to maintain vital bodily functions even when no exertions are undertaken. Above this level there is a linear relationship between food intake and ability to produce useful work up to an intake level of about 4000 calories a day, such that an intake of 3000 calories permits twice as much work to be performed as an intake of 2250 calories. At a normal level of nutrition, therefore, about half of the consumption of food was needed to keep the 'machine' viable, while the balance was available to carry out work. See, for example, F. Cottrell, *Energy and society: the relation between energy, social change, and economic development*, New York, 1955, p. viii; or E. Cook, *Man, energy, society*, San Francisco, 1976, pp. 27–8.
20. C.P. Kindleberger, *Economic development*, 2nd edn, New York, 1965, fig. 4.4, p. 70.
21. Wrigley, *Continuity, chance and change*, esp. chaps. 2 and 3.
22. E.H. Phelps Brown and S.V. Hopkins, 'Seven centuries of the prices of consumables compared with builders' wages', in E.M. Carus-Wilson, ed., *Essays in economic history*, II, London, 1962, pp. 179–96.
23. Fluctuations in the PBH series reflect the volatile behaviour of wholesale prices. Retail prices tended to be far less volatile, and therefore the 'true' standard of living of that part of the population chiefly dependent on wages probably moved up and down less violently, especially in the long term, than the PBH series suggests. See S. Rappaport, *Worlds within worlds: structures of life in*

*sixteenth century London*, Cambridge, 1989, ch. 5, 'The standard of living'.

24. The fallibility of the index of Phelps Brown and Hopkins is widely recognised, not least by its authors. It is unrealistic to assume that the proportionate share of items within the 'shopping basket' should remain the same over such a long period of time. The prices are wholesale prices but for the family budget retail prices were the relevant statistic, and retail prices were much less volatile than wholesale prices. The wage data were drawn largely from the south of England for very long periods and relate only to craftsmen and labourers in the building trade. Some important elements in the budget of every family, notably the cost of accommodation, could not be included in the index for lack of relevant data. And so on. It is tempting to suppose that the series may fail to capture an improvement in the real wage in the early modern period, if only because the marked change in employment structure away from agriculture in the seventeenth and eighteenth centuries suggests that an increasing proportion of income was available for the purchase of comforts and even luxuries after meeting the continued requirement for necessities.

25. On the extent of the contrast between England and the continent in the degree to which urbanisation increased in the seventeenth and eighteenth centuries, see Wrigley, *People, cities and wealth*, ch. 7, 'Urban growth and agricultural change: England and the Continent in the early modern period', esp. tab. 7.7, p. 179. On the Continent there appears to have been remarkably little change in the extent of urbanisation over almost half a millennium between 1400 and 1800; at both dates the proportion of the population living in towns with 5000 or more inhabitants was about 13 per cent. P. Bairoch, J. Batou and P. Chèvre, *La population des villes européennes. Banque de données et analyse sommaire des résultats*, Geneva, 1988, tab. B2, p. 255.

26. Smith, *Wealth of nations*, I, p. 106.

27. Putting some of Gregory King's data into a modern national income accounting framework, for example, Stone has estimated that social welfare provision through the poor law represented about a fifth of the combined total of central and local government expenditure in England in the late seventeenth century. R. Stone, *Some British empiricists in the social sciences* (the 1986 Mattioli Lectures, forthcoming), ch. on Gregory King.

# PART II

# Transitions to the modern world

# CHAPTER 4

# On a little known chapter of Mediterranean history

## Karl R. Popper

Our civilisation, which is, essentially, the Mediterranean civilisation, derives from the Greeks. This civilisation was born in the period from the 6th century before Christ to the 4th century, and it was born in Athens.

The Athenian miracle is staggering. Here we have, in a short period, beginning with Solon at about 600 BC, a peaceful revolution. Solon saved the city by shaking off the burden of debt from the exploited Athenian citizens, and by forbidding that any Athenian could be made a slave because of his debts. It was the first constitution ever designed to preserve the freedom of the citizens; and its principles were never forgotten, although the history of Athens shows abundantly clearly that freedom is never secure but always threatened.

Solon was not only a great statesman; he was the first Athenian-born poet of whom we have knowledge, and he explained his aims in his poetry. He spoke of 'eunomia' or 'good government', and he explained this as balancing the conflicting interests of the citizens. It was, no doubt, the first time, at least the first time in the Mediterranean region, that a constitution had been shaped with an ethical and humanitarian aim. And what was here at work was the universally valid ethical imperative that Schopenhauer brought into the simple form: *Neminem laede, imo omnes, quantum potes, juva!* That is: Hurt no one, but help all, as well as you can!

Like the American revolution, which came over 2000 years later, Solon's revolution had in mind the freedom of *citizens only*: the slavery of the bought slaves (largely barbarian slaves) was overlooked.

After Solon, Athenian politics were far from stable. Several leading families were contesting for power, and after some unsuccessful attempts, Peisistratos, a relation of Solon's, established himself as a monarch or tyrant in Athens. His great wealth derived from silver mines situated outside Attica, and he used his wealth largely for cultural purposes and for stabilising the Solonian reforms in Athens. He instituted festivals, among them especially theatrical festivals; to him is due the founding of the performances of tragedies in Athens. And, as we know from Cicero, he organised the writing down of the works of Homer, the *Iliad* and perhaps also the *Odyssey*, which previously seem to have existed only as oral traditions.

It is the main thesis of my address that this was an act that had the most far-reaching consequences; that it was an event of focal significance in the history of our civilisation.

For many years, ever since I wrote my *Open Society and its Enemies* (first edition 1945), the Athenian miracle has been a problem that has fascinated me. It is a problem that follows me around and does not let me go. What was it that created our civilisation in Athens? What made Athens invent art and literature, tragedy, philosophy, science and democracy, all in such a short period of time?

I had one answer to this problem, an answer that was undoubtedly true but, I felt, quite insufficient. The answer was: *culture clash*. When two or more different cultures come into contact, people realise that their ways and manners, so long taken for granted, are not 'natural', are not the only possible ones, neither decreed by the gods nor part of human nature. It thus opens a world of new possibilities: it opens the windows and it lets in fresh air. This is a kind of sociological law, and it explains a lot. And it certainly played an important role in Greek history.

Indeed, one of Homer's main themes in the *Iliad* and even more in the *Odyssey* is, precisely, culture clash. And culture clash is of course a main topic also of Herodotos's *History*. Its significance for Greek civilisation is very great.

Yet this explanation did not satisfy me. And for a long time I felt that I had to give up. A miracle like the Athenian miracle, I felt, *cannot* be explained. Least of all can it be explained by the writing down of the works of Homer, although this certainly had great influence. Books, indeed great books, had been written down before, and at other places, and nothing comparable to the Athenian miracle had happened.

But one day I read again Plato's *Apology of Socrates Before His Judges* – the most beautiful philosophical work I know. And re-reading a much discussed passage, I had a new idea. The passage (26 D-E) implies that there was a flourishing book market in Athens in the year 399 BC, a market, at any rate, where old books (such as Anaxagoras's book *On Nature*) were regularly sold, and where they could be bought quite cheaply. Eupolis, the great master of the old comedy, even speaks (in a fragment cited by Pollux, *Onomasticon* IX, 47; cp. VII, 211) quite explicitly of a book market 50 years earlier. Now, when could such a market have arisen? It was clear: only after Peisistratos had the works of Homer written down; and not only written down, but published.

Slowly, the whole significance of this event dawned on me: the picture began to unfold. Before Homer had been written down, there were books, but no popular books that were freely for sale at a market: books were, even where they existed, a great rarity, not commercially copied and distributed, but (like the book written by Heraclitus) kept in a holy place, under the surveillance of priests. But we know that in Athens Homer became popular: everybody read Homer, most knew him by heart. Homer was the first public entertainment ever! And this was the case mainly in Athens, as we can learn from Plato, who in his *Politeia* complains about this dangerous entertainment, while in his *Nomoi* he satirises Sparta and Crete for their lack of literary interest: in Sparta, he indicates, Homer's name is just barely known, and in Crete, he indicates, Homer has hardly been heard of.

The great success of Homer in Athens led to something like commercial book publishing: books, we know, were dictated to groups of literate slaves, who wrote them down on papyrus; the sheets were collected in scrolls or 'books', and they were sold on the market, at a place called 'the Orchestra'.

How did all this start? The simplest hypothesis is that Peisistratos himself not only had Homer written down, but had him copied and distributed. By a strange coincidence I stumbled about six years ago across a report saying that the first and very considerable export of papyrus from Egypt to Athens began in a year in which Peisistratos was still ruling in Athens.

Since Peisistratos had been interested in having public recitals of Homer, it is very plausible that he started distributing the newly edited books; and their popularity led to the emergence of other publishers.

Collections of poems written by other poets, and tragedies and comedies followed. None of these had been written with the intention of publishing them; but books written with that intention followed as soon as publishing became an established practice, and the book market (*bibliōnia*) in the Agora became an established institution. I conjecture that the first book written deliberately for publication was Anaxagoras's great work *On Nature*. Anaximandros's work appears never to have been published, although it seems that the Lyceum had a copy – perhaps a summary, and that Appollodoros, much later, discovered a copy – perhaps the same one – in an Athenian library. So I suggest that the publication of the works of Homer was the first publication ever, at least in the Mediterranean region. It not only made Homer the bible (*biblion*) of Athens – it made him the first instrument of education, the first primer, the first spelling book, the first novel. And it made the Athenians literate.

That this was highly significant for the establishment of the Athenian democratic revolution – the expulsion of Peisistratos's son Hippias from Athens, and the establishment of a democratic constitution – may be seen from one of the characteristic institutions of the democracy that was established about 50 years after the first publication. I mean the institution of ostracism. On the one hand, this institution assumed that an Athenian citizen was able to write, for it assumed that he would *write*, on a potsherd, the name of the citizen he thought dangerously popular or otherwise prominent. On the other hand, the institution of ostracism shows that the Athenians, at least during the first century after expelling the tyrant Hippias, regarded as the central problem of their democracy the prevention of a tyranny.

This idea comes out very clearly when we realise that the institution of ostracism did not regard the banishment as a punishment. By being ostracised, a citizen retained his honour unblemished, he retained his property and indeed all rights except his right to remain in the city. This right he lost, first for ten years and later for five, though he could be recalled. In a sense, ostracism was a tribute, since it recognised that a citizen was outstanding; and some of the most outstanding leaders were ostracised. Thus the idea was: nobody is irreplaceable, and much as we admire leadership, we must be able to do without any particular leader; otherwise he may make himself indispensable, and by steps become our master; and it is the main task of our democracy to avoid this. It should be noted that ostracism was not long in use. The first known case was in 488 BC, and the last in 417. All the cases were tragic for the great men who were banished. The period almost coincides with that of the greatest works of Athenian tragedy, with the period of Aeschylus, of Sophocles, and of Euripides, who banished himself.

So it is my hypothesis that the first publication in Europe was the publication of Homer, and this fortunate fact led to the Greek love of Homer and of the Homeric heroes, to popular literacy, and to the Athenian democracy. But I think it did more. Homer was of course popular before; and almost all the vase paintings had for some time been illustrations of his work; so had been many sculptures. Homer himself had been a detailed and realistic *painter in words* of many vivid and interesting scenes, and as Ernst Gombrich has pointed out, this challenged sculptors and painters to emulate him in their own different media. And the challenges became even greater as a detailed knowledge of the Homeric text became more widespread. So the influence upon the arts of the power to read cannot be denied. The influence of Homeric themes upon the Athenian tragedians is evident; and even when they used non-Homeric themes, they still continued to choose themes with which their audience could be assumed to be familiar. So I can claim that the cultural influence of the book market was indeed incalculable. All the components of the Athenian cultural miracle were greatly influenced by it.

But to crown all these arguments, we have a kind of historical experiment. The great invention that, as it were, repeated the invention of the publication of books on a far larger scale was the invention of book printing by Gutenberg, 2000 years after Peisistratos's invention of book publishing. It is interesting that, even though the invention was made in the north of Europe, the majority of printers who acquired the skill brought it quickly south to the Mediterranean – to Italy. And there they played a decisive role in that great new movement called the Renaissance, which included the development of the new humanist scholarship and the new science that ultimately transformed our whole civilisation.

This was a movement on a much larger scale than the movement that I dubbed 'The Athenian Miracle'. It was, first of all, a movement based on very much larger editions of books. In 1500, Aldus printed editions of one thousand copies. It was, obviously, the size of the printed editions that was the salient point of this new revolution. But otherwise there is an astonishing analogy, or similarity, between what had started in Athens in, say, 500 BC and had spread from there over the Mediterranean, and what happened in Florence or Venice in, say, 1500. And the new humanist scholars were aware of this: they wanted to renew the spirit of Athens, and they were proud of their ability to do so, and of their success.

As in Athens and later in Grecia Magna – and especially in Alexandria, but indeed all over the Mediterranean – scientific and, in particular, cosmological speculation played an important role in these movements. Renaissance mathematicians, such as Commandino, successfully recaptured the lost works of Euclid, Archimedes, Apollonius, Pappus and Ptolemy, but also of Aristarchus, which led to the Copernican Revolution and so to Galileo, to Kepler, to Newton and to Einstein. If our own civilisation is correctly described as the first scientific civilisation, then it all comes from the Mediterranean and, I suggest, from Athenian book publishing, and the Athenian book market.

In all this I have badly neglected the contribution of the Arabs, who brought an Indian number system to the Mediterranean. They gave much, but when they reached the Mediterranean, they received as much as they gave, if not more.

I have briefly retold a well-known story – well known except for one small yet, I think, significant contribution: the decisive role played by books, and especially by published books, from the very beginning. Our civilisation is, indeed a bookish one: its traditionality and its originality, its seriousness and its sense of intellectual responsibility, its unprecedented power of imagination and its creativity, its understanding of freedom and its watchfulness for it – all these rest on our love of books. May short-term fashions, the media and the computers never spoil or even loosen this close personal attachment!

But I do not wish to end with books, however important they are for our civilisation. It is most important not to forget that a civilisation consists of civilised individual men and women, of individuals who wish to live good lives and civilised lives. It is to this end that books and our civilisation must make their contributions. I believe that they are doing so.

## NOTE

This is a slightly shortened version of a lecture delivered on 24 May 1989 at the Palace of the Generalitat de Catalunya on the occasion of receiving the first Catalonia International Prize. It has not been previously published (eds).

# CHAPTER 5

# Ernest Gellner and the escape to modernity

## Alan Macfarlane

Ernest Gellner is in the great tradition of European thinkers. Poised between social systems, he is compelled to analyse the chasms that he straddles. Few writers in this century have been better placed to see and explain the peculiarities of modern industrial-capitalist civilisation.

The early clash between eastern and western Europe in his upbringing has been reinforced by at least three further intellectual and social experiences which have heightened his awareness of the peculiarities and precariousness of our civilisation. One of these is his professional interest in the great philosophical watershed between the *ancien régime* and modernity which took place in the eighteenth century and particularly in the Scotland of his beloved David Hume. Here Gellner finds a specification of the foundation of the new world and all its strangeness, which was given further precision by his other mentor, Kant.

The second reinforcement comes from his professional involvement with Islam. This provides him with an invaluable counter-model. He approvingly quotes De Tocqueville on the fact that 'Islam is the religion which has most completely confounded and intermixed the two powers . . . so that all the acts of civil and political life are regulated more or less by religious law'.[1] Islam makes Gellner deeply aware that the mixing of religion and politics is the normal state of mankind; their separation is a recent peculiarity.

Thirdly, there is Gellner's continuing work with the only other major 'totalitarian' or 'closed' system that still exists, communism. Whereas Islam embeds politics within religion, the Soviet world where Gellner has worked tries to embed economy, society and religion within the polity.

Put in another way, Gellner has experienced the stark contrast between Open and Closed societies three times, once historically and twice in his own experience. It is no surprise that his specification of the uniqueness of modern western civilisation is so compelling.

The repeated insistence on the uniqueness and lack of inevitability of modern western civilisation often takes the form of praise of Max Weber. Weber's *Protestant Ethic* 'is a masterpiece . . . for its superb sketch of what it is that distinguishes the modern world from the other possible and actual social worlds . . . he knew full well that the modern world was but one of many possible ones and very different from the others . . .'[2] Weber's central point was, 'what were the specific preconditions and consequences of this unique kind of man, who was also responsible for that fascinating monstrosity, the modern world?'[3] This reality of the 'uniqueness of the West' is one of the ironic consequences of a new and less Europocentric vision. We have had a 'very odd and distinctive historic development . . .'[4]

The consequence of this unique transformation are immense. Western industrial-capitalist society is 'without any shadow of doubt, conquering, absorbing all the other cultures of this Earth'.[5] The single occasion when men escaped from the embedded pre-industrial world has 'transformed the entire world'[6] for 'the modern industrial machine is like an elephant in a very small boat . . . [it] presupposes an enormous infrastructure, not merely of political order, but educationally, culturally, in terms of communication and so forth'.[7]

What then *is* this unique and unprecedented civilisation, and how does it differ from all its predecessors and the two major alternatives today, Islam and communism? Much of Gellner's work, in numerous volumes, is concerned with specifying this, so it is impossible to do more than single out a few of the most important theories.

One central theme is the growth of rationality or disenchantment of the world. There is a 'radical discontinuity' which exists 'between primitive and modern mentality'.[8] This is the 'transition to effective knowledge', which Gellner describes many times. There is 'the great transition between the old, as it were non-epistemic worlds, in which the principles of cognition are subject to the pervasive constitutive principles of a given vision, and thus have little to fear, and a world in which this is no longer possible', a 'fundamental transition indeed'.[9] This is, of course, not unlike the work of Popper and Kuhn. But Gellner's stress is on the fact that 'the attainment of a rational, non-magical, non-enchanted world is a much more fundamental achievement than the jump from one scientific vision to another'. Popper 'underestimates the difficulty' of establishing an Open Society.[10]

Again, some of the most illuminating statements come in the exposition of Weber's similar work. The modern world of rationality has two central features: coherence or consistency, and efficiency. Coherence means 'that there are no special, privileged, insulated facts or realms'. Efficiency means 'the cool rational selection of the best available means to given, clearly formulated and isolated ends'. This is 'the separation of all separables . . . the breaking up of all complexes into their constituent parts . . .'; it creates 'a common measure of fact, a universal conceptual currency . . . all facts are located within a single continuing logical space . . . one single language describes the world . . .'[11]

Put in another way, 'rationality' means that spheres have become sufficiently disentangled for the mind to move without constantly bumping into wider obstacles created by impenetrable barriers whether of religion, kinship or politics.

This 'freedom of thought' is, of course, bought at a price. Gellner takes from Kant and Weber, among others, his analysis of the consequences of this disenchantment. The modern world 'provides no warm cosy habitat for man . . . the impersonality and regularity, which make it knowable are also, at the same time, the very features which makes it almost . . . uninhabitable.'[12] Our world is 'notoriously a cold, morally indifferent world'. It is notable for its 'icy indifference to values, its failure to console and reassure, its total inability to validate norms and values or to offer any guarantee of their eventual success . . .'[13] The open predicament is one where logical consistency and openness is bought at the price of social and moral inconsistency. We are simultaneously strictly rational and open-minded, and totally lost and confused. Within the new world 'there also is and can be no room either for magic or for the sacred'.[14]

What has happened is that thought, cognition, has been set free from its usual masters – politics, religion or kinship. We are open to all thought and to all doubt. God is dead, the father is dead, and the king is dead. We are our own masters, to think what we please. The barriers are down and everything is levelled onto one plane (as Simmel described the effects of money). This is one feature of 'modernity' for Gellner.

The second main theme concerns the separation of institutions or balance of powers. Gellner notes that in the majority of human societies, there is no separation of institutions. For instance, in tribal societies there is no distinction between economic and political: 'in acephalous or near-acephalous segmentary society, what you own and what you can effectively defend can hardly be distinguished'.[15] But 'under capitalism, this unity disappears; productive units cease to be political and social ones. Economic activities become autonomous . . .' This separation of the economic from the political and social is one of the important features of western industrial capitalism. 'The really fundamental trait of classical capitalism is that it is a very special kind of order in that the economic and the political seem to be separated, to a greater degree than in any other historically known social form.'[16] In this situation, 'Production replaces predation as the central theme and value of life'.[17]

The second major separation is that between religion and politics. We saw earlier that the confusion of these two is the hallmark of Islam. But in the modern West, perhaps partly because 'a kind of potential for political modesty has stayed with [Christianity] ever since those humble beginnings',[18] politics is not embedded in religion. Nor is economics. The famous Weber–Tawney thesis concerning the separation of the market from religion is largely endorsed: 'the separation of the economic from other aspects of life, in other words the untrammelled market, is highly eccentric, historically and sociologically speaking'.[19]

This separation of spheres, where politics, economics, religion and kinship are artificially held apart, is the central feature of modern civilisation. None of the institutions is dominant. There is no determining infrastructure, but a precarious and never to be taken for granted balance of power. This, Gellner believes, is the key to the difference between Islam and the

West. 'The difference would seem to be less in the absence of ideological elements than in the particular balance of power which existed between the various institutions in that society.'[20] We have a polity with 'an unusual balance of power internally and externally'. This 'miraculous political and ideological balance of power in the non-economic parts of society made the expansion [industrialisation – A.M.] possible . . .'[21]

This 'insulation' of various spheres of life has its own costs as well. Although it allows people to think 'freely' and to act 'rationally' it is, of course, caught in the deeper contradiction that the real world is not separated into watertight compartments. We have to believe that religion and politics, morality and economics, kinship and politics are separable and can live amicably alongside each other. But the garment is thereby torn apart arbitrarily: reality is a seamless web, as the majority of human societies have realised. Marx recognised this in his concept of 'alienation', Durkheim in 'anomie'. Gellner adds some further dimensions to these contradictions.

We have seen already the Kantian clash between a cold mechanistic controllable world, and the desire for social cohesiveness. Put another way, 'the world in which we think is not the same as the one in which we live . . . the colder the one, the more fanciful the other, perhaps'. Hence the manifestly irrational features, romantic love, obsession with nature and feeling, modern paganism and astrology, and so on. There is a huge contradiction between the orderly, rational 'society', and the arbitrary, bizarre, random 'culture'.[22] As we have gathered logical cohesiveness, so we have lost social cohesiveness. We live in a 'cognitively powerful, and socially disconnected' world.[23] This insight Gellner partly owes to another of his sources of inspiration, Ibn Khaldun, who showed that you 'could have communal, civic spirit, or you could have civilization – but not both'.[24]

So far so good. Gellner has clearly elaborated the problem: the unique and peculiar nature of modern civilisation needs to be explained. How did it emerge? Once and once only mankind escaped from the Malthusian world of poverty, into the cold sunlight of a rational, expanding but divided civilisation.

Critics might argue that there is nothing particularly new here. It is true that if we add together the best insights of the

Scottish Enlightenment, Durkheim, Weber and Marx, and then add Ibn Khaldun, we could have independently arrived at the same conclusions. What is unusual is that Gellner has rescued this vision. The new world has become so much part of the air we breathe that the shock of newness felt by Hume, Smith and Ferguson, or of comparative strangeness best exemplified in Weber, has been forgotten by most of us. Islam and the Soviet bloc, and perhaps memories of Czechoslovakia before the Second World War, have constantly reminded Gellner that none of this is to be taken for granted, that it is indeed not the normal condition of man. An 'open' society is a miraculous, unique and precarious phenomenon. 'That all men are created equal and independent' is for from being a universally 'sacred and undeniable' truth.

The less good news is that Gellner cannot explain *why* this happens, what caused this once-only exit into modernity. To be fair, Gellner is quite aware that he does not understand the reason why. 'The origins of industrial society continue to be an object of scholarly dispute. It seems to me very probable that this will continue to be so for ever.'[25] 'The first miracle had occurred when men *for obscure reasons* persisted in working a set of levers not yet known to work.' 'On one occasion and in one area, the message did prevail, *thanks to very special circumstances . . .*' which are not specified.[26] These successfully capture the essential point about the uniqueness and lack of inevitability of the process. But miracles are also difficult to explain, as are accidents. 'The notion of a unified orderly Nature . . . led, by a miracle we cannot fully explain . . .'; yet Gellner does attempt to explain the inexplicable, while implicitly recognising the impossibility: 'we have striven to explain how one society, and one only had, by *a series of near-miraculous accidents . . .*',[27] escaped into modernity.

At heart, Gellner's story is as follows. There are three types of society, hunter-gatherers, agrarian, industrial. His problem is how, against all the odds, the first society escaped through a gate from Agraria to Industria. It was miraculous, for 'almost everything in the ethos, and in the balance of power of the society, generally militates against the possibility of an explosive growth in either production or cognition'. The Agrarian Age 'was basically a period of stagnation, oppression and superstition'; all these are reversed as one civilisation miraculously 'escaped' from this rural idiocy.[28] Having rejected economic determinism, how can this transformation have occurred?

Gellner's first major attempt to explain the escape stresses three factors. The ideological force of Protestantism was important for the reasons Weber gave – the accumulative ethic. An expanding technology was important, but the really important thing was that it was a feeble technology, not powerful enough to threaten the rulers. Finally there was a peculiarly modest but powerful State. 'The suspension of coercion arose because there was a state strong enough to prevent private coercion, yet at the same time willing or obliged not to expropriate and exploit the producers . . .'[29] All this is important, but only *describes* a few of the necessary causes, without saying either that any or all of them are *sufficient*, or how they came about. At best it is redescribing aspects of the miracle.

A new factor which becomes increasingly important in Gellner's work after this early attempt is literacy. Literacy, for instance, 'means in effect the possibility of cultural and cognitive storage and centralization', so that 'the truly crucial step in the cognitive development of mankind is the introduction of literacy'.[30] But, of course, Gellner is well aware that this will not help him to solve his problem, for literacy is a phenomenon co-terminous with the *first* transition to Agraria, rather than with the transition from it. Mass literacy, however, is indeed a feature of industrial societies.

The most sustained attempt to solve the problem is contained in a section headed 'Conditions of the Exit'.[31] The use of the word 'Conditions' is indicative. This turns out to be a set of possible, maybe necessary, pre-conditions. It is a useful checklist of 'factors'. But none of them is determining and Gellner is too auto-critical to be really convinced by any of them. There are fifteen of them, from 'Feudalism as the matrix of capitalism' through 'the restrained state' and 'the direct Protestant ethic thesis' to 'a national rather than civic bourgeoisie'. Most are thought provoking, and some, such as 'the availability of an expanding bribery fund', are original. Probably Gellner's favourites, if weighting has to be attached, remain those of his earlier attempt, the restrained state, the multiplex role of Protestantism and the growing yet modest technology.

Yet the best that he can draw from this analysis is really a list of possible ingredients. The precise weightings are not specified nor the ways the elements should be combined. We are left, as Gellner is himself, unsatisfied. It is still a miracle, the way through the gate is still obscure.

A few thoughts might be offered to help Gellner out of this impasse. The first is a particular point, indicative of a larger one. The curious nature of feudalism is only half understood, as a 'matrix of capitalism'. While recognising that the 'relationship between members of various levels in this stratified structure . . . are . . . contractual' and 'even affirms a curious free market in loyalty', Gellner still believes that feudalism is 'governed by status and not contract'.[32] It is thus difficult for him to see how strange and powerful feudalism was. If the major transformation which Gellner analyses is rephrased in other terms as the movement from status-based to contract-based societies, or from *Gemeinschaft* to *Gesellschaft*, then according to Gellner, feudal societies are still 'governed by status' and hence on the wrong side of the divide.

Yet the greatest thinkers on this subject are united in placing feudalism after the great divide. The first and second of these are Sir Henry Maine and F. W. Maitland, whose views can be encapsulated in a remark by the latter: 'the master who taught us that "the movement of the progressive societies has hitherto been a movement from Status to Contract" was quick to add that feudal society was governed by the law of contract'. Maitland added his endorsement as recognition of this: 'there is no paradox here'.[33] In other words that very element of 'progress' and 'growth' which Gellner singles out is present in feudalism. We already have the peculiarity he is searching for well *before* the supposed 'capitalist revolution' of the fifteenth or sixteenth century let alone industrialisation in the eighteenth and nineteenth.

This misapprehension is indicative of a deeper difficulty of Gellner's framework, which lies in his rigidly tripartite model. Quite early on in his intellectual life Gellner seems to have convinced himself that three-stage models are the best and that world history can be fitted into such a model. This becomes a dogma in his book on nationalism, for instance, where he writes that 'mankind has passed through three fundamental stages in its history: the pre-agrarian, the agrarian and the industrial'. Or again he writes, 'my own conception of world history is clear and simple: the three great stages of man, the hunting-gathering, the agrarian and the industrial, determine our problems, but not our solution'.[34] Trinitarians who subscribe to the 'elegant and canonical three' stages (Comte, Frazer or Karl Polanyi) are praised.

This is certainly clear and simple, and it becomes the frame-work for the whole of *Plough, Sword and Book*, where we are told that 'mankind has passed through three principal stages . . .', each of which is then briefly characterised.[35] A section on 'Trinitarianism' is then included to give support for such a theory. But the difficulty is that such a model does indeed determine not only the problems, but also the nature of the solution. If we believe with Gellner that there are these three types, each distinct and different, it is indeed difficult to see how the movement from one to the next occurred. But attractive as three-stage theories are (they are probably an 'idol of the mind' in Bacon's sense, for from the definition of the novel as having a beginning, middle and end, to Hegelian dialectic or the demographic transition, we tend to think in three stages), they are stifling and blinkering when applied to such a complex story as the history of mankind.

Let us start with the beginning. There is not one generic type of 'hunter-gatherer' society, but numerous types. Gellner is quite aware of the major divisions, immediate-return and delayed-return hunter-gatherers, but there are many others. For instance, Australian hunter-gatherers with their elaborate kinship and mythical systems are very different from the cognatic and mythless African bushmen; or forest-dwellers in the Amazon are enormously different from the Inuit of Canada. From very early on there is enough variation to start mankind moving in all sorts of directions, some leading to Tehran, others to Los Angeles.

In Gellner's scheme there is then tremendous lumping together of differences in 'Agraria'. Here we have everything from pastoral nomads to densely settled India and China, almost every conceivable kind of kinship system, numerous religious and political organisations. If they are all lumped together or generically similar, it makes the emergence of modern individual civilisation totally inexplicable. But once we allow for the possibility that, say, tenth-century England, though 'agrarian', was very different from, say, tenth-century Poland or Ghana or Peru (or the approximate places where these names would later apply), then we can open up the discussion.

Instead of being locked in the hopeless task of trying to see how it was that out of a uniform mass one part 'broke away', we can look at the historical record to see what the major differences were and how long they have existed and where they come from.

We could keep a very rough general external framework, which might be Gellner's, or might be the more conventional anthropological one of the hunter-gatherer, tribal, peasant and industrial-capitalist, yet we could also recognise that each of these is an artificial and arbitary mnemonic device, an attempted 'as if' classification which really only highlights the difficulties and differences. If we do this, we are free to speculate on possible exits in any way we like. One speculation might look like this.

Suppose Gellner is right in describing the central feature of 'modernity', which is the separation of spheres or, put another way, the 'restraint' of each. The characteristic feature of most civilisations and societies is that over time one or other of the major institutions gains weight and dominates. 'Kinship is king' on the whole in hunter-gatherer and tribal societies, and all the rest is embedded. Religion or politics, or a mixture of the two, dominates in peasantries, as in Hindu or Islamic civilisation. All these are instances where society 'freezes', to use Lévi-Strauss's metaphor, so that status comes to dominate, whether kinship status as in unilineal kinship systems, or religious status, as in caste societies, or political status as in communism. What is peculiar is a situation where *nothing* dominates.

In 'modern' societies, kinship regulates a small sphere, reproduction, but does not organise politics, economics or religion. Religion provides solutions to some philosophical problems and minimal ethical guidance, but is kept well back from important matters like politics or the market. Politics is restrained and should allow the citizens plenty of 'freedom' to carry on their economic, family and religious business secured only by the 'night-watchman' state. Even the market and economic activity should be held in check and prevented from 'corrupting' emotional life, art, sport, leisure, nature, or buying its way too openly into politics and religion.

Now this peculiar position of balance of institutions or interests, of moderation, caution, tolerance, lack of passionate intensity, of trust and single-stranded rationality, is another characterisation of 'modernity'. By Gellner's three-fold model it is entirely antithetical to the major features of the hunter-gatherer and agrarian stages. Tribal societies are not based on Hobbesian individualism, but on embedded segmentary structures where kinship dominates all. Agrarian civilisations are again based on status, but this time the status of a hierarchy of religious and political power.

In fact, once we drop the three-fold model and simple characterisation, it is possible to find almost perfect anticipation of much of this characterisation in all 'stages' of human civilisation. It has long been noted that African hunter-gatherers, and hunter-gatherers in general, are curiously 'modern' in many ways. Though they lacked the technology, literacy and so on, they often seem to have had the essential quality that nothing dominated ('free' individuals were not slaves to one institution) – religion, polity, economy or even kinship. From the start, then, it may be that 'modernity' existed a very long time ago.[36]

The normal course of affairs was for this 'modernity' to be crushed during the long intervening years. As populations grew more dense and wealth was congealed, hierarchies emerged and mankind became dominated by religious or political institutions or, usually, a mixture of the two. This *ancien régime* world was to be found in most of Asia or pre-Revolutionary Europe or South America. It seemed a necessary 'stage' in the famed transition between tribal and 'modern' societies. Its social concomitant was peasantry.

Yet, apart from our own imposed model-building tendencies, there is no need to believe that this was the only and *necessary* course. It is quite conceivable that the path has varied all over the world. In western Europe, for instance, it could be argued that after the fall of the Roman Empire, there was a strange mixture of several elements. The survival of traces of

Romanism, the contractual political system of Germanic feudalism, the ascetic and individualistic (and, according to Gellner,
modest) religion of Christianity, the non-segmentary kinship
system made, over the centuries between about the fifth and the
eleventh, a new and potentially 'modern' system in terms of the
division of spheres outlined above.

Put another way, the secret must lie in the properties of the
four main institutions, all of which must have a non-exclusive
and limited character. This seems to have been the case. Christianity, especially in its heretical forms and later in Protestantism, was not too deeply involved in this world, allowing people
to render to Caesar that which was Caesar's. The bilateral
kinship system cannot form the basis of the society since it built
up no discrete political or social groupings. The political system,
based on the contractual feudal system, was powerful enough to
guarantee some order, but was always held in check by the
countervailing devolution of power that is a necessary feature of
feudalism. The ruler is the first among equals, unable to rule
without consent, a limited monarch. The economy in this technologically backward and varied landscape was not strong
enough and produced too little wealth to allow it to dominate.

During the centuries after the eleventh, of course, much of
this changed and the widespread tendencies which have been
found in older civilisations, such as those in India, South East
Asia and China, manifested themselves. Over much of central,
eastern and southern Europe, a caste-like society arose with
hereditary nobility, a King above the Law, a Church in alliance
with the state. The usual reconfusion of economics, moral,
political, social and religious spheres occurred.

Yet for reasons which are strictly historical and accidental, this
widespread tendency did not occur in northern Europe to the
same extent; in particular in England much of the 'modernity'
implicit over much of Europe in the tenth century survived. It
continued and provided the balanced platform for the emergence of a new technology (industrialism) and society (urban-
ism) which we know and love. There was no inevitability about
this. But nor is there any particular mystery. By failing to
gravitate towards absolutism, inquisition or familism, part of
northern Europe preserved a balance which allowed free-
floating individuals to make themselves wealthier in peace,

within a secure framework. This was what the Pilgrims took to America.

Now Ernest Gellner has already heard most of this story, and while conceding that the case 'has not been demolished by its critics', he is reluctant to accept it. It is worth examining his reason for this.

The greatest difficulty this thesis faces, perhaps, is that it merely pushes the question one step further back. Just how did it come about that this privileged set of people developed, and were allowed to develop and maintain a spirit which, in the context of wider history, is so very unusual? How did they escape the logic of the agrarian situation, which prevails in most other parts of the world?[37]

This is difficult to answer if we accept Gellner's three-stage model, because all the argument does is to squeeze the first two stages, pushing them backwards in time. If the simple three-stage model is accepted, then there must have been hunter-gatherer segmentary systems, these then evolved into Agraria, which was then broken down. All this merely happened earlier than before. But we are still left with the puzzle of *why*.

Yet, if we drop the three-stage model, except as a model (that is, a benchmark against which to judge *exceptions*) this *is* the 'exception'. First there were peoples who already had a politico-kinship system which was not segmentary and which already had a contractual, law-based element. These people settled a wide area without becoming 'peasants'. They adopted a religion that did not fossilise into an intensive ritualistic system. In other words, they were agriculturists and traders, but they never went through a proper 'Agraria'. Like the gibe about Americans moving from barbarism to decadence without the intervening stage of civilisation, certain peoples of northern Europe (and possibly the Japanese as well) moved from barbarism to modernity, without the intervening stage of Agraria.

Many paths through time are possible. Ernest Gellner has achieved the difficult goal of remembering that though it seems from our vantage point looking backwards that there was some *necessity* about the path that was taken, this is not the case. We should not lose that insight. I am therefore not suggesting any inevitability. It is still a miracle, and hence still largely fortuitous, accidental. But this does not preclude us from measuring the distances after the accident. Even if we would not have predicted it, we can give some picture of how it happened.

We can also see what is the most crucial ingredient, the separation or balance of power. This was recognised by many of the most perceptive commentators of the eighteenth and nineteenth centuries, and with a little testimony from them, we can end.

The first is Montesquieu, whose remark in the *L'Esprit des Lois* that England 'had progressed the farthest of all peoples of the world in three important things: in piety, in commerce and in freedom', was commented on by Max Weber as follows: 'Is it not possible that their commercial superiority and their adaptation to free political institutions are connected in some way with that record of piety which Montesquieu ascribes to them?'[38] Thus Montesquieu and Weber saw that it was in the interconnections, in the *balance* between religion, polity and economy, that the secret lay, and that autonomy or 'freedom' of spheres, was essential. David Hume independently noted something similar in his *Essays*. The English had a mixed political system, 'mixture of monarchy, aristocracy, and democracy'; they were religiously pluralist, 'all sects of religion are to be found among them'. And consequently, though speaking one language and subject to one set of laws, 'the great liberty and independency, which every man enjoys, allows him to display the manners peculiar to him'.[39]

The essential characteristics are beautifully summarised in the middle of the nineteenth century by Taine. When trying to compare England and France, he found that the climate, distribution of wealth, and family and communal life of France were preferable. England was superior in three ways. Firstly, its political system 'is liberal, and calls upon the individual citizen to take an active part in public life . . . British citizens enjoy full freedom of speech and association . . .' Politics, in other words, knows its limits; so does religion. 'It subordinates ritual and dogma to ethics. It preaches "self-government", the authority of conscience, and the cultivation of the will. It leaves a wide margin for personal interpretation and feeling. It is not altogether hostile to the spirit of modern science nor to the tendencies of the modern world.' Finally, the economy is allowed to flourish in peace and security. 'England has suffered no invasion for eight hundred years, and no civil war for two hundred years . . . Evidence of comfort and opulence is more plentiful in England than in any other country in the world.'[40] This is an (unconscious?) reflection of Montesquieu's 'piety, commerce and freedom'.

We can combine this balance with Adam Smith's view, as recorded by Dugald Stewart, that 'Little else is requisite to carry a state to the highest degree of opulence from the lowest barbarism, but peace, easy taxes, and a tolerable administration of justice; all the rest being brought about by the natural course of things.'[41] We then have a Thatcherite picture that describes *how* things happened. What it leaves out is the fact that the art of maintaining such a balance, as many societies and civilisations have learnt, is not as easy as it looks. It is certainly far from 'natural'.

## NOTES

1. Gellner, *Muslim Society*, Cambridge, 1981, p. 1.
2. Gellner, *Muslim*, p. 89.
3. Gellner, *Legitimation of Belief*, Cambridge, 1974, p. 191.
4. Gellner, *Plough, Sword and Book: The Structure of Human History*, London, 1988, pp. 259, 44.
5. Gellner, *Plough*, p. 200.
6. Gellner, *Plough*, p. 277.
7. Gellner, *Spectacles and Predicaments: Essays in Social Theory*, Cambridge, 1979, p. 288.
8. Gellner, *Plough*, p. 42.
9. Gellner, *Legitimation*, pp. 169, 173.
10. Gellner, *Legitimation*, p. 182.
11. Gellner, *Nations and Nationalism*, Oxford, 1983, pp. 21, 20, 22, 21.
12. Gellner, *Legitimation*, p. 184.
13. Gellner, *Plough*, pp. 64–5.
14. Gellner, *Plough*, p. 66.
15. Gellner, *Muslim*, p. 37.
16. Gellner, *Spectacles*, p. 285.
17. Gellner, *Plough*, p. 158.
18. Gellner, *Muslim*, p. 2.
19. Gellner, *Spectacles*, p. 286.
20. Gellner, *Muslim*, p. 6.
21. Gellner, *Plough*, pp. 277, 132.
22. Gellner, *Legitimation*, pp. 194–5.
23. Gellner, *Plough*, pp. 61, 70.
24. Gellner, *Muslim*, p. 17.

25. Gellner, *Nations*, p. 19.
26. Gellner, *Plough*, pp. 222, 112; my italics.
27. Gellner, *Plough*, pp. 199, 277; my italics.
28. Gellner, *Plough*, pp. 103, 22.
29. Gellner, *Spectacles*, p. 286.
30. Gellner, *Nations*, p. 8; Gellner, *Plough*, p. 71.
31. Gellner, *Plough*, p. 154.
32. Gellner, *Plough*, p. 158.
33. Sir F. Pollock and F. W. Maitland, *The History of English Law Before the Time of Edward I*, 2nd edn, Cambridge, 1968, vol. 2, p. 233.
34. Gellner, *Nations*, pp. 5, 114.
35. Gellner, *Plough*, p. 16.
36. For a general account of this balance see Elman R. Service, *The Hunters*, New Jersey, 1966.
37. Gellner, *Plough*, p. 163.
38. Max Weber, *The Protestant Ethic and the Spirit of Capitalism*, London, 1970, p. 45.
39. David Hume, *Essays, Literary, Moral and Political*, London, n.d., Essay XX, 'Of National Characters', p. 122.
40. Hippolyte Taine, *Notes on England*, London, 1957, trans. Edward Hyams, pp. 290–1.
41. Quoted in John A. Hall, *Powers and Liberties; the Causes and Consequences of the Rise of the West*, Oxford, 1985, p. 141.

# CHAPTER 6

# The emergence of modern European nationalism

### Michael Mann

The story is often told against the citizens of West Hartlepool, on the northeast coast of England, that during the Napoleonic Wars a ship was wrecked offshore and a ship's monkey, dressed in uniform, was washed ashore alive. The good people of Hartlepool hung it as a Frenchman.

This story may be apocryphal, but I will show that it aptly symbolises much of the rise of nationalism. I define nationalism conventionally as an ideology which asserts the moral, cultural and political primacy of an ethnic group (real or constructed). This conventional definition allows for two main sub-types of nationalism, cultural and political, each of which has its peculiarities. In Europe the assertion that an ethnic group had distinctive cultural virtue often preceded agitation to secure its own state – as in 18th century Ireland[1] or Germany (discussed here). Yet it was typically espoused by only a few intelligentsia. Political nationalism was often more broadly based where the ethnic group did not have its own state (Italians or Czechs in the 19th century), yet was almost invisible when it did (England in the 19th century). In both cases, however, political legitimation was vested in what were supposed to be the peculiar virtues of 'the nation', in fact of 'this particular nation', in the sense of 'the people'. I shall therefore look for the emergence of 'popular' national ideological elements and for evidence of popular support or mobilisation in both cultural and political movements.

My aim is to establish when and why such nationalism first emerged as a mass phenomenon in Europe, beginning with and then revising Ernest Gellner's explanation of this. Unlike Gellner, I do not claim a general but a local theory of nationalism – though it was a locality of some significance in the world. I concentrate on four 18th and 19th century Great Powers: Britain, France, the lands of the Austrian Monarchy and Prussia/Germany.[2] These give a good range of the varied nationalisms that arose in modern Europe. They are also states on whose activities I have collected systematic statistical data – which we find later to be significant in explaining the rise of nationalism.

I start with where I am indebted to Gellner. Like him I am a 'modernist', believing that nationalism – like class ideology, the other great ideology of modern times – was capable of spreading across large social and geographic spaces only from the 18th century to the present day. True, I must qualify that statement, acknowledging that elements of 'ethnic consciousness' identified by Anthony Smith existed in earlier times. But in large-scale societies such consciousness was generally of the distinctive sub-type labelled by Smith as 'lateral' and aristocratic, confined within the upper class. Even Smith, who argues more strongly than Gellner and I for the existence also of some 'vertical' (that is cross-class) ethnic communities in agrarian societies, concludes that 'nationalism, both as ideology and movement, is a wholly modern phenomenon'.[3]

Gellner developed an original explanation, both negative and positive, for why nationalism is modern. Negatively, he argues that prior agrarian societies, termed 'agro-literate polities', were based on the cultural insulation of ruling class from peasant masses. Political units could not be defined by the sharing of culture: there could be no nationalism.[4] I agree with this reasoning.[5] I will explore and amend his positive explanation: how did modern societies encourage nationalism (as well as class ideology)?

Gellner argues that the nation is an abstract, universal community. It presupposes a modern rationalised society in which an impersonal communications system allows context-free messages to pass both vertically and horizontally across extensive social spaces. It requires what the 18th century called a 'civil society'. But, he continues, this flow of context-free messages also implies a 'universal, standardised and generic' education system, and therefore requires state supervision and funding. Modern society depends on a state-defined sense of community: the nation. 'A modern, industrial state can only function with a mobile, literate, culturally standardized, inter-changeable population.' Thus with modernisation local popula-tions 'yearn for incorporation into one of those cultural pools which already has, or looks as if it might acquire, a state of its own, with the subsequent promise of full cultural citizenship, access to primary schools, employment and all'.[6] He still adheres to this argument.[7]

But Gellner adds a further detail, as one sentence quoted above reveals. He tells us what specific aspect of modern society requires the new culture and generates nationalism: *industriali-sation*. Industry requires interchangeability, mobility and state-supervised education. That is the key stimulant. There are two elements here: firstly, interchangeability – or, as I prefer to term it, 'universalism'; second, the requirement that such universalism be given authoritative organisation over a ter-ritorially-delimited area – that is, by a state.

Gellner's theory therefore constitutes economic materialism of the industrial society school. He rejects (or rather ignores) the rival Marxian school of materialism which emphasises capitalism – usually its uneven economic development – and its social classes as the progenitors of nationalism.[8] He also rejects non-economic theories, such as the politically-centred theory of Anthony Smith[9] who sees nationalism as emerging from a crisis of state modernisation. And the theory constitutes evolutionary functionalism: industrialisation requires a diffuse, universal culture, linking the inhabitants of a territory to their state. That culture is nationalism.

We might object to the very strong functionalism of the argument. Does industrialisation really *require* nationalism? Will nothing else do as a substitute? Later I argue that national-ism was rather more contingent than this, more dependent on specific inter-relations between a diversity of power relations, not merely economic ones.

However, the stress on industrialisation also raises the prob-lem of dating nationalism. For a cursory review of the historical evidence might suggest that industrialisation – and state-funded universal education – came a little too *late* to explain nationalism. Let us overlook for the moment the controversial view that English nationalism can be found in the 1760s. But from the 1790s we can find incontrovertible demonstrations of

nationalism: the French army at Valmy in 1791, shouting
'Vive la nation' as the Prussian cannon rained fire into them,
the revolutionaries' cry 'la patrie en danger', the creation of
self-styled 'patriot' revolutionary movements across Europe
(though the Americans had actually started this in 1776), then
the conversion of European resistance to the French, especially in Prussia, to more mobilised, popular forms and the
emergence of national movements in some of the most
backward Habsburg lands across the mid 19th century. Aren't
all these expressions of nationalism too *early* to be accounted
for by industrialisation? It is dubious to call even Britain
'industrial' in the 1790s, let alone France; it would be
ludicrous so to style Prussia in 1810 or Hungary in 1848. And
no state possessed effective mass state-funded education until
well after 1850.

Gellner might defend himself in three ways. He does say that
nationalists may be acute and anticipate industrialisation.
Indeed 19th-century nationalists in quite backward countries
often did advocate industrialisation as a central part of their
modernisation projects. But so did most power groupings of
the 19th century, since industry was obviously necessary to
progress and power. Why should industrialisation be specifically nationalist? We must remember that the first wave of
industrialisation, lasting until after the mid 19th century, was
actually predominantly transnational. Technical inventions,
capital and skilled workers diffused from England right
through state boundaries, with little state intervention.[10] List,
the great advocate of national protectionism, was not widely
read until after mid century. Tariffs were still matters of
pragmatic, sectoral interest, applied sparingly and without
ideological backing, except from traditional mercantilism. Nor
was mass education – on which Gellner places such reliance –
yet seen as specifically useful to industrialisation. That push
came from 1850, and especially around 1880 with the advent of
the Second Industrial Revolution, more capital- and science-
intensive. Economic and industrial nationalism came after
earlier forms of nationalism and were fitted into their mould.

Second, Gellner might amend his argument to include
'proto-industrialisation', that earlier diffusion of small handicrafts and artisan manufactures through 18th century Europe,

rural as well as urban. Did such sectors generate nationalism? I will examine below whether they did.

Third, he points to the 20th century to observe how, even in the absence of capitalism – that is, in state socialist societies like the Soviet Union – the logic of industrialism has exerted the same pressure for mobility, inter-changeability and context-free education sponsored by the state, and therefore for nationalism. This is a valid point. Once industrialism did move into its second, post-1880 phase, its pressures became more generalised than those of the capitalist form that had originally sponsored it. Thus my critique applies on this point only to the first emergence of nationalism.

In fact, though I explore different routes for the emergence of nationalism, I do so by taking seriously Gellner's more general way of conceptualising nationalism. Nationalism is an elaborated ideology shared by many people right across a territory. It therefore depends on the extensive communication of discursive literacy – that is, the ability to read and write non-formulaic texts. In Benedict Anderson's words, the nation is an 'imagined community' in time and space.[11] People who have never met, who have no direct, particularistic connection – even the living, the dead and the yet-to-be-born – became linked by what he calls 'print culture'.

We should add, however, what Anderson, a Marxist, does not: that if the nation was an imagined community, its main ideological competitor, class consciousness, might seem to have been even more metaphorical, an 'imaginary community'. Nations were usually conceived and actually created as being coterminous with at least one of living historical traditions, state boundaries (past or present), or linguistic or religious communities. How were classes, with no significant prior histories (apart from ruling classes), which always live among and co-operate with other classes, to be conceived and created? We shall see that the two imagined or imaginary communities arose together, conjoined, in the same process of modernisation.

The insights provided by Gellner and Anderson give my method in this essay. I focus on how discursive literacy diffused across societies beyond the particularistic upper-class networks to which it had been hitherto confined. In tracing how nationalism and class ideologies became possible, I analyse the growth of specific media of discursive communication. This is in line with the more general 'organisational materialism' of my work – if ideologies are to spread, they must be organised through specific channels of communication.

This method will lead to a substantive explanation of the rise of European nationalism. After being early dominated by religion, discursive literacy then expanded in a first phase in two distinct ways, as a response either to the spread of commercial (not at first industrial) capitalism or to the expansion of states.[12] Both routes encouraged the diffusion of broader, more universalistic ideologies. One centred on class consciousness and/or class collaboration through political reform; the other centred on state modernisation. Through the 18th century both were then affected in a second phase by the intensification of geopolitical rivalry between the Great Powers. As states vastly increased their rates of extraction of taxes and military manpower, they politicised emerging ideologies. Over matters of political representation and state reform, class and national consciousness developed and fused. This was hastened on in a third phase by the particular power relations set in train by the French Revolutionary Wars. Nationalism emerged as this hastened fusion – thus sealing the fate of the monkey.

### THE 18TH-CENTURY GROWTH IN THE MEDIA OF DISCURSIVE COMMUNICATION

Literacy grew against the backdrop of the 16th-century technical revolution in printing which made possible the duplication and circulation of texts into the thousands. However, as Anderson notes, these inventions only become socially revolutionary with the emergence of 'print culture' when people outside the upper classes, the Church and royal administration felt they actually *needed* to read and write standardised discursive texts. The usual measure of the rise of literacy is 'signing literacy', the ability to sign one's name in the marriage register. This increased enormously through the late 17th and the 18th centuries, in most cases more than doubling over the period, resulting in about 90 per cent male and 67 per cent female signing literacy in Sweden and New England, 60 per cent and 45 per cent, respectively, in Britain, down to 50 per cent male literacy in France and Germany.[13] The male rise preceded the female, but by 1800 females were catching up. Signing is not a good measure of discursive literacy – many signers could do little other writing and no reading – but it situates discursive literacy amidst a larger basic literacy which we can perceive massively broadening in certain social settings in the late 17th and the 18th centuries. Let us concentrate on those settings.

I now list the principal media of discursive literacy in the late 17th and the 18th centuries. If nationalism, and other ideologies, emerged at the end of this period, they must have been carried by one or more of these media, for there were no other means of discursive communication.

### 1. The Church

– the main traditional home of a confined 'craft literacy'. Churches began to export literacy to the laity from the 16th century. First Protestant churches, then Catholic ones encouraged the ability to read and reproduce simple catechisms and to read the Bible. Their programmes were the main instrument in the surge of 'signing literacy' among the masses. The churches' control of schooling also probably made them responsible for the largest growth in discursive literacy, and this is evidenced by the predominance of devotional works among the best sellers up to about 1750 in the literary media listed below.

### 2. The State

– which developed two principal administrative needs for discursive literacy.

### 2a. Armed Forces

The 'Military Revolution' of 1540–1660 created more centralised, yet more functionally differentiated armies and navies. Its effects on literacy were felt right through the 18th century. Drills and logistical support became more standardised; technology became more complex and scientific, especially in artillery and navies; the division between staff and line institutionalised written orders and map-reading. Drill manuals became common reading among young officers and also spread among NCOs and ordinary soldiers who wished for promotion; quartermasters and artillery and naval officers needed full literacy and numeracy; and higher officers increasingly 'studied' in the modern sense. Evidence on the 18th-century French army reveals that its signing literacy was much higher than the overall population's, probably because it was recruited disproportionately from the towns. Once in the army, this basic level of literacy was expanded upon.[14] The great increase in the size of the armies – trebling from 1650 to 1750, trebling again during the French Revolutionary and Napoleonic Wars, then reaching up to 5 per cent of contemporary total populations – made this a significant channel of discursive literacy.

## 2b. Civil administration

– another traditional home of craft literacy. We do not find a large quantitative increase until the mass expansion of the lower bureaucracy in the second half of the 19th century. Before then, however, there was probably a modest increase in fiscal departments supplying the vast armies and navies. And we must note that the literacy of administrators had become largely formalised and secularised, as universities replaced churches and upper class family life as the trainer of government administrators. Absolute monarchs, first Protestant, then Catholic, developed ambitions to take over the main educational role from the Church, though none was able to realise this in more than rudimentary fashion.

## 3. Commerce

Its massive 17th- and 18th-century expansion spread discursive literacy as contracts, accounts and marketing methods became more formalised. Signing literacy was thus greater in commercial areas and occupations than among either agriculture or manufacturing industry.[15] The lower level of literacy in industry also goes against Gellner's 'industrial society' theory. Commerce also involved women, though perhaps less so as the workplace became separated from the household from the end of the 18th century.

### 4. The Profession of Law

occupied the ideological interface between church, state and commerce. Where commerce dominated, law generated broader contractual notions of rights; where church or state dominated, law remained corporatist yet generated more universal notions of rights and duties, as in the central European notion of 'the well-ordered police state'.[16] The law profession seems to have doubled in size in most 18th-century countries and its education broadened in discursive scope.[17]

### 5. The Universities

Controlled either by church or state and supplying young adults for them and for the law profession, the universities rapidly expanded in the 18th century, especially in continental Europe, to become the principal trainer of high-level discursive literacy.

### 6. The Literary Media

– the creation, printing, circulation and reading of literary products. Another traditional home of discursive literacy, it rapidly expanded from the late 17th century, its organisation transformed by capitalist production and market methods. It diffused down through households and middling classes and uniquely began to involve as many women as men, at least as readers.[18]

### 7. Periodical media

Newspaper, periodicals and secular pamphlets virtually began at the end of the 17th century and expanded rapidly through the 18th century. In England their numbers went up tenfold over the course of the 18th century.[19] Near the end of the century, Tom Paine's *The Rights of Man* could sell 200,000 copies in two years in Britain, while his *Common Sense* sold 120,000 copies in three months in the American colonies.

## 8. Discursive discussion centres

Academies, clubs, libraries, salons, taverns and coffee-houses all rapidly expanded as discussion centres of printed discursive materials. Even barbers and wig-making shops stocked newspapers and pamphlets and served as discussion centres. All but salons were male dominated.

It is difficult to convert this mixture of broad trends and specific quantitative increases into an exact overall measure of discursive expansion. Nonetheless, I hazard the guess that through the 18th century discursive literacy was probably expanding faster than basic literacy. Its media carried more universalistic ideologies. Right across Europe, nationalism was preceded by a number of self-consciously modernising ideologies like Cameralism, the Enlightenment, social contract theory, political reform and (in Britain) 'Improvement', which were more universal in their claims than prior secular ideologies. Who were now being brought into these media to communicate such broader ideologies?

We might be tempted to reply that 'the bourgeoisie' was emerging into communication networks that had hitherto been dominated by 'the old regime'. But we must be more precise than this. Discursive literacy was increasing through a variety of media, some of which were obviously connected to the rise of capitalism, others of which appear somewhat removed. The Church (medium 1) began the process; states, especially their armies (2a), and commercial capitalism (3) then added weight; their discursive demands then fuelled the other media. The expansion of discursive literacy could thus take different routes in different countries. I suggest two broad alternative routes by which 18th-century countries expanded discursive literacy. I take Britain as the prototype of one, Austria and Prussia as the other, with France mixing the two.

### ROUTES TO DISCURSIVE LITERACY

#### A. Commercial Capitalism

Britain, the most commercialised society in the 18th century, is the paradigm case, though the American colonies and the Low

Countries would follow not far behind. By 1760 only about one third of the English population lived and worked in agriculture; one third lived in the countryside but worked in commercial and proto-industrial occupations; and one third lived in the towns.[20] The massive increase in discursive literacy occurred amid those 'middling classes', generated primarily by the commercialisation of agriculture, and secondarily by the expansion of overseas trade.

This may seem like 'the rise of the bourgeoisie'. But it was actually complicated in two principal ways (plus the further complications of religious sect and region). First, the newly-literate groups were varied – from lawyers and other professionals (from whom naval and artillery officers were also disproportionately drawn), through merchants and shop-keepers to petty traders, and a diversity of artisans, including both 'masters' and 'men'. Modern writers might be tempted to use a class label for all these, but to begin with they themselves rarely did. How could they emerge as an 'imaginary or imagined community'? Second, the rise of commercialism also transformed the old regime itself, many of whose members were now connected by economic ties to merchants and professionals – for example, solicitors fuelled their savings into commercial ventures.

The overall trend and its two complications impacted on the media of discursive literacy. Overall they were expanded more by commercial capitalist than by state demand. But both complications reduced what might have been the 'bourgeois class consciousness' of the media of literacy. At the top, the profession of law, the clubs, libraries and some of the newspapers and literary media intermingled old regime and 'bourgeoisie'. Lower down, coffee-shops, taverns and pamphlets brought a rather diverse 'bourgeoisie' and 'petty bourgeoisie' (including artisans) together.

The ideologies being carried by such media were thus somewhat mixed. Brewer argues that by the 1760s the expanding infrastructures of a literate consumer society were conveying a distinctively petty bourgeois ideology, contrasting the moral virtue of work and free markets with the idle luxury of privilege and patronage.[21] This was linked, he says, to the radical politics of John Wilkes, and then to the subsequent political and 'economical' reform movements (demanding reform of the franchise and the end of the corrupt holding of government offices as private property). But reform tendencies were also present in old regime politics, among both of what came to be the main rival political factions, Foxites and Pittites, and even in the Anglican Church, among Evangelicals. Cities without pronounced class antagonisms, like Birmingham, also saw the joint participation of 'old' and 'new' classes in the literary media and discursive discussion centres. There mild reform politics, seeking to extend the franchise somewhat and eliminate 'old corruption' from the state, tended to be a cross-class movement acting partly inside, partly outside established politics.[22] Though towns as big as Manchester saw greater class segregation and antagonism, they exerted insufficient national pressure to carry forward a class-conscious reform movement – without considerable assistance from war (as we shall see). Overall, commercialism brought broader discursive ideologies, but they diffused across as well as within what we might be tempted to view as class barriers.

## B. The Old Regime State

In relatively backward economies like Prussia and Austria, commercial capitalism exerted feebler pressures which depended more upon the supply and demand of large agrarian estates and the demand of states and capital cities. Here old regime states led the way in the expansion of discursive literacy. Their officer and NCO corps were proportionately bigger; their civil administrations were probably no bigger, but their bureaucratisation began earlier and included university training and/or written examinations for higher administratoгs by the 1770s, virtually a century before this reached Britain. In this context broader ideologies emerged as more statist: Cameralism promoting efficiency in administration, and military professionalism among armed forces, both subsumed under Enlightened Absolutism. State-sponsored universities, rather than private salons or academies, were among the principal media.

But even so, these ideologies were not wholly confined within the state. They emerged outwards into a broader penumbra of

Enlightenment modernisation carried especially by educated nobility (especially the service and court nobility), clerics and the professional bourgeoisie, concentrated around capital cities and university towns. Their more radical discussions could not easily take political forms (because of absolutism and their own dependence on state hierarchies). So creativity seems to have been displaced into literature, philosophy and enquiry into the principal technique of literacy itself – that is, language and philology. Where the language explored was that of state administration, they were merely giving greater historical and scientific status to the dialect that statism had already elevated and standardised. Where it was not, they were engaged in a more subtly subversive activity. Literary revivals and cultural and linguistic 'proto-nationalism' among German academics or Polish nobles were not anti-state and they did not command popular support, but they were creating a more universal community of identity, the cultural or linguistic 'people' – though the people did not yet identify with it.

It was yet to be seen whether this was inimical to statism. State sponsorship used distinctive mechanisms of control. It attempted tighter censorship of discursive literacy and control through formal army and administrative hierarchies. Regimes' attempts to limit the ideological range of the new media would depend crucially on the effectiveness of these hierarchies.

In Austria there were two additional problems of hierarchical control. First, Habsburg government operated at two levels, the royal administration centralised in Vienna and the provincial administrations and Diets such as those of Hungary, Bohemia and Inner Austria, each with distinct privileges and historic legitimations. Second, unlike in the other states, the media of expanding literacy carried multiple languages. As the Habsburgs sought modernisation they changed the language of administration from Latin to German, the most widely-spoken language of their domains. Yet they recognised that Magyar (after a delay during which the Hungarian nobility continued to cling to Latin), Italian and French should have some official status in their provinces, and Czech and Polish, and Slovak, Ruthene and other dialects, were all in practical use as officials interacted with local populations. At first the Habsburgs welcomed the efforts of the intelligentsia to codify these languages and dialects. Yet Austrian statism would have to cope with formidable domestic diversity.

## C. The Mixed Route – France

The greatest 18th-century power does not fit neatly into either category. France was an absolute monarchy with a large army, navy and Church, yet also with a relatively commercial (if predominantly agrarian) economy. Thus the expansion of French discursive literacy was mixed – with the hindsight of 1789 we can see that it was contradictory.

At first sight the social composition of the expanding media (at least at their better-documented upper levels) does not appear mixed. Research has shown that the profession of law, the officer corps, salons, academies and masonic lodges were predominantly noble.[23] Yet by the late 18th century nobility in France denoted wealth more than ancient lineage.[24] At the upper levels old regime and bourgeoisie were merging, relatively smoothly. The bourgeoisie appeared to recognise that the way to greater wealth lay in acquiring public office, privilege and title (either by purchase or by marriage). Thus class tensions were rarely overt – except for the peasantry.

Instead class tensions appeared indirectly within the old regime, expressed ideologically in terms of the contradictory ideals of the French Enlightenment, and politically in terms of disunity over the state's fiscal crisis. The state's control structures faltered. Censorship weakened in the face of Ministers, like Malsherbes and Necker, who were also Enlightened reformers. Administration became more ramshackle as fiscal pressures turned it over to tax farmers. The army had its own problems. After the Segur decrees of 1781, bourgeois and recently ennobled officers' promotions were blocked, while the aristocratic higher officers saw very little of their junior officers and even less of their men.[25] Similarly the clergy became divided between high aristocratic prelates and 'professional' lower clergy. These discursive media became divided. Before 1789 this was not very evident, but then the divisions exploded.

In this first phase it is too early to talk of popular nationalism or class consciousness in any country. Yet the creation of broader discursive networks and ideologies was a necessary condition for what followed. It also involved an ideological ferment in which a diversity of cultural messages could develop their coteries. Perhaps the biggest were still religious revitalisation movements, as diverse as Methodism or Evangelicalism in Britain, the Great Awakening in the American colonies or Jansenism in France. But we can also detect small groups of petty bourgeois political radicals and cultural nationalists. To analyse their emergence and growth we must also look abroad.

## THE INTENSIFICATION OF GEOPOLITICAL RIVALRY

So far I have treated countries as independent cases in a comparative analysis. Yet they also interacted, most obviously in terms of geopolitical rivalry, and this impacted on every stage of the development of nationalism. It is rather curious that though nationalism asserts the moral virtue of one ethnic group over another, most theories of nationalism pay so little attention to geopolitical causes of its rise.

The dominating 18th-century rivalry was between France and Britain, who fought four major wars against each other. Austria and Prussia were also embroiled in this and other rivalries, and in fact the very existence of both states was threatened in mid century. Under the impact of the Military Revolution, traditional geopolitical rivalries now became vastly more relevant to the lives of the people, as taxpayers and as combatants. We cannot accurately measure the size of economies before the 18th century, yet their state expenditure could hardly have comprised more than 3–5 per cent of GNP before the 17th century and 5–10 per cent during it. By contrast 18th-century estimates for my four countries range upward from around 10 per cent in peacetime, to 15 to 30 per cent at time of war (all references to state revenues and expenditures, size of armed forces and civilian administrations, and GNPs derive from data contained in the forthcoming second volume of my *The Sources of Social Power*). This is a massive increase in the size and relevance of the state to the life of its people. Moreover, in the 18th century most states relied for the bulk of their revenue on indirect customs and sales taxes, which impacted immediately upon trade and which were highly regressive. Thus the state became especially relevant to 'the people' because it was taking away their means of subsistence.

Thus as discursive literacy and broader ideologies grew, they became more politicised. Two issues began to dominate. The more radical, 'bourgeois' and 'popular' movement focused on political representation, to oversee who would be taxed and for what purposes. It was exemplified by the American slogan of 'No taxation without representation'. A more conservative and modernising old regime movement sought to cut costs with greater state efficiency and reform from within of state particularism and the excesses of 'corruption'. Political reform, economical reform and state modernisation became major and conjoined issues everywhere, thus beginning the process of fusion between emerging class and statist ideologies. Political pressures, arising primarily from fiscal-military pressures, enabled diverse groups to imagine themselves as 'proto-national' and 'proto-class' communities. Specific, mobilised geopolitical rivalries then converted this fusion into overt class consciousness and nationalism. Let us follow the variety of fusions that developed in the individual countries.

INTENSIFICATION

A. Britain

I have left British discursive literacy at a stage where broader ideologies, primarily the product of commercial capitalism, were diffusing more widely, partly as bourgeois class ideologies, partly as a broader, cross-class reform and state modernising movement. But, as Newman has shown, from the mid 18th century both were also influenced by the French bogey.[26] Since old regime aristocratic culture had cosmopolitan and French overtones, popular 'proto-class' sentiments for political reform also acquired a 'proto-national' coloration. English sincerity, bluntness and hard work were contrasted with French/ aristocratic luxury, decadence, superciliousness and idleness. Newman concludes, perhaps with some exaggeration, that by 1789 English nationalism was fully in place. What he has established is that a key element of English nationalism was in place: many intellectuals and reform politicians argued that

English moral virtue lay in the qualities of its 'people'. But who qualified as the people in the political sense was still contested. This state still legitimated itself by the doctrine of 'virtual representation' whereby the monarch, the titled and some of the propertied ruled on behalf of the rest. Most of those in the mixed bourgeois and cross-class reform movement wanted rule by 'the people', by which they meant all male property owners. A few predominantly petty bourgeois radicals wanted rule by what their opponents called 'the populace', that is, universal manhood suffrage.

The Revolutionary and Napoleonic Wars hastened on popular class consciousness and nationalism while changing their tone. Britain was stretched to its limits by the Wars. Its naval-commercial domination faltered, the invasion threat was real, the War absorbed up to a staggering 31 to 43 per cent of GNP (according to whose estimate we believe) and the armed forces absorbed more than 5 per cent of total population (neither figure remotely approached previously, or indeed subsequently until World War I). The War dominated politics and politicised social life. It was broadly popular – at least among those with discursive literacy whose growth I have been charting. Nationalist sentiment, focused on the British–French contrast, now became widely and overtly expressed, as Colley has argued – and as the monkey would testify![27]

Revolution, as Reign of Terror and Dictatorship, became the new French bogey. This at first stigmatised all reformers, enabling the government to repress class radicalism. But the fiscal stress of war forced Ministers like Pitt into administrative 'economical reform' measures. 'Old corruption' was abandoned, largely from within. After the end of the War, old regime modernisers sided with popular pressures and completed political reform with the Great Reform Act of 1832. Particularism, monarchical patronage and the power of the House of Lords were now largely broken. Though the Reform Act only conferred the vote on about 20–25 per cent of males, it did so on a single, universalist criterion – property ownership. Though Parliament was still dominated by landowners, it legislated in the interests of this new homogeneous class of capitalists.[28] In the language of the time, power was vested in 'the people' – that is, the propertied people. Through the entwining of the politics of class representation and geopolitical rivalries, Britain was ruled by what we might call a 'class-nation'. Britain was as a result a nation-state.

## B. France

Nationalism emerged differently in France, to produce a more obviously popular and assertive nationalist ideology. During the Revolution, statist and class ideological currents fused to produce the first overt nationalist and class-conscious statements of modern times. The Revolution began as a fiscal crisis, pressured by earlier military commitments. The *cahiers*, documents of complaint drawn up by local communities in 1788, indicate some minimal extension of the sense of France as a single kingdom in which some universal reforms were necessary (though some communities asserted their particularistic local privileges). But the emphasis is on the practical necessity for reform of taxes and privileges to ease the fiscal burden.

It was because of the King's three-year obduracy from 1789 that pragmatic issues of state finances and partial political representation turned into principles and ideologies. Since he would not compromise, the Revolution moved left. Latent 'proto-nationalism' and 'proto-class consciousness', presumably already lurking but largely concealed, sprang into life. Seeking an alliance between quite diverse reform groups – peasants, non-noble substantial bourgeoisie, the petty bourgeois crowd, frustrated junior officers and clerics – leaders sought the cover of broad ideologies. The reform party styled itself 'les patriots', and claimed to speak against privilege and particularism for 'le peuple', then 'la nation'. Then liberal aristocrats, prominent old regime lawyers and dissident clerics were replaced by bourgeois and petty bourgeois factions, expressing some class consciousness against privilege and idleness. Throughout the Revolution the leaders were prominent members of those discursive networks of literacy noted earlier, the largest group changing twice, from being royal officials to being independent lawyers to being the professional intelligentsia. Of the final 'Twelve who Ruled', the core members of the Committee of Public Safety, eleven published at least one literary, scientific or social-scientific work (excluding political works and *memoires*).[29] These intelligentsia articulated the broadest fusion of class and national ideologies. The revolutionary process lodged legitimacy with the nation, and all political factions now claimed to speak for it.[30] But national mobilisation also accelerated when monarchy and revolutionaries took their differences onto the geopolitical arena. The Brissotin faction hurled the first popular, national army of modern times (no foreign mercenaries, saturated with political clubs, mobilised by national slogans) at the foreign dynasts and emigré nobles.

The national army was astonishingly successful, not only defending France but carrying revolution into neighbouring states. Domestically, of course, the Revolution collapsed amid class-factional dispute, and Bonaparte backtracked on much. But he retained the national army and the national legitimation. At home French nationalism endured, threatened by monarchism and clericalism, but triumphing completely in 1848. Republicanism and Bonapartism still contested its soul but both brought together essentially bourgeois and peasant alliances to vest legitimacy in the nation. Though French history seems very different to British, we see the same conjunction of the politics of class representation and geopolitical rivalry to produce a more overt nationalism and a more self-conscious nation-state.

### C. Prussian Germany

The French had sought to export revolution and found sister-republics, mobilising patriots in a common cause. Then Bonaparte sought to incorporate them into his personal Empire. I am concerned in this essay with what happened in Germany and across the Austrian lands. There 1789 triggered off two types of 'patriotic' demonstrations, the first more relevant to Prussia and Germany, the second to Austria.

First, among those ruled by dynasties from their own ethnic/linguistic community, such demonstrations (generally centring on the professional bourgeoisie) were sparsely supported and easily crushed. Across Germany none of the several hundred state regimes was toppled, except later by French armies. Those linked by a predominantly statist discursive literacy were unlikely to seek modernisation by overthrowing the state.[31]

Also, though Prussia extracted a high proportion of GNP in revenue (around 25 per cent in 18th-century wars), it depended least on taxation for its revenue. It entered the 19th century with the greatest income from its own royal estates; it left it with the greatest income from its own railways. Thus political reformers, generated as everywhere by fiscal issues, were less enraged than in other states.

The full force of the French military threat was revealed in the battles of Jena and Austerlitz, which crushed the armies of Austria and Prussia. But the 'proto-nationalist' sentiment unleashed was the reverse of what the French had expected. Reformers argued that the existing state could be modernised and strengthened by attaching popular mobilisation to its hierarchies. In Prussia this was accompanied for a time by a reform movement for greater political representation, coming largely from within the university-educated administrators.[32] Though defeated over effective parliamentary representation, reformers did ensure that the Prussian state embodied the rule of law and a state administration whose offices did in a sense allow the educated bourgeoisie a form of 'inner representation' alongside the nobility. But the final phase of Austro-Prussian resistance to the French, during 1813–1815, involved no political reform concessions, only the strengthening of a more mobilised military hierarchy as popular militias were brought into the armies.

What we regard as a distinctively 'Prussian–German nationalism', the linking of cultural and political national sentiments to loyalty towards a strong state, was becoming established. The ground had been prepared by a movement of cultural nationalism, sweeping through the discursive university and literary media at the turn of the 19th-century. In North Germany this became harnessed (sometimes somewhat uneasily) to the administrative and legal structures of the Prussian state. The 19th century then saw competition between two rival German political nationalisms, one prepared to ally with a centralised authoritarian state, the other advocating a liberal, confederal state. As Prussia gobbled up the confederal states and humbled (though it did not absorb) their protector Austria, it acquired this statist (and *Kleindeutsch*) nationalism.

Thus in Prussia the representation of the bourgeoisie became conjoined to geopolitical rivalry in a further distinct way, to produce a third type of nation-state and nationalism. The statist route to discursive literacy here led directly to statist nationalism. Its hierarchical controls, though buffeted by the reform movement of 1806–8 and the 1848 Revolution, and though modified by compromise with the National Liberals in the 1860s, remained intact. This was in marked contrast to Austria.

### D. Austria

For Britain, France and Prussia major war ended in 1815 and the fiscal pressures were largely over by 1820–1825 (with debt repayments down to manageable proportions). By then, however, nationalism was largely established in all three countries, its precise coloration determined by 19th-century politics and geopolitics. Austria differed, however, for the pressures on the Habsburgs remained greater and produced plural, disrupting nationalisms.

The second type of patriotic response to the French Revolutionary Wars involved risings by a local population against distant, 'foreign' dynastic rule. It was influenced by the slogans of the French revolution and then aided by French armies. Habsburg Austria was the main sufferer, facing revolts in the Low Countries, Poland and Italy. It continued to be the main sufferer right up until its final collapse in 1918, for losing the Low Countries and Italy seemed only to encourage other 'national' movements, in Bohemia (the Czech part of Czechoslovakia), Hungary and the Balkans.

These anti-Habsburg movements are generally considered as the prototypical European cases of overt political nationalism, which asserts that a people, defined by ethnic-linguistic culture, but ruled by foreigners, should have its own state. I will therefore dwell longer on the Austrian cases. It is difficult to attribute them primarily to civil society forces, more specifically to the development of capitalism or industrialism (as Gellner or Marxists tend to do). Their most striking feature was the diversity of their economic development and class composition. The Low Countries and Northern Italy contained much commercial capitalism at the time of their ferment and the Czechs were largely industrial by the time ferment reached them. But throughout the century Poland, Hungary, Slovakia and the Balkans remained predominantly agrarian and backward. Even in the more advanced countries national movements were not significantly 'bourgeois' until well after mid century. The major national movements in the 1848 Revolution (apart from more backward Hungary) were in the Northern Italian provinces and in Bohemia – but there, as elsewhere, the leadership and organisation was predominantly noble.[33] Later the class basis of national movements varied: some remained predominantly aristocratic, others became popular among peasants and workers (especially in the Balkans where the Turks had earlier removed local aristocracies and stifled economic development), and only the Czech movement was predominantly bourgeois.[34] Yet all proclaimed themselves as national movements. What did they have in common?

Gellner's notion that the backward countries were anticipating industrial society seems too teleological. But there were two real grievances which could be expressed in common political terms even amongst such diverse groups, and which could receive wider support if expressed in more universalistic 'national' terms. Both concerned the Habsburg state: its fiscal exactions and its office-holding spoils – respectively the costs and benefits of the state.

Fiscal problems loomed larger at first because of the rise in the 18th century state's fiscal-military extraction rate. The Habsburg state extracted about 17 per cent of GNP in 1780, about 27 per cent in 1790, and probably between 30 and 40 per cent around 1810 (GNP estimates are not available for then, but the size of the army and of expenditure rose considerably). During the reign of Maria Theresa (to 1783) the Habsburgs could get most of their fiscal needs from a legitimate, traditional tax, the Military Contribution, and they could borrow most of the rest.[35] But this proved insufficient and inflexible to increased fiscal needs. The regime had few of its own royal domains and its credit declined. It declared bankruptcy in 1811. To prevent a repeat, economies and new taxes were required.

But taxes had to be obtained through a confederal structure of government: its major provinces either possessed active

Diets, as Hungary did, or possessed traditional but inactive Diets and assemblies which were revived at times of fiscal crisis – as did Bohemia, Moravia, Silesia, Croatia, Inner Austria and the two Italian provinces. These 'parliamentary' institutions, usually representing only the nobility, made Austria peculiarly comparable with the Anglo-American world rather than with the other Absolute Monarchies like Prussia or 18th-century France. Thus the Habsburgs encountered slogans of 'no taxation without representation', coming from the diversity of social classes dominant in each province.

Indeed the Habsburgs faced more serious economic and fiscal subversion than other states. Discontent in Britain might produce class-based riots in Nottinghamshire or Manchester which the local gentry and yeomanry would usually handle. But fiscal discontent in the Habsburg lands was expressed *territorially*, in the form of a revolt of a whole province, including its armed forces. Political representation was also the major issue in Austria, but it was structured less by class than territory. It was not unique in this respect. The American colonies had revolted against British taxation territorially; the United States' mid 19th century political crisis still concerned territorial issues (states' rights, specifically over slavery). And just as in America (twice), the territorial expression of issues of political representation was more severe than those of mere class representation: it led to civil war in which the rebels could usually call for aid from foreign Powers. For Austria war did not go away in 1815: it occurred in 1821, 1830, 1848–9, 1859, 1866 and 1908. Economies were difficult to effect. The level of taxation remained high and this further fuelled territorially-based representative struggles.

The second common grievance concerned office-holding rights, which were connected to nationalism by way of language disputes. Gellner stresses this connection and gives two explanations. The first is that industrial society needed a context-free means of communication. When industrialism arrived it did indeed encourage linguistic nationalism. By about 1890 it may have dominated advanced parts of the Monarchy like Czechoslovakia (where Gellner's own origins lie). But earlier and elsewhere linguistic nationalism appeared as predominantly a 'statist' issue: what should be the language of central, regional and local government? This fed back into a second language issue: what languages should be taught in public schools? This brings in Gellner's second argument. As he notes, the acquisition of literacy in a modernising society is a form of cultural capital, realisable in employment. Across the mid 19th century this meant predominantly state employment, in army and civil administration (and the latter began to expand substantially from about 1880). It was important to all literate persons – noble, bourgeois and petty bourgeois – that their language of literacy was also that of the state. In a European-wide trend the supply of highly educated men rocketed at the beginning of the 19th century, and then continued to hold up.[36] Linguistic capital thus became a more vital political issue over the period. Gellner's second argument might have more explanatory power than his first.

Habsburg language policy was not consistent. Yet when the regime failed to get consent to taxation, it generally tried to impose its demands from the centre. This meant relying on its loyalist core, predominantly Austro-German, and particularly on the officer corps and central administration, both predominantly Austro-German. Thus in periods of authoritarian rule (most of the time between 1815 and 1848 and in the 1850s) the regime discriminated in favour of German-speakers, and blocked the access of other linguistic communities to administration and the law courts. This became the principle grievances of non-German dissidents in 1848,[37] and was from then on a perennial grievance of movements for political and national representation.

After mid century Habsburg centralisation policies collapsed under the pressure of internal discontent and the disastrous defeats of 1859 and 1866 against the French and Prussians. Near-bankruptcy and geopolitical humiliation forced constitutional concessions, especially to the powerful Hungarians. But the failure to produce a comprehensive constitutional settlement meant that the fiscal issue remained, fuelling nationalist discontents. And the near-capitulation to the Hungarians, embodied in the 1867 switch from Empire to Dual Monarchy, merely ensured that there were now two Imperial languages – German and Magyar – instead of one. The Hungarians attempted Magyarisation in their half of the Monarchy.

Across mid-century the fusion of the two issues occurred under the initial leadership of the main dissident nobilities, in Italy, Hungary and Bohemia. In fighting for their traditional political privileges, they sought popular support. They sought this with especial fervour after 1846, when the rebellious Polish nobility were slaughtered by their own peasants, apparently in the mistaken belief that the Emperor had ordered them to his rescue. The cultural nationalism of often quite small professional bourgeoisies was the obvious universalising ideology, stressing community, usually linguistic community, between classes. They gradually, and mostly sincerely, articulated an ideology of national resistance against 'foreign' German–Austrian domination. After 1867 Slavs used these proven methods to resist Magyar domination in the Hungarian half of the Monarchy. All these movements legitimated themselves in terms of 'the nation', even where, as in Hungary, they permitted only the nobility active political citizenship, and even where, as in Slovakia, 'the nation' was initially only a tiny group of intelligentsia.

The geopolitical threat to the Habsburgs also continued longer, in a distinctively 'multi-national' form. Dissident nationalities located right across the Habsburg borders were encouraged by Austria's Great Power neighbours – notably Italians by Piedmont and France, and Slavs by Russia. Geopolitically-assisted nationalism culminated in the last year of World War I, when the Entente finished off the Austrian Monarchy by offering independence to all nationalities should the Entente win the war. As an Entente victory would ensure the humbling of Germany, and as Russia had already collapsed, there seemed no further justification for a large confederal central European state (how short-sighted that view seems today!).

As I noted earlier, the Austrian example of the statist route to discursive literacy and ideologies would have to surmount distinctive threats to its hierarchical controls. It failed as the state hierarchy disintegrated into plural nationalisms which were fundamentally the product of the territorialisation of struggles over state finances and officeholding.

CONCLUSION

I have started from Gellnerian principles of examining the preconditions for the emergence of a rationalised society in which impersonal, universalistic, context-free communication can spread across and down large social spaces. Yet I have arrived at different conclusions. Industrialisation was not a principal cause in this period (it may have been subsequently). It arrived too late and too unevenly. There were two principal causes: on the one hand, the emergence of commercial capitalism and its universal social classes; on the other, the emergence of the modern state and its professional armed forces and administrators. Conjoined by the fiscal-military pressures exerted by geopolitical rivalry, they produced the politics of popular representation and these formed several varieties of modern nationalism.

I have only considered four cases, and I do not claim that these exact causes have operated in other places and later times. However, let me convert this from a limitation into a more general argument. Other and later cases of nationalism have all had their peculiarities – especially, perhaps, what might be termed the second great wave of nationalism and nation-states, in the Third World after World War II. But all other cases also differ because they have been structured by and conscious of the very cases I have described. My cases comprise not only the earliest popular nationalisms, but also the most powerful. These four were the greatest European Powers of the mid 19th century. Historical actors recognised that the three most successful Powers embodied nationalism, and that the least successful was declining precisely because it could not devise a more mobilised nation-state and was instead beset by divisive nationalisms. The future lay with more unitary, mobilised states, as Italians, Turkish and Japanese élites notably realised (and as American élites independently realised through their Civil War). In touching upon the later complexities of the Austrian tragedy, I also mentioned other conscious responses and adaptations. The attainments of the powerful Hungarian nobility could be emulated by rather feebler nationalists. President Wilson's notion that geopolitical instability could be reduced by 'national self-determination' has been institutionalised by the Superpowers across the Third World.

The rise and rise of nationalism has constituted a dominant secular trend of the last two centuries until very recently. But it has been a specific historical trend in one part – though the most powerful part – of the globe, with which the rest of the globe has had subsequently to contend. It was produced by dynamic interaction between knowledgeable actors, principally classes and states. It has not been as regular and as evolutionary as perhaps Ernest Gellner suggested. Furthermore, its partial regularity has been provided less by industrialism, than by the way capitalism and states conjoined to produce greater concentrations of power which first defeated more confederal powers and then allowed national minnows their own little spaces.

There have always been two principal elements of nationalism, the notion of virtue and legitimacy vested in 'this particular people' and the notion that this should constitute a state. It is surely no surprise that the former would be affected by the rise of popular classes and that the later would be affected by the principal historical activity of states, warfare. The history of classes, of nations and of war cannot be told separately. The monkey perished in their joint venture.

## NOTES

1. J. Hutchinson, *The Dynamics of Cultural Nationalism*. London, 1987.
2. Given the limited space available to me here, I hope I can be permitted two elisions. Britain/England and Prussia/Germany will not be disaggregated into their component 'nations' or states. But the national complexities of the Austrian lands will be discussed.
3. A. Smith, *The Ethnic Origins of Nations*, Oxford, 1986, pp. 18, 76–79.
4. E. Gellner, *Nations and Nationalism*, Oxford, 1983, ch. 2.
5. M. Mann, *The Sources of Power. Vol I: A History of Power from the beginning to A. D. 1760*, Cambridge, 1986, pp. 527–30. And J.A. Hall. *Powers and Liberties*, Oxford, 1985.
6. E. Gellner, *Nations and Nationalism*, p. 46.
7. E. Gellner, *Plough, Sword and Book. The Structure of Human History*, London, 1988, p. 210.
8. For example T. Nairn, *The Break-Up of Britain*, London, 1977.
9. A. Smith, *Theories of Nationalism*, London, 1981.
10. S. Pollard, *Peaceful Conquest: The Industrialization of Europe*, Oxford, 1981.

11. B. Anderson, *Imagined Communities*, London, 1983.
12. Benedict Anderson also distinguishes commercial capitalism and state administrations as the two major causes of nationalisms arising in the British and Spanish New World colonies. But the rest of his book privileges 'official' statist routes to nationalisms, without the fiscal-military and geopolitical pressures which I emphasise.
13. F. Furet and M. Ozouf, *Reading and Writing: Literacy in France from Calvin to Jules Ferry*, Cambridge, 1982; K. Lockridge, *Literacy in Colonial New England*, New York, 1974; M. Schofield, 'Dimensions of literacy in England 1750–1850' in H.J. Graff (ed.), *Literacy and Social Development in the West: A Reader*, Cambridge, 1981; E.G. West, 'Literacy and the Industrial Revolution' in J. Mokyr (ed.), *The Economics of the Industrial Revolution*, London, 1985.
14. S. Scott, *The Response of the Royal Army to the French Revolution*, Oxford, 1978.
15. R. Houston, 'The development of literacy: Northern England 1640–1750', *Economic History Review*, vol. 35, 1982; 'The literacy myth: illiteracy in Scotland, 1630-1760', *Past and Present*, no. 96, 1982.
16. P. Raeff, *The Well-Ordered Police State*, New Haven, 1983.
17. For example, France – R. Kagen, 'Law students and legal careers in eighteenth-century France', *Past and Present*, no. 68, 1975.
18. I. Watt, *The Rise of the Novel*, Harmondsworth, 1965.
19. G. Cranfield, *The Development of the Provincial Newspaper, 1700–1760*, Oxford, 1962.
20. E.A. Wrigley, 'Urban growth and agricultural change: England and the Continent in the early modern period', *Journal of Interdisciplinary History*, vol. 15, 1985.
21. J. Brewer, *Party Ideology and Party Politics at the Accession of George III*, Cambridge, 1972; J. Brewer, J. McKendrick and J.H. Plumb. 'Commercialization and Politics', in N. McKendrick, J. Brewer and J.H. Plumb (eds), *The Birth of a Consumer Society: The Commercialization of 18th Century England*, London, 1982.
22. J. Money, *Experience and Identity: Birmingham and the West Midlands, 1760–1800*, Manchester, 1977.
23. R. Darnton, *The Business of Enlightenment: A Publishing History of the Encyclopedie, 1775–1800*, Cambridge, Mass., 1979, pp. 273–99; A. Le Bihan, *Francs-macons et ateliers parisiens de la Grand Loge de France au XVIIIe siècle*, Paris, 1973, pp. 473–80; A. Roche. *La Siècle des lumières en province: Academies et academiciens provinciaux, 1680–1789*, Vol. I, Paris, 1978, chapter 4.
24. G. Chaussinand-Nogaret, *La Noblesse au XVIIIe siècle. De la feodalité aux Lumières*, Paris, 1985, pp. 23–24.
25. S. Scott, *The Response of the Royal Army to the French Revolution*, pp. 4–45.

26. G. Newman, *The Rise of English Nationalism. A Cultural History, 1740–1830*, New York, 1987.
27. L. Colley, 'Whose Nation? Class and National Consciousness in Britain, 1750–1785', *Past and Present*, no. 113, 1986.
28. F. Thompson, *English Landed Society in the Nineteenth Century*, London, 1963, p. 298; H. Perkin. *The Origins of Modern English Society, 1780–1880*, London, 1968, p. 315–16.
29. M. Mann, *The Sources of Social Power. vol. II: A History of Power, 1760–1914*, Cambridge, forthcoming, chapter six.
30. F. Furet, *Penser la Revolution Française*, Paris, 1978, p. 83.
31. T. Blanning, *Reform and Revolution in Mainz. 1743–1803*, Cambridge, 1974, pp. 305–334.
32. M. Gray, 'Prussia in Transition: Society and politics under the Stein reform ministry of 1808', *Transactions of the American Philosophical Society*, vol. 76, Part 1, 1986.
33. For a review of the evidence, see A. Sked, 'Historians the nationality question, and the downfall of the Habsburg Empire', *Transactions of the Royal Historical Society*, vol. 31, 1989, pp. 41–88.
34. P. Sugar, 'External and domestic roots of Eastern European Nationalism', in P. Sugar and I. Lederer (eds), *Nationalism in Eastern Europe*, Seattle, 1969.
35. P. Dickson, *Finance and Government under Maria Theresa, 1740–1780*, Oxford, 1987.
36. L. O'Boyle, "The problem of an excess of educated men in Western Europe, 1800–1850," *Journal of Modern History*, vol. 42, 1970.
37. A. Sked, 'Historians, the nationality question, and the downfall of the Habsburg Empire', pp. 41–88.

# CHAPTER 7

# Sovereign individuals

## Ronald Dore

Many years ago I showed Ernest Gellner a review I had written of a Barrington Moore book. It began with some remark about most of us from time to time harbouring the ambition to spend a few years licking history into shape. I remember his comment: you've hit on my secret weakness! We should be grateful that he finally indulged this weakness – and glad that *Plough, Sword and Book*[1] had been gestating over such a long period of time in such a lively iconoclastic mind inhabiting such a diversity of worlds: anthropological, philosophical, sociological; metropolitan, Oxbridgean, Muslim, Eastern and Central European. Where the intellectual historian will eventually place the book in the Gellner *oeuvre* it is hard to predict; its ambitious scope and its comprehensiveness make it less easily summarisable as message than his *Thought and Change* of twenty years earlier, though the style has anything but mellowed; the sharpness of the epigrams and the imaginative leaps of the analogies, the punning on proverbs, the playful reifications of abstracts are as beguiling as ever.

And in the end, he is too much social scientist to turn prophet and offer us a *real* philosophy of history, complete with a guide to what the *meaning* of it all is, and an indication of where we are going. As schematisation and explication of the past it is a *tour de force*; his trinity of cognition, coercion and production proves so much more useful an instrument than a simple base/superstructure dichotomy. He doesn't quite stop there, at explication and schematisation. But his extrapolation of a limited number of trends of the present and near past goes only a little way into the future and serves only to pose and not to answer the big questions; whether, for instance, leisured masses, incapable of elevated thoughts, will need to turn to faith; whether the state which is needed to run the vast infrastructure will turn coercive.

The sense of wonderment which puts the fire in the belly of a philosopher of history is there all right but it is directed, in Gellner's case, not to the whole sweep of history, nor to the working out of some idea, some providence, some spirit of progress, but to a single 'miracle', the 'single occasion' when one group of societies made the 'great transformation' – 'from concept-implementation to generalised instrumental rationality, from a norm-conception of truth to a referential one, from rule of thugs to rule of producers, from oppressed subsistence farmers to a free market economy', in another formulation, from a society whose central theme and value is predation to one which honours production.[2]

Somehow, I find myself a bit resistant to this miracle story, while still lost in admiration for Gellner's neat encapsulations of the fifteen possible reasons why it took place. Can one really compress what was, after all, some centuries of cumulative change to the status of an event? If one reads David Landes's history of clock-making[3], even the eighteenth-century spate of inventions in textile machinery takes its place in a long history stretching back into medieval times – a history of slow acceleration in invention and slow evolution of the capitalist exploitation thereof. What gives the illusion of suddenness is the fact that one particular cluster of inventions, which produced the steam engine, had such widely ramifying consequences for everything else – but that is more a function of the physical interrelatedness of things, not of some discontinuous change in the institutional environment.

But that, perhaps, is a quibble; the 'miracle', the 'single occasion', after all, is more a rhetorical device than an assertion of discontinuity; the 'transition to the modern industrial scientific world' is, in the Gellner scheme of things, a generic concept, to use his term for what Weber called an ideal type; it is a matter of 'stylizing' the facts as economists, honouring Kaldor, call it when they are taking liberties with empirical reality.

But the other reason why I do not feel too happy about the Gellner account is more serious. Was it really only in Europe that those trends of cumulative change were at work – trends

towards the rule-bound civility which could tame the swords-
man and debunk the cleric, towards rule by rules rather than by
people, towards reflective attempts at understanding nature
and at using that understanding for productive ends, towards
the acceptance, indeed the celebration, of individual choice and
market contract?

I think for example of Matsudaira Sadanobu, the man who
cleaned up the central Japanese bureaucracy in the 1790s –
who insisted, for example, that officials should draw a proper
distinction between the office files and their personal files and
take only the latter when they left office; a model piece of
Weberian rationalisation. He kept an occasional book, part
reflective diary, part jottings on odd etymologies, travellers'
tales, natural phenomena – in a style reminiscent of other
cultures' expressions of leisured gentlemanly curiosity – a kind
of Japanese anthropological *Notes and Queries*. So did many of
his contemporaries, and modern collections of these writings
run to many volumes. Matsudaira describes in one how he and
friends got into an argument as to whether there were tides in
wells. They settled the matter with a float attached to a bamboo
pole with a piece of string to mark the level. Soon after, of
course, thanks to the two Dutch ships which came every year,
the diffusion to Japan of European medicine and metal technology began to accelerate even though it required the threat
of Western coercion to open the floodgates – or, better metaphor, to start up the suction pumps of a state-led national effort
to industrialise Japan. But meanwhile, throughout the first,
non-revolutionary half of the century, the wholly indigenous
processes of rationalisation, of social and organisational engineering proceeded: the invention by merchants and bankers of
what are today called new financial instruments; new means of
financing land reclamation; various experiments and much
argumentation about the incentive effects of different kinds of
guild regulation and taxation; experiments with official mono-
polies and infant industry protection; increasingly careful use
of precedent in the administration of justice. There was a good
deal of polemical debate about these things, as well as about the
nature of the universe, and considerable tolerance of diverse
opinions. Probably there was mechanical invention, too, though
it was already being swamped by the process of absorbing

Western techniques through treatises translated from the Dutch. To say that the pace of innovation was accelerating through the first half of the nineteenth century would be to assume the possibility of some kind of quantification; suffice it to say that the Japan of 1850 was already a significantly different Japan from that of 1800.

To be sure, it hadn't quite made the transition from a state which drew its legitimacy from its reverence for the past to a state legitimated by its promise for the future. That required the short civil war of the Meiji Restoration, a momentary and slightly half-hearted burst of coercion – swords unsheathed in earnest instead of for carefully choreographed displays, for the first time in generations. And it is probably true that that precipitating acceleration of change would not have happened – or would not have happened so soon – without the external threat posed by all those European and American warships in Japanese waters. When it happened, though, and the drive for modernisation began (albeit that the new state also claimed a legitimacy deriving from its *restoration*, at least formal and ritual restoration, of an older and more authentic past), the ground had been sufficiently well prepared for the future-orientation to take over far more completely than it ever did in Victorian England.

For all the complexities and imponderables, I see no reason not to suppose – though the nature of the necessary counter-factuals is mind-boggling – that without the West, or rather without the West's prior development of a deliberate and cumulative science applied to production – the Japanese, or, rather, the inter-communicating societies of the Chinese cultural complex, would have done it themselves. They too would eventually have got to the steam engine, and to the institutionalisation of the invention process which brought so many other things in its train, and to some sort of social organisation which would have used all these things for the enrichment of people's consuming lives.

After all, given the non-appropriability and diffusibility of technology – once well-maintained literacy traditions are established, at any rate – it *could* only have been once in history that a nation or cluster of nations achieves, through a burst of inventions, such a superiority of national power vis-à-vis the rest of the world that the other nations seek to imitate – however unpromising their original 'ethos'. I find no reason to suppose that it could never have been in Japan that they happened – certainly nothing in Weber's ahistorical meanderings around Chinese Confucianism, nor in Gellner's few references to China (puzzlingly precocious chaps who managed already to come out of the axial age ready to dispense with theology, but then didn't *do* anything with their rationalism).

And if it *had* been in Japan or Japan/China that self-conscious and progressive science and its practical applications had taken off, would a Gellner, a couple of centuries later, be writing: 'only an individualist and instrumentalist society, committed to toleration as part of its internal compromise, can provide the required milieu',[4] for the great transition? Instrumentalist, yes; early nineteenth-century Japan already was that. Tolerant, yes; certain brands of Confucianism were banned from official schools in theory, but flourished in practice. Ideological battles sometimes led to assassination; but, by the mid nineteenth century, it was already two hundred years since state or church had killed anyone for heresy.

But individualist? Compared with the Anglo-Saxon countries, compared even with Germany, (and one has to make *some* comparison, since individualist is a relative term), Japan was certainly not that. Nor, in the process of industrialising – late and rapidly and under the aegis of the state – has it become so. Supposing that it had industrialised endogenously and slowly on a mere trickle of inventions as Britain did, would its, also, have been an individualistic capitalist form of industrialisation? There would certainly have been free markets in goods, and free markets in labour – there already were such, in effect, despite nominal feudal restrictions, by the middle of the nineteenth century. But would there have been the complete capitalist package, including free financial markets and free markets in land? Maybe, but maybe not. It is possible to imagine all kinds of more collectivist alternatives – different from all the collectivisms we know at least in being organic growths, not reaction formations defining themselves in contra-distinction to a hegemonic capitalism.

## AN ALTERNATIVE PATTERN?

About the (relatively) non-individualistic nature of modern Japanese capitalism, I take it that there is no dispute. (And it is not just a matter of compartmentalisation, of separating culture from cognition and production. Japanese business behaviour – the long-term obligated ties of employee to company; of scientific worker to his lab, of company to its subcontractors and its banks, even to its competitors, neighbours in the industry and fellow-members of its industry association – is suffused with values and assumptions about personal relations and the purpose of life which are very different from those of Britain or the United States.) Let us grant that the lesser degree of individualism (relative to UK/US) owes a good deal to the late development effect and to the racial effect – the fact that the Japanese were collectively conscious not only of coming up from behind, but also of coming up as alien and disparaged outsiders, differing both in physiognomy and in culture from all the leading insider member states of the concept of powers/ civilised world/international society/the free world, call it what you will. That consciousness (plus some other factors like the greater clarity, for late-developers, of the need to build an infrastructure, and to mobilise capital resources) enhanced the role of the state in industrialisation, and the willingness of businessmen to accept it. And even where the state was not involved, national consciousness could sometimes induce a spontaneous collectivism which altered the terms of market competition; representatives of rival trading companies in London or Dar-es-Salaam were more conscious of their common interest in promoting Japan's trade and less conscious of company and personal rivalry than would have been the traders of top nations.

Let us grant the importance of these factors. I still think that the difference in degrees of individualism as between Japan and Europe goes well beyond what they can explain. Take, as an example, economic change in an area where late development and racial effects had very little bite: agriculture. Compare Marc Bloch's classic account of the way technical change brought individualism (increased the frequency of individualistic behaviour) in French villages in the eighteenth century,[5] with the response to technical innovation of Japanese villages.

Community control in the open-field villages of eighteenth-century France was highly constricting. 'Ownership' of land represented only a limited bundle of rights. At a certain date of the year the grazing animals of all the village were let loose on your field, so you had to be sure that your planting time and harvest time left nothing but stubble by the time that day arrived. The community likewise dictated the rotation in which you left your fields fallow every third year. You could only take one crop of hay from your fields; thereafter it was free-for-all grazing again.

What changed these practices was new science, new techniques; new knowledge of the determinants of soil fertility, of new types of cultivated grasses and other fodder crops like alfalfa and clover, of new late strains of wheat with longer growing seasons and higher yields, of means of fattening stall-fed cattle. The *potential rewards* for any individualist who would break out of the bonds of neighbourly custom steadily increased. If he put hedges round his fields, chose times of planting and harvest which catered for the new crop strains, used fertiliser instead of fallow, took three crops of fodder – and if the more careful conscientiousness and attention to detail which these techniques required spilled over into carefulness in accounting methods and self-discipline in his consuming life – he had a good chance of riches. The incentives were made stronger by news from England where it was already happening on a larger scale, and by the emergence of new technology elsewhere in the economy; as new methods of transport and new sources of income from manufacture strengthened demand for commercial crops and meat.

It was, of course, the more powerful local magnates who had surer access to the knowledge of these possibilities, the capital for the initial hedging outlay plus, perhaps, compensation to the community, the clout to get the courts to support them when they were challenged, and the capital to take advantage of the new methods. There was vigorous debate about the propriety of these developments through the latter half of the eighteenth century. Arguments about individual rights, the sacredness of property and the barbarity of feudal restrictions were pitted against claims that it was above all the poor who would suffer. In the end, it was the Constituent Assembly after the Revolution which made sure that it was liberty and equality of opportunity which won out over fraternity and equality of substantive outcomes.

The story of the modernisation of Japanese agriculture is a very different one. In the great burst of mechanisation in the 1960s, for instance, Japanese writers on agriculture were apt to write of the deplorable 'egoism' of Japanese farmers who insisted on buying their own powered cultivators for their tiny farms (which by then they could well afford) instead of accepting the time and other constraints involved in sharing ownership of a bigger and more fully utilised machine. Their strictures were a revealing assumption of the extent to which cooperative neighbourly activity still remains the norm. In large numbers of villages irrigation systems are still laid out in such a way that no farmer can change his cropping pattern without the agreement of the community organisation, and the water-control plan dictates the day a farmer may plant his rice. Acceptance of the government's set-aside subsidies is made conditional on arrangements to control weeds on the idle fields that might spread to those of neighbours. Collective marketing through agricultural cooperatives remains the norm; the cooperatives now provide a full range of contract cultivation services for those too old to till their fields, and are the initiators in a good proportion of experiments with new crops. Forest commons which have lost their earlier economic significance have often, to be sure, been divided and sold, and the villages are, of course, far more heterogeneous communities than they were; many have been largely transformed into dormitories for those who work elsewhere, but even many of those villages still have the wired broadcast service – loudspeakers in every home which you have to disconnect to turn off. The national news at 6.30, followed by physical jerks, then announcements from the co-op – the arrival of fertiliser stocks, meeting times, news of crop pests discovered – followed by announcements from the clinic or the village office.

## INDIVIDUALISM

I have taken the concepts 'individualism', and 'individualistic'
for granted, but the words are, of course, used in a wide variety
of senses. Several people have tried to sort out its different
referents and evaluative implications. My own best list of
relatively distinguishable meanings goes something like this.

Methodological individualism, ever since I became aware of
it from debates between Gellner and Watkins thirty years ago,
has always seemed to me sensible and in no way prone to rule
out appreciation of the importance of shared collective representations. But it does not have very much to do with any
other kind of individualism, except, possibly, that it has a
logical affinity with what one might call ontological individualism – namely the utilitarians' belief that the only criterion for
judging the relative desirability of different states of the world
is what is happening to individuals – that there is no such thing
as a collective good which is not in some sense an aggregation of
the goods of the constituent individuals, no such Hegelian
thing as the transcendant destiny, the collective mission of the
nation, for example.

The ethical implications of this kind of ontological individualism and the extent to which it can permeate a society and
affect its moral judgements are not trivial. An example is the
way different capitalist societies think of the business firm.
What counts as enlightened doctrine in American business
schools questions both the appropriateness and the social
reality of the legal doctrine that companies are the property of
their shareholders, and of which they can dispose at will. They
speak of 'multiple stakeholders' in the company – employees,
suppliers, distributors and local communities as well as shareholders. In this view the company is often in practice seen by its
managers – and properly so, they would add – as an arena for
the reconciliation of the sometimes converging, sometimes
diverging, interests of the various stakeholders.

What this 'arena' view of the firm does not admit is the notion
that the firm constitutes, for some people in the United States,
an 'entity', which can be harmed or benefited in ways that
cannot be disaggregated into the harm or benefit of individuals. When a company chairman talks about 'the future of our

great firm' he often means just that – just as Presidents do when they talk about 'the future of our great country'. And that reification has obvious social uses – read, if nothing else, Gellner's summary of the Durkheim effect. American normative theorists, however, regard it as mere muddle-minded obfuscation – and some American judges have explicitly described it as such in their judgements.[6] In Japan, by contrast, the 'entity view' is very much taken for granted – not, perhaps, in business schools which tend to stick to American mainstream doctrine – but in the practice and rhetoric of daily life the difference between the two countries is marked. It is a difference which can be ascribed to the differential acceptance in the two countries of ontological individualism as a philosophical foundation for ethics.

Methodological, ontological and, thirdly, behavioural individualism – what one means when one says that a person's behaviour, or attitudes, or ethical judgements are 'individualistic'. One can, I think, distinguish at least six separable strands of meaning.

First there is stress on autonomy or, if you like, the rejection of subordination. This may take the form of what may be called the Buncist strain in British trade unionism – after Trollope's Mr Bunce who had no particular grievances against his employers who prized his services and treated him well. He nevertheless started a union to set himself in opposition to his employers 'because some such antagonism would be manly, and the fighting of some battle would be the right thing to do'.[7] An alternative form in Thatcherite Britain is liberal hostility to the state – the village Hampden tradition of firm rejection of state authority.

The second variety involves stress on independence, a rejection not of subordination, but of dependency. This is the self-reliance – the proud sense of self-sufficiency and expectation of that sense in other people – celebrated by Emerson.[8]

Somewhat different is, to coin an ugly phrase, emotional ungroupishness. This is, if you like, the emotional, psychological correlate of the philosophical doctrine of ontological individualism – the disposition of an individual to feel deeply about, to be made sad or glad about, things which happen to himself personally, or to other individuals to whom he is personally attached, rather than things that happen to some group in which he belongs – his firm, his nation, his family, his favourite team and its supporters' club.

Parallel to that, but in a calculative and instrumental rather than an expressive, consummatory mode, is the primacy of the pursuit of self-interest – selfishness. This is the rational-choice individualism – assumed by writers like Olson to be universally characteristic of man[9] – of the free rider who not only does not recognise intellectually, but also does not feel in any way conscient of, duties towards any collectivity to which he may belong.

Among those who have thoroughly absorbed the doctrine of the invisible hand and turned Smithian marketism into a religion, it *is* just possible for this last form of individualism, the single minded pursuit of self-interest, to become a moral *duty* – not, except in certain rather bizarre milieux, via the tortured reasoning of 'calling', predestination and demonstration of elect status on which so many millions of words have been expended, but more commonly from some notion of a social duty to promote social efficiency. But there is another and much more common form of equally self-regarding behaviour which is much more commonly moralised – made dutiful – and deserves separate listing. That is the pursuit of self-fulfilment, self-development, self-realisation; the individualism of the religious recluse or of the Californian cultist. The dutifulness may have its rationale in some notion of an obligation to one's Maker to develop the potential He has given one, or of not squandering one's good fortune in being born with a good potential, but it clearly does not need that. 'I owe it to myself to try to . . .' may not be a phrase which bears close logical analysis, but one hears it frequently enough. One would intuitively suppose that what determines whether a *real* rather than a specious claim to dutifulness lies behind the pursuit of self-fulfilment is the extent to which it involves self-discipline and the pursuit of some distant goal of achievement, or alternatively a more instant gratification.

And finally, in a somewhat contrasting sense because nothing if not moral, there is the individualism of moral consistency, the adherence to principle. This is closely related to the stress on autonomy, but involves resistance not only to superordinate authorities but also to peer pressures – to thine ownself be true.

It is clear that these are not such highly intercorrelated charac-teristics that it is legitimate to talk of a general syndrome of individualism of which they are partial manifestations. The vociferous welfare claimant, for example, may be high on autonomy, but not much concerned to avoid dependency. Self-interestedness, the pursuit of self-fulfilment and moral consistency clearly differ along a spectrum of relative morality-loadings, to a degree that hardly makes them compatible. Bell's perception of the cultural contradictions of capitalism, for instance, rests plausibly on the assumption that the pursuit of expressive self-fulfilment in consumption erodes both the moral consistency, the self-discipline and the residual groupish-ness which even capitalism, let alone other forms of industria-lism, needs to survive. Autonomy, self-interestedness ought, one would think, to be logically related to ungroupishness, but empirically one saw, even before the Falklands War in Britain – as well as in Reagan's America – how a strong revival of patriotism and military spending could be combined with a drive to roll back the state to give more room for self-interestedness and autonomy.

So individualism is a messy concept, and before moving to the last sections of this paper there is one other useful notion to be introduced as relevant to discussions about the 'growth of individualism', namely that of 'individuation'. Whereas 'indi-vidualistic' is a characteristic of individual behaviour 'individu-ated' is a characteristic of social structures. Its measure lies in the answer to the following question: how much of the things people do and say is the result of individual conscious choice, as opposed to being the unthinking repetition of habit, or the performance without question of 'the proper thing to do', or the acceptance of the decision of some state authority or of some group to which one belongs, or – though here we begin to shade into the choice category – the following, possibly against inclination, of what seem unassailably prescribed social norms? Thus a mobile society in which children are asked what they want to be when they grow up is more individuated than one in which they automatically follow their parents, or than one in which their destiny is decided by a family council, or by their work brigade. A society with frequent and easy divorce is more individuated than one where divorce is rare and discouraged by strong social pressures. A rich society with supermarkets is more individuated than an Indian *jajmani* village where consumption as well as production is regulated by custom.

### AN INDIVIDUATED FUTURE?

This multiplicity of meanings accounts for our ambivalence about individualism. On the whole, in Anglo-Saxon societies at least, it has had a good press. 'Sturdy individualism' has had a stronger image than 'ruthless individualism'. But both forms – or rather, if one accepts the more discriminated quiver of meanings set out above, all forms – of individualism are a function of – indeed, an increase in individualistic behaviour is almost a synonym for – society becoming more individuated. And that depends, as the example of Bloch's French village made clear, on how far the technology a society uses provides *opportunities* for choice and what, within the constraints of that technology, the economic and political structure makes of those opportunities.

Dominant assumptions about the way the accumulation of technological knowledge and the concomitant changes in organisation in advanced industrial societies change the nature and structure of such opportunities have fluctuated in recent decades. David Riesman and William Whyte[10] together in the 1950s created a widespread assumption that the age of individualism – of the autonomous, independent, ungroupish but morally consistent individual – was a function of family farming and small-scale entrepreneurship, and that the growth of large organisations put a premium on a different type of personality – the conformist careerist, ever-ready with his radar antennae to sense the best way of securing the approval of big brother organisation.

In the 1980s, by contrast – and again this is preeminently an Anglophone-country phenomenon – the Friedmanite backlash has created a general impression that sclerotic big organisation has had its day; that we have entered a new age of small business and individual entrepreneurship. Big corporations have reduced employment, substituted subcontracting relations and experimented with devices to introduce quasi-market competition within the enterprise itself. Public corporations have been privatised. Bits and pieces of the health and education and municipal services have been broken up into private franchises. The entrepreneurs of Silicon Valley and the venture capitalists who created them were the new heroes, the ingenious pirates, not the captains, of industry. Even the left came to celebrate the virtues of small businesses,[11] flexibly combining their specialised efforts, partly through cooperatives, partly through decentralised local government stimulation.

And all this was linked to – indeed, in part consequence of – political trends. Most dramatically in Britain and the US, but more generally throughout the industrialised world, the decade of the 1980s was a decade of vigorous attack on all forms of state collectivism. The assumptions were explicit. Hayek is one of Mrs Thatcher's favourite authors. Individualism = self-interestedness is the dominant characteristic of modern man and the only reliable form of motivation for economically useful activity. Politics increasingly proceeded on the assumption that the promise of tax cuts was the only way to win an election. Civil service wage structures were revamped to provide performance incentives. The solidaristic assumptions of welfare services were steadily weakened as notions of entitlements gave way to resurrected nineteenth century notions of charity. The politics of collectivism receded so far into the past that suggestions for a revival of national service as a means of dealing with both youth unemployment and the loss of social cohesion were laughed out of court.

But how much does this reversal amount to? Has the world of Riesman and Whyte really passed away? By the 1990s it does not seem quite so simple. In spite of the ringing endorsement of market liberalism provided by the collapse of Eastern European collectivisms at the end of the decade, the growing social divisions produced by the unleashing of individualism = self-interestedness had prompted second thoughts. The new American president promised to be kindlier and gentler, in a nation where drugs and crime are a dominant preoccupation. Worries about social cohesion continue to blunt the British attack on the welfare state.

And it becomes obvious that high technology has not changed the structure of production all that much either. The big corporations are alive and well, and still the dominant centres of innovation. After a decade of privatisation and deregulation, the involvement of the state in industry seems not much diminished, and has even grown in the high technology fields where risks and lengthy lead times inhibit private development activity. The number of self-employed has increased somewhat in some economies, while continuing a long-term secular trend of decline in others. Overall there has been only a marginal reversal of the crucial switch which played the central role in the Riesman/Whyte scheme of things – from income derived directly from the market to an employee salary (the salary of what official Italian statistics define as *dipendenti*) fixed according to bureaucratic rules.

All these changes concern the values and behavioural dispositions of man as *producer*. But in the 'me-decade' of the late 1960s to 1970s, discussion of individualism issues tended, instead, to focus on what affluence was doing to the values and habits of man as *consumer*, on questions of identities, self-realisation in leisure pursuits, the cultivation of personal relationships, doing 'what you feel comfortable with'. School education in the Anglo-Saxon countries became increasingly 'child-centred', increasingly concerned to avoid coercive discipline and instead evoke the essential spark of the spontaneous *individual* desire to learn. When unemployment of an apparently structural, technology-induced, kind began to grow at the beginning of the 1980s, there were left-wing educators who talked of the absurdity of an education still concerned to prepare children for production when schools ought to be about making sure that in leading their inevitably leisured life they knew how to lead a good life. That individualism = self-fulfilment would become a dominant value was taken for granted. The question of concern was only: would it be disciplined, achievement-oriented 'worthwhile' self-fulfilment, or sloppy instant gratification?

The syllogism was simple. Consumerist values were coming to dominate over productivist (producerist? productionist?) values. (The fact that 'the production problem has been solved' made that possible; the social need to maintain demand and the

profit drive of the advertising industry made it necessary.) This
trend was a product of growing affluence. Therefore as affluence
increased, the dominance of consumerism would increase.

But it is clear that it is not necessarily so. The resurgence in
productivism is apparent in more than the disappearance of
the three-martini lunch. The desperate political effort to end
the era of permissive education in the US and the UK, to
emphasise disciplined effort, the achievement of accepted
standards and the meritocratic cultivation of talent is one sign.
The productivity drive in industry is another, requiring, as it
does, more intense work effort as well as work efficiency –
flexible deployment of labour to reduce idle time, just-in-time
manufacturing to reduce inventory costs, meticulous production planning, perpetual vigilance to maintain quality. On the
bookstalls the plethora of books about national competitiveness
signals the new preoccupations of the chattering classes.

It is not hard to guess the reasons for these symptoms. One
lies directly in technology; the rapid cheapening of transport
and communications. This has combined with the postwar
reduction in trade barriers to intensify international competition. World trade has grown twice as fast as world GNP over the
last five years. The result has been a steady increase in the
exposure to competition of firms which once enjoyed oligopo-
listic security within their own national borders. They have
been forced to become more efficient in order to stay ahead.

Moreover, as world markets become more integrated, the
competition in some markets – in aerospace, in branches of
computers and pharmaceuticals, for example – becomes
increasingly competition between three teams of national
champion firms – American, Japanese and European. States
become involved; competitiveness becomes the order of the
day; multiple ways are found of giving subsidies for research
and development; there is an outcry about the failure of the
education system to create the right 'infrastructure'.

And it is on the managerial élites that these competitive
pressures weigh most heavily and are translated into performance pressures within their organisations.

There is moreover another technology effect. As the technology we use becomes more sophisticated, the job structure changes. The jobs that almost anybody could learn to do begin to disappear. The jobs which are so complex that they require not just extended periods of training but also levels of learning ability, levels of general intelligence, which only a limited proportion of the population possess increase in number. Once, brains were not particularly scarce. Thousands of people who had, say, the intellectual capacity to become first-class doctors, lived and died as farmers and carpenters. Today numerous professions and employing organisations are tapping the 'pool of ability' at lower levels than they would like. The pattern of scarcities has changed.

One consequence seems to be a clear tendency for the primary, pre-transfer, income distribution to be moving towards greater inequality. Another is change in the distribution of working time as well as of income. It might be objected to the 'resurgent productivism' thesis that hours of work continue to shorten and weeks of annual holiday continue to lengthen. But while total work hours may be diminishing, their distribution seems to be more skewed – partly because of the shortage of skills, partly because the jobs done by people with the higher and scarcer intellectual abilities are also the more interesting jobs. Once, hours of work were inversely correlated with pay. The 'hands' came in at 7.30; the boss arrived around 10. Today top managers may well be doing double the shop floor's 35 hours. It is no longer 'conspicuous leisure' but the 'conspicuous busyness' of the filofax executive, settling down to his files after a hectic day of appointments, which validates claims to élite status.

And, minority though the conspicuously busy may be, it is likely to be their values, the values of busy organisation men, which form the dominant ethos of society. Consumerist individualism and the self-fulfilment of instant gratification are for drop-outs.

THE NEXT STAGE

So *is* society set to become more individuated? Are some, or all, of the values of autonomy, independence, moral consistency, ungroupishness, self-interestedness and so on likely to rise or fall in the priority scale? I am no more disposed than Ernest Gellner to map out the further course of evolution and certainly less capable of doing so.

I offer only one final, wild, schematic thought. It *does* seem to be somewhat anomalous that people who are getting richer and richer should be working harder and harder. Surely, eventually, the resurgent productivism phase will pass. Cartelisation and oligopoly, this time at the global rather than the national level, will blunt the forces of competition which have been responsible for it. And by then, with instant computerised translation and all the rest, there should be something of substance which can really be called a global culture.

What values will dominate in *that* culture? Will it be those of the Anglophones whose language will presumably be the key language of that global culture? Or will it be those of the nation which is strongest in the competition and ought, thereby, to have the strongest influence in shaping the global economy? At the moment, whether one looks at growth in market shares *or*, more significantly, the capacity to innovate, that looks like being Japan, a nation which managed to found its industrial efficiency on being, in every one of the term's many senses, less individualistic than its competitors.

## NOTES

1. E. Gellner, *Plough, Sword and Book*, London, 1988.
2. *Plough*, pp. 158, 171, 258, 277.
3. D. Landes, *Revolution in Time*, Cambridge, Mass., 1983.
4. *Plough*, p. 132
5. M. Bloch, 'La lutte pour l'individualisme agraire dans la France du XVIII siècle', *Annales d'histoire economique et sociale*, 1930.
6. R.E. Freeman and D. L. Reed, 'Stockholders and stakeholders: A new perspective on corporate governance', *California Management Review*, 25, iii, Spring 1983.
7. A. Trollope, *Phineas Finn*, London, 1972, p. 107.
8. R.W. Emerson, *Essays and lectures*, New York, 1983.
9. M. Olson, *The logic of collective action*, Cambridge, 1965.
10. D. Riesman, *The Lonely Crowd: A study of the changing American character*, New Haven, 1950. W.H. Whyte. *The organization man*, New York, 1956.
11. M.J. Piore and C.F. Sabel, *The second industrial divide*, New York, 1984.

# PART III

# Modernity and its discontents

# CHAPTER 8

# Science, politics, enchantment

Perry Anderson

The two addresses given by Max Weber on 'Science as a Voca-tion' and 'Politics as a Vocation' occupy a special position within his work. In a body of writing often cumbersome and diffuse, they stand out as masterpieces of literary economy and passion, sudden distillations in a few glowing pages from the sprawling mass of Weber's scholarly thought. Here the themes of rationali-sation, religion, value-freedom, power, bureaucracy, charisma, ethical responsibility are all present, with a rhetorical intensity that has made these texts two of the most influential intellectual statements of this century. Yet it is as if their classical status has tended to shield them from close inspection. For beneath their surface clarity, each reveals signs of a turbulence that escapes logical control, generating a series of aporia which form a signifi-cant pattern.

Weber delivered his lecture on 'Science as a Vocation' on 7 November 1917, the day the Bolsheviks seized power in Russia. To his student audience in war-time Munich, he explained the sternness and strangeness of the scientific enter-prise. Quite apart from its external drawbacks in the lottery of academic life, it afforded no inner satisfactions of a traditional sort either. Irremediably specialised, it excluded any possibility of general cognitive achievement; inherently impersonal, it for-bade temperamental self-expression of the kind normal in art; perpetually developing, its progress ruled out any lasting achievement. Nor could it acquire meaning from any other sphere of life. For modern science had stripped the world of those fictive harmonies where it was once believed to be united to eternal truth, or to nature or divinity or happiness. Structurally disappointing for the scientists and disenchanting for society, what value then attached to it? At least, Weber argued, it was the

187

indispensable means of technical efficacy and conceptual clarity – of practical control or clear thinking, to whatever purpose. The vocation of science, so understood, had nothing to do with politics – the principles of the two were absolutely separate, permitting of no mixture.

Pronounced to the same audience just over a year later, on 28 January 1919, in the midst of the Bavarian Revolution, 'Politics as a Vocation' spelt out the differences. The role of the politician was to exercise independent leadership in the conquest of state power, defined by its monopoly of legitimate violence. Such legitimacy, assuring the obedience of those subject to it, could be traditional, charismatic or legal in character. Its enforcement required a permanent administrative staff, in whose historical development lay the origins of the modern professional politician. Unlike the functionary, however, the statesman takes personal responsibility for his political action, initially as a leader among notables, later as plebiscitary commander of a popular following organised in a mass party. Where such figures failed to emerge, electoral machines operated by mere officials over the heads of equally passive constituencies were the only alternative – leaderless democracy. The true politician, by contrast, not only relished the exercise of power for its own sake, but was distinguished by a combination of passion, judgement and sense of responsibility. Such passion could be for any cause – the choice of a faith was unarguable. But once made, the vocation of politics imposed its own rules. Since the decisive medium of politics was violence, with its peculiarly unpredictable consequences – force breeding force – the only appropriate code to guide it was a secular ethic of responsibility, judging actions by their consequences, not by their intentions.

In outline, such is the substance of the two lectures. The connection between them is at first paradoxical. For the theme they most conspicuously share is also that which Weber intended to separate them – the idea of the vocation as such. In the formal organisation of Weber's discourse, whatever else the term may come to mean, it always denotes the exclusive pursuit of *one* goal – be it science, art, business, politics – at the expense of all others. What makes it serious is *specialisation*. The central message of the two addresses appears to be that politics and science obey distinct laws, which must on no account be commingled or confused.

The term *Beruf* is, of course, pervasive in Weber's sociology. But what has been insufficiently noticed is its extreme semantic instability – the drastic shifts in its meaning from one context to another. Its original sense was a religious calling; as Weber himself noted, it was first introduced into Germany by Luther, in his translation of the Bible.[1] *The Protestant Ethic and the Spirit of Capitalism* freely mines this usage for its account of the high spiritual purpose and rigid moral discipline of the early Calvinist merchant. It is this register, now detached from its religious background, which dominates the Munich addresses – science and politics conceived as strenuous existential callings. But by Weber's time, the normal German meaning of the term was quite different: *Beruf* was simply a profession. That sense too recurs in the lectures, and Weber occasionally senses the difference, but without at any point theoretically fixing it, or realising its consequences for his construction as a whole. Thus, in a famous passage, he spoke of 'two kinds' of *Berufspolitiker* – those who lived for politics, and those who lived from them. The former could devote themselves to public life in economic independence from it, typically as rentiers or landowners; the latter, without major property of their own, derived their income essentially from offices of party or state. This would seem a sufficiently clear-cut contrast. No sooner is it made, however, than it is undone, when Weber goes on to remark that politically dominant strata invariably exploit their power for private economic ends, while the most unconditional political idealism is normally displayed by the propertyless.[2] The antithesis of 'living for' and 'living from' is incoherent here in part because it does not coincide with an opposition that is more important to the argument. For Weber starts by defining the vocation of the politician 'in its highest expression' as pure charismatic leadership – *hier wurzelt der Gedanke des Berufs in seiner höchsten Ausprägung*.[3] After tracing the rise of various kinds of administrative staff, he then proceeds to a catalogue of political roles in which the idea of *Beruf* finds, so to speak, its lowest expression. These include the party official and the machine boss, parliamentary herds (*Stimmvieh*) or municipal cliques: in short 'professional' politicians in the perjorative sense of the word. To these Weber finally applies the disgraced term *Berufspolitiker ohne Beruf* – in effect, a *reductio ad absurdum* of the contradictions in the concept.[4] For what

Weber had yoked together under the single rubric of his title were three completely opposite meanings: charismatic leadership in the pursuit of high ideals, bureaucratic service under orders in the state, and mercenary competition for spoils of office. In *Wissenschaft als Beruf* the oscillation of meaning is scarcely less severe. On the one hand, the vocation of science is to serve the moral purpose of 'self-reflection' – *Selbstbesinnung* – by instilling 'a sense of duty, clarity and responsibility' in the individual who answers to its intellectual standards. On the other hand, it simply furnishes the techniques for 'calculable control of external objects and human behaviour', much as a Mid-West grocer's wife supplies cabbage across the counter.[5] The second function is in fact more plausibly presented by Weber than the first, which would not seem to require any specialised scientific knowledge at all. Here too the notion of *Beruf* dilates and fissures in the course of the argument. This process is not confined to the formal exposition of the lectures. The same pattern can be observed in Weber's informal accounts of himself. Explaining his refusal late in life of the compromises demanded of a politician, he could declare proudly: *Ich bin von Beruf: Gelehrter.* But he could equally express thorough contempt for the whole notion, as too narrow for him: *irgendeinem Respekt vor dem Begriff des 'Berufs' habe ich nie gehabt*, he wrote as a young man of his attitude to his prospects.[6] Ironically, the great final peroration of 'Politics as a Vocation', climactically conjuring up once again the mission of 'the leader and the hero', also involuntarily lets out that same dreary underside of the concept. What will become of you? he challenged the students before him, listing their possible life-failures: *Verbitterung oder Banausentum, einfaches stumpfes Hinnehmen der Welt und des Berufes?*[7] Here, with the further connotation of philistine routine, the fall – across the same term – of 'calling' into 'career' is complete.

There are a number of ways of seeing this particular strain in the structure of the two lectures. It can be related to Weber's more general difficulty in negotiating the relationship between the 'ideal' and 'material' elements of his social theory, where the actual balance or connection between the two is rarely if ever confronted. Typically, rather, the former acquires a tacit predominance through the formal volume of its elaboration, suddenly interrupted by uncompromising reminders of the weight of the latter – often all the more brutal, as if a way of compensation for steadier treatment. But there was another, and more specific, reason for the anomalies in Weber's treatment of the concept of vocation. The term had one unambiguous force, common to its ideal and material registers alike. It spelt specialisation – whether as higher calling or lowlier profession. It was this which rendered the notion a firebreak between science and politics. What was then its antonym in Weber's vocabulary? The answer is readily to hand. Strewn throughout his political writings is a set of obsessive references to 'literati' and 'dilettantes'. These function as nearly interchangeable imprecations. However indiscriminate in their polemical application, they always contain at least one fixed charge: the slur of amateurism. Over against the man of a vocation or profession, there was the dabbler and the dilettante. The *literaten* against whom Weber so tirelessly thundered varied over time. They included the sycophants who enthused over Bismarck's mere violence and cunning, as well as the carpers who impotently resented them; the parasites who advocated a relaxation of German diligence after the war, and the demagogues who demanded too many territorial annexations during it; the dreamers of democratised industry, alongside the confectors of new religions.[8] But by the time of his second lecture in Munich, in its dramatic political setting, previously diffuse referents had narrowed to one overwhelming target. The German Revolution had put power into the hands of 'absolute dilettantes', whose only claim to it was 'their control of machine-guns'; all that distinguished the rule of Bolshevik or Spartacist ideologues, workers' or soldiers' councils, from that of any military dictatorship was their 'dilettantism'.[9] Eisner was a prize example in Bavaria. Another was Trotsky, who had displayed 'the typical vanity of the Russian literati' in questioning the good faith of Germany at Brest-Litovsk, forcing the Reich to impose its own peace.[10] In these years, the familiar terms of earlier dislike become fused into a figure otherwise elusive or absent in Weber's sociology of modernity – the 'intellectual'. Identified with revolutionary socialists of all persuasions – USPD, Spartacists, Syndicalists, Bolsheviks – the figure of the intellectual, lacking the specialised aptitudes for either science or politics, bespeaks generic irresponsibility and incompetence.

This theoretical contrast, at least, seems hard and fast enough.

Yet the notion of what it is to be an intellectual, too, suffers a curious sideways disturbance in Weber's writing. For one of the central themes of his later thought – unforgettably developed in 'Science as a Vocation' – is what he termed the 'intellectualisation' of modern life.[11] By this he meant just that process of specialisation which divided life into separate and incompatible spheres of value, draining meaning from it as a whole. 'The fate of our age, with its characteristic rationalization and intellectualization – above all disenchantment of the world – is that the ultimate and highest values have withdrawn from public life'.[12] In other words, here the character of the process is the very opposite of the figures who should logically embody it. Intellectualism portends just what intellectuals forego. Crucially, moreover, Weber deplored the consequences of the process as he described it. After invoking the 'unending and inconclusive struggle' between different outlooks on life in the disenchanted world, he told his audience that he too 'hated intellectualism as the worst evil' of modern times.[13] The strongest expression of that dislike is, of course, the scathing final verdict of *The Protestant Ethic*: 'Of the last stage of this cultural development it might truly be said: "Specialists without spirit, sensualists without heart; this nullity imagines it has attained a level of civilization never before achieved."'[14] The Nietzschean scorn for the *Fachmensch* here was one that could extend to the *Berufsmensch* – the two indeed being equated as products of the bureaucratisation of power and culture,[15] whose long-run effects threatened something like an Egyptian bondage of the spirit. Weber, who was sure that he himself 'could in some measure perform in rather a large number of positions',[16] had reason to say that he detested this kind of intellectualism.

Yet the problem posed by the bane of 'intellectualism' – value-disintegration – remained. It was the strong sense of vocation that was uppermost in Weber's mind when he gave his Munich addresses. Science and politics were callings – a summons to the right conduct appropriate to each. But how was an ethics possible in either, once the process of intellectualisation had divested the world of all objective obligations? Within the texts themselves, two kinds of response can be found. The first attempts to formulate a morality proper to each calling in terms of the immanent logic of its practice. The pursuit of science assists or forces individuals to confront the logic of their life-choices, 'to render account of the ultimate meaning of their actions', even while it cannot prescribe it. In so doing, Weber declared, it served the *sittliche Mächte* – social-moral forces – of 'duty, clarity and responsibility'.[17] The practice of politics, for its part – because its principal means was violence – required sober reckoning of what might come of any action contemplated: not the morality of pure intention preached on the Mount, but the civic responsibility defended by Machiavelli. In each field the ethic enjoined – one of intellectual clarity, the other of practical consequence – is of a technically formalist type, stipulating no substantive ends. Moreover, Weber conceded, neither could motivate their adoption.[18] A decision external to, and unwarrantable by, each was necessary for that. This decisionism, with its markedly Nietzschean background, has been sharply criticised by Habermas and others: its irrationalist cast is obvious enough. What has been less noticed is the incoherence of each of the formal prescriptions themselves. After defining contemporary science as inherently *specialised* knowledge, Weber has ruled out in advance any possibility of arguing that it can perform the completely generic task of logical clarification he eventually ascribes to it; and, in fact, there is a predictable slippage at this point in the text to *philosophy* as the indicated help-meet – that is, just the opposite of the sciences as depicted by him, or the most general of intellectual disciplines. Similarly, his case for an ethic of responsibility in politics centres essentially on the claim that in the world of power it is the case that good ends can be achieved by bad means, that is by the use of force prohibited by the Sermon on the Mount. It is on 'this problem of the justification of means by ends that an ethic of convictions inevitably founders'.[19] But since for Weber the decisive means in politics, as he never tires of repeating, is violence, the means are by definition *always* bad: they therefore cease to be discriminative – so that within this schema policies can paradoxically only be judged by their ends, in other words precisely the maxim of an ethic of conviction. At the same time, in remarking that the 'tragedy of all political action' is that 'as a rule' – in other words, whatever ethic is adopted – outcomes not merely fail to coincide with intentions but contradict them, he renders ends themselves incalculable, and the lessons of statecraft he adduces from

Chandragupta onwards irrelevant. In a remarkable non sequitur, Weber draws the conclusion that 'precisely because' of this unreckonability, political action 'must serve a cause if it is to have inner strength' and not 'bear the curse of creaturely nullity'. But 'what cause the politician adopts in his drive for power is a matter of faith'.[20]

If Weber's endeavours to deduce a morality specific to the pursuit of science or politics want much cogency, there is a more consistent theme that is partly screened by them. This is a psychology of practical success, which provides the real voltage of the account. What is striking is the similarity of its formula in each calling. The first requirement of the scientist, Weber explained, was passion – 'a strange frenzy' that was the condition of inspiration. The second was hard work, which normally prepared the ground for it.[21] Intoxication on the one hand, application on the other, were the keys to scientific insight. In politics, likewise, the first essential quality of the statesman was passion – devotion to 'the god or demon' of a cause. The second was detachment, the capacity for a cool gaze at the world and the self, which demanded a 'firm taming of the soul' that set the true politician apart from the dilettante.[22] The duality is echoed in the concluding flourish which evokes the 'immeasurably moving' spectacle of the 'mature man' at a crossroads of conscience whom Weber represents – ignoring an earlier claim of their incompatibility – as suddenly synthesising the ethics of responsibility and of conviction in his person: 'that is truly human and affecting'.[23] The recipe for the two vocations is thus basically the same – a combination of intense passion and iron discipline. The recurrence of this trope, across the separation of science and politics, had deep biographical sources. For it corresponded, of course, to Weber's sense of himself.

The scientist is a teacher, and his work is necessarily impersonal. The politician is a leader, whose authority can only be personal. Vanity in the former, however frequent, is innocuous; in the latter, it is ruinous. These contrasts are designed to underwrite the segregation of the two activities. But in Weber's account, the fundamental difference between the two lies elsewhere. Science is the main force for that rationalisation of the world which has denuded it of objective values, and must itself abstain from the expression of subjective preferences. Modern politics operates within the disenchanted world created by science, but necessarily pits subjective causes against each other. The cardinal error for the scientist is to stray across this line into value-judgements in public life. 'Politics has no place in the lecture-room.' The proper duty of a public speaker on democracy, Weber declared, is to use words not as 'ploughshares for loosening the soil of contemplative thought' but as 'swords against opponents, instruments of struggle'. Such language would, however, be 'an outrage in a lecture'.[24]

The most cursory glance at the two addresses reveals how far Weber was from practising these precepts. Value-judgements abound in each, giving them their peculiar rhetorical force. The whole structure of 'Science as a Vocation' builds up to an impassioned final warning against the 'swindle or self-deception' of new religious cults fabricated by intellectuals 'without a new and genuine prophecy' – as distinct from the 'sublime values' to be found in the transcendental realm of 'mystical life' or in the intimate realm where the 'pulsations' of immediate community recall the sacred *pneuma* of old.[25] What could be the scientific criteria for demarcating these, on Weber's own terms? The polemical ends of 'Politics as a Vocation' are still more insistent and overt. Far from being the neutral survey promised by Weber in his opening sentences, in which all advocacy would be 'completely excluded' – *ganz ausgeschaltet* – it is filled with furious attacks on the revolutionary socialists of the time, in Russia and in Germany.

Weber's inability to separate science and politics in his practice, radical though it was, matters less than the nature of the relationship actually at work between them in his thought as a whole. The central themes of his sociology of modernity are disenchantment and bureaucratisation – the loss of meaning and the loss of freedom paradoxically brought by that process of rationalisation which gave Western civilisation its lead over the rest of the globe. Science is the principal author of the demystification of the world. But what is the nature of the waning of enchantment that it causes? In perhaps the best-known of all his passages, Weber described it as a new polytheism in which 'the many gods of old, no longer magic but become impersonal forces, rise from their graves and contend for powers over our lives in unending mutual struggle'.[26] Which are these deities?

Weber amalgamates two answers in his account that are logically independent of each other. One is that they represent, as in the pantheon of antiquity, rival ideals of wealth, power, art, love, knowledge – in other words a *multiplicity* of value-spheres. There might then exist binding norms specific to each, inherent in the nature of their domain. This is the version, derived from Mill, on which Weber relies in arguing for an ethic of responsibility in politics – whose morality he contrasts with those that govern the spheres of eros, commerce, family or administration. 'We are placed into various life-spheres, each of which is governed by different laws.'[27] But there is, of course, a second answer: that the strife of the gods means – not because there are many of them, but because they have lost their magic – a general *indeterminacy* of values within each sphere. This is the more radical version, derived from Nietzsche, to which Weber would revert when discussing the general logic of modern culture, whose 'every step leads to an ever more devastating senselessness', a 'meaningless bustle in the service of worthless, self-contradictory and mutually antagonistic goals'.[28] In other words, the intellectualisation of the world could lead to either ethical pluralism or nihilism.

What were the consequences of this conception of the impact of science for Weber's politics? He was an early twentieth century liberal, of a distinctively German kind. Civic rights, electoral competition and private enterprise were conditions of individual freedom. If universal male suffrage had probably come too early in Germany, the censitary franchise in Prussia was an obstacle to national unity. Parliamentary responsibility was needed, but did not have to extend to the choice of Chancellor. Academic life should be free from political control, and trade unions encouraged. Neither natural rights nor free trade entered into this liberalism, whose basic concern was the formation and expression of the free personality. Before the war, Weber believed that strong leadership was best nurtured by competitive selection of independent élites in parliamentary settings; after the war, by plebiscitary mandates overriding parliamentary divisions. He identified himself with the German bourgeoisie from which he came, but was an uncompromising critic of what he held to be its cowardice in the Wilhelmine order. He assailed the conservatism and egoism of the Junker class, but much of his outlook was markedly aristocratic: few terms are so cherished in his political vocabulary as honour. Wounds to that, he told his audience in Munich, a nation could never forgive.

For his deepest political commitments were, of course, national.

Weber never retracted his inaugural address at Freiburg, which announced at the outset of his scholarly life that the 'power interests of the nation are the ultimate and decisive interests' for the study of economic policy, 'a science in the service of politics' for which *'raison d'état* is the final measure of value'. In famous phrases, he declared: 'it is not to peace and human happiness that we must show the way to our descendants, but to the endless struggle for the preservation and higher breeding of our race' – 'in the hard and clear air in which the sober work of German politics flourishes, yet pervaded too by the serious splendour of national emotion'.[29] Critical of the diplomatic ineptitude of the Wilhelmine regime, he was a strong advocate of German naval and colonial expansion. When the First World War broke out, he greeted it with jubilation: *'Whatever* the outcome, *this war is great and wonderful'.*[30] It had led to 'the inner rebirth of Germany', for the country had a *'responsibility before history'* to become a great power, as a nation of seventy million whose 'calling as a master people' was to 'turn the wheels of world development'. The cause for which Germans were fighting was 'not changes on the map or economic profits, but *honour'* – the honour of our nationality'.[31]

Weber's nationalism was more important to him than his liberalism. But the two were connected, since for most of his life he believed that only a liberal political order could equip Germany to play its appointed imperial role. If they conflicted, however, within the horizon of his own experience nationalist principles came first. How did he justify these? There are two basic themes in his bellicist writing. One is the cultural mission of the German people to save the world from Russian diktat and English etiquette, equally stifling of inner authenticity. This was a standard *topos* of war-time literature, capable of a number of individual variations. By comparison with the extended constructions of Thomas Mann or even his brother Alfred, Weber's use of it is quite cursory: unlike them, he never spelt out the contrasting virtues of German *Kultur* – on the contrary, conceding that small nations often produced better art and displayed more community than large ones – and never opposed Anglo-French *Zivilisation* to it, Russia always remaining the most dangerous enemy for him.

The real mandate for Germany's world-historical embrace of war lay elsewhere. It was fate – *Schicksal* – that decreed it. Since 'the mere existence of a great power, such as we have become, is an obstacle in the path of other great powers', the European conflict was inevitable.

The fact that we are a people not of seven but seventy millions – *that* was our fate. It founded an inexorable responsibility before history, which we could not evade even if we had wished. We must make this clear again and again, when the question of the 'meaning' of this endless war is now raised. The magnetic force of this fate drew the nation upwards, past the perilous abyss of decline, onto the steep path of honour and fame, from which there could be no turning back – into the clear hard air of the realm of world history, to look its grim majesty in the face, as an imperishable memory for our remote descendants.[32]

The significant crux here is the linkage of *meaning* and *fate*. It recurs again, in a particularly revealing way, when he compared the life of the masses in peace and war, speaking of

that loveless and pitiless economic struggle for existence, which bourgeois phraseology calls 'peaceful cultural labour', in which hundreds of millions wear out body and soul, sink under, or lead a life infinitely more devoid of any perceptible 'meaning' than the engagement of all (including women – since they too 'wage' war, when they do what they must) in the cause of honour, *that is* – the historical duties of the nation decreed by fate.[33]

For Weber, in other words, nationalism was above all meaning regained. Pacifism was a Gospel mentality incompatible with any action in this world, which included not only 'beauty, dignity, honour and grandeur', but also 'the inevitability of wars for power', and the different laws binding each of these domains. He who enters the world 'must *choose* which of these Gods he would serve, or when one and when another'.[34] Fate and Choice are thus exploited side by side, in the same rhetorical construction. The oscillation between them corresponds, one might say, to the two poles of Weber's political outlook. The idea of a free choice between the locally valid codes of this world, allowing for temporal negotiations between them, answered to Weber's liberalism. It followed the logic of the mild version of disenchantment. The idea of a sheer fate imposing one value, without appeal ('we could not evade it if we wished'), inspired his nationalism. In a paradoxical way, it followed the logic of the strong version of disenchantment. For if there are no specifically valid codes, in any sphere of life, there are no grounds for selecting or negotiating between them. Choice that is purely arbitrary then swivels into another form of facticity. A pure decisionism is thus always liable to be shadowed by a radical fatalism. Nietzsche had already displayed this paradox, as he moved from the death of god to *amor fati* – the will to power operating simultaneously as metaphysical challenge and physical destiny. So it was with Weber. If choice between values is rationally impossible, the chance of nationality becomes unanswerably valuable. The intellectualisation of the world which strips it of meaning here prompts just that sacrifice of the intellect Weber otherwise scorned, in the discovery of supreme meaning in fate, and its moral decoration as duty. Weber, of course, was not alone in the headlong rush to the Great War. But it is striking how unconscious he was, sociologically, of his own solution to the disenchantment he feared. The extent of his self-reflection was the solitary sentence at which the few scant paragraphs on the 'nation' in the vast mass of *Economy and Society* peter out: 'Intellectuals are in some degree predestined to propagate the "national" idea'.[35] The most powerful political force of his day, and central passion of his public activity, is all but absent from his theoretical sight. It is as if nationalism had to be exempt from the light of science, as the consolation for what it wrought. It was immune, too, to the maxims of politics Weber ostensibly defended. The sermons to the left on the ethics of responsibility have their irony. For it was Weber who welcomed the carnage of the First World War 'whatever the outcome' – with a cult of expressive community and a pathos of military power heedless of all consequences. The cost of those ethics of conviction was about eight million lives.[36] But on the battlefield, such deaths were enchanted. 'War grants the warrior something uniquely meaningful: the experience of a sense in death that consecrates it' – 'the community of the standing army today feels itself a community unto death: the greatest of its kind'.[37] The *Sinnlosigkeit* of the world dissolves in the modern sublime, the *Sinnhaftigkeit* of national destiny.

To move from the pages of Max Weber to those of Ernest Gellner is a large change in atmosphere. It is not just that the two belong to such different epochs. Their temperaments and tones are so contrasted – what could be more antithetical than Weber's heroically elevated pessimism and Gellner's deliberately plain-man optimism: the high rhetoric of the one, and the low jokes of the other. The distance between the cultivated middle classes of Berlin under Bismarck and those of Prague under Benes have their part in this – Czech manners, in the absence of a nobility, were no doubt always more egalitarian. But there is also a marked opposition of philosophical background. Where Weber was deeply affected by German vitalism, above all the legacy of Nietzsche, Gellner comes out of British empiricism and utilitarianism as it culminated in Russell. The gulf between the two traditions speaks for itself: Gellner is a shining example of the 'eudaemonism' Weber scorned. Ironically, on the other hand, Weber professed a variety of methodological individualism for the social sciences, even if his practice – to its advantage – ignored it; whereas Gellner has been a trenchant critic of the doctrine, which for obvious reasons has rarely appealed to anthropologists. Last but not least, of course, there is the striking divergence in the forms of their corpus: the massively detailed scholarship of the one, monuments of historical erudition and taxonomic improvisation, compared with the insouciantly reconnoitred forays of the other, travelling light over the most variegated terrain to unexpected theoretical effect. In all these respects, the two are evident antitheses.

Yet there is another sense in which, of all the sociological thinkers of the subsequent epoch, Gellner has remained closest to Weber's central intellectual problems. Some have sought to develop his formal analytic of action, building it into large new systems theories. Others have taken up the unfinished tasks of his historical encyclopaedia, giving it a superior narrative direction or typological consistency. But none has addressed themselves with such cogency to the core cluster of his substantive concerns. If we take Weber's great terminating themes of science and politics, this becomes readily apparent. Gellner's account of the 'structure of human history', like Weber's, is essentially one of the pilgrimage of reason through the world, from magic through religion to science. It is, of course, more tightly – also more selectively – focused: not 'rationalisation' as a whole, which in Weber is a process differentiating and transforming all the domains of life from the economic and administrative to the aesthetic and erotic, but 'cognition' as such – that *Reich des denkenden Erkennens* which forms only the last, if most important, of Weber's reflections in the *Zwischenbetrachtung* – is the leading theme of *Plough, Sword and Book*. Philosophy and science are foregrounded in this version with greater overall force. But the new situation created by the advent of modern science is the same in both accounts – a decline of meaning. For Gellner, consistently with his starting-point, this is however in the first instance an epistemological crisis, where for Weber it was unmediately ethical and existential. In the general problem posed by *Legitimation of Belief*, 'What can I know?' logically commands 'What should I be/do?'[38] Here there are two problem-areas to which Gellner returns again and again: the original validity-basis of modern science, and the contemporary forms of philosophical relativism. The former, he has argued, can best be seen as a – not wholly natural or easy – union of an empiricist sense of the self and a mechanist view of the world: an atomism of evidence, and structuralism of explanation. The fit between them is never quite sealed in Gellner's writing, which tends to fall back on professions of faith for the autonomy of the first – the ghost always rattles somewhat in the machine. When Gellner treats of the classical tradition of modern philosophy, the scientific universe is the cold mechanical environment of impersonal causation, scoured of value as Weber held it to be. But when Gellner tackles the lax conceptual relativism of so much late twentieth-century culture, science – the precipitant of the crisis of meaning – *reverses out to become its solvent*. This is the basic intellectual move which distinguishes him from Weber. It is one that in part reflects their different historical situations. Where Weber jousted no more than briefly with Spengler in the last months of his life, Gellner confronted the luxuriance of the latter's descent forty years later, as it was mediated through Wittgenstein. Gellner's reaction to the doctrine of the incommensurability of the 'forms of life' embodied in different communities was to emphasise the universal cognitive and *therewith moral* power of science. In substance, his argument has consistently been that science – and science alone – brings modern industry, which yields mass prosperity, which permits effective morality. It is the material affluence afforded by scientific reason that is its epistemological trump-card.[39] No community, once exposed to the benefits of industrialisation, has ever resisted them; and once gained – hunger and disease overcome – ethical decency for the first time becomes generally possible. This is the change of thought of *Thought and Change*, in which – one might say – premises derived from Weber somersault into conclusions close to Holbach.[40] The political force of the argument is entirely sympathetic; but its philosophical form is one Gellner himself criticises in others. To rest philosophical truth on technological success is to veer towards the pragmatism he rebukes in Quine;[41] while to tie moral decency to material ease is to assume more than to found its content. The role of industrial progress in Gellner's thought is rather like that of human rights in the world at large: a value whose only normative foundation lies in the extent of its *de facto* acceptance. The distance between this position and Weber's is not just a question of temperament. It also reflects the immense transformation of life-conditions brought by industry since the Second World War, creating levels of popular consumption in the advanced countries – and promising them to the less developed – unimaginable at the time of the First. It is difficult to imagine Weber, relaxed before a television set, greeting the festivities of the time as a new Belle Epoque.[42] But his sociological realism would have respected the empirical strength of Gellner's case.

Where does this leave disenchantment? Among the most striking of Gellner's ideas is, of course, the thesis of the Rubber Cage. Industrial modernity, far from constructing houses of an iron bondage excluding all meaning, provides open ground for constant new flowerings of it. Re-enchantment, indeed, becomes an industry in its own right with a multiplication of self-indulgent fads and subjectivist creeds, from the Oxonian cult of ordinary language to the Californian mysteries of daily conversation.[43] The disciplines of industrial production prove more than compatible with these fantasies of ideological consumption – both increased leisure, and the effortless technical aids to it, actually encouraged them. Gellner likes to invoke Weber's contempt for the sham spiritual furnitures of his time, while pointing out that he never conceived they could become so widespread. But, of course, in Gellner's scheme of things, the proliferation of bogus meanings can occur because *real* meaning has already been restored. Science provides the grid of all our effective beliefs, leaving us the luxury of symbolic creeds that can be retracted as easily as a video-cassette.

Or so it would seem at first sight, from Gellner's main doctrine. In fact, it is part of the interest of his work that it contains certain contra-indications. In his final reflections on the crisis of meaning, Weber showed particular concern with two domains of value: the religious (artificial or authentic) and the interpersonal (erotic or convivial).[44] It is no accident that Gellner should have devoted major studies to each of these. The results are not entirely consistent with the ironic harmonies of his general theory of re-enchantment. Of the major world religions, Weber wrote least on Islam, and it is this lacuna Gellner has filled to pointed contemporary effect. For all its imaginative brilliance, it is true that his sociology of Muslim societies themselves models them too heavily on the Maghreb, the backward Wild West of the Islamic world, rather than the core zones of settled agriculture in the Middle East. But this limitation is less significant for his more general theoretical programme than his contention, often reiterated, that Islam is so soberly monotheist, scriptural and egalitarian that of all the world religions it is most compatible with the requirements of an industrialising age, and will perhaps alone survive intact into it. Khomeini himself – certainly the nearest recent approximation to a 'prophet' in Weber's sense – is presented as theologically true to this singular Muslim modernity.[45] Here Gellner, scathing about ersatz religions, is curiously uncritical about the original article. The claim that Islam is uniquely egalitarian forgets entirely the position it accords women (always something of a blind spot for him). More generally, it overlooks the obvious fact that precisely because it is a traditional religion – that is, a set of dogmatic beliefs about a supernatural order – it is bound to be decommissioned by contact with modern science and mass consumption, like every other such faith, for just the reasons Gellner elsewhere insists on, ending up like them in the symbolic rather than effective economy of belief. Intercontinental hysteria over blasphemy expresses not unusual congruence with modernity, but exceptional fear of it. With good reason: there will be no special reprieve for the integrity of the Koran.

Gellner's treatment of the realm of the interpersonal is very different in character. If *The Psychoanalytic Movement* is the most wittily sustained of all his polemics, it is also his most serious and searching: arguably his finest single book. In conditions of material security, social fluidity and moral anomie, it suggests, traditional fears and anxieties projected onto the natural world become concentrated on the social, at the sensitive points of the individual's most intimate relationships with others. Here, where the greatest share of life's happiness or misery is now decided, all seems unpredictable, yet often unfathomably patterned, an arena of tension, mystery and danger. Freud's doctrines owe their success to a combination of ostensibly scientific explanation of this domain of experience, with covertly pastoral ministration to it, condensed in the unique confessional mechanisms of transference. Of all the modern forms of re-enchantment psychoanalysis, offering personal salvation through an austere theoretical medication, is the strongest. In a considerable adversary literature, Gellner's critique of it is unmatched. His principal concern, however, is less with its intellectual shortcomings than with its cultural influence. If he exaggerates this – psychoanalysis has never been a 'movement' in the normal sense of the term, with a mass following – the error paradoxically stems from an acknowledgement of the scale of the distress it promises to relieve. For the other main theme of the book – vindicating Nietzsche against Hume – is the intrinsic crookedness and unruliness of the human psyche, contorted in so many involuntary directions by multiple unconscious forces that Freud naively simplified, assimilating them to the workings of the conscious mind.[46] Weber, expressing interest in psychoanalysis as a new field of research, found its clinical material still 'alarmingly thin', and looked forward to the development in two or three decades of an 'exact casuistics' of the instinctual dynamics it had started to explore.[47] These are essentially the demands that remain for Gellner still unsatisfied today – more and better evidence, more precise and complex theory, for the study of what is not conscious. The stress that falls on the painful precariousness of this zone of experience, and the intensity of the need to wrest meaning from it, nevertheless contradicts the portrait of the Rubber Cage. On Gellner's own showing, here the bars are truly cold and hard; and it is desperation, not distraction, that shakes them in search of escape.

If such are the sequels of Weber's view of science in Gellner's work, what of politics? Much more straightforwardly and unreservedly, he too has been a liberal. That liberalism is a primary commitment, unaffected by dreams of imperial power. But the view of democracy that issues from it has sociological points in common with Weber's, and might be described as a benignly updated version of it. Popular will can only exist within a concrete social structure that cannot be willed: democracy reposes on principles that are not based on consent, but limit it. Parliamentary government therefore is most effective where decisions to be taken are relatively marginal. The essence of democracy is perhaps no more than civic rights garnished with symbolic participation in the Durkeimian community – the ballot essentially limiting the life of governments, and so indirectly cautioning their conduct.[48] The Western exemplars of it should inspire no smugness: they overlook unnecessary enclaves of poverty and preserve archaic areas of hierarchy. But can they really be much improved? Egalitarian in mores, if perhaps less so in structure, they can allow reveries of yet greater equality because the danger of these being implemented is so small that their compatibility with liberty is unlikely to be tested. No one has yet shown how power might be more diffused in an industrial society.[49] Compared with Weber, there is a much more central attachment to the openness of liberal institutions to criticism and reform as values in their own right; and much less (scarcely any) interest in the leadership presiding over them, a difference that follows from the tasks of the epoch: the mission of the state is not to conquer world power, but to manage growing affluence.

With this sanguine outlook, Gellner reacted to the upheavals

of the late sixties with sardonic good humour, treating student
rebellion as little more than the obverse of establishment
conservatism – both equally facile ideologies, the one rejecting
all general ideas in the name of common sense, the other
trumpeting any number of them as a *dérèglement des sens*;[50] each
comfortably ensconced in a costless realm of make-belief typical
of advanced industrial societies. Uncharacteristically, his ser-
enity briefly deserted him in the seventies, when industrial
unrest and oil price rises seem to have disproportionately
agitated him. Texts of this period strike an apocalyptic note
found nowhere else in his writing: the horizon suddenly
becomes menacing, civilisation undermined by rot and
betrayal, England itself doomed – all, apparently, because of
the blackmail of miners and sheikhs. These addresses are his
modest version of Weber's forebodings at Munich: a liberalism
under threat of social unrest, at home and abroad, fearing if
not a polar night, at any rate a 'dark and lowering sky' before
it.[51] One imagines a Conservative vote in 1979. Return to
normal service, with the boom conditions of the eighties, has
restored Gellner's natural sang-froid. Other and more lasting
preoccupations have since dominated.

   The main one, of course, has been nationalism. Here lies the
most significant and paradoxical of all the relationships
between the two sociologists. For Gellner has made good
Weber's central omission, with a vengeance. His work contains
the boldest and most original theory of nationalism to date.
Prompted by his fieldwork in the Third World, it explains the
emergence of nationalism as a breakwater of differential industrialisation. Modern technology demands occupational mobility. But the more fluid the social structure, the more unitary is
the culture it requires of its agents, as they shift and intermesh
across its positions in an increasingly complex and mutable
division of labour. This is a universal imperative of industrialism. But its advent is not only historically staggered; it hits a
world already ethnically and linguistically divided. On the one
hand, no single culture is yet powerful enough to encompass
the globe; on the other, the later a region comes to industrialisation, the more it risks subjugation to those that arrived
earlier, and exclusion of its inhabitants from the local fruits of
the process. The result is nationalism: or the spread of the

drive to create states whose political frontiers roughly coincide with ethnic boundaries. Nationalist movements are typically recruited from a disaffected intelligentsia and an uprooted proletariat – the former standing to benefit from monopoly of public office in an independent state, the latter at least to be exploited only by fellow-citizens. Contrary to received preju- dices, the diffusion of nationalism throughout the globe is a salutary process, which has certainly improved the lot and perhaps bettered the conduct of humanity. For the nation- state, however fortuitous its original demarcation (there are far fewer than the possible linguistic candidates), is the necessary general framework for the unitary culture – also preliminary protection – required by modern industry, which is in turn the only passport to prosperity for individuals, and equality between peoples.

This explanation of the nature of nationalism is an outstand- ingly powerful one on its own ground. But that ground is self-confessedly less than the whole phenomenon. Gellner's theory can account for the rise of nation-states in Eastern Europe, and the decolonisation of Asia and Africa, even if it runs into difficulties with the earlier liberation of Spanish America. But what it completely skirts is the really spectacular manifestations of twentieth-century nationalism – not the independence of Czechoslovakia or Morocco, but World War and Nazism. Such catastrophic processes cannot be blandly tidied away as anomalies, with the discreet assurance that 'exceptionless generalizations are seldom if ever available'.[52] It is difficult not to sense a *parti-pris* here, as if Gellner has over-reacted to previous depictions of nationalism as a destruc- tively irrational, atavistic force – producing something like a mirror opposite, in which it becomes to all intents and purposes a wholesomely constructive and forward-looking principle. The huge world-historical ambiguities of nationalism are not captured by either; they call for an account that is temporally and spatially more differentiated. But what Gellner leaves out casts into a sharp light what he puts in. The most arresting feature of his theory of nationalism is its single-minded econo- mic functionalism.

The economy needs the new type of cultural centre and the central state; the culture needs the state; and the state probably needs the

homogeneous cultural branding of its flock . . . The mutual relationship of a modern culture and state is something quite new, and
springs, inevitably, from the requirements of a modern economy.[53]

Gellner early on defined his sociological position as a 'multi-
form materialism', with a clear-sighted insistence on the
general (not invariable) priority of the (several) physical and
material determinants of social existence.[54] Whatever its varia-
bility over time, this moderate materialism has generally distinguished him from Weber, to whom such clarity of outlook was
foreign. Ironically, however, there is a sense in which Gellner's
theory of nationalism might be described as immoderately
materialist. For what it plainly neglects is the overpowering
dimension of collective *meaning* that modern nationalism has
always involved: that is, not its functionality for industry, but its
fulfilment of identity. In his tour of re-enchantments, Gellner
inexplicably has missed far the most important of all in the
twentieth century. There are surely reasons of sensibility for
this. That same Enlightenment optimism which made him
avert his gaze from the threat of nuclear war during his own
Belle Epoque, as 'not easily amenable to rational consideration',
has also probably stopped it before the Great War of the
original one: the founding episode of the century simply seems
'in retrospect sheer madness'.[55] Where Weber was so bewitched
by its spell he was never able to theorise nationalism, Gellner
has theorised nationalism without detecting the spell. What was
tragic fate for the one becomes prosaic function for the other.
Here the difference between idealist and utilitarian backgrounds tells.

But if Gellner's view of nationalism focuses so calmly – at
times blithely – on cause at the expense of meaning, it does so
consistently with the structure of his sociology as a whole. For as
we have seen, the serious business of *Sinnstiftung* has already
been taken care of, in the scientific provision of affluence.

Nationalism is a means to the values of abundance, not a
value-force in its own right. There is a political pre-judgement
behind this. Gellner's liberalism has been resistant to any
crossing of the division between public and private spheres –
critical of all hopes of a more expressive community than we
now have, in which individuals would find a larger share of
their identity in collective life. That for him, it would seem, is

dangerous romanticism.[56] The public realm is instrumental, for the management of prosperity – the more marginal its meanings (he takes monarchy as an ideal) the better. Private life, where the fruits of ease are to be enjoyed, is the proper sphere of self-expression.

It would look as if with this, Gellner's universe has – at any rate potentially – solved all its major problems, save those mishandled by psychoanalysis. But there is a serpent in the garden. Science may unexpectedly have brought peace among Weber's warring gods – by installing Pluto as unchallengeable master over them. But what if its progress should move on from triumphant transformation of the world to that of the self?[57] The rickety fit of the ghost in the machine, noticeable at the epistemological start of Gellner's enterprise, returns as a sociobiological shiver at its end. Perhaps genetic engineering might one day cancel the illusions of the empiricist ego, leaving only mechanist laws for its manipulation. Loss of meaning affected the objective world, and proved curable – or tolerable – with the *de facto* appearance of subjective consensus about the one major meaning after all. Loss of self could attack the stability of subjective agreement about anything – prosperity, liberty, knowledge – at all. In these moments, it is as if Gellner is caught wondering whether Weber did not under- rather than over-estimate the long-term problems of science for public and private life alike.

## NOTES

1. M. Weber, *Wirtschaft und Gesellschaft*, Tübingen, 1972, p. 344; *Economy and Society*, Berkeley and Los Angeles, 1978, p. 569. Henceforth WG and ES.
2. M. Weber, 'Politik als Beruf', *Gesammelte Politische Schriften*, Tübingen, 1971, pp. 513–515; H. H. Gerth and C. Wright Mills (eds), *From Max Weber*, New York, 1958, pp. 84–86. Henceforth GPS and FMW.
3. GPS, p. 508; FMW, p. 79.
4. GPS, p. 544; FMW, p. 113, which renders this as 'professional politicians without a calling'.
5. 'Wissenschaft als Beruf', *Gesammelte Aufsätze zur Wissenschaftslehre*, Tübingen, 1992, pp. 550, 549 – henceforth GAW; FMW, pp. 152, 150.
6. Letter to the Chairman of the German Democratic Party,

explaining his withdrawal from it, of April 1920; Wolfgang Mommsen, *Max Weber und die deutsche Politik*, Tübingen, 1974, p. 334 – English translation *Max Weber and German Politics*, Chicago, 1984, p. 310, rendered as 'I am a scholar by profession' – henceforth MWDP and MWGP; letter to Marianne Schnitzger of 1893; Marianne Weber, *Max Weber – ein Lebensbild*, Tübingen, 1926, p. 197 – English translation *Max Weber – A Biography*, New York, 1975, p. 185, rendered as 'I have never had any respect for the concept of a "vocation"' – henceforth MWL and MWB.

7. GPS, p. 560; FMW, p. 128 – which gives; 'Will you be bitter or banausic? Will you dully accept world and occupation?'.

8. GPS, pp. 311; 189, 217–218; 249; GW, p. 314.

9. GPS, pp. 521, 550; FMW, pp. 91–92, 119.

10. 'Der Sozialismus', *Gesammelte Aufsätze zur Soziologie und Sozialpolitik*, Tübingen, 1924, pp. 513–515 – henceforth GASS.

11. GPS, pp. 545–546; FMW, p. 115.

12. GAW, p. 554; FMW, p. 155.

13. GAW, pp. 550–551; FMW, p. 152.

14. *Gesammelte Aufsätze zur Religionssoziologie*, Tübingen, 1934, p. 204; *The Protestant Ethic and the Spirit of Capitalism*, New York, 1958, p. 182 – henceforth GAR and PE.

15. WG, p. 576; ES, p. 987.

16. MWL, p. 197; MWB, p. 185.

17. GAW, p. 550; FMW, p. 152.

18. GPS, p. 558; FMW, p. 127; GAW, pp. 550–551; FMW, p. 152.

19. GAW, p. 550; FMW, pp. 151–152; GPS, p. 553, FMW, 122.

20. GPS, pp. 547–548; FMW, p. 117.

21. GAW, pp. 530–532; FMW, pp. 135–136.

22. 'Jene starke Bändigung der Seele': GPS, pp. 545–546; FMW, p. 115.

23. GPS, p. 559; FMW, p. 127.

24. GAW, p. 543; FMW, p. 145.

25. GAW, pp. 553–554; FMW, pp. 15–155.

26. GAW, p. 547; FMW, p. 149.

27. GPS, p. 554; FMW, p. 123.

28. 'Zwischenbetrachtung', GAR, p. 570; FMW, pp. 356–357.

29. 'Der Nationalstaat und die Volkswittschaftspolitik', GPS, pp. 14, 25.

30. 'Gross und wunderbar' – he repeated the phrase like a refrain: MWL, pp. 527, 530, 536; MWB, pp. 519, 521–522, 528.

31. 'Deutschland unter den europäischen Weltmachen', GPS, pp. 170, 176; 'Parlament und Regierung im neugeordneten Deutschland', GPS, p. 442.

32. GPS, pp. 143, 177.

33. GPS, pp. 144–145.

34. GPS, p. 145.

35. WG, p. 530; ES, pp. 915–916.
36. At the end of it all, Weber could still speak of the war in the language of the gaming-table, applauding Ludendorff as a *wahnwitziger Hasardeur*. Only 'old women' could ask who was responsible for massacre and defeat, for it was 'the structure of society that produced the war': MWDP, p. 317; GPS, p. 549; FMW, p. 118.
37. GAR, p. 548; FMW, p. 335.
38. E. Gellner, *Legitimation of Belief*, Cambridge, 1974, p. 30.
39. E. Gellner, *Cause and Meaning in the Social Sciences*, London, 1973, pp. 71–72.
40. Thanks to science, 'for the great majority of mankind, current politics is a transition from the certainty of poverty, short life, insecurity and brutality, and the strong likelihood of tyranny, to a condition containing the near-certainty of affluence and at least a reasonable possibility of security and liberty'; so that whereas moralising in the past was a rather sterile exercise, 'today the situation is different. A fairly modest 'annual rate of growth', sustained over time, can do more to alleviate human misery than all the compassion and abnegation that past ages could muster': E. Gellner, *Thought and Change*, London, 1964, pp. 46, 219.
41. See E. Gellner, *Spectacles and Predicaments*, London, 1979, pp. 234–237, 253–254.
42. Gellner's term for the era 1945–1973: *Culture, Politics and Identity*, Cambridge, 1987, p. 111.
43. Gellner's earliest statement of this idea is perhaps to be found in *Cause and Meaning in the Social Sciences*, pp. 132–133; the formal treatment of it is in *Spectacles and Predicaments*, pp. 152–165; its most coruscating application is the essay on ethnomethodology: *Spectacles and Predicaments* pp. 41–64.
44. GAR, pp. 556–563; FMW, pp. 343–350; GAW, pp. 553–554; FMW, pp. 154–155.
45. E. Gellner, *Muslim Society*, Cambridge, 1981, pp. 4–5, 62; *Culture, Politics and Identity*, pp. 145, 148.
46. E. Gellner, *The Psychoanalytic Movement*, London, 1985, pp. 99–107.
47. MWL, pp. 379–380; MWB, p. 376.
48. E. Gellner, *Contemporary Thought and Politics*, London, 1973, pp. 29–39.
49. *Contemporary Thought and Politics*, p. 172; *Thought and Change*, p. 119.
50. *Contemporary Thought and Politics*, pp. 8–19, 84–85.
51. *Spectacles and Predicaments*, pp. 39, 280; *Culture, Politics and Identity*, pp. 111, 123.
52. E. Gellner, *Nations and Nationalism*, Oxford, 1983, p. 139.
53. *Nations and Nationalism*, p. 140.

54. *Cause and Meaning in the Social Sciences*, p. 127.
55. *Culture, Politics and Identity*, pp. 113, 11.
56. *Spectacles and Predicaments*, pp. 38–40.
57. E. Gellner, *Plough, Book and Sword*, London, 1988, pp. 267–268.

CHAPTER 9

# Deconstructing post-modernism: Gellner and Crocodile Dundee

Joseph Agassi

ABSTRACT AND INTRODUCTION

This essay is an attempt to dispense with the negative aspects of Romanticism and examine whatever positive it has to offer – in the light of ideas scattered through diverse writings of Ernest Gellner.

A paragraph on the negative side of Romanticism, however, is in order, since Romanticism is negative at base: it developed in understandable disillusionment over the excessively optimistic claims of the Enlightenment after the fiasco of the French Revolution and its aftermath. Its discontent was wider than the Enlightenment, however: it was a discontent with civilisation as such, as was argued by Sigmund Freud in *Civilization and its Discontents*. The discontent, Freud suggested, was understandable: civilisation is repressive: we inculcate in our charges a disastrous distaste for food and for sex. There is no dissent from Freud on this; it is obviously in our tradition to create in our charges distaste for the appetites we share with other animals; thus the continuing appeal of these appetites creates 'animalism,' the desire to emulate other animals all the way, expressed, for example in the writings of Count Gobineau and of D.H. Lawrence. This negativism, understandable as it is (and Lawrence's autobiographical *Sons and Lovers* makes it hard not to sympathise with it), has no saving grace. Yet Romanticism also has something positive to offer: a search for integration, meaning, de-alienation. Can the positive ideas of Romanticism possibly be detached from the negative? Post-modernism is an attempt to answer this affirmatively and in detail. The question deserves a better treatment.

The Modern Vision was the vision of the Enlightenment Movement of the Age of Reason. It was a vision of a peaceful world governed by scientifically-oriented sweet reasonableness. The Romantic Movement gained its popularity more through its criticism of the Enlightenment Movement than through its positive substitute for it. The Romantic Movement presented the Enlightenment as alienating, as contributing to the alienation and tedium which are characteristic of the modern world.

Still, the Romantic Movement did attempt to offer an alternative to the Modern Vision, or at least a semblance of one: the Romantic Vision. This was a vision of integrated communal life, governed by tradition and by meaningful traditional values, yet decidedly not opposed to progress. It is hard, if not impossible, to hold a consistent, workable model of a society run by a mixture of tradition and progress. Critics of the Romantic Movement rightly noted that traditionalism forced the Romantic Movement into the Reactionary mould: its progressivism was a ruse. Even its nationalism, its advocacy of national autonomy, was a ruse for its Reactionary hostility to individual autonomy: it supported the national right to self-determination as a substitute for the individual right to self-determination (which the Enlightenment Movement supported and the Reaction rejected).

The mixture that Romanticism offered, of tradition and progress, was naturally fascinating; it offered a reasonable challenge to generations of Reactionary sociology and anthropology, including Durkheim and Töennies. The Post-modern Vision thus slowly evolved into its present state. It is cheap, but it cannot easily be dismissed. Perhaps it can best be symbolised by *Crocodile Dundee*, a popular mythological hero: unlike the Modernist Superman, Batman and their likes, who are firmly rooted in science fiction and 'the American way', Dundee is both modern and primitive (Australian bush style) and, of course, he incorporates the virtues of both the Modern and the Romantic visions in a fashion as vulgar as the public can tolerate: he is a true Post-modern.

The fantastic character of popular mythology stems from its admitting the impossible or the barely possible as facts; the post-modern mythology offers as fact the suggestion that the Enlightenment and Romanticism can be fused to yield a blend of the best of each. To deconstruct a myth, then, may be the proper way to examine its ingredients for their quality while suspending judgement on the possibility of realisation. Crocodile Dundee is perhaps the best mythical expression of the Post-modern Vision; as such he is a comic-strip version of what Gellner presents as the new Promethean Vision.

Gellner offers a way of dismantling the various characteristics of modern industrial society which our predecessors have accepted and which we have inherited from them, in order to see if we cannot reconstitute it differently. The contrast between the superficiality and vulgarity of the Dundee myth and the depth and breadth of Gellner's works should not blind us to their shared vision. It may be the best we have, anyway. This is my plea for discussing the very possibility of its realisation.

## THE ROMANTIC AND THE POST-MODERN VISIONS OF INTEGRATION

Perhaps the most famous criticism of the Modern Vision of society in which classical social science is embedded is this: the vision is atomistic; thus, naturally, pursuing it leads to a society of disjointed individuals. This criticism is valid. Atomos and individuum are etymologically synonyms, after all, the latter term being the former Greek term Latinised. And the Enlightenment's individualism was thoroughly reductionist: all social phenomena, it taught, should be analysed in terms of individuals and their non-human environments. The Romantics had no theory beyond the claim that rootless individuals are alienated, that is, they have lost direction; unless they are endowed with characteristics of both heroes and geniuses and are engaged in the growing of new roots for some future societies, they are lost for good. The scantiness of this idea led to the proposal to neglect social studies, especially economics and rational political theory, not to mention cognitive psychology, and to concentrate instead on historical studies, especially of one's roots, namely folklore and such. This suggestion bloomed into a vision of a golden age of the integrated communities of our forefathers. This vision was first taken as frankly mythical, yet it has become a more realistic and informative part of an overall image which is provided to us by social anthropology. The myth of the golden age became the empirical scientific study of pre-literate society; pre-literate society, with all of its severe shortcomings and limitations and defects and even ugliness, with all of its undesirable aspects, has one enormous superiority over the modern world. It is a unified community: one cannot separate the religion of pre-literate society from its art, technology, or daily life; they are all one. Industrial society, in contradistinction, is atomised; its diverse aspects are as fragmented or compartmentalised as possible by a strict division of labour that has replaced the integrated happy farmer and artisan with the self-alienated conveyor-belt worker.

This image is one which was first offered philosophically, not empirically; only after its philosophical variant, the Romantic Vision, was thoroughly discredited (see below) was it rendered empirical, enabling it to have a come-back, without suffering summary dismissal, as the Post-modern Vision. In both variants, Romanticism and Post-modernism, it was opposed to the Modern Vision of the Enlightenment Movement. The most recent example cited in Gellner's writings is a quotation from Marshal Sahlins, wherein the classical philosophical, perhaps even moralistic, criticism of the Economic Man of the Enlightenment Movement as selfish, self-centred, lost and self-alienated, is replaced with the image of the hunter and gatherer as the Uneconomic Man; want not, lack not. It follows from the empirical descriptions on which Sahlins relies, Gellner observes, that the agricultural revolution, viewed traditionally as a great boon, 'was a catastrophe, both moral and material, not a glorious achievement' (*Plough, Sword and Book*, p. 32).

Gellner himself is a supporter of progress, but he comes to examine its cost, and the possibility of cancelling ancient debts so as to be able to retrieve some old lost property. There is no doubt that Gellner has no patience for the campy anthropologists who pretend that magic is equal to science in descriptive and technological power. Nor does he consider the relativist claim that the truth is divided, that our truth may equal theirs: to the contrary, we live in one world, is his slogan. Nevertheless, he tries to exonerate magic. Though science in his view caused 'the great divide' between the advanced and the less advanced parts of the one world, there is value to the magic that was lost with the advent of literacy and more so with the rise of science: magic-systems are vague, 'non-referential' (not endorsing the ideal of clear reference of words and clear truth-value of statements and refutability of even grand theories), and this way they manage to permit their followers a higher degree of integration than is to be found in the modern scientific-industrial society. 'What on earth, literally,' he asks (*Plough, Sword and Book*, p. 78), 'could ever induce or enable the various tentacles to cut themselves off from the non-referential main body?' His answer to this question makes his philosophy new. The chief target of his criticism is the Modern Vision, even that vision updated. Those to whom he sounds Romantic, however, do not hear his intended message: limited in their choice of options they fail to entertain, or even to comprehend, his proposal to consider the cost of atomisation and the cost of moving forward, not backward.

The Romantic Vision came first as a philosophical vision because it was a backward gaze, and so a fake one, not given to empirical examination, if only because it was openly anti-scientific; hence it was not given to empirical support. In the present age, when science is highly prestigious, it is a handicap to be anti-scientific. This handicap was removed only very recently: the peak of the Post-modern Vision, of the empirical variant of the Romantic Vision, is the recent work of Paul K. Feyerabend (*Philosophy of the Social Sciences*, 1988), in which Western science is viewed as a tradition and is placed within a set of systems of knowledge so-called, all traditional. The scientific tradition is not always the most advantageous, Feyerabend observes. Also, it is supremacist and even imperialistic and thus highly objectionable: it ruthlessly destroys other systems of knowledge (especially the pre-literate, magically oriented ones, those better conforming to the Romantic Vision).

These, then, are the philosophical Romantic Vision and the (pseudo-) empirical Post-modern Vision. The enormous cost of our having entertained its philosophical variant in the recent past is the topic of the next paragraph; the cost of continuing to entertain it will be discussed in the rest of the next section.

### THE ROMANTIC AND THE POST-MODERN VISION

Humanity has paid dearly for the Romantic Vision, for the Romantic quest for integration: in the period between the Reaction to the French Revolution (1814) and the end of World War II (1945), in the period which may be called the Romantic Era, the quest for integration was the main feature of the Romantic populist ideology; it played almost the same role in all Reactionary politics, official, semi-official, unofficial and academic, and culminating with Fascist and Nazi politics. The exceptional variant was, of course, official Soviet politics which, though populist and Reactionary, had a veneer of progressive ideology. An episode in Soviet history, known as Zhadanov-schina (after the name of its official advocate André Zhadanov), epitomised this populism, which deviated from the Romantic Vision in its placing of the golden age not in the (primitive) past but in the (technologically advanced) future. Yet, like all other Reactionary lands, Soviet Russia, too, made use of chauvinist and other supremacist theories, and they all did so on the ground that these were at the time scientifically respectable. (This is an argument in favour of Feyerabend's criticism of science; he does not use it, however, preferring to speak of Europe's recent past only elliptically.) So much for the incalculable damage caused by the populist adherence to the Romantic Vision, to the quest for integrated society.

All this evil is past history: the Post-modern Vision, the new variant of the Romantic Vision, is certainly not European supremacist: it is routinely understood as a criticism of supremacism and of any other form of parochialism (see I. C. Jarvie, *The Revolution in Anthropology*, and Gellner's preface there). It has been accused of Reactionary tendencies, but if this is so, then it is a new kind of Reaction: those social anthropologists who write scientific progress-reports and make documentary films extolling pre-literate tribes in accord with the Romantic Vision present propaganda, but not as political activity. Therefore, the Post-modern Vision is treated these days as a respectable doctrine, though as a mere idle dream, just because it is a nice dream – nice in that it is friendly to pre-literate people and so not imperialistic nor racist nor whatever else is associated with supremacist Reactionary politics. Taking it for granted that the Post-modern Vision is benign, lending it respectability has its cost; the cost may be assessed and possibly reduced.

The cost of taking the Romantic Vision and its diverse variants, including the Post-modern Vision, to be respectable is a broad topic. The cost of the very indulgence towards the Post-modern Vision as an idle dream is easier to assess, at least in part: taking it as a respectable but idle dream precludes the discussion of the possibility that the dream is not utterly impracticable, that at least to some extent it is practicable under certain circumstances. Of course, it may nevertheless be judged undesirable, at least as a plan to execute only in part and at a great cost. Nevertheless, is it advisable to take seriously the question, is the Post-modern Vision desirable or not? This question is shelved too, and for the same reason: the vision is treated as unserious: it is even resented when viewed as more than a mere fantasy whose whole function is strictly to insure some anti-racist anti-colonialist sentiment, as well as some entertainment in the form of idle romances not in conflict with the Western way of life (*Crocodile Dundee*).

What is the source of this hostility to taking the Post-modern Vision as an inspiration for action? Why is it so obviously unthinkable that we should live in a modern, highly technological, democratic, civilised society and yet have a high level of integration of our different functions? Are we so convinced that the modern world must be atomised or regress? Is it attested that toying with magic systems in a high-brow fashion is dangerous? Why do we insist on the separation of different functions even when it is already demonstrably possible to merge or integrate some of them? For, no doubt, it has been shown that learning, play and work need not be as separated as they traditionally are in our society, that we can integrate them – not ever fully, but to a large extent – in a manner more characteristic of magically-oriented societies, yet beneficially so by our own standards.

## TAKING INTEGRATION SERIOUSLY

Taking integration seriously means, at the very least, doing so responsibly – without populism and irrationality. Here comes a thesis that has created much controversy, and I wish to dodge a part of the controversy. Karl Popper noted that one obvious way to avoid responsibility is to go for the jackpot or for nothing. Speaking of social and political engineering (the terminology is that of John Dewey), he distinguished between a total or utopian engineering and a partial or piecemeal one; and he recommended the latter, as the former is irresponsible (*The Open Society and Its Enemies, passim*). Since he did not mean by piecemeal small-scale, and since today some total, non-utopian plans to save our planet are urgently required, it is better to avoid distraction into the controversy about how irresponsible utopian engineering in general is; suffice it if it is admitted that Popper has scored against the irresponsible revolutionaries who advocate revolutions even if these are avoidable. It would then be also admitted that it is irresponsible to recommend going after integration only and always through the barricades. Even if one admits that there is little chance to go to the barricades just now, it is irresponsible to insist on the choice between the barricades and inaction.

The discussion here is not an attempt to defend any specific concrete program for partial integration. There are such programs, and some of them were mentioned earlier, especially the partial integration of study and play or study and work (not to exclude the partial integration of work and play). The point mentioned here is advisably general: there is a traditional hostility to the mixture of work and play (in the name of discipline), for example, and there is a traditional proposal that atomising society is for the good, that excessive division of labour (Taylorism) is excellent for many reasons, and so on. Without going into detail, we may observe that, as in all matters, the truth may go hither and thither, and so there is an understandable hankering for integration that deserves study – for both theoretical and practical purposes. Even the hostility to integration as magically oriented deserves study. Let me then discuss magic, since many scientifically-oriented writers, such as Gellner, agree that integration is historically rooted in magic.

## BETWEEN RELIGION AND MAGIC

Why is magic integrated and religion not? The question deserves a better formulation since, evidently, we have integrated and atomised cases of both magic and religion. For magic is integrated in pre-literate societies and atomised in industrial societies in which it appears. (Jarvie and I have argued empirically that we know of no magic-free society;[1] Gellner is amused by our incomprehension of the view of a cucumber as an ox to be carved coupled with our acceptance with the wafer as the flesh of Christ to be cannibalised.) And religion is atomised in modern society because modern society is atomised (on which more soon), but it is highly integrated in the relatively pre-literate societies of Medieval Europe (as our Romantic historians keep reminding us) and to some extent even of contemporary, still pre-industrialised pockets of Europe. So the question is, why is industrial society so atomised, at least by comparison to pre-industrialised, especially pre-literate, societies in general? This takes us away from the fact that most pre-industrialised societies are primitive and that primitive societies are governed more by magic than by religion, where magic is viewed as a combination of magic rites with an animist–fetishist religion of sorts, and that magic is more prevalent in pre-industrial than in industrial societies.

This leads to the question, though, is there something in magic that makes it a good social glue? Is magic, because of its animism and fetishism, a specifically integrating characteristic of its society? Despite our rejection of Voodoo, may we approve of its integrative aspect and declare that its practitioners are more integrated under its influence than they are after they lose it? This question is seldom asked, because of the interference of the Post-modern Vision. This is but one example of the fact that this vision is less innocuous than it seems. Indeed, the benefits of research into questions that it blocks can scarcely be assessed; in my opinion the loss is great.

The question is, then, how does magic act as a social glue?

This question received an answer from anthropologists, especially from those under the influence of the British school. It is very clear, even though I do not think this fact has been noticed before sufficiently critically: their answer is, magic is more integrative than religion, because the former is much more directly related to the empirical world than the latter.

How, then, can magicians hold an obviously false view of the world and keep it integrated with their empirical experience?

This question has two traditional answers: The Bacon–Frazer answer and the Durkheim answer. Both require some background explanation, I am afraid. The Durkheim answer is easier to present: it is well within the sociology of knowledge, whereas the Bacon–Frazer is within the psychology of science.

BACON AND FRAZER ON MAGIC
AS PSEUDO-SCIENCE

The Bacon–Frazer answer is based on two classic discoveries of Sir Francis Bacon, the one that we refuse to accept empirical refutations of our preconceived notions, and the other that we constrain the meanings of terms we use in order to escape these refutations. Both of these discoveries are significant and they are rediscovered repeatedly and attributed to diverse thinkers, though they are clearly and forcefully stated in Bacon's immensely influential *Novum Organum* (1620).

Bacon lived in Elizabethan society, a society permeated with both magic and religion. He took it for granted that magic as he knew it, as well as religion as he knew it, were sets of dogmas, prejudices and superstitions. For he proposed that any hypothesis one entertains long enough becomes all three: a dogma, a superstition and a prejudice. He did think magic was possible, in the sense that many wondrous claims of magicians, to do with the transmutations of metals, with wonder cures and with longevity, are lies, but they can be approached scientifically and rendered successful. (He reported observations of magical cures.) As to religion, he did think that (since it is not science) of necessity it is dogmatic, and so he preferred its claims to be utterly non-factual.

In Bacon's view, in short, magic is pseudo-science. Bacon considered almost all extant intellectual activity spurious: university scholars are engaged in endless, ridiculous disputations. They did so because, he said, their views are refuted by empirical observations; and, quite generally, refuted errors are not rejected as they should be. This theory led him to suggest the varieties of ways in which apologetic thinkers argue. One of these is particularly sophisticated: the false theories undergo change: they have their scope narrowed so as to exclude the refuting instances as irrelevant to them; the narrowing of scope is done either by altering the intended scope explicitly, or, more often, covertly, by the narrowing of the meaning of the terms used to state them. (Karl Popper called this move the conventionalist twist and surreptitious change; Imre Lakatos called it monster-barring and concept-shrinking.)

Frazer, together with most thinkers accepted all this as a matter of course. Also, he took it for granted that religion is magic emptied of its contents. He therefore declared religion inferior to magic, as it is a step in the wrong direction the way Bacon described it: the retraction of meaning instead of the relinquishing of error. (The evolutionist aspect of this theory will explain why magic is ancient in origin, religion its newer replacement; this is highly seductive, until articulated, and then it becomes clear that this is just the Post-modern Vision: magic rites are extremely hardy and prevalent in all pre-industrial societies and in many industrial ones, whereas Christianity absorbed the animism–fetishism of pre-Christian Europe to a surprisingly large extent; ironically, this last point about the survival of animism–fetishist faith and of magic rites in Euro-pean Christendom is the very point extensively and excitingly illustrated in Frazer's *The Golden Bough*.)

The Bacon–Frazer theory, that refutation of the factual claims of religion empties it of its factual content, is extremely popular. Its latest growth is Gellner's elaboration of Russell's view of communism as a religion: Gellner proposes in *Thought and Change* that Marxism was emptied of all factual content as a result of clashes between theory and facts. This is a bit harder on Marxism than on Christianity, where the counsel, Render unto Caesar what is Caesar's is replaced by the Praxis Theory of the Unity of Theory and Practice. This is quite remarkable in view of the fact that the theory in question is a psychological view of magic and of religion, according to which both are mere matters of opinion, and inferior competitors to science at that. (Taking science as the body of true, demonstrated opinion, or even as merely the best opinion around, one cannot but see them as ousted by science and their adherents therefore as the rear-guard. Feyerabend's just complaint is rooted in this fact.)

The Bacon–Frazer theory of religion and magic has been ousted by a more sophisticated, positivist, institutional theory of magic and of religion, which is better, though also quite

inadequate (as shown in detail by both Gellner and Jarvie[2]) in
that it altogether ignores all doctrines as opinions. (This inadequacy indicates that Gellner is groping for a third theory that
includes elements from the two traditional ones: indeed, it calls
for a theory of institutionalised opinions proper, a theory I
have suggested an outline of in my *Towards a Rational Philosophical Anthropology*.)

## DURKHEIM ON RELIGION AND MAGIC

The most influential variant of the positivist theory is that of
Durkheim. Durkheim answered the question, how do religion
and magic act as social glue? His answer began with the
acceptance as a matter of course of the Baconian thesis that
taken literally religion either has no empirical content or it is
bunk: it is mere superstition and prejudice. The true meaning
of religion (magic included), then, is not literal but metaphorical: it is society extolling itself. (This theory of Durkheim is a
variant of what Friedrich Nietzsche warned against under the
title of 'secular religion'.) (All philosophers who sanctify ordinary language, and who have incurred the wrath of Russell,
Popper and Gellner, take this theory for granted when they
notice the prevalence of religious contentions in everyday
discourse.) Durkheim's disciples have admitted that his theory
has been most uncomfortably confirmed by the advent of
Fascism and Nazism (see Stephen Lukes's scholarly monograph, *Emile Durkheim*). Yet the critic of this doctrine has to take
account of the fact that in his wisdom Durkheim clearly stated
that religion is more integrative than magic. Admittedly, this
same fact is usually overlooked by Durkheim's disciples, and
with some justice: when he declared religion more integrative
than magic he was not reporting any empirical observation; he
was conveying a vision of a highly integrated society, as
described, say, at the end of his classic *The Division of Labour in
Society* and a faith in progress of sorts.

   Is there then at least a difference between degrees of
integration which magic and religion offer? Yes; and this
depends on the division of labour in society, since pre-literate
society is dominated by magic and has a coarse division of
labour. True or false, this is a move back to Durkheim all the

way: we do not know where to stop. And then we have swallowed Durkheim's view that religion is more integrative, whereas according to his positivist disciples magic is (so that possibly the Post-modern Vision is nowadays more a part of social anthropology and the loveliness of remote pre-literate tribes rather than a political theory and a Reactionary pretence of a return to our own lovely folkways). Moreover, Durkheim (and his collaborator Mauss) feared that we must include as social glue, not only magic and religion, but also science: is science too, they asked (the end of *Primitive Classification*), a mere matter of ritual? Hopefully not, they said.

Durkheim's followers among the anthropologists do not raise his question concerning the status of science. His followers among the sociologists, however, do. Some of them are true Romantics; they play anthropologists and say, 'Yes: science, too, is a (magic) ritual'. Some of these Romantics still endorse the claim of science to truth: it is both a ritual and a valid opinion. Others stick to the ritual: science has no exclusive right to be the true opinion; no more than magic. Of course, the former have an over-determination on their hands (that is, too many sufficient causes cooperating in harmony), the others have the success of industrial society to make science a particularly potent magic.

Be it so. Is industrial society better integrated than pre-literate society, though? Durkheim said, yes. The Post-modern Vision says, no. Assume that vision, and Durkheim is out. Elaborate on the argument in favour of that vision, and Durkheim slips in. We are stuck.

The confusion is very interesting, and was pointed out, as far as I know, only by Bertrand Russell, in his *Science and Society*: technologically primitive society has its household provide most of its necessities and so the individual is more integrated, whereas pre-literate society is more atomised in comparison to technological society since the latter enjoys a higher degree of division of labour and is therefore more integrated – at the expense of its members being less economically integrated. Moreover, we see here that economic dependence and moral dependence appear as opposites of sorts: members of pre-literate society have more of the one, members of civilised society have more of the other. Here, incidentally, Russell is making use of Georg Simmel's theory of the web of affiliation. His theory is also akin to Simmel's in that it neither reduces the individual to society nor society to the individual, since it views the integration of the standard individual as different from that of the society as a whole; it is thus systemic (ascribing to a system and to its members different characteristics).

## WHY IS INDUSTRIAL SOCIETY SO ATOMISED?

In which manner is industrial society less integrated than pre-literate society? This question is at the heart of the discussion and it is unavoidable; it is usually avoided due to the Post-modern Vision, which is fuzzy; and then the discussion on it, when at all attempted, becomes equally fuzzy. The answer that can be given the status of an observation report is that in modern industrial society activities are fragmented or compartmentalised, so that members of such a society, even if quite uneducated, can choose to be engaged now in work, play, study, prayer, magic, or name any other recognised sort of activity; whereas members of a pre-literate society can hardly do so or even notice the distinction between the different activities. And religious thinkers have always looked with awe at people who consider themselves engaged in the worship of God no matter what activity holds their attention in addition to that. Moreover, the fragmentation or compartmentalisation observed in any situation whatsoever is but a matter of degree, and its high degree is not a matter of industrialisation or civilisation but of the puritanical ethos that has traditionally gone with the industrial or modern ethos.

The early Romantic philosophers who put great value on the integration that was later observed in pre-literate society, take it for granted that individuals who live in a more integrated life-style are more at peace, more economically autonomous, belong to a more stable and integrated society, and so on: they are allegedly in a better position in all respects except science and technology. The distinction between culture and civilisation was introduced by somewhat Romantic writers in various ways, but always as a means to suggest that in matters of culture the uncivilised is superior to the civilised. This has made it difficult for these thinkers to say what exactly culture is; it made their writings difficult and so deep; in brief, they hoodwinked their readers.

This leads naturally to a group of questions about modern society, especially whether modern society is necessarily industrial, rather than technologically advanced, and whether it is necessarily, or at all, puritanical, rather than hedonistic. The classical answer is Marx's technological determinism, so-called: history had to progress, if at all, more or less according to the observed scheme; in particular, industrialisation is the only path to modernisation. It seems that an increasing number of thinkers now break increasingly further away from technological determinism and find it not difficult at all to imagine a society which is technologically advanced, yet not industrial in the sense in which Karl Marx or Alfred Marshall described the major traits of trade and industry (as large-scale production process utilising hired labor at the machine's controls and trading its products in relatively free markets). As to the question of puritanism, the situation is still controversial.

And so, the prime hypothesis for the atomisation or fragmentation or compartmentalisation of modern society is this: the cause of fragmentation is only indirectly industry or modernity: it came with the modern lifestyle in a package deal (Gellner, *Plough, Sword and Book*, p. 103), and the package can now be disentangled; we may then choose from the packet what we like, and we may declare, if we wish, that increased integration of one sort or another should play the role of a criterion of choice. But we may also use a different criterion, and even if we choose this criterion, the outcome is not uniquely determined thereby, at least not as long as we go for increased integration, not for total integration.

The package deal was a complex matter. Even on the question of integration and fragmentation it offered a complex alteration. As was mentioned already, the economic autonomy had to give way to moral autonomy. Moreover, as Gellner notices in *Nations and Nationalism*, ethical attitudes within integrated societies are always complex due to the very integration of the group: there were always multiple sets of rights and duties between two members; yet relations with strangers had to be highly simplified and each side of a transaction had to prove its reliability. Now this simplification had to destroy many kinds of loyalties, and, indeed, traditional society itself. Yet the crisis went deeper. The new attitude required deference both to traditional religion and to the facts of science, thereby imposing a separation between religion and science. It was the 'mixing' of religion and science that Sir Francis Bacon so vociferously blamed for so many of our ills. He thus viewed compartmentalisation as the cost of modernisation; and he was in error – at least if we are allowed to choose a religion that may very well go with science.

## DECONSTRUCTING THE PACKAGE DEAL OF INDUSTRIALISM

The package deal required an attitude of utter and complete personal autonomy which was then taken over by the early Romantic philosophers as the vision of the Hero: only a saint or a genius or an otherwise exceptional person can be truly autonomous in the sense of the philosophers of the scientific and industrial revolution. This led to reenchantment, to use the term of Max Weber and Ernest Gellner, and then the hedonists had to hide behind the theory of deferred gratification, or behind any other flimsy excuses for conventional conduct, in order to endorse harsh, puritanical modes of education and lifestyle, harsh 'capitalist' attitudes to workers as lazy, and so on.

The question will arise at once, how much can one separate the items in the package deal? Moreover, what will be the cost of giving up some items in it?

Here Gellner's philosophy comes as a straight answer. On the one hand, in his view science and technology are inseparable (not in the sense that we cannot imagine a society with science and yet without scientific technology; this has been proposed in Samuel Butler's *Erewhon*; rather they are inseparable in that Erewhonian society is not likely). On the other hand they are separated from almost every social institution, especially those belonging to alternative ways of life, more sophisticated or less so: there is a Great Divide between science and all else. Moreover, thought and change are interwoven. In particular, 'the growth of knowledge forces a "trans-valuation of values" whether we like it or not' (Gellner, *Thought and Change*, p. 217).

It is this transition which he deems essential, the crossing of the Great Divide, from the traditional (pre-literate or literate) ways of life and values to modern, science-and-technology-based ones.

We still face the question raised here: what do we have to give up in order to overcome the Small Divide between integrated and atomised or fragmented or compartmentalised society? What can be done in order to render our societies increasingly integrated, though not necessarily in the same manner everywhere?

The first answer is autonomy: we have to educate the citizen to be able to choose and to exercise choice freely. The great modern division between philosophers, social thinkers, authors, political leaders and so on, is that between those who advocate autonomy and those who oppose it. All else is secondary. Customarily, the advocates of autonomy see autonomy as natural and as easy, and their opponents oppose autonomy on the ground that it is an impossible burden. One of the great insights of Karl Popper's *The Open Society and Its Enemies* is that attitudes for and against autonomy signify more than assessment of the ease or difficulty of its implementation: the valuation of autonomy as an important asset will bring about the search for ways to implement it with as much ease as possible. The ones who oppose such experiments are the ones who value social stability over against autonomy.

If so, and if social stability is deemed less important than tradition everywhere claims, then the future of religion is wide open, and so is the future of any factor, integrative or atomising. The choice as to how integrated our society should be, then, is not the choice between civilisation and culture, but of the way we prepare our package deal. We may therefore institute a variety of experiments in devising social glues of diverse sorts. We may then find that the main question is, do we really need social stability, and if not, do we really want it and at what price?

It is the question of price that makes the difference between the responsible and the irresponsible programme – or between the programme and the enjoyable harmless myth. Myths are at least indicative of what we would like to have were the price right. This explains the success of some cardboard popular heroes as compared with others. And on the basis of this contention we may bring the latest popular cardboard hero, Crocodile Dundee, as a witness testifying to our deep wishes. Though there are only two movies about him, it is clear what has caught the fancy of vast crowds on many continents. Crocodile Dundee is a Westerner, not a Westerner like you and me, but like any Western hero. He also is at home in the Australian bush. He does not move in the bush like a hero in an ordeal: Western mythology, including many myths that have been created for the silver screen, are full of ordeals in primitive terrain of all sorts. Dundee is different. The bush is his home – his second home, no doubt, but that matters little. He has friends in the bush, who are at home in the civilised world: it is their second home. There is no hint that primitive culture and magic are exempt from criticism, and they are certainly not presented in a relativist fashion as equal to Western science. But the image is suggested that there are valuable and reprehensible aspects to each society, that one can move freely from one to another with a little human under-standing, that a sense of proportion does a lot to bridge gaps. More one cannot possibly ascribe even to serious movies, let alone to trash. And trash these movies certainly are, as there is not even a glance at the problems raised in these movies. They are mere pastime, they entertain. They could not be found that entertaining were they not able to tickle our fancy the right way, even if only as a mild joke. The Post-modern vision may be vulgar, but it presents a strong yearning.

## NOTES

1. J. Agassi and I.C. Jarvie, eds., *Rationality, the critical view*, The Hague, 1988.
2. E. Gellner, *Cause and meaning in the social sciences*, London, 1973, ch. 6; I.C. Jarvie, *The revolution in anthropology*, London, 1964.

# CHAPTER 10

# A methodology without presuppositions?[1]

## John Watkins

Re-reading some of Ernest Gellner's pieces of thirty or more years ago has been giving me a double enjoyment; it has been a little like seeing a Buster Keaton film one hadn't seen for years: as well as enjoying it afresh, one also enjoys the re-awakening and filling in of one's memories of it. This nostalgia-factor was particularly strong with 'On being wrong',[2] a piece which I heard Gellner give as a radio talk on the Third Programme in about 1954. I had retained an audible memory of him suggesting that some kind of theological doctrine was invented to deprive the Devil of an unfair advantage, but I had forgotten what the doctrine was, though I remembered very well what the Devil's unfair advantage was. The theme of the piece was an asymmetry that crops up in various contexts, conferring an advantage on the bad opposite of something good, given mankind's preference for certainty and finality over precarious uncertainty. Consider life and death. Life, with its ever-present possibility that today will be your last, is essentially precarious, whereas with death one attains a stable and perfectly unprecarious state. 'Death', I remembered Gellner saying, paying Ryle a back-handed compliment, 'is an achievement word' (p. 47). And he cited a story by Gorki about a peasant whose longing for finality incited him to multiple murder. (I don't know whether the man could have been dissuaded from his murderous course by being told that according to some well-known metaphysical views there need be nothing final about death. Thus classical atomism implies that it is in principle possible to restore a dead man to life by collecting the atoms that constituted his body at a time when he was alive and arranging them just as they were then. That nothing is absolutely dead was also an implication of Leibniz's monadology; he claimed that

various phenomena, such as hibernation, support it empirically. For Leibniz, 'death' is not an achievement word; rather, to
be dead is to be more or less permanently indisposed.)

Gellner found another example of the above asymmetry in
Karl Popper's philosophy of science, according to which an as
yet unfalsified scientific hypothesis is in ever-present danger of
losing this status, but a falsified one can never lose *that* status. (It
is here being assumed that no previously accepted basic or
observation statement will later be rejected.) Gellner likened
this to a woman's virtue, which is always in danger of being lost,
but once lost is in no danger of being regained. And here comes
the bit of theology whose precise content had escaped me:
'Theological doctrines concerning the ever-present possibility
of Grace are perhaps cunning attempts to deprive the devil of
his advantage, by making sin infinitely corrigible also, and
hence equally precarious' (p. 50). I am not entirely confident
that such a doctrine ever was formulated by a card-carrying
theologian; I was under the impression that theologians either
regarded grace as earned, say by devotion and good works, or
else, if they regarded it as unearned, as a matter of predestination. Perhaps Gellner was giving theology a nudge.

But rather than make this a topic for the present occasion,
and rather than revive the debate on methodological individualism in which we were both involved, on opposite sides, a
good many years ago, I prefer to concentrate upon a serious
problem about the status of any proposed methodology for
science which Gellner raised in his 'An Ethic of Cognition'.[3] He
presented it as follows. A (non-empty) methodology is more
than mere logic; it has a substantive content:

> But if it asserts, or presupposes, something over and above the formal
> requirements of logic, will not that *something else*, whatever it may be,
> have some implications concerning *the world*? And if so, can one not
> imagine or construct a possible world within which those implications
> are false, and within which consequently [its] recommendations are
> misguided? And if such a world is conceivable, obviously we cannot
> say, in advance of all inquiry, that such a world is not the *real* world.
> What use is a methodology that prejudges the nature of the world we
> are in . . . before we have any right to an opinion about it.[4]

Gellner's own response to this challenge was to grasp the nettle:
'Yes, method is more than logic; consequently it does indeed

prejudge some results of inquiry prior to the very start of the inquiry, eliminating certain possibilities, excluding certain imaginable worlds; *and rightly so*' (p. 162, his italics). He claimed that since empiricism asserts the sovereignty of experience, it must rule out a priori any theory that seeks to elude the check of experience; more specifically, it rules out what he called 'Ideologist's Worlds'. As I understand it, a theory that depicts an Ideologist's World endows believers in it with various cognitive and other privileges, enabling them to feel at home in this 'world', and has built-in methods for disarming criticism and discrediting opposition to itself.

As I see it, a methodology for science has a twofold task: first, to lay down necessary conditions for a propositional entity to be a candidate for being the best scientific hypothesis in its field; and then to lay down sufficient conditions, given the evidence and any other relevant information, for being the best scientific hypothesis in its field at the present time. For example, Popper's methodology performed the first task by means of its demarcation criterion, and the second by means of its theory of corroboration: to be a candidate it has got to be a testable (corroborable) hypothesis, and to be a winner it has got to be better corroborated than its competitors.

Now I am quite ready to fall in with Gellner's claim that the kind of empiricist methodology that he had in mind *rightly* excludes Ideologist's Worlds a priori; but as depicted by him it discharges only the first of the above two tasks. There remains the possibility that, were such a methodology strengthened sufficiently to fulfil the second task, it would exclude worlds other than Ideologist's ones, worlds that ought not to be excluded a priori.

But is it true, as Gellner assumed, that all (non-empty) methodologies have factual presuppositions, whether of a legitimate or illegitimate kind? Well, there surely are *unsatisfactory* ones that do not. There are two main ways in which a methodology may be unsatisfactory: it may be ineffective, failing to effect selections among the contenders in the field; or it may effect wrongful selections. The injunction 'Accept a proposition if and only if it is true' does not, so far as I can see, involve any factual assumptions about the world, but it is ineffective; nor, so far as I can see, does Descartes's first rule of

method, namely to accept no proposition that was not 'presented to my mind so clearly and distinctly that I could have no
occasion to doubt it'.[5] This rule is not ineffective, but as a
methodological rule for empirical science it is unsatisfactory,
since apart from the *Cogito* what it would select is only tautolo-
gies and certain autopsychological present-tense reports.

So the question becomes: is it true that a satisfactory methodology for science is bound to have factual presuppositions?
Let us mean by *rationality–scepticism* the thesis that there is never
any good cognitive reason to prefer one (unrefuted) scientific
hypothesis to its (unrefuted) rivals. Then one thing that a
satisfactory methodology must do is to dispel rationality–
scepticism: it must sponsor rational choices between competing
scientific hypotheses. But how is it to do this? Well, rational
choices are possible only in the light of an aim; so a satisfactory
methodology will have to be linked to an aim for science. But
now the question arises whether the choice of such an aim
could be rational. Popper once said that such a choice 'must, of
course, be ultimately a matter of decision, going beyond
rational argument'.[6] That seems to open up the possibility that
the republic of science might split into warring tribes, each
adhering to its own peculiar aim. Rationality–scepticism would
not have been defeated if it were 'rational' for one tribe to
prefer theory $T_1$ to theory $T_2$, given their aim, and equally
'rational' for another tribe to prefer $T_2$ to $T_1$, given their
different aim.

But wasn't Popper right? How could the choice of an aim for
science be controlled by rational argument? Well, I argue in
*Science and Scepticism* (henceforth *S & S*)[7] that, given certain
rather obvious adequacy requirements (for example that the
aim should be coherent, and feasible), there is one quite
definite aim that constitutes *the optimum aim* for science: of the
aims permitted by the adequacy requirements, this one
includes everything contained in them and is the highest, or
most ambitious, of them. To aim higher would be to run foul of
one or more of the adequacy requirements (for example it
would be incoherent, or unfeasible), as would aiming in a
different direction; while to aim lower would be to forgo some
legitimate aspiration.

Assume for the sake of the present discussion that my claims in *S & S* concerning the optimum aim are in order. What is its content? What, for a start, does it say about truth? It says that science should aim at theories that are, not certainly or even probably true, but only *possibly true* in the sense that, despite their best endeavours, scientists have not succeeded in discovering them to be false.

In addition to this demand, the aim for science defended in *S & S* calls for theories that are increasingly *deep, unified, and predictively powerful.* A long chapter was given over to an attempt to make this aim reasonably precise by providing comparative measures for depth, unity, and predictive power (or testable content). It turned out that the demands for increasing depth and increasing unity are really demanding essentially the same thing. Thus the aim simplifies to the requirement that for a new theory to be an advance, it should be possibly true and both deeper and wider than its predecessor(s) (where 'wider' means having more explanatory-cum-predictive power).

I partition the premises of a more or less deep scientific theory $T$ into its theoretical core $T_H$ (in which only theoretical predicates occur) and its auxiliary assumptions $A$ (in which observational predicates occur). $T_H$ on its own will not have any testable content, while $A$ on its own may; but when married together, their testable content should far exceed any that $A$ alone may have. That is what I call organic fertility. I take the *corroborable content* of $T$ to be the testable content of the conjunction of $T_H$ and $A$ minus any testable content of $A$ on its own; in other words, that part of the theory's testable content in which its theoretical core is implicated. A theory gains a corroboration only from a favourable outcome of a test on its corroborable content. I say that theory $T_2$ is better corroborated than theory $T_1$ if no result of an experimental test favours $T_1$ over $T_2$, while at least one favours $T_2$ over $T_1$. (A result favours $T_2$ over $T_1$ if either (i) it refutes $T_1$ without refuting $T_2$ or (ii) it corroborates $T_2$ without corroborating $T_1$.) And it turns out, given a realistic assumption concerning what kinds of tests have actually been carried out, that if $T_2$ is better corroborated than $T_1$, then $T_2$ will indeed be deeper and wider than $T_1$. (I allow that there is sometimes no one best corroborated theory, the scientific situation being messy, but I deny that scientific situations always are messy.)

So the methodological rule, 'Of competing scientific theories, prefer the one that is best corroborated', gains a new justification. My answer to a challenge raised by many critics of the Popperian school – namely, why should we anti-inductivists regard the best *corroborated* theory as the *best* theory? – is that the best corroborated theory is, at the present time, the one in its field that best fulfils the optimum aim for science.

So for me the present question becomes: does Gellner's point hit this methodology? And for me this is a rather ominous question. Not all philosophers of science need be too squeamish about allowing a little factual content into their methodology; does it really matter so much, they might reply to Gellner, that one's methodology makes a few uncontroversial assumptions about the world? But I cannot take that line. If factual presuppositions are smuggled in by my methodology, then I have not, after all, succeeded in doing what I tried to do in *S & S*, namely to uphold the rationality of science within a non-inductivist and strictly deductivist framework and while endorsing Humean scepticism concerning induction. Humean scepticism could easily be defeated if it were permissible to slip in one or two factual postulates. (One that would do the trick nicely says that God constructed the world in such a way that the truth about it could be learnt by inductive procedures.) My claim to have purged Popperian philosophy of science of all traces of covert inductivism would obviously be hollow if it turned out that factual assumptions were covertly presupposed by the aim and method of science that I proposed. Forgive my understandable concern to look into this.

Let us say that a property of a theory is *extrinsic* or *intrinsic* according to whether the theory's possession of it does or does not depend on factors external to the theory. Thus for (non-analytic) theories, truth is an extrinsic whereas consistency is an intrinsic property. Some physicists and mathematicians are much concerned with the *elegance* or otherwise of theories; although I do not use this concept myself, it would presumably be an intrinsic property. This distinction can be extended from absolute 'either-or' properties, such as truth and consistency, to comparative 'more-or-less' properties, such as simplicity and verisimilitude. Suppose that we have a well-defined measure for simplicity (say, a 'paucity of parameters' measure à la

Harold Jeffreys). Then the claim that theory $T_2$ is simpler than theory $T_1$ points to an intrinsic difference: we can verify it by just a comparative examination of the two theories (say, by counting their adjustable parameters). Now suppose that we have a well-defined measure for verisimilitude, or truth-likeness. Then the claim that $T_2$ has more verisimilitude than $T_1$ points to an extrinsic difference: we cannot verify *it* by just a comparative examination of the two theories; we would need in addition to compare them with $T^*$, where the latter is either the whole truth or what Graham Oddie calls the *target theory* in their field[8] (roughly, a true theory that answers all the questions that $T_1$ and $T_2$ seek to answer). But normally we will not know what $T^*$ contains.

Extrinsic properties are open to a further distinction, drawn by Fred D'Agostino,[9] between those that are, and those that are not, *observable*. A property is said to be 'observable' if appropriate evidence would enable us to tell whether the theory has it, or has it to a higher degree than some rival theory. For example, D'Agostino holds (and I agree with him) that $T_2$'s being *better corroborated* than $T_1$ is an observable difference between them: it can be ascertained by examining the relation of the historical record of experimental tests to the corroborable contents (see above) of $T_1$ and $T_2$. A property might be said to be 'quasi-observable' if, although not itself observable, it is linked to one that is.

We may likewise distinguish, in the case of intrinsic properties, between ones that are, and ones that are not, determinable. For instance, simplicity as defined by a 'paucity of parameters' measure, is determinable, whereas elegance might be a matter of taste.

A methodology that is to be effective will have to base its appraisals of theories on properties each of which is either intrinsic and determinable or else extrinsic and observable (to which a quasi-observable one might be linked). A methodology that sought to appraise competing theories solely in terms of intrinsic properties would be unsatisfactory, since the question of their truth or falsity would have dropped out. One of the adequacy-requirements in *S & S* for a proposed aim for science is that the aim involves the idea of truth in some way. Although I hold that this requirement should be met by demanding only that all accepted theories be possibly true in the sense indicated above, I want here to allow a hearing to the rival demand that all accepted theories be probably true in some sense which we will assume to be well-specified.

If a methodology that seeks to appraise competing theories in terms of extrinsic properties is to be effective, the latter must all be observable or quasi-observable. Popper's methodology, as it stood from about 1960 until the mid 1970s, treated verisimilitude as quasi-observable; it claimed that there is reason to expect the better corroborated theory to have the higher verisimilitude. This is hit by Gellner's point, just because it involves an inductive assumption: that $T_2$ is better corroborated than $T_1$ means only that $T_2$ has performed better than $T_1$ *so far*; but if $T_2$ has more verisimilitude than $T_1$, then $T_2$ should, other things being equal, continue to perform better than $T_1$ *in the future*.

If the link between corroboration and verisimilitude is severed, as it should be by a non-inductivist philosophy, verisimilitude becomes a non-observable property. A methodology that simply said, 'Of two or more competing theories, prefer the one with the highest verisimilitude' would no longer be hit by Gellner's point, but it would be ineffective. It would be as if navigators were told to steer by a star which, however, turns out to be permanently behind cloud.

A methodology that said, 'Of two or more competing theories, prefer the one that is best corroborated' would not be hit by Gellner's point, and nor would it be ineffective, but it would have no answer to the question, 'Why is the best corroborated theory the best theory?' While one tribe may worship corroboration, may not another worship something different, such as high probablity?

Now consider a methodology that appraises scientific theories in terms of both an extrinsic and an intrinsic property. For purposes of presentation I will, to begin with, take these to be, respectively, simplicity and probable truth; this methodology, I will suppose, endorses Leibniz's assertion that 'a hypothesis becomes the more probable as it is simpler'.[10] Such a methodology surely is hit by Gellner's point. It involves, among others, the metaphysical presupposition that God did not construct the world according to an arcane and complex plan.

Now consider a methodology that appraises scientific theories in terms of simplicity combined with possible rather than probable truth. In *The Logic of Scientific Discovery*, before he had taken up with verisimilitude, Popper required, so far as the truth or otherwise of an accepted scientific hypothesis is concerned, only that it be possibly true (though he didn't use this term) in the sense that it has survived severe attempts to falsify it. He also held that we should, other things being equal, prefer $T_2$ to $T_1$ if $T_2$ is simpler than $T_1$; but he repudiated the suggestion that this is because $T_2$ will be more probable than $T_1$: on the contrary, on his view of simplicity, $T_2$ will be less (or at any rate not more) probable than $T_1$. Popper's reason for preferring the simpler hypothesis was that it will, typically, be easier to test.[11] This is an example of a preference for an intrinsic property receiving a methodological justification that involves no metaphysical presuppositions. Irrespective of how the world is, a testable theory with two adjustable parameters, say $a_1$ and $a_2$, is from a logical point of view easier to test than one with the three adjustable parameters $a_1$, $a_2$ and $a_3$. Popper's methodological preference for simplicity involved no methodological presuppositions. A methodology can combine the aim of increasing simplicity with that of possible truth without being hit by Gellner's point.

The optimum aim for science propounded in *S & S* is structurally analogous to the above. Simplicity gets absorbed into the demands for increasing depth and predictive power. Like simplicity, these are intrinsic, and determinable, properties of theories; and there is no suggestion that if $T_2$ is deeper then it is more probable than $T_1$; on the contrary, if they are both unrefuted, then the deeper $T_2$, having more testable content, will be less (or at any rate not more) probable than $T_1$. The only extrinsic property invoked by this aim is possible truth, and to require of a theory that it be possibly true is not to smuggle in some metaphysical principle.

So I don't think that Gellner's point hits this methodology, which advises us to prefer the best corroborated of a set of competing and well tested scientific theories on the ground that it is the one, at the present time, that best fulfils the optimum aim for science. Gellner might reply, in line with the passage of his that I quoted at some length earlier, that if 'Ought' implies

'Can', then our aim presupposes that a reality, more specifically a multi-levelled reality, exists independently of our thoughts and perceptions; hence the methodology associated with this aim *prejudges the nature of the world we are in*. And he might add that this, of course, renders it vulnerable to Humean scepticism.

This is not the place to go into it in any detail, but I hold that *'Ought' implies 'Can'* should be replaced by *'I ought' implies 'I don't know that I can't'*. A man who is a strong swimmer sees a small girl fall into the water. He dives in in an attempt to rescue her; but unknown to him, she has a weak heart for which the shock of immersion has proved too much: she cannot be saved. Was his action irrational? Of course not. He was attempting what was actually impossible, but he had no reason to realise this. And even if he had had some reason to suspect that she could not be saved, he would not have acted irrationally in attempting to save her so long as his suspicion fell short of certainty.

I claimed in *S & S* (pp. 349ff) that, although knowing that one cannot fulfil an aim would render pursuit of it irrational, not knowing that one can fulfil it does not render pursuit of it irrational; if it did, the adoption of any aim that is at all ambitious and risky would be irrational. A great explorer aims to discover an unknown continent. An adherent of a strong version of *'Ought' implies 'Can'* might say that his adoption of this aim presupposes that he knows that there is an undiscovered continent 'out there', awaiting discovery, although he could not know this before he sets out on his voyage of discovery. I say that it presupposes only that he does not know that there is no such continent. One can adopt an aim without a prior commitment to the claim that the preconditions for its fulfilment are satisfied. More specifically, we can hope that science will make ever deeper discoveries about a multi-levelled reality without a prior commitment to the claim that such a reality exists.

## NOTES

1. I am grateful to Mr Aliabadi for criticisms of an earlier draft.
2. 'On being wrong', *Rationalist Annual*, 1955; reprinted in *The devil in modern philosophy*, edited by I.C. Jarvie and Joseph Agassi, London, 1974, pp. 45–51.
3. Published in R.S. Cohen, P.K. Feyerabend and M.W. Wartofsky,

(eds.), *Essays in Memory of Imre Lakatos*, Dordrecht, 1976, pp. 161–177.

4. P. 161. At around this time Feyerabend was making the stronger claim that 'every methodological rule is associated with cosmological assumptions, so that using the rule we take it for granted that the assumptions are correct' (*Against Method*, London, 1975, p. 295). This claim is clearly too strong; what specific cosmological assumptions are associated with, for instance, the methodological rule that one should reject empirically falsified hypotheses?

5. *Philosophical Works of Descartes*, ed. H.S. Haldane, and G.R.T. Ross and 2nd edn, Cambridge, 1931, p. 92.

6. Karl R. Popper, *The Logic of Scientific Discovery*, London, 1959, p. 37.

7. John Watkins, *Science and Scepticism*, Princeton: Princeton University Press; London: Hutchinson, 1984.

8. Graham Oddie, *Likeness to Truth*, Dordrecht, 1986, p.11.

9. 'The aimless rationality of science', *International Studies in the Philosophy of Science*, 4, 1990, pp. 33–50.

10. *Gottfried Wilhelm Leibniz: Philosophical Papers and Letters*, ed. Leroy E. Loemker, 2 vols, Chicago, 1956, p. 288. It is surprising that Leibniz held this thesis in view of his own metaphysics, according to which the actual world is the richest possible world; which means that it will contain counter-examples to every simple or not so simple law-statement. For references, see my 'Minimal Presuppositions and Maximal Metaphysics', *Mind*, 87, April 1978, pp. 208–209.

11. For references, see *S & S* § 3.44.

CHAPTER 11

# *Gellner's positivism*

## *I.C. Jarvie*

A colleague of mine who was both a product of Oxford and an 'Oxford philosopher',[1] once described Gellner to me as a sociologist. This colleague affected some disbelief when I offered the information that Gellner had, as a Balliol under-graduate studying PPE, won the John Locke Prize in philosophy. Some years later, my correction notwithstanding, that colleague was still wont to characterise Gellner as a sociologist. I took it that this resistance was social: the Oxford commonroom circuit, as it were, had decisively characterised this most dangerous critic as 'not really a philosopher, a sociologist'.[2] They had evidence. Four fifths of Gellner's critique of Oxford philosophy, *Words and Things*,[3] was an entirely orthodox marshalling of arguments to show the incoherencies and inconsistencies of that school of thought. It displayed a detailed familiarity with the profes-sional writings of all of the most influential of the British language philosophers of the time. The last chapter of the book, however, broke new ground. After demolishing the Oxford philosophy movement on its own terms, a sociology of it was advanced. Gellner's claim was that the content of the doctrine and its successful entrenchment in Oxbridge could best be explained by examining the social institutions which gave it nurture, and the social mechanisms which perpetuated it. One convenient way for those in the movement to erase the memory of Gellner's searing philosophical critique was to remember only his sociological analysis, which they endeav-oured to neutralise by declaring it unfairly *ad hominem*. This warranted dismissing it with the equally *ad hominem* argument that its author was not really a professional philosopher, rather a sociologist unable to appreciate philosophical matters.

Gellner, of course, would not refuse the title of sociologist

243

and would certainly not wear it as a badge of shame. He has a University of London PhD in social anthropology. More importantly, Gellner's life and work contest the very idea that there is some sustainable contrast between philosophy and sociology. Gellner was first, and in my view is still, a philosopher. That is, he works on philosophical problems, uses philosophical apparatus, and offers a vision of the human condition that is unmistakably philosophical. The attempt by some philosophers to characterise (and hence dismiss) him as a sociologist gains merely a dubious credence from the fact that he is also a professional social scientist. The temptation to think of what he does as sociological analysis of philosophy is in my view profoundly mistaken. It rests on the premiss that the narrow construction of philosophy which excludes his work is defensible. In fact his work undermines any defence of that narrow construction of philosophy and, indeed, proceeds on the basis of a quite different construction. Gellner's own practice is to treat sociology as a specialised branch of philosophy. The important results achieved in this branch feed back on and alter philosophy as a whole.

It is my contention, *contra* that Oxford philosophy colleague of mine who characterised Gellner as a sociologist, that in his close study of the implications of Marx, Weber and Durkheim, Gellner operated primarily as a philosopher, that the greatest bulk of his output is philosophy, and that his major books are almost all philosophical. This is not a verbal move based on some arbitrarily broad construction of philosophy as comprehensive. It also happens to be true even on the narrower traditional construction of philosophy held by my Oxford philosophy colleague. That some of the professional philosophers Gellner has criticised refuse him the label is not just an amnesia brought on by the pain his critique inflicted. It has in addition a more intellectually interesting source.

As Gellner construes philosophy, it should be a very different sort of activity from what is done by those who try to exclude him from the professional ranks. It should, among other things, be partly empirical: the facts of the world make a philosophical difference. The overwhelming fact of the modern world makes a decisive philosophical difference. Furthermore, the particular philosophy of the facts so scorned by

the Oxford disciples of the later Wittgenstein, namely positivism, seems to Gellner the correct philosophy – even if it was
seldom properly worked out by those who adhered to it (for
example the logical positivists). This last qualification merely
points to the fact that Gellner is a positivist yes, but something
of a positivist *sui generis* because modern positivisms are 'trite
and scholastic'.[4] However that may be, the hostility at Oxford
may have had a rational source in the recognition that Gellner
was a philosophical enemy. He was sympathetic to a philosophical movement, positivism, which Oxford philosophers thought
had been overthrown by the later work of Wittgenstein in an
event they referred to as the Revolution in Philosophy.[5]

Although Gellner never describes himself as a philosopher of
science, that is an illuminating way to approach his work: his
concerns centre on problems traditionally ascribed to this field.
There are at least two streams of philosophy of science,
depending upon on what problem they centre. The deeper and
more interesting problem stems from an interest in the part
science has played in the emergence of the modern world: how
is it to be explained? In particular, what can explain the
attractions of the modern world when its scientific underpinning means that it offers a world-picture with no human
comfort whatever? Gellner often heaps scorn on intellectuals
who seek cosy community and revalidation of their own
resistance to the modern world, a warm holism, the re-
enchantment of the world, and he emphasises instead a bleak
vision of the granular, mechanical and soulless world-picture
offered by science.[6] In this Gellner reveals clearly enough the
source of his own mordancy. The choice forced upon us he
finds uncomfortable, but the self-deception involved in rejecting science and modernity he finds risible. And it is self-
deception to try to reject the powerful cognitive and practical
tools modern science places in the hands of mankind. These
tools make such a difference that even those who want to resist
the accompanying bleak world-view try to postpone that issue.
It is the affluent insulation of intellectuals from the harsh
realities of the pre-modern world that make their (albeit
theoretical) rejection of modernity possible, but those less
privileged are mostly unequivocal about wanting to participate
in modernity, and the hold-outs will not last.[7]

Upon this deep and central problem of the philosophy of science, then, Gellner takes the position that science has fostered modernity at a cost, the cost of a comfortless world-view that no one relishes, but which is rationally unavoidable. The other main problem which is the source of philosophy of science is the narrow technical quest for some kind of formal or abstract characterisation of science, a methodology that will render it distinct from and discontinuous with any of the thought-styles (such as folk-knowledge, myths or religion) that preceded its emergence or which continue to exist alongside it. In his major essay stating his positivism, and touching on methodological questions, 'An Ethic of Cognition', Gellner willingly borrows a transcendental argument of Paul Feyerabend, one intended to show that the project of a pure methodology indifferent to all content is impossible.[8] Feyerabend seems to have held that implicit presuppositions about how the world is underlay all efforts at methodology that went beyond mere restatement of the principles of formal logic. Gellner accepts this point and goes one step further with the transcendental objection to the methodological characterisation of science by arguing forcefully that the theoretical/methodological presuppositions also involve moral presuppositions. Science and modernity make moral demands and are themselves moral goods.[9]

According to Gellner, those philosophers whom tradition has (mis-)characterised as no more than social scientists – namely Marx, Weber and Durkheim – enjoined upon us a reframing of the problem of knowledge. The change was from the question of how does the individual consciousness gain knowledge of the world, to the question of which social formations are conducive to the growth of knowledge, and which are not. Knowledge so considered is a social product and a social possession and is not reducible to the sum of the contents of the consciousnesses of knowing individuals. By contrast, most orthodox philosophers of knowledge such as Oxford philosophers, formulate the problem of knowledge in a way that begs individualist and justificationist answers. They ask, what does it mean to say that I know that $p$? They answer along the lines that, I know that $p$ if and only if $p$ is some form or other of justified true belief. This reveals at once the enormous gulf between their approach to epistemology and Gellner's. And perhaps we also see how it is possible for some to conclude, as I do, that there is a congenial confluence between tbe central epistemological strategies of Popper and of Gellner. Thus Gellner is to be taken quite literally to be Popperian, and not only in that place where he says Popper (whom he hails as a fellow positivist and the best of the bunch) is right (on the first problem), if for Hegelian reasons.[10] He is also very close to the Popper of 'On the Sources of Knowledge and of Ignorance'.[11]

This *sui generis* positivism which Gellner espouses was articulated in many of his works and hinted at in others. Some of the broadest hints lie in the sympathetic attention Gellner gives in his writings to registering carefully his appreciation of and dissents from the greatest living positivist, W.V.O. Quine. The central text that I shall stick to here, however, is the aforementioned 'An Ethic of Cognition', originally a contribution to the 1976 volume in memory of Gellner's LSE colleague Imre Lakatos.[12] Gellner there tries to characterise science in a new way. Having accepted Feyerabend's argument that scientific method is a substantial rather than a methodological commitment, and suspecting that such a choice is a moral one, the obvious move would be to proceed to characterise the scientific or modern world-view which morally recommends itself. This was difficult to do because Gellner had previously argued that, unlike pre-modern systems of thought, scientific thought underwent great changes, but those changes did not necessarily have social ramifications similar to what followed comparable changes in pre-modern thought.[13] A radical shift of world view such as between Aristotle and Darwin, or between Newton and Einstein, could take place without any discernible social consequences of the kind that accompany breakdown and replacement of world views in traditional or pre-scientific societies.

Gellner's ingenious solution was to try to characterise science by the sorts of worlds it rejects, rules out of court, forbids. Just those sorts of world-views were excluded by science which tied society and a world-view together, which provided cosy community, unity and wholeness, which offered comfort and an enchanted locality. Empiricism, he argued, whether Baconian or Popperian, enjoins us to face up to the way the world is regardless of how we would like it to be. This is, of course, a moral position. In its decision to exclude from the start certain options it is also a priori. This paradox obviously tickles Gellner. Can we a priori establish the sovereignty of experience? How?

Gellner, instead of trying to define experience, a project which he thinks has dim prospects for success, suggests working by contrast: stressing what is forbidden:

> The essence of empiricism is that all, but *all*, theoretical structures are accountable; that none can claim such an awful majesty as to be exempt from the indignity of inquiry and judgement; and that substantive theoretical systems so constructed as to elude and evade this indignity, are out. *Out*.[14]

To this I would only want to add that the radicalism of Bacon consisted partly in his recognition that the tribunal of experience which was to exercise this inquiry and judgement was to be peopled on a broad and egalitarian basis. This is the connection of empiricism with Enlightenment for all of humankind. Both cognitive sovereigns and worldly and religious sovereigns had to face the same tribunal. Bacon's egalitarianism failed if experience did not reveal the truth, so Bacon, like his radical rival Descartes, glibly reached for God, who so constructed our selves and the world that the truth about it would be revealed by experience. Gellner thinks the modern world cannot put so much trust in God.

It follows, Gellner goes on, that experience of the given is to be understood as 'that which is not under the control of any theoretical system, but independent of them all'. Or, rather, only experience that abides by this demand is admissible in the tribunal. If we push Gellner's tribunal metaphor in a slightly different direction than he does, this amounts to saying that all who come before the court of experience should be equal in the face of experience. This then explains the atomistic or fragmented account of experience so characteristic of empiricism, and so impoverished as a psychology. It is not that experience happens to be that way, but it is the court's way of individuating the accused and the charges which are being tried (much like the way law courts do not deal indiscriminately with charges against a lot of people for doing criminal things, but rather identify the accused separately, even if they are part of a gang or conspiracy, and itemise the alleged offences one by one). This facilitates the work of the tribunal and rules out the defence of: we are all guilty; so why pick on me? That defence is impregnable once allowed, just as the kinds of world-views empiricism rules out are irrefutable from the inside and as a whole.

What is the attraction of the tribunal of experience, a tribunal set up to condemn a priori all the reinforced dogmatisms that constitute the great majority of the received world-views? Gellner offers five suggestions, which I shall give first in his words, and then offer comment, critique and supplement upon them in my own.

1.    The plausibility of the empiricist model.
2.    The correct (sociological) argument from illusion.
3.    The lessons of the Big Divide.
4.    The extension of Neutral-speak.
5.    Kantian–Protestant ethics.[15]

Insofar as I offer supplement it will be to reiterate the political appeal of intellectual weapons and tribunals against intellectual and social oppression. This does not at all cut against Gellner's view that empiricism is fundamentally an a priori moral imperative, it simply stresses what a broad appeal that has, an appeal testified to by the countervailing fear and derision the empiricist vision evokes from a great many intellectuals.

(1) Gellner says teasingly little about the appeal of empiricism, what he calls 'the plausibility of the model', the notion of bits of factual brick out of which knowledge can be built. He does not notice that the metaphor of bricks into buildings may itself go to the plausibility. Indeed, he says that an a priori holism lumbers itself with a virtually insoluble problem: the apparent pre-established harmony between mind and reality. I don't quite see this. Bitty bricks go to make up whole buildings, yes; but then it is equally intuitive that whole acorns grow smoothly into great oaks. Mind and harmony may grow together. Indeed, the refusal of empiricists to accept narratives has to be highly counter-intuitive to most of the thought-systems to which humankind has given birth. The mind has to learn to harmonise its tendency to narrative with the absence of narrative in reality.

Perhaps another metaphor, language itself, may offer clues

to the plausiblity and appeal of empiricism. Language is constructed from bits: sounds, words, expressions, sentences and so on (although they too tend to be acquired in clumps, clusters or structures). All languages can be decomposed into such bits for explication, teaching and translation. Perhaps such dismantling to component parts is a metaphor for successful communication as such, namely a system that can be dismantled far enough to reach the point where there can be mutual understanding and agreement, and from which basis the whole system can be put back together again. Empiricism, like language or, for that matter, like counting or like money or like names, fragments experience as far as is necessary for communication ('intersubjective testability', Popper calls it). The appeal of empiricism, then, again like that of language and of money and of counting, is that it is a very powerful tool for being critical of those systems you are trying to reconstruct from the level reached: it is like taking a clock apart so as to see what makes it tick.

(2) This directly connects to Gellner's sociological formulation of the argument from illusion as amounting to the recognition that since the views of others contain blatant and pervasive error, and contradict one another and their own past, there can be no reasons to privilege ourselves and our current stock of assumptions (does this recommend what Popper calls 'friendly-hostile cooperation'?) As we sink down the levels of language or bits of experience trying to convey our meaning to the other, we may see the way in which those bits of experience challenge and hence emancipate us from our own system, not just them from theirs. I would stress again that this is both enormously attractive (because of the sense of power it gives) and very frightening (because it threatens certainty and security with uncertainty and insecurity).

(3) That same ambivalence is generated by what Gellner has called the Big Divide, the Big Ditch or, more recently, the transition. This is the radical disjunction between the modern or advanced world and all previous and contemporary worlds. The modern world is one based on industrialisation, an industrialisation connected in some intrinsic way with science. Knowledge and the consequent control of nature have grown radically since the seventeenth century in one sort of society,

which thus stands out in contrast to the cognitive stagnation characteristic of all the others. When Gellner formulates his objection to relativism he notices that relativism holds true for cognitive systems that came before the Big Divide fairly well: as near as no matter they are equal in their cognitive feebleness. Relativism across the divide, between modern scientific cognition and traditional thought, he finds patently absurd. While it is not easy to give a satisfactory account of the exact connection between empiricism, experiment and the growth of science, Gellner accepts the usual view that there is such a connection and that it is sociologically of overwhelming importance.

Point (4) is subtle and controversial. Gellner notes that traditional belief systems are always bilingual in a specific sense. Although they are officially closed systems, with answers to every doubt, answers that, fully worked out, form a closed circle in which, in the end, premises are simply reasserted and revalidated; in fact all the defenders and expositors of such systems are equipped with means of talking to the unconverted, unwashed, unpersuaded, sceptical, and so on, to offer them ways in and to offer those on the way out means of assuaging their doubts and difficulties. This contradicts the idea that sense can only ever be made within a thought-system (attacked by Popper as 'the myth of the framework'[16]). Clearly the edges of the thought system are permeable, allowing access to a discourse in which meaningful contrasts can be drawn with other systems as well as with doubts and difficulties with the system itself. Gellner asserts as a sociological fact that this Neutral Zone has enormously expanded in the modern world, so that it fills most of the available space, and the closed systems have shrunk to Sunday morning rituals. Gellner clearly has in mind the so-called secularisation thesis, as well as his own field experience in Eastern Europe and the Soviet Union where he claims the official communist faith is similarly *pro forma*, and this also explains perhaps his fascination with the great exception to his view in the modernising world, namely the pre-scientific thought system of Islam.

It is difficult to dispute these factual claims and of course Gellner's sociology allows for religious revivals – but only as a kind of last ditch hold-out against modernity. Unlike Popper, who thought Nazism made possible a return to the closed tribal society, even a return to the beasts,[17] Gellner sees modernity as unstoppable, partly because it is highly appealing to the masses not yet enjoying it. This is a field to which he has made a special contribution, the rise of the nationalist faith. He does not explain it as a last-ditch effort to resist modernity, but rather as a legitimation exercise for some who wish to claim the benefits of the modern world, even though it frequently happens to articulate a bitterly anti-modern outlook (perhaps partly because the moderns misunderstood it or overlooked it).

Nationalism is usually a secular movement, however seriously or playfully we compare it to a religion. While I am impressed by Gellner's argument that nationalism is not a tribalist refusal of the benefits of modernity (as intimated by Popper), I am not sure that he can get around the counter-example of religious revivals. Some of those seem to me direct resistance to aspects, at least, of modernity. If there can be successful resistance to aspects of modernity perhaps there can also be resistance to its totality as well.

One interpretation of this split attitude between resisting science and technology and embracing it is that the revivalist resistance to modernity is partial or inconsistent. Another is that their resistance is total, but that they try to insulate themselves from some of the implications of science and technology while also turning it to their advantage where possible. In so far as the embrace of the technology of destruction stems not from apocalyptic but from nationalist sources, revivalism can be brought under Gellner's account of nationalism. There remain the apocalyptic scenarios which are to be found in both Christian and Islamic revivalism. Because of the ambiguity of these cases I resist the conclusion that we are witnessing an inexorable expansion of the realm of scientific Neutral-speak and an irreversible retreat of the closed systems of thought.

(5) Gellner's final point is to note the existence of an ethic which does not seek legitimation in other-worldly or totalising systems of thought but which stands alone. 'Let the facts be what they will; our norms are not at their mercy.' This tough-minded refusal to be intimidated by a recalcitrant world is clearly an ethic which appeals to Gellner. Where he feels sheepish is that the overall picture is, philosophically 'untidy

and messy', because empiricism is a circular ideology also – 'in a sense'.[18]

Gellner is admirably candid in drawing out the implications and the difficulties in his view. He chastises 'the falsificationists' for spurning verificationism and Baconian inductivism.[19] It is my duty to report, alas, 'that these falsificationists are a Lakatosian caricature, followers of the imaginary leader Popper. Gellner notwithstanding, the real Popper of the writing and teaching was never the leader of 'the cult of falsification' or 'the cult of criticism'[20] or of any cult at all.[21] In the sense in which Gellner wants to appreciate inductivist empiricism this real Popper did not and would not dissent at all. But Gellner's vulgarisation of Popper as what Lakatos called a 'naive falsificationist' and his criticism of this distortion does not succeed in being a criticism of the real thing.

In the very last paragraph of the important paper under discussion Gellner wobbles between affirming the primacy of each of the two components of empiricism as he reads it, namely the exclusion of certain kinds of worlds, or the sovereignty of experience. In this passage and in his critical remarks on Quine's rejection of any prior philosophy, he raises the spectre of a cognitive crisis, a dramatic revolutionary discontinuity, instability and rapid change with the line of succession far from obvious. Here, he thinks, a negative exclusionism is not good enough (he means falsificationism as he reads it), the situation demands an independent and extraneous talisman, and so we look to experience to guide us, however hard it is to give a philosophically adequate account of it. The tribunal, having condemned certain world-views out of court, is now to be called upon to give us positive guidance from experience. It is at this point, I think, that Gellner's love of empiricism would seem to have blinded him to just how unreconstructed a positivist he is. The reason he cannot give an account of experience that satisfies his own philosophical standards is precisely that those standards are positivistic, whereas he needs them to help him in the task of finding a positive account of experience, that is one that explains how knowledge arises from sense-experience: such an account should distinguish factual or experiential statements from theoretical statements, develop a language of experience neutral between theories and world-views, and so on. As Gellner is well aware, all of these succumb to determined criticism, hence his unease at his own yearnings for them.

Yet the execution of the task of providing an empirical theory of experience was to hand in Popper's philosophy, a system of thought Gellner at times showed evidence of having studied carefully and thought deeply about, and at other times of refusing to appreciate. Popper chose as one of the mottoes for *Conjectures and Refutations* a *bon mot* from Oscar Wilde: 'Experience is the name every one gives to their mistakes'. This way of putting the matter points us in the direction of an understanding of a profound point Popper argued about experience. This was to abandon the notion of a sensing individual constantly in touch with what one might call 'positive' experience about the world. Any model of this kind is subject to precisely the objection Gellner calls the correct formulation of the argument from illusion: namely that when we contemplate the alleged experience of others we are struck by the amount of blatant and pervasive error. Attempts to cope with this have usually fastened on the idea of specifying some mechanism whereby experience is reliably transformed into knowledge. But again all such efforts issue in traditions with blatant and pervasive error. No account of a veridical mechanism of perception will overcome this sceptical objection.

What Popper put in place of such 'positive' accounts of experience was his idea that we very seldom come into genuine contact with the world, that is to say we seldom have what the traditional account calls experience. The *problem of experience itself* then changes from being that of giving an account of how we make knowledge out of this plentiful flow of experience to that of showing how those small numbers of times when we bump into the world do in fact nudge us into rebuilding our conjectures about the way the world is. Our conjectures lead us to move about and act in the world in the way we think it is and hence to bump into the world, when our preconceptions have led us to expect something that turns out, sometimes painfully, not to be the case. This makes experience contingent on a careful construction of expectations: we have to think hard before we can see; perception is not a pure or neutral act as traditional empiricists thought. We have to construct the world as we think it is, not from vast amounts of positive data which flow all by themselves, inundating our usually reliable perceptual apparatus, but from those odd and important occasions when we see that the world cannot be like this, because of our failures to conjecture it correctly.

This new account of experience, horribly truncated here in order not to make this an expository paper, solves at one stroke Gellner's dilemma: 'I find myself vacillating on this'.[22] Popper's account of experience as primarily a negative achievement places a general sceptical question against all received views, folk knowledge and wisdom, belief systems, and so on. Some are totally immune to ever making mistakes and thus they *never achieve contact with the world* and hence they are *out*; in crisis situations the account of experience as mistakes corrected at least forms the basis of a policy, one of caution, tentativity and testing step by step any candidates that come forward for leadership.[23] Thus Popper finds no need to vacillate as Gellner does between empiricism as an exclusionary policy and empiricism as an attempt to bring ideas before the tribunal of experience. In his system these two become one and the same: those that cannot lead before the tribunal because they say nothing, are not tried until they speak up; most of those who do speak up will be condemned by the tribunal; the views that do not get quickly condemned receive a stay of their execution . . . but only *pro tem*.

We notice at once that Popper is operating with experience as a tribunal in way that should be very agreeable to Gellner. Gellner's argument about the inadequacy of falsificationism was that positive guidance was needed in crisis situations. At the end of the old order the question becomes, how shall we go about building the new? We see here that Gellner is an epistemological radical in the traditional empiricist mould. Popper is not. Popper thinks that the tribunal of experience is not always as unequivocal as we might wish, sometimes it is positively delphic. False theories, he argues, can for long periods be reliable guides to action. Our ideas never face the tribunal alone and hence if they are convicted of crimes they may be convicted *en bloc* when in fact not all are responsible. Assigning responsibility may then become a major task in itself. So crisis situations may themselves be a matter of dispute.

Where they are not, Popper's philosophy is that we should qualify and modify the old views while we search for or test the new ones. There is no algorithm to experience that guides us towards new brainwaves any more than there is one to make the tribunal of experience unambiguous. There is no doubt that this is a conservative epistemological doctrine. We advance by conjectures and refutations, which may be equally rare. A conjecture in trouble is not to be dumped but used circumspectly where trouble has been detected.

Perhaps it is this underlying conservatism in Popper that has alienated Gellner, who is a vigorous advocate of modernity, whereas Popper is a qualified critic. Furthermore, Popper found the Big Ditch in a pre-Socratic methodological attitude: Thales's relation to his pupils Anaximenes and Anaximander, whereas, Gellner found it only in the rise of industrial society. Here lies a deep quarrel, Popper holds that the Socratic method of critical rationality, which is the basic method of science, was discovered, lost (or suppressed) and rediscovered a few times, most recently in the Renaissance. Nurtured and practised, it yielded the edifice of science and the immense social changes the ideals of science and the application of science made possible. Under this description modernity becomes not an unstoppable transition, but a fluky and delicate achievement, not least because its principles were not understood. The better our grasp of those principles the better we can help sustain it. This makes the problem of method the central and fundamental one, and dispenses with the search for a positivist theory of experience.

## NOTES

1. 'Oxford philosophy' was one of several nineteen-fifties terms of art for members of the school of language, linguistic or ordinary language philosophy described and criticised in Gellner's *Words and Things* (London, 1959. Second edition London, 1979). R.H. Hare, an Oxford philosopher, without mentioning Gellner, argued that Oxford at the time was a school for philosophers and not a philosophical school in 'A School for Philosophers', *Ratio*, 2, 1960.
2. I have deliberately phrased this in a neutral way, although sociology was not then a degree subject at Oxford, and the word 'sociologist' was often preceded in conversation by a voiced or implied 'mere'.

3. See note 1, above.
4. 'An Ethic of Cognition' in *Spectacles and Predicaments*, Cambridge, 1979, p. 175. (The paper was originally published in R.S. Cohen, P.K. Feyerabend and M.W, Wartofsky, eds. *Essays in Memory of Imre Lakatos*, Dordrecht, 1976.) The positivism to which Gellner gives almost unqualified approval is d'Holbach's *Le Système de la Nature* to which he devotes a lengthy encomium in 'French Eighteenth-Century Materialism', chapter 10 of *The Devil in Modern Philosophy*, London, 1974.
5. Gilbert Ryle, ed., *The Revolution in Philosophy*, London, 1956.
6. The scorn perhaps reaches its wittiest and most devastating in his paper on Hannah Arendt, 'From Königsberg to Manhattan or Hannah, Rahel, Martin and Elfriede or Thy Neighbour's *Gemeinschaft*', chapter 5 in *Culture, Identity and Politics*, Cambridge, 1987.
7. See especially the controversial passages in *Thought and Change*, London, 1964, pp. 68–73.
8. Gellner, 'An Ethic of Cognition'.
9. Gellner, *Thought and Change*, p. 69.
10. See the end of 'Positivism against Hegelianism', in Ernest Gellner, *Relativism and the Social Sciences*, Cambridge, 1985.
11. This was the Annual Philosophical Lecture to the British Academy in 1960, reprinted in *Conjectures and Refutations*, London, 1963.
12. Gellner, 'An Ethic of Cognition'.
13. See Gellner, *Legitimation of Belief*, Cambridge, 1974, chapter 8, pp. 166–7.
14. Gellner, 'An Ethic of Cognition', p. 170.
15. Gellner, 'An Ethic of Cognition', p. 174.
16. See K.R. Popper, 'The Myth of the Framework' in Eugene Freeman, ed., *The Abdication of Philosophy: Philosophy and the Public Good*, La Salle, 1976.
17. K.R. Popper, *The Open Society and Its Enemies*, London, 1945, chapter 10.
18. Both quotations from Gellner, 'An Ethic of Cognition', pp. 177–8.
19. Gellner, 'An Ethic of Cognition', p. 179.
20. Gellner. 'An Ethic of Cognition', p. 180.
21. He was so anti-cult that he would not even admit that he had a position of his own. 'Popperian', 'Popperite', 'falsificationist' and so on all entered the language under the auspices of Lakatos.
22. Gellner, 'An Ethic of Cognition', p. 180.
23. Agassi has attempted to describe this in his 'Sir Karl Popper in Retrospect', in *The Gentle Art of Philosophical Polemics*, La Salle, 1988.

# CHAPTER 12

# Left versus Right in French political ideology
## A comparative approach

*Louis Dumont*

My main theme here is going to be the chronic division of Left versus Right in French political ideology and political life. But before coming to it, allow me to recall one or two definitions and some of the results of a previous comparison between France and Germany. I call ideology a system of ideas and values current in a given social milieu. We shall speak of a certain ideology as being *predominant* respectively here and there. What is a predominant ideology? It is not exactly the ideology of a majority of the people nor something stable that would be seen to underline historical changes. It is rather something that comes spontaneously to the mind of people living in the cultural milieu considered, something in terms of which those people speak and think, and which is best revealed by comparison with other cultures.

Thus, there is a difference between what it means to be a Frenchman and to be a German. We may state a basic contrast. 'In his own idea of himself, the Frenchman is a man by nature, and a Frenchman by accident, while the German feels he is first a German and then a man through his being a German'.[1] For the French side, I can quote a statement made by a French historian and adopted without ado by another historian: 'Nous n'avons pas à rougir qu'un hasard nous ait fait naître français . . .' In English that means something like 'There is no cause for blushing in having been born a Frenchman, for it is a matter of chance'. Here is a naive dissociation of one's individual identity from one's collective identity that would be hard to match from the German, or even the British, side – not to speak of the Iranian or Japanese.

A German, on the contrary, is immediately conscious of his collective identity as a German, and it is a matter of culture. We shall say that he has a feeling of *cultural* belonging. We cannot say the same, on the same level of representations, or ideology, of the Frenchman. This poses a problem. I think the answer is that it is essentially as a citizen that the Frenchman feels and acknowledges himself as French. His sense of belonging lies at the *political* level. The collective identity is cultural in the former case, political in the latter. (I do not pretend, of course, that politics is not part of culture at large, but here we need to distinguish.)

For our Frenchman, France means first of all democracy, the Republic. If he is somewhat educated, he will say that the French have shown the world the way of the Rights of Man and the Citizen, and will be inclined to add that the destiny of France is to be the teacher of mankind.

After all, this is only a particular form of a feeling that is universal: people everywhere believe that their own society is superior to others. That is what is called ethnocentrism – I prefer to say sociocentrism. It would be wrong to suppose that modern societies do not harbour such feelings, under modified forms. The corresponding trait in Germany for long was Pangermanism, that is to say the belief that Germany was called to dominate the world, by reason of the excellence of its culture and organisational powers.

Let us make the picture a little more precise on the French side. To reiterate, we are considering here the major or maximal level of the most common ideology. On that level, I maintain that only the individual human being on the one hand, and the human species on the other, are acknowledged – and nothing in between, nothing like different nations or different cultures: the French tend naively to identify their own culture with culture at large, universally considered. Anything that differs from that model is either strange or defective.

This may seem unbelievable, and at this point loud protests must be expected: isn't it clear that the French, like anybody else, recognise the existence of boundaries, distinct states, and so on? They do of course, but this does not impinge on what is essential. To open a parenthesis, we have to take into account that there are different *levels* of thought: if we fail to do so in such matters we wipe out all differences, all specific patterns, we are back to the Hegelian night where all cows are black. For the Frenchman, the existence of boundaries, of different languages, of conflicts of interest between nations, is negligible in relation to man's essence as expressed in his watchword: Liberty, Equality, Fraternity. The basic or global French ideology is as powerful as it is simple, and devoid of concrete elements. At bottom it consists of a single principle: the human subject as universal. The creed has come down to us from the Enlightenment, of course, through the dispensation of the great Revolution that marks the beginning of the establishment of truth on earth.

If this is so, then the next question one will be expected to ask is surely how it has been possible for such an ideological configuration to endure, and in particular how it could survive the numerous and bloody confrontations with the world as it really is?

To answer that question, it is necessary to know more about French internal politics. Therefore we reserve the question for later consideration and we now turn to the Right–Left dichotomy.

Two features go to characterise France's internal political history since the 1789 revolution: one is political instability, the other an all-pervading ideological rift between Right and Left. Already in the 1830s Tocqueville was struck by the contrast between the happy implementation of democratic values in the US and the permanent strife and chronic instability that had followed their introduction in France, and he went to America to compare the two cases more closely.

It is only in the 1870s, after the Franco-Prussian war, that a democratic regime – the Third Republic – was securely established. Until then, the nineteenth century had seen three revolutions – the Three Glorious Days of 1830, the Revolution of 1848 with the ephemeral Second Republic, and the Paris Commune in 1871 – and three different kinds of monarchy. Raymond Aron graphically summed up this dramatic course of events, saying that France had been 'suffering in turn under the sordid egoism of the rich, the rage of the Revolutionaries, and the despotism of one man'. Can we, long after Tocqueville and with a richer store of dearly bought experience, take up again the question to which he provided a first answer: how can the introduction, in one particular country, of what was thought to be rational human values have ushered in such a train of evils?

Is it only due to the resistance of entrenched privileges and vested interests, within the country and outside it? The question is rarely asked in such terms and current explanations are only partial, for it is generally presumed that no relation prevails between the predominant ideology of the period and the course of events. The same may be said about all the undesirable phenomena that have occurred in the political world at large in our own era, even the massive ones that would appear particular to it, such as world wars or totalitarianism. We believe, and always imply, that our modern ideology is good, and it follows by definition that it can have nothing to do with such scourges. Yet all this belongs to one and the same world, and if only we would admit that there are more things on earth than are dreamt of in our ideology, and that, whatever its excellence, it may have its shortcomings – that is, if we were to look at it comparatively – we would be prepared to face such questions as this: can any understandable relation be discovered between the particular form of democratic ideology inaugurated by the French Revolution and the unfortunate course of history that prevented the establishment of a stable democratic regime in France for almost a century?

Moreover, even during the Third Republic we note that all instability did not disappear. It was only transferred to a relatively minor level: cabinets changed in rapid succession until the end of the régime in 1940. It was then, moreover, with the paramountcy of Parliament over the other agencies of government, that the Right–Left division, of much older origin, became all-embracing and assumed the form under which we still know it today.

The distinction between Right and Left in politics has spread far and wide in the world. Nowadays it is perhaps understood everywhere, and used more or less intensively in many places. It originated in France in 1789 and it began to spread only relatively late, first in the mid-century to Italy with Parliamentary Democracy, and, remarkably, in the Socialist movements after 1920.[2] Nowhere, probably, has it acquired the degree of pregnancy, the intensity and the scope that it has in France. Nowhere has it become the kind of Manicheism – a twofold Manicheism – deplored by the French on occasion as an obstacle to consensus, although it is something like the warp on which their political life is woven.

Everyone in France speaks of the Right and the Left (the words are substantified), and yet one is hard put to it to say what that distinction is really about. A concrete reference is implied, for only a human body has a right and a left side. That suggests interdependence. And yet the distinction is abstract, each side being supposedly self-sufficient and excluding the other as an enemy. It is simple when compared with the direct designation of the different political parties, but it is highly complex as to the issues it evokes. It appears as a stable dichotomy whereas in actual fact much water – or should we say blood? – has flowed between those two rival banks over the last two centuries.

At any given moment those two little words allow us to reduce the political nebula to a straight line, a single axis along which all qualitative differences become a mere matter of degree. One forgets that there are three distinct 'Rights', as was the case around 1875, and several kinds of Socialism – even revolution is but an 'extreme' reform. Moreover, the distinction can be segmented at will. All parties, and even the Centre, have their Right and their Left.

Although the distinction is familiar to all, it is diversely used and nuanced in different environments. For a Parisian worker of my generation, it was even more social than political. He saw himself as belonging to the Left with his trade-union, and the party of his choice, probably a Socialist one. On the Right were the employers, the rich, and of course the Church and the Army. On the parliamentary level, one reaches the utmost sophistication, as in this formula of 1930: 'A Republican of the Left is a man of the Center whom our hard times compel to sit on the Right'.[3] We shall not grapple with such subtleties but only try and grasp what is comparatively essential.

First, let us go back to the beginning. As you know, the French Revolution broke out in 1789, when the king, for the first time after a long interruption, convened the Estates General of the realm. When the king, Louis XVI, solemnly opened the Estates General on 5 May 1789, he sat above the Assembly. Below him were first the members of his house, on his right side the Princes, the Princesses on his left. Lower down sat the Deputies: to the right the Clergy, to the left the Nobility, and further off, in between, the Third Order. Soon after, the three orders mixed in a single assembly where the Deputies began to group according to their affinities, debate after debate. The result was to polarise the Assembly from the extremes: the adepts of change were on the Left, the supporters of tradition on the Right. Historians note that the disposition is fully established on 28 August 1789, when the vote on the Royal veto is taken.[4]

We see here the origin of a reversal of values. It is generally observed that the right hand has preeminence over the left hand. The Revolutionaries, insofar as they opposed tradition and worked to change the established institutions, were compelled to assemble on the Left. The Revolution established a preeminence of the Left. Henceforth the Left would represent the Revolutionary legacy. To quote a political scientist: 'French politics developed in the 19th century in terms of a kind of Manicheism, a permanent conflict between the adversaries and the partisans of the principles of the Revolution'.[5] The word 'principles' should be underscored, for, as we shall find again and again, everything here is a matter of principle.

In the first place, the stress on 'principles' makes understandable how for two centuries the Right-versus-Left division could survive all the changes that took place on the political stage and in the objects of political debates. It is clear that at any moment the Right and the Left have something in common (beginning with a common language, including the use of the distinction itself, which allows for the integration of the *other* as an adversary). It is also clear that that common basis has significantly changed over time. In 1789 all Deputies certainly had in common something of the Enlightenment philosophy which pervaded the minds at the time and especially inspired the reformers. But the Rights of Man, and even more so, popular sovereignty, were not accepted without a struggle. And yet, who today would call in question universal franchise? It is obvious that a considerable part of the initial values of the Left have become common to all. But if the themes have changed, if the locus of debate has shifted, the principle of opposition stands. It is sometimes possible to pinpoint the migration of a theme from one camp to the other. Thus we shall see that the word 'nation' passed from the Left to the Right between 1792 and 1890. One could even speak of a fluctuation of ideological contents between Left and Right. Thus the Assembly of the 2nd Republic elected by universal suffrage in 1849 decided to return to limited franchise, with the result that Louis Napoléon, who put an end to the Republic through a coup d'état, could give himself an air of the perfect Democrat by organising a plebiscite. Even a few years ago, we have seen our socialists exchange at short notice (1981–83) a mystique of nationalisations for the apology of the daring individual entrepreneur.

But to come back to principles. The Revolution itself was characterised by an absolute disjunction between principles on the one hand and the empirical state of things on the other. I noted earlier a remark by Condorcet which is the more interesting as he had worked with Thomas Paine.[6] Regarding the Constitution, he criticises the Americans for having stressed identity of interests rather than equality of rights: here is the difference between an orientation towards utility and practicality, and the assertion of naked principle.

Our Left has inherited this exclusive attention to principles, to the neglect of the difficulties of their factual application, and it is still alive with us. There is no doubt that this is what characterises France in contrast to the Anglo-American Democracies, and which explains why our Right/Left opposition is as absolute, irremediable, indeed almost as inexpiable as it is.

On this point, I shall quote Emile Littré. Littré is known as the author of the most authoritative dictionary of the French language. He was also trained in medicine, and as a positivist philosopher and political analyst was a disciple of Auguste Comte. He wrote in June 1851, about the watchword Liberty, Equality, Fraternity:

Considered in itself the Revolutionary formula reveals immediately its metaphysical origin. I mean that it does not represent how things actually are, but rather a subjective notion, an idea that came to the mind at the end of the 18th century of what a normal society should be.[7]

Littré added that the Revolutionary motto was completely inapt 'to represent the actual existence of any society', that it was inapplicable to the present and the future as well as to the past.

By and large, Littré was right: the 'actual existence' of any society, whether past, present or future, is not reducible to the individualistic principle.[8] I have directly demonstrated the fact elsewhere. There are only two points on which Littré's dictum, illuminating as it is, must be corrected or modified. First, Littré's positivism misled him into thinking that the eighteenth-century ideal was becoming obsolete; it is quite alive at present in the whole world. Second, we should introduce a distinction, which Littré does not make, as to the applicability of the ideal. He is right in saying that the revolutionary principles are inapplicable *in toto* and instantly. But history shows that they have not been altogether ineffective either. The truth is that they have managed to become reality in some measure, gradually, in some respects. Only the price that had to be paid for this slow and incomplete implementation may be judged a high one. One positive result of this limited applicability is that the ideal, remaining unrealised in its perfection, may be invoked again and again as fresh as ever.

Let us recall that the Positivists thought that the Revolutionary watchword had presided over a destructive, negative stage of the Revolution, and expected the Revolution to close with a second positive, constructive stage, whose motto would be 'Order and Progress', and which Littré saw dawning in 1878 with the Third Republic. From 1789 until then the country had been torn between progress without order, or rather against order, that is, Revolution, and order without or against progress, that is, Reaction and Conservatism. To these two terms, and in conformity with the historical record, Raymond Aron's formula adds a third one, 'despotism'. It has often been observed that it is natural to have recourse to one man to maintain unity in a deeply divided society, but the point requires analysis.

We have in our country a recent example of such a resort. I am thinking of de Gaulle in 1958. Looking back, one sees France, facing the Algerian crisis, on the brink of civil war, so much so that her saviour needed a measure of machiavellism to avoid it. (Jean Lacouture wrote recently that the Prince had increased tensions by overdoing it, but this is perhaps not the last word in the matter.) Let me note in passing that the French intellectuals on the Left, distrusting de Gaulle as a man of the Right, were mistaken to the end about his real intention, and that today our ideological blinkers have the effect of throwing the event into oblivion, for neither side has been able to retain the lesson. To do so, we must define politics, or the political domain. The French tend to be suspicious of the State, and they have for long lent an ear to the theory that reduces politics to a secondary category dependent on economics. Fortunately things have changed in the last decades, and the political category is now better acknowledged as a fundamental one. What is the grounding principle of the political domain in relation to society at large? We shall posit that the political level appears when a society is seen as a unit facing other societies (whether empirically as in war, or ideologically). The society taken as *one* is *ipso facto* superior to the society seen in its multiplicity and legitimately commands over it. This is found even with Rousseau, who opposes the general will to the will of all, the citizen as participating in sovereignty to the subject.

Once the political category is thus defined in its very principle, we are reminded that the immediate figure of this unity is its incarnation in a person. This is not only true of the past, but of the present as well, except that for contemporary nations the function is no longer generally conceived as hereditary. On this point alone – excepting the United Kingdom and a few others – history has vindicated the sarcasms Marx once directed at Hegel's justification of monarchy.

What interests us here is the case where an insoluble ideological conflict, rooted, if not in different rationalities, yet in different rationalisations, leads to the supremacy of one man. Most commonly, attention is paid exclusively to the concentration of power; I should like to draw attention to another aspect, the one for which Max Weber borrowed from theology the word, widespread today, of charisma. The word by itself obscures the matter rather than clearing it up. Actually the mere introduction of a human being reopens a world of perceptions and sentiment that had no place in the ideological debate. The citizen-subject may again feel respect, admiration, attachment, devotion, identification and he may even feel alleviation from a tension that had been experienced as at once extreme and narrow. I am here only expressing in terms of human feelings what is called a shift from a rational to a traditional orientation, or, in Talcott Parsons's terms, from universalism and specificity to particularism, and diffuseness. Given the strength of universalism among the French, the change may be deemed a fall, or self-disavowal. Let us not forget that they had put to death in the person of Louis XVI the figure history had given to their particularity.

This seeming digression was intended to set the third term of Aron's dictum, 'despotism', in its proper relation to the two others. Long before Aron, in 1848, Littré again, calling the period 'an eternal halt between anarchy and disorder', laid bare the vicious circle of its dynamics:

Ever again reactionary successes would in the end discredit order and open the way to new commotions; ever again revolutionary successes would in the end discredit progress and open the way to new reactions.[9]

The problem for us is to get out of the dilemma, to master the alternation. This Aron did not do, for in his well-balanced formula he was content with looking at the Left with the eyes of the Right, seeing 'the fury of the Revolutionaries', and at the Right with the eyes of the Left, seeing 'the sordid egoism of the rich'. We must, on the contrary, as Littré hinted, be able to identify positive content on both sides.

It is possible to do so by finding a hierarchical relation between the two terms. To start with, we know full well that generally speaking the right hand and the left hand are never equal, and we have seen that the Revolutionaries have not abolished the hierarchical relation between the two, they have only reversed it for their own use. The problem for us is to find whether one or the other of the two opposed 'preeminences' has been underwritten by history, can be taken as historically established. To this question the answer is plain, there is no place for doubt. We saw earlier that comparison delivers a picture of French *global* ideology which is by and large that of the Left. History tells us something similar, for the point of arrival is not identical with the point of departure, and all the intervening dramas that have occurred should not hide from us the final result. As we already stated in passing: *in the long run*, some of the fundamental themes of the ideology of the Left have imposed themselves, political institutions have been transformed and even in some measure social institutions. In retrospect it cannot be denied that the motive force in our history was on this side. We must conclude that the ideology of the Left has been and still is predominant as such, that is to say on the ideological level.

In good method, this ideological predominance authorises a hypothesis, namely that the historical development was determined in its general shape or rhythm by the characteristic, or idiosyncratic features of the ideology of the Left. Indeed we already touched on that point when we said how the divorce between the ideal and the actual made impossible a global implementation of the principles and condemned them to be translated into facts only slowly and piecemeal.

Now the theory of hierarchy prepares us to find a reversal when passing from the ideological to the empirical level: whatever is preeminent ideologically will be disadvantaged empirically. This is very much the case here. As the Left did not concede ontological status to anything that then existed and that was not in conformity with its principles, it left out all that was just actually given in the society, backed by tradition and history, except for the points or restricted domains where the legislator intervened. It is as though the Left had, by its extreme one-sidedness abandoned to the care of the Right, and put at its disposal as a store of strength most of the complex interrelations that made for the functioning of the society. Hence the proverbial figure, in this century, of the Leftist voter, who supports anti-Church policies, but goes to Church for his family ceremonies. Only after they had fought side by side in the trenches of the First World War were the village curate and the state schoolteacher reconciled enough to act together in an association of veterans.

The Revolutionaries thought they were building everything anew, from scratch, while they were actually busy grafting a scion onto a live tree. That is why the Right, ideologically impotent, has been empirically powerful in the long run. Yet, if such was the balance of forces in general, we should not forget that changes have taken place. The permanence of the oversimple vocabulary of French political struggles should not mislead us into exaggerating the continuity and into surmising that the balance of forces has remained stable except for short-term oscillations. Looking at the scene today, it is obvious that the enormous increase of state power has corresponded with an increase of the relative weight of the Left through the recurring intervention of the State in economic and social life.

A clear discontinuity was marked by the establishment of the Third Republic, actually the first viable one. In the words of an historian, the word 'Republic' then ceased to be 'that mythical opening into Hell and Paradise that it had been ever since 1792',[10] it ceased to be a utopia and became something real. Its birth was slow and difficult (1870–78), it was the fruit of a series of compromises between politicians of the Right and of the Left. To accept compromises was for people of the Left an absolutely new occurrence. It was done thanks to a handful of shrewd men in whom the values of the Revolution were quite alive but who had learned from history, and probably from the recent humiliation of being defeated by the German armies, that principles were not everything.

From that time onwards, the process of slow implementation of Leftist values went on more smoothly under the institutional dominance of the Left, eroding in succession the strongholds of the Right: the army, the Church, and the power of wealth.

In order to size up our subject-matter through two centuries of political life, we have neglected hitherto the changing contents of the ideological struggle. Let us now consider a concrete example of confrontation. We shall choose one of the deep crises the régime went through, the Dreyfus affair. The Republic was twenty years old when Captain Dreyfus, an artillery officer born in Alsace of a Jewish family, was accused by the Intelligence Branch of the army of having passed confidential information to the military attaché of the German Embassy in Paris. First degraded and banished to Guyana for life under especially cruel confinement conditions, he was finally rehabilitated, after many years and several trials, his accusers and the army hierarchy having been convicted of forgery and complicity. This was achieved thanks to an unprecedented mobilisation of public opinion where Leftist intellectuals played a decisive role, for the first time, of which the famous pamphlet by the novelist Emile Zola entitled 'I accuse . . .' was the starting point and can serve as the epitome. The intensity of the strife caused by what was simply called 'the Affair' can hardly be imagined, as it divided the whole country, best friends and otherwise united families. It can conveniently be read from an excellent recent monograph which I shall use.[11]

A diplomat who was commissioned to attend all the sessions of the Courts and had witnessed the development of the Affair from beginning to end, Maurice Paléologue, gave the most condensed definition of it. He saw it as a struggle between what he called 'two sacred sentiments, the love of justice and the religion of the fatherland'. We need not speak of something 'sacred', but two supreme values were actually at stake. In one camp were the high officers of the Army, fearful of the German neighbour and later on committed by esprit-de-corps and raison d'état to cover up any blunder their subordinates might have committed, backed by vibrant patriots respectful of the army and more often than not sensitive to antisemitic propaganda. In the other camp was most of the Left, suspicious of the army as a reactionary corporation and rallying all those who cared above all for the dignity of man and for justice. Adrien Dansette expressed well that it was a matter of the paramountcy of one value or the other: he saw 'on one side the principle that everything had to be judged in relation to France' (that is, nationalism, still in a nascent state after the 1870 defeat); on the other, the principle that 'the Rights of Man are above any institution and any conviction'. And still more clearly Jaurès, a great Socialist leader who, as a Socialist, did not take sides immediately soon declared: 'The human individual is the measure of all things, of fatherland, family, property, humanity, or God. Here is the logic of the Revolutionary idea'. And, he added, 'here is Socialism',[12] a dictum to which we shall have to come back.

This declaration of Jaurès tracing Leftist values to their ultimate principle is valuable for us insofar as the principle applies beyond the Left alone and therefore throws light upon the concrete situation of the Right. If individualism, properly defined, is the cardinal value of modern times, and especially of post 1789 France, then it is clear that its systematic development

by the Left has ensured its ideological supremacy. And, furthermore, who would pretend that the adepts of what Maurice
Paléologue called 'the religion of the fatherland' were absolutely immune to the individualism? They could only limit its
application, admitting it here – say in economic matters – and
excluding it there – in matters of national import. This sort of
disposition explains how the Right was somehow inferior and
weaker ideologically, as *encompassed* in the Left, and felt itself to
be so, taking on occasion a defensive or shameful attitude and
appearing insecure and self-conscious.

A strange feature of the Affair is found in the very personality of its involuntary hero. In the end he disappointed his
champions as well as his enemies through his modesty, his
reserve, his refusal of any affectation or rhetoric, to the point
that he tended to pass for an insipid character, someone
deprived of any strong conviction or courage – despite the
fact that his having withstood the terrible conditions of his
transportation would be enough to demonstrate the contrary.
Bredin notices this, and in the last page of his book he reflects
that this startling quality of Dreyfus is due, at least for a large
part, to his having housed in peaceful association within
himself the two ideologies that he saw so fiercely assaulting each
other around him. Deeply attached to France and to its army –
never distrustful of his superiors until their indignity was made
clear to him, he would never separate the cult of his fatherland
from that of justice and the dignity of man. For him both were
but one thing, and he witnessed in incredulity and bafflement
the deadly fight of which he was himself the occasion. His
humility was that of a saint who did not know the reason of his
martyrdom.

But let us go back to the beginning. The volunteers of Valmy
in 1792 would have found as incomprehensible as did Dreyfus
a conflict between 'the Nation', that is, France, and the Rights of
Man. The clue to Dreyfus's attitude is perhaps that, as a
perfectly assimilated Jew, he was a kind of neophyte to the
Republic, who had not gone beyond the Valmy stage. He was
blissfully ignorant of the checkered history of the intervening
century, of the ever recurring struggle between the universalist
ideal and the forces of conservation, that struggle which
Littré, and with him Gambetta and Jules Ferry, the founders of

the Third Republic, had been so intensely conscious of having inherited.

In fact, we are led to conclude that something that was united at the dawn of the Republic, in Valmy, and that remained united for Dreyfus himself, had become divided when put to the test of history in the nineteenth century. This is reflected in the vocabulary, as what Claude Nicolet has described as the migration of the word *nation* from the camp of the Left to that of the Right.[13] The proud outcry of the troop at Valmy, 'Vive la nation', expressed the identity of the community (*Gemeinschaft*) with the new society of free and equal individuals (*Gesellschaft*). In other words, at that exceptional historical moment the individualism of the Revolution asserted itself as the heir, which implicitly carried on the holism of the traditional society. The people of one land, one territory, gave itself over to universal values. It was this enthusiastic and paradoxical identification that would not stand the test of history. Hence a shift of the word 'nation' itself. It began with the Right slowly accepting the term in the course of the century, so that it became part of the common vocabulary. Then the trauma of 1870–71 intensified the feeling and there appeared a new phenomenon, a French nationalism. To quote Nicolet:

This nationalism [which Renan, Taine, Fustel de Coulanges occasionally discuss] will not renounce anything of the Revolutionary patrimony but at the same time, by dissociating the nation from the transitory regimes, – especially from the Republic –, by rejecting universalist and cosmopolitan ideologies, finally by recovering the ethnic roots of the nation of the Ancien Régime [let us call it the holistic perception of the French community] ( . . .), it will become a Rightist, mostly anti-Republican ideology.[14]

Such a nationalism nourished the ephemeral popularity of General Boulanger, who seemed for a short time to represent a threat to democracy, and after the crisis the Left decidedly preferred the words 'patriot', 'patriotism'. The shift was then complete: the word 'nation' had accomplished its migration.

This shift can be seen to be the trace of an ideological fission: the particularistic holism which the 1792 Revolutionaries encompassed in their universalistic individualism asserted itself independently from and in opposition to this universalism. That is what Dreyfus was blind to.

Did nationalism become the essential content of the Rightist ideology in the days of the Boulangist crisis and the Dreyfus affair? In the perspective adopted here, it is one fundamental element. Thus, for instance, what was in the same period in Germany the core of global ideology was in France only a relatively minor component of the global ideology. This does not mean that the Right has a monopoly of patriotism, for the Left participates in it in some way, just as the Right does not totally escape the individualism which is at the core of the Left. It is only a question of the relative rank attributed, on either side, to the peoccupations of universal justice and national destiny, as in the formulas of Paléologue and Dansette that we quoted. In other words, the relative rank of France as a community and as a society.

The Dreyfus affair is important in many respects. For our present concern, it confirms our analysis insofar as its final solution went according to the hierarchy of values that we have acknowledged here. The fact that the Republican regime was able to weather such a shattering storm shows the wisdom of its founders. The Constitution itself had issued from a difficult conciliation between some Royalists on the one hand, some Liberals and Republicans on the other, and the great republican statesmen chose to govern through a union of moderate Republicans and those of the Conservatives who were nearer to them. Claude Nicolet underscores the role of three men. The influence of Positivism was important, especially through Littré, who had lived through all the great conflicts of the century and had the courage to republish his old articles with commentaries, including some painful recantations (he died in 1881). Gambetta and Jules Ferry, despite their Republican zeal, were also sages who were able to postpone their most cherished reforms – the 'Separation between Church and State' – and to introduce at first only those the country was prepared to admit. It is thanks to them, and to the public education which they introduced, that a series of victories at the polls, first of the Republicans and then of the Radicals, secured the Republic and made possible the 'Separation' at the beginning of the twentieth century.

The wisdom of a few statesmen has of course not brought to an end France's ideological dichotomy. The Republic only assuaged it and made the Parliament the arena of choice for its exercise. Very soon, for instance, the Republicans were divided into 'opportunists' and 'radicals'. The preeminence of the Left among the representatives of the nation was so marked that latter day political scientists have coined the word 'sinistrism' (or *sinistrose*) to designate it. Nicolet aptly defines the phenomenon as a

> double movement: with age most Leftist parties and labels evolve towards the Center, towards the Right ... On the other hand formations periodically appear on their left, which play the same structural role towards them as they themselves played one generation earlier.[15]

The party called 'Radical' is a case in point. Soon doubled by the 'Radical-Socialists', it opposed at first, between 1875 and 1885, the opportunism of Gambetta and Ferry. Its chief figure was Clemenceau. And just as Clemenceau then opposed Ferry, so in the 1890s the Socialist Jaurès would oppose Clemenceau. The evolution of the latter was spectacular. He actually exchanged one camp for the other, being a libertarian anarchist at the beginning of the Dreyfus affair, and a minister who implacably repressed the workers' strikes in 1906 – not to speak of his incarnating the war effort in the last years of the First World War and dictating the harsh conditions of the Peace of Versailles. Equally clear is the Socialist shift from intransigent opposition to participation in the government, beginning with that of Millerand in 1906, which appeared as an act of treason to the party.

The whole affair has sometimes been summed up by saying that a politician had to belong to the Left to get elected, and had to move towards the Right to attain a government post. In brief: 'One gets elected on the Left, and one governs on the Right'.

Nicolet admits that this 'sinistrism' had deep social and ideological causes. Actually, we can show that it results from the ideology itself as analysed here. The disjunction between principle and actuality, on which we insisted, implied, under the Third Republic a dynamic of political life. For if the ideology cannot be implemented in its pure state, then people of the Left cannot govern without compromising with the

existing order, without, that is, betraying their initial commitment. And as long as the ideology remains alive and strong, it
will revive as a phoenix under the form of a new party, ever
more radical than its forerunners, rising to the left of the Left:
after the Radicals so called, the Socialists, then the Communists.

It can be objected that the political ascension of Socialism in
the widest sense, no doubt a major ideological event of the
period, introduced a new, heterogeneous element, for, as I
stated elsewhere,[16] socialism does not merely continue the
French Revolution, it also goes against it in some of its aspects –
in varying degree in its diverse tendencies. Yet Socialists like to
think of themselves as its direct heirs. Karl Polanyi saw in
socialism the end product of Christian individualism (*The Great
Transformation*). In France this was ideologically decisive. Thus
Jaurès, in the passage quoted, identified with the individualistic
principle both 'the Revolutionary idea' and Socialism. From
1920 onwards, the supporters of the Bolshevik Revolution
presented it as the sequence and the achievement of 1789. As
unlikely as the thesis may look, the wide audience of the
Communists in France up to the Second World War was due to
their having thus managed partly to confiscate for their own
purposes the Leftist ideology which was so strongly alive among
the common people.

Apart from the peculiar pattern called 'sinistrism', many
general features of political life under the Third Republic may,
we believe, be understood through the existence and the
strength of the ideological configuration we have outlined. This
is true of the notorious shortcomings of the political system. We
cannot here enter into details, but only mention government
instability, the frequent ineffectiveness of policies, the weakness
of the executive. With respect to the latter, it is characteristic
that the dissolution of the Chamber by the executive, although
explicitly provided for in the Constitution, was not resorted to
one single time. More important perhaps, the particular path
taken by the progress of legislation and political action on the
society, the fact that such and such measures – and not others –
were taken, in such and such an order, should be amenable to
our analysis, but we can here only sketch an approach. On the
one hand one can discern the main stages that secured the
foundations of the régime, and thus laid the basis, at one

remove, of the present-day political and social system. On the other hand, it has been stated, and it is fairly obvious, that social progress has been relatively slow in comparison with other countries. Thus, it is remarkable that Bismarck established a social security system in Germany, while France had to wait for it until after the Second World War. At the same time Bismarck failed against the Catholic Church, where the French succeeded. Political action in France in that period was oriented more to ideological and political aims than to social welfare.

Summing up the course of this study, I think we have acquired two perceptions: the predominant ideology in France is that of the Left. It implies the commonly held belief that whatever is easy to conceive should be easy to realise in practice. But in actual fact, and contrary to this belief, that ideology was so foreign to social actuality that the efforts to implement it issued in recurring disappointments and setbacks, with the final result that a Republic based on universal suffrage – or almost so – could be really established only after a century of hardships and trials. We have thus enabled ourselves to understand, in general terms, the kind of fatality recalled by Raymond Aron, and also to acknowledge how the Right, though being ideologically subordinate, has nevertheless been in charge of a part of the common patrimony.

This latter point will come out still more clearly if we contrast individualism, in which, as Jaurès put it, 'the individual is the measure of all things', and holism as the reverse case, where the social totality, the global society is valued above and against the individual.

If we compare France with its neighbours regarding the respective place of individualism and holism in the global ideology (and the institutions) of the country, we find that France is characterised essentially by the exclusive affirmation of the individualism inherited from the Enlightenment. In contrast, England possesses an altogether similar form of individualism, but has been able to combine with it a good deal of traditional, older, holistic inheritance. Thus it has no written Constitution but relies much on precedent, in its jurisprudence and in general; it keeps a monarchy, and has a state religion, although not a national one. As for Germany, it acculturated intensely to the newest form of modernity around 1800 and built up a culture in which, in contrast with England, enlightened individualism figures as an element partly modified by a new and original combination of holism and individualism.

If now we ask where in the French configuration the holistic aspects present elsewhere are to be found, those aspects which the encompassing French values, those of the Left, ignore, and without which the society could probably not exist, the political domain offers an answer: these aspects are found on the Right, mostly in a subordinate position, sometimes shamefaced or self-conscious, and reasserted now and then in unexpected and sometimes violent ways.

My aim here has been to elucidate an ideological configuration and some of its factual concomitants. If I may submit a methodological conclusion: in my view the study of such general representations requires three conditions: (1) they should be identified through comparison: (2) they should be considered in a long-range historical perspective: (3) the analysis should follow a hierarchical method, going from the global level to the local and not the reverse.

## NOTES

This chapter is the text of a lecture given in the University of North Carolina at Chapel Hill in October 1988. It is an English version of an earlier communication in French to the Société d'Ethnologie Française, summary in *Ethnologie Française* vol. 18, 1988, No. 1, pp. 82–84). As alluded to in the text there is a complement on 'The Impact of War', to be published.

1. Louis Dumont, *Essays on Individualism*, Chicago, 1986, p. 130.
2. J.A. Laponce, *Left and Right. The Topography of Political Perceptions*, Toronto, 1981, pp. 52–56.
3. Fr. Goguel and A. Grosser, *La politique en France*, Paris, 1981, p. 27.
4. Laponce, *Left and Right*, pp. 47ff.
5. Goguel in Goguel and Grosser, *La politique*, p. 26.
6. Dumont, *Individualism*, pp. 94–96.
7. Emile Littré, *Conservation, révolution, positivisme*, 2nd edn, Paris, 1879, pp. 330–31.
8. Louis Dumont, 'Collective Identities and Universalist Ideology', *Theory, Culture and Society*, vol. 3, 1986, p. 33.

9. Littré, *Conservation*, p. 161.
10. Claude Nicolet, *L'idée républicaine en France. Essai d'histoire critique*, Paris, 1982, p. 204.
11. Jean-Denis Bredin, *L'affaire*, Paris, 1983.
12. Bredin, *L'affaire*, p. 631.
13. Nicolet, *L'idée républicaine*, p. 16.
14. Nicolet, *L'idée républicaine*, pp. 17–18.
15. Nicolet, *L'idée républicaine*, p. 184.
16. Dumont, *Individualism*, p. 103.

# CHAPTER 13

# Property, justice and common good after socialism

*John Dunn*

In his recent and impressively lucid analysis of *The Right to Private Property*, Jeremy Waldron takes as his central challenge a question which extends back at least to Plato and Aristotle.[1] As Aristotle expressed it in the *Politics*: 'What are the best arrangements to make about property, if a State is to be as well constituted as it is possible to make it? Is property to be held in common or not?'[2] In the present century the contest between defenders of private and common property has frequently appeared as the principal issue in world politics; and it has long been a pressing concern in the domestic politics of Great Britain. (It would certainly take more than Mrs Thatcher to eliminate it from the latter arena.) In the course of the Presidencies of Ronald Reagan and Mikhail Gorbachev and of the Premiership of Mrs Thatcher it has come to be widely assumed that this contest has reached a decisive outcome. Economies organised largely on the basis of common property, it is now all but universally agreed, cannot assure the prosperity of modern populations; and because they cannot assure their prosperity they cannot, in the long run, guarantee their security either. Since the overweening claims to authority made by modern states depend directly for their cogency upon these states' capacity to secure the welfare and safety of their citizens,[3] the custodians of modern state power have little choice in eschewing common ownership as a dominant principle in the organisation of production. They may still choose to acknowledge this practical constraint with better or worse grace. But they flout it at their peril.

Common ownership as the organising principle of a system of production might in due course be resuscitated by a clear demonstration of its practical efficacy (a demonstration that may or may not lie within the bounds of natural possibility – be compatible with the laws of nature – but which is scarcely imminent).[4] What is decidedly less clear is that common ownership can be as readily abandoned as the ultimate justifying principle of a system of distribution. Modern liberal theories of social justice, as classically expressed by John Rawls and as powerfully elaborated over the last decade by writers like Ronald Dworkin and Brian Barry, cannot be said to have had much practical impact upon the historical process. But the demise of common ownership in the field of production has not appreciably lessened its imaginative appeal in the domain of distributive justice, despite the intensive political exertions of those who deplore it in either guise or who deny that it can coherently operate in the one domain without covertly doing so in the other also. Yet why should it prove any more durable in the one case than it has in the other?

One simple and reasonably cogent answer is that common ownership signifies something entirely different in the two domains. What renders the principle of common ownership of most of the means of production massively unattractive in the late twentieth century is a strictly causal matter: that it appears at present levels of human comprehension and skill (and perhaps at any naturally possible levels of these) to preclude efficient production.[7] But the principle of common ownership in the domain of distribution is not in itself a causal hypothesis. It does not predict definite consequences for given actions: still less assert a guaranteed benefit from particular lines of conduct, or even from the pursuit of particular social goals, instead, it simply affirms a criterion for publicly avowable and morally defensible social goals: the interests of at least all the human beings concerned. This criterion certainly raises clear problems about the scope of putative ownership, jeopardising the status of the territorial state as the uniquely appropriate frame of distributive responsiblity,[8] and questioning the normative adequacy of an exclusive concern with the needs and purposes of members of the human species. But it also establishes a powerful claim to normative authority, and one with considerable historical depth. The central premiss of Christian natural law understanding of human claims to own and enjoy economic goods was the presumption that God had given the world to human beings in common, and given it for their use. That was what the world was for. The secular heirs of the tradition of natural jurisprudence are understandably ill at ease with the presumption that the world really is *for* anything: that it has a clear telos independent of the historical vagaries of human purpose. But they still find it difficult to develop any coherent normative viewpoint without tacitly readopting the Christian natural law presumption, despite the apparent absence today of appropriate foundations for that presumption. Even utilitarians, for example, in effect treat as the telos of the world at least the full set of the historical vagaries of human purpose (along, perhaps, with the balance of pain and pleasure for every other sentient creature).[9] The Christian impetus towards inclusiveness within the human species itself is extended in its secular descendants, apparently under the sole impress of rationality, across the borders of the species, and perhaps eventually even to non-sentient entities.[10]

Modern liberal theorists of justice offer an appreciably more powerful and coherent viewpoint at present than any of their socialist or conservative critics. (They are better, that is to say, at moral theory.) But their lack of impact upon the historical process has not been fortuitous.[11] To consider the assignment of natural goods and of the products of historically developed human powers as morally answerable to at least the needs of all living humans[12] is a plausible precondition for any rationally defensible theory of ownership, use or enjoyment. But it is grimly distant, both imaginatively and practically, from the gritty and confused settings in which actual conflicts over ownership, use or enjoyment invariably occur. Robert Nozick's criticism of the ahistorical unreality of modern liberal theories of distributive justice lends no real support to his own whimsical construction of the normative implications of the history of human production.[13] But it does pick out a profound weakness of these theories: their singularly equivocal treatment of economic causality.

Aristotle's question – what are the best arrangements to make about property if a state is to be as well constituted as it is possible to make it? – is still a central question in modern politics. Indeed it is hard to see, short of the termination of all human politics, how it can ever cease to be such.[14] But, as

Aristotle himself firmly realised it is as much a question about
the probable consequences of human actions as it is about the
rational justification of particular evaluative beliefs or aspirations. Right wing and left wing critics of modern liberal theories
of social justice have both pilloried the unreality of these
theories and the distressing range of unintended consequences
of attempts to embody even a minimal version of them in the
institutions of post-war welfare states. (It should be noted that
these two lines of attack are not obviously compatible.) But
these critics have had far less success in contesting their
standing as moral theories, being reduced for the most part to
efforts to break up or dissipate systematic moral thinking about
the domains of economics or politics.[15] These are old ideological quarrels (Machiavelli against the residues of medieval
Christianity and civic humanist blandness; Burke against Paine;
Weber against Marx). But the form which they take today is
remarkably stark and has yet to be captured at all commandingly. Is the choice which we now face really a choice between a
world of practical causality that simply repudiates the claims of
moral rationality (though it continues to take the precaution of
professing a desultory array of good intentions) and a practice
of reflexive moral rationality which either has no detectable
purchase on the practical world at all or (still worse) affects the
latter where it does so only in ways manifestly at odds with its
own intentions? Can there still be morally informed and
grounded political agency? Or must any claim to act politically
in a morally informed and grounded manner be ultimately
self-deceptive, where it is not offered in conscious bad faith?

The key issue in modern politics is the issue of agency. The
great modern traditions of political understanding – the liberal
conceptions of constitutionally protected personal liberty and
market-generated prosperity, and the socialist conceptions of
the effective pursuit of the interests of exploited class majorities
– all depend fundamentally on the validity of their assessment
of the nature and efficacy of particular forms of agency. They
are all theories of how to act with predictably desirable consequences. Each of these traditions has been subjected to the most
corrosive criticism, though it is fair to say that the second has
for the present worn decidedly worse than the first, and it
ought by now to be possible to explain this disparity with some

clarity. Much recent thinking, too, has sharpened longstanding demotic suspicions about the prospects for effective collaborative action under any possible normative inspiration. The intellectually baffling problems of collective action – of coordinating interests which are always partly in conflict, on the basis of highly imperfect information and for the greater benefit of the majority of those affected – have been explored with great tenacity in recent decades.[16] The better these problems are understood, the less plausible the expectation that they could be resolved even in principle by clearer thought or better devised institutions. The sense of human collective life as an unmasterable but inescapable strategic predicament, at every level from the single individual to the most populous, powerful or wealthy of contemporary states, presses hard upon modern political consciousness. It does so, not because humans today are less generous or psychologically resilient than their forbears, but because they have been taught to see their lives in this way and because the instruction, however partial it may be and however potentially destructive its results, is also essentially valid. It is the purely cognitive weight of the interpreted causal complexity of the world in which we live that numbs our capacity to conceive political agency with any force and clarity: let alone to enact it effectively in the always refractory world of political practice.

It is an important historical question (as yet very poorly answered) how far such constitutionally protected personal liberties, market generated prosperity and effectively realised interests of previously exploited class majorities as exist today have come to do so as a result of political action premised on valid causal understanding. The historical sequences from which these human benefits have emerged have always contained many other and distinctly less reassuring elements: spasms of savage and destructive violence, mass murders, unyielding cruelty and obtuseness. The economic mishaps of socialist production may well in the end prove to outweigh every human benefit credibly attributable to the great twentieth-century revolutions. But even if they do not do so, no serious analysis of the trajectory of these dramatic episodes can present even their more encouraging features as the intended consequences of a political agency informed by valid understanding of the context in which it was acting.[17]

Nor, to take what is for the present a less dispiriting example, can the recent economic triumphs of Liberal Democrat Japan be realistically understood as the outcome of clearly conceived and steadily implemented collective goals by an integral political agency that knew what it was doing. Despite almost four decades of rule by a single democratically re-elected governing party in intimate symbiosis with a polished and widely admired public bureaucracy, despite a sustained economic dynamism unmatched on such a scale within the last half century, and despite highly intelligent and illuminating celebrations of its prowess as a developmental actor,[18] the political vicissitudes of the post-war Japanese state defy interpretation in terms of unified and clairvoyant agency.[19]

There are one or two countries whose recent political development has been reassuring enough for most of their inhabitants and steady enough when seen from abroad to encourage the view that their states at least are relatively rational and integrated agencies operating in pursuit of clearly conceived goals. Sweden is still a much cited example,[20] indispensable for sustaining the hopes of Social Democrats in less fortunate lands. The Federal Republic of Germany, Holland and perhaps Canada are other and less ideologically emotive cases. It is not only employees of OECD who see the operation of the world economy over the last forty years as a massive extension of the rewards of modern liberty.[21]

The maintenance and expansion of the world economy has been, and remains, a political as much as an economic process. It is caused by (reinforced or imperilled by) the agency of states and supranational entities as well as by economic actors in quest of personal or corporate profits. There has been sharp dispute over the last decade as to how far the post-war success of the world economy was a product of the unparalleled power of the United States and the relatively coherent purposes (in this respect at least) of its successive national governments, and more urgent disagreement over just how far the world economy can continue to flourish in the absence of a single global hegemon and in conditions where coercive power and wealth become increasingly discontinuous.[22] It takes some optimism to discern relatively coherent purposes in the United States government at present (as it does in the government of the Soviet Union or Romania, or indeed Great Britain). Since politics is an inherently competitive activity (at least after the era of absolute monarchy), most holders of governmental power are provisionally united at least against those who aspire to replace them. But that degree of unity of purpose is plainly insufficient to secure much harmony in practical judgement or in choice of either strategy or goals. It is not necessary to study game theory to appreciate that the worst possible outcome for all in a given predicament can sometimes result from actions that make the best possible sense for each. Effective political agency over any length of time is principally an exercise in the reimagining and practical reconstruction of given predicaments: in the identification and maintenance of compelling solidarities premissed upon the reinterpretation of these predicaments. It is not necessarily the best way of enhancing political understanding to concentrate on the attractions of effective political agency for keenly desired ends.

To insist on the importance of efficacy in politics is no novelty: it is more in the nature of a truism. Most serious political thinkers have paid at least lip service to this imperative. The great eighteenth-century Scottish theorists of commercial society[23] and their modern heirs shared with later Marxist critics a clear commitment to it. The need to consider the efficacy of action with as much care as the desirability of goals formed the core of Max Weber's understanding of politics and lent a notably acerbic quality to his nationalist reading of the goals of economic policy.[24] But except as a device for belabouring political opponents, it is extremely difficult to adopt the premiss and think on at all commandingly on its terms. This does not mean that adopting minimalist[25] (or publicly unavowable)[26] goals in political agency is guaranteed to do more good or less harm than any more ambitious alternative. (Consider the economic consequences of Mrs Thatcher.)[27] But it does highlight a distressing tension between reasonably rich conceptions of social purpose and accurately understood practical expedients. In this sense the recent political travails of Keynesian macroeconomics (whatever the ultimate verdict on their purely cognitive sources) are perhaps better understood primarily in terms of the degree of political exposure and vulnerability intrinsic to any attempt to do something complicated generous, lasting and worthwhile through the agency of a modern state.

In a prosperous, just and secure society there is everything to be said for minimalist goals in political agency. (Why imperil what is already very good?) But there are at present no societies that are genuinely prosperous, just and secure, and little reason for confidence that there ever will be any: let alone that there is much danger of all human societies eventually becoming such. The international consequences of Mr Gorbachev have already diminished some appalling dangers; but they have also unleashed plenty of novel perils too. The domestic consequences of Mr Gorbachev[28] are not merely for the present utterly imponderable: they also plainly demand, sooner or later, a relatively ambitious political response. In a society that is neither prosperous, just nor secure and which confessedly cannot go on in the old way, the choice of minimalist political goals (staying in power, prolonging the real political monopoly of the ruling party, maintaining urban food supplies) would demonstrate not sober prudence but a truly Neronic irresponsibility. Yet a relatively ambitious political response is always a perilous adventure. (That is why revolutions almost always, sooner or later, end in tears, whether or not their ultimate consequences prove to be on balance benign.) The reconstruction of an entire state, society and economy cannot on principle be an instance principally of a definite set of human beings (let alone one human being) knowing just what they are doing. But such reconstructions sometimes have to occur; and there is good reason to see the existence of every modern state, society and economy as undergoing a more muted version of such transformation virtually all the time. The view that even the less turbulent passages of this transformation can be aptly understood in terms of reassuring homeostatic mechanisms, popular amongst American social scientists in the post-war decades, now looks staggeringly credulous: blankly at odds with such vestiges of causal understanding as the modern social sciences have contrived to accumulate. (In the last instance game theory will face down any version of systems theory whenever the going gets rough.)

It is an open secret that political leaders in the modern world operate in a setting of which they can hope to have only the shadowiest knowledge and comprehension. No doubt political leaders have always done so; and no doubt the more imaginative and analytical of contemporary political leaders (like Mr Gorbachev) know and understand markedly more than the less diligent and intellectually gifted (like Mr Reagan). But it requires no undue personal despondency to infer from the political experience of the last decade that the real (efficient rather than ceremonial) function of political leaders in modern societies is often principally to sedate the political awareness of the subjects of whose destiny they are nominally in charge.

But however far it may be from the fluent implementation of clearly conceived intentions, modern political agency remains eminently consequential. It matters how state power is exerted, and how states deal with one another. The outcome of the Uruguay round of the GATT negotiations will affect the economic prospects of most of the world's population; and it will affect very many of them very deeply indeed. The economic, coercive and diplomatic practices of the American government in the face of the trade in illegal drugs will reshape the lives (or occasion the deaths) of many millions, both at home and abroad. To understand politics today would be to understand a reality as urgent and alarming as it has ever been in human history. But it might well also be to understand with quite new clarity how devastatingly narrow and practically unhelpful the human understanding of politics must always remain.

This is not a matter about which modern thinkers have yet had the courage to think very hard. But it deserves more serious attention. One major instance which evidently demands this is the recent and remarkably rapid collapse in the political credibility of socialism, even for those who found it credible in the first place. What has collapsed, to be sure, is not (as yet) in all cases a series of entrenched political interests (in organisations, prebends, rallying symbols and turns of phrase). Nor is it a range of decently avowable social intentions. Rather, it is a rationally assessed and reasonably integral structure of social, economic and political institutions and practices linking the organisations, rallying symbols, turns of phrase and avowable social intentions at all plausibly to the predictable consequences of intended actions.[29] Without such links, the socialist residues may in the short run prove more lasting than the feudal residues of the ancien régime: but their eventual prospects must be every bit as unpromising. Socialism is especially vulnerable to clear gaps between predictable consequences and agents' intentions because it embodies such a profoundly intentionalist vision of the nature of a good society.[30] (The gloomy history of Marxist politics underlines the fact that this profoundly intentionalist vision of the nature of a good society is far from being the only conceptual element that socialism can embody. But the telos of history for Marxists, as much as for admirers of Benjamin Constant, is still a world of concrete human freedom. What is lethally misguided about Marxism is less its interpretation of the nature of this telos (which has seldom been very specific) than its gratuitously euphoric estimate of the means for approaching it or the prospects for eventual arrival.

The collapse in the political credibility of socialism is widely seen by its longstanding opponents (and not altogether unjustly) as the collapse of a distinctive and congenitally imprudent tradition of political action. But however natural and agreeable this perspective may be for those who share it, it does risk not merely eventual historical refutation (probably a pretty slight risk) but also an immediate and ill-advised superficiality. Socialism is far from being the only modern repository of political imprudence. It may be peculiarly ingenuous in its hopes to embody moral perception and sentiment directly in the texture of collective social life and it has certainly often proved remarkably maladroit in its choice of techniques for effecting this embodiment. But the sad contrast between consequence and (at least avowable) intention is as easy to draw for the avenging government of Mrs Thatcher as it was for those of her post-war Labour (or Tory) predecessors. The intentions which it is easy to embody effectively in the consequences of political practice are characteristically negative and destructive: the dismantling, for example of the fiefs of political opponents. It is worth pressing the question of just which techniques for embodying moral perception and sentiment even indirectly in the texture of collective social life have proved predictably deft in modern history, or indeed even in the past ten years.

Some candidates for this schedule have worn distinctly better than others: the conception of moderate government explored in Montesquieu's *L'Esprit des Lois*[31] and entrenched so durably in the representative system established by the American constitution of 1787, the vision of expanding market exchange and deepening division of labour classically set out in Smith's *Wealth of nations*. But it is a very nice question how far the undoubted and protracted services of the United States constitution to the promotion of modern liberty have issued from its formal structure and how far they rested essentially on the unique and successive historical advantages of its physical separation from other powerful states, its vast open land frontier and deep internal market for industrial goods. Certainly, both before and after emancipation, the fate of its black and Indian populations has proved beyond reasonable doubt that moderate government as such is no guarantee of the even-handed extension of the blessings of modern liberty. By the same token, the post-colonial history of Africa and Asia has shown decisively that the best designed of constitutions are at the mercy of economic weakness and intense social and political conflict.[32] Even the palpable collective benefits of capitalist production on a world scale, since by definition they are never collectively appropriated, have continued to serve some so much more handsomely than others, that to conceive them as collective benefits can seem wilfully perverse. (The case for so conceiving them was as well understood by Marx as it was by Adam Smith[33] and it has not served modern socialists in the Third World or elsewhere (still less their hapless subjects) to have gone so far in forgetting it. Under the Ricardian theory of comparative advantage, the gains from international trade would on the whole be justly allocated on a genuinely open market. But Ricardian comparative advantage starkly misrepresents the strategic manoeuvering to appropriate rents that dominates international trade today and it is likely to prove more irrelevant than ever to the increasingly manipulated and protectionist markets of the late twentieth century.[34]

There is one very simple answer to offer, in the late twentieth century, to Aristotle's question. The best arrangements to make about property, the arrangements that will render a state as well constituted as it is possible for it to be, are those that will maximise aggregate utility (or collective well-being) for the population of the state in question. But there are an endless series of difficulties with this answer, from vexed issues of distributive justice, through doubts about the capacity of any human agencies (governmental or otherwise) to judge the utility or well-being of others with minimal accuracy, to the blunt and obtrusive fact that no holders of state power today happen to know which arrangements will in practice maximise aggregate utility or even avoid diminishing it very drastically. (It is not plausible, even of Mrs Thatcher, that she intended to deflate the British economy as harshly as she did in the opening years of her Premiership, merely because of the incidental political conveniences of having done so.) Few, of course, would be fool enough to explain the level and distribution of fiscal extraction in the United States of America at a given time solely by its government's choice of a particular normative criterion for political success. But even the most disabused vision of policy-making as acrimonious bureaucratic and interest group feuding will have to recognise sooner or later the impact within it of dramatic miscalculations of economic causality. No doubt the practice of good government in any society at any time has always been more or less at the mercy of effective lobbying. But a pessimistic observer of the American or Russian (or perhaps even Japanese) political process today might easily view its practice of government as virtually dissolved into a practice of effective lobbying. The state as ideological fiction is the principal contemporary mode for articulating conceptions of social and political value.[35] (Its sole serious competitor in the modern world, despite the Babel of dissonant verbiage with which they share the airwaves of modern politics, is the large-scale capitalist corporation as ideological fiction.) But the view that the state in concrete reality might actually correspond to the ideological fiction and serve to implement any clear conception of political and social value is harshly at odds with virtually every aspect of our causal understanding of its concrete reality.

If we reconsider the demise of socialism in this light its implications must appear very different. Production on the basis of common ownership appears not to work. The presumption that it would work has proved to be a vast and humanly expensive causal miscalculation. But there have never been compelling reasons for regarding common ownership as an unmediated good in itself. The case for applauding it has always rested on comparisons between the putative consequences of establishing some variety of it with those of establishing a variety of private ownership: on its presumed effects on moral personality, social peace or conflict, productivity, distributive justice. The proven demerits of socialism as a technique for achieving these ends does not in itself establish the delusory or malign character of the ends themselves (though of course it leaves that possibility entirely open). Still less do the proven demerits of socialism establish the desirability of resigning a given community in its entirety to the supposed requirements of a fetishised and grossly misdescribed process of economic causality (a process which may itself prove a very poor technique for achieving most avowable ends).

In this context it is important to recur to the persisting imaginative force of the presumption of the common ownership of the goods of nature and the accumulated productive powers of human beings in the theory of distributive justice. The underlying normative premiss of socialism is simply the intuition that, despite the dominant role of power and exploitation in human history thus far, every human being remains entitled to a just share of the human opportunities that can be made open to her or him and that human society must be refashioned so that she or he can secure this right. This is a stupendously ambitious causal project; and no one at present has the dimmest idea of how it could be carried out. But the socialist tradition has kept a better imaginative grip on both its extremity and its moral power than even the most impressive liberal theorists of social justice. It is at least in part because they have sensed the scale of it and tried to implement it in practice that socialists have sometimes done such fearsome harm. Where they have not been wrong is in hearing it as a demand for action.

'What are the best arrangements to make about property?' is still the central question of modern politics.[36] (If we are obliterated in thermonuclear war, we should still be so in the last instance because of the epic misadventures of modern answers to this question.) A socialist command economy has proved a disastrous technique for implementing the premiss of common ownership as criterion for just distribution. But it has done nothing to show that it is not the correct criterion. A sound criterion for distributive justice unaccompanied by any credible technique for realising this in practice can be little more than a taunting and brutal mockery of our limited capacities for shame. To see how any such criterion can be brought to bear upon the texture of collective social life requires an accurate judgment of social, economic and political causality. (To see that it cannot be so brought to bear would be to see that we must keep our moral sensibilities firmly out of politics and adopt the most minimal or private goals within it: a more austere conclusion than Professor Hayek appears to appreciate.) The political question is still 'What is to be done?' Socialism, it seems, was the wrong answer. But it was at least an answer to the right question.

## NOTES

The immediate stimulus for this essay was provided by a talk by Ernest Gellner in Kings College, Cambridge in October 1989 on the prospects for perestroika in the USSR.

1. Jeremy Waldron, *The Right to Private Property*, Oxford, 1988.
2. Aristotle, *The Politics*, 1262b (Tr. T.A. Sinclair), Harmondsworth, 1962, p. 62.
3. Cf. John Dunn, 'Political obligation', in David Held (ed.), *Political Theory Today*, Cambridge, 1991; 'Liberty as a substantive political value', in J. Dunn, *Interpreting Political Responsibility: Essays 1981–89*, Princeton and Cambridge, 1990.
4. Cf. for example, Frank Hahn, 'On some economic limits to modern politics', in J. Dunn (ed.), *The Economic Limits to Modern Politics*, Cambridge, 1990.
5. John Rawls, *A Theory of Justice*, Oxford, 1972, and many subsequent articles.
6. Ronald Dworkin, *Taking Rights Seriously*, London, 1977, and *A Matter of Principle*, Cambridge, Mass., 1985; Brian Barry, *Theories of Justice*, London, 1989.
7. For the overwhelming importance of this judgement see J. Dunn, *The Politics of Socialism*, Cambridge, 1984.
8. See especially Barry, *Theories of Justice* and compare J. Dunn, 'Unimagined Community' in J. Dunn, *Rethinking Modern Political Theory*, Cambridge, 1985, chap. 6.
9. It is extremely difficult to see how this framework of assessment can generate any coherent and cogent practical conclusions.

Compare Derek Parfit's 'repugnant conclusion': Derek Parfit, *Reasons and Persons*, Oxford, 1984.

10. Cf. Parfit, *Reasons and Persons*; Peter Singer, *Animal Liberation*, London, 1977; James Griffin, *Well-being: its meaning, measurement and moral importance*, Oxford, 1986 and the extremely interesting review of this by Samuel Scheffler, 'Making the best of Utilitarianism', *Times Literary Supplement*, 7 August 1987, pp. 835–36.

11. Cf. Dunn, 'The Future of Political Philosophy in the West', in Dunn, *Rethinking Modern Political Theory*, chap. 10.

12. This is plainly an indefensibly parsimonious standard to adopt. Why not those of future generations of human beings? Why not other sentient species?

13. Robert Nozick, *Anarchy, State and Utopia*, Oxford, 1974; and cf. the review by Dunn, *Ratio*, 19, 1977.

14. Cf. Dunn, *Economic Limits to Modern Politics*.

15. Compare, for example, Dworkin's harsh appraisal of Michael Walzer's sensitive *Spheres of Justice*, Oxford, 1983 in Dworkin, *A Matter of Principle*, chap. 10, pp.214–20.

16. For a helpful introduction see Russell Hardin, *Collective Action*, Baltimore, 1982; Robert Axelrod, *The Evolution of Cooperation*, New York, 1984.

17. J. Dunn, 'The Success and Failure of Modern Revolutions', in Dunn, *Political Obligation in its Historical Context*, Cambridge, 1980, chap. 9 and 'Understanding Revolutions', in Dunn, *Rethinking Modern Political Theory*, chap. 4; Theda Skocpol, *States and Social Revolutions*, Cambridge, 1979.

18. See especially Chalmers Johnson, *MITI and the Japanese Economic Miracle: the growth of industrial policy 1925–1975*, Stanford, 1982.

19. See especially Kent E. Calder's dogged and cumulatively decisive *Crisis and Compensation*, Princeton, 1989.

20. Cf. Gösta Esping-Anderson, *Politics against Markets: The Social Democratic Road to Power*, Princeton, 1985.

21. Cf. Benjamin Constant, *Political Writings*, ed. Biancamaria Fontana, Cambridge, 1988, pp. 309–28.

22. Robert Keohane, *After Hegemony*, Princeton, 1984; Robert Gilpin, *Political Economy of International Relations*, Princeton, 1987.

23. Istvan Hont and Michael Ignatieff (eds.), *Wealth and Virtue*, Cambridge, 1983, especially the Introduction.

24. Max Weber, 'Politics as a Vocation', in *From Max Weber*, ed. H.H. Gerth and C. Wright Mills, London, 1948, pp. 77–128: 'The National State and Economic Policy', *Economy and Society*, 9, 1980.

25. For example, enhance the dynamism of an economy by retracting the direct exertion of governmental power from the operations of the economy.

26. For example, sharply increase the proportion of national income accruing to the wealthier members of the population.

27. Ken Coutts and Wynne Godley, 'The British Economy under Mrs Thatcher', *The Political Quarterly*, 60, 2, 1989.

28. This formula is simply a way of referring to what is happening within the Soviet Union: not a recommended approach to its causal analysis.

29. Cf. Dunn, *The Politics of Socialism*. The prebends, perhaps, were never very plausibly linked in this way.

30. For the importance of this see the forthcoming work of Anthony Butler of Kings College, Cambridge. See also Adam Przeworski, *Capitalism and Social Democracy*, Cambridge, 1985.

31. Bernard Manin, *Du Libéralisme à La Terreur*, Paris, 1992.

32. J. Dunn, 'Representation and Good Government in Postcolonial Africa' in Patrick Chabal (ed.), *Political Domination in Africa*, Cambridge, 1986.

33. Cf. Bill Warren, *Imperialism: Pioneer of Capitalism*, London, 1980; Keith Hart, *The Political Economy of West African Agriculture*, Cambridge, 1982; John Sender and Sheila Smith, *The Development of Capitalism in Africa*, London, 1986.

34. Cf. Gilpin, *Political Economy of International Relations*, esp. chaps 5 and 10.

35. Cf. Dunn, *Interpreting Political Responsibility*, Introduction. It is not, of course, necessarily the practical instrument most favoured by all for realising these conceptions.

36. Cf. Dunn, *Economic Limits to Modern Politics*.

CHAPTER 14

# Social contract, democracy and freedom

*Gerard Radnitzky*

Political liberty is good only so far as it produces private
liberty.

Samuel Johnson[1]

While Dr Johnson's eighteenth-century optimism about human
nature – the thought that Nature will rise up and . . . overturn a
corrupt political system'[2] – cannot be shared by those with
experience of twentieth-century history, his concern for individual freedom/private rights will be shared by all those who
believe in some modern version of classical liberalism. James
Buchanan and Friedrich von Hayek give, for the public arena,
priority to freedom. Buchanan thinks that with the help of a
contractarian approach it is possible to arrive at a Constitution
of Liberty without recourse to non-instrumental value judgements, while Hayek's evolutionary approach to the Constitution of Liberty acknowledges the necessity of taking a stand on
value issues.[3] Can a contractarian approach deliver the goods?
What kinds of problems is it intended to solve, and what kinds
of problems can it solve? What is the proper role of the State?
Classical liberalism views the State as an instrument: 'an instrumental State, one charged with the performance of a set of
tasks which, however do *not* include responsibility for ultimate
human fulfilment, or for the rule of righteousness'.[4] But, how
to define that 'set of tasks'? Can the social-contract type of
theory in combination with the democratic method help to
secure freedom? What is the relationship between economic
freedoms, civil liberties and political freedom?

## 1. A SOCIAL-CONTRACT TYPE OF THEORY CANNOT EXPLAIN THE ORIGINS OF THE STATE.

Yet, since time immemorial myths of contractual origins have
been used for ideological purposes: by offering a causal

297

explanation of the emergence of a particular state – an *ad hoc* explanation – they simultaneously legitimise that state. Often it is claimed that supernational entities have been part of the contract – from the totemic animal of the tribe to various gods and divine law givers. The modern versions of social-contract type of theory no longer attempt to provide a historical explanation of the origins of the State as an institution. Instead they attempt to legitimise the State in terms of public goods: law and order being viewed as the supreme public good.

Very likely the institution of the State evolved as a spontaneous order, like, for example, the market order and money. The successful individuals, families or clans who founded states intended to cement their power by means of edicts and laws; they did not intend to contribute to bringing about a particular form of social organisation. The modern State evolved from the monopolisation of coercion and violence and by placing them in the service of protecting and securing the possessions and lives of individuals against intruders from outside (national defence) and against intruders from inside (internal security, later equality before the law). Nozick's invisible-hand explanation of the rise of the 'ultraminimal' state is suggestive.[5] He focuses on the evolution of more and more efficient solutions to the problem of enforcement, from mutual-protection associations and professional private protective agencies to the single protective agency that dominates a particular area. After the institution of the State has emerged in cultural evolution, it becomes conceivable that people may sign a Social Contract. Perhaps the founding of the colony of Plymouth in the seventeenth century is the only known example of such an event.[6]

The evolution of the institution of the State should be viewed against the foil of the development from the face-to-face group to the anonymous society, the development from the 'solidarity' norm system to the new rule system consisting of 'abstract' rules. Rules are 'abstract' in the sense that they apply to any individual chosen at random (including government and state) by abstracting from all concrete particular circumstances. The choice example of such a development in Hayek's theory of cultural evolution is the development from personal exchange to an impersonal market order based on abstract rules.[7] It enabled the individual to transcend the experience based on personal acquaintance, the social world of the face-to-face group. Another well-known example of an evolutionary explanation of a feature of that development is the emergence of money.[8] Money is an asset with low marginal costs of acquiring information; it has social productivity because its use helps to save resources and makes possible the extension of the market system precisely because of the reduction in the cost of making exchanges. It is a substitute for the specialised market skills that are part of a particular transactor's epistemic resources and 'human wealth'. It too qualifies as a public good.

## 2. A NON-NORMATIVE SOCIAL-CONTRACT THEORY CANNOT PRODUCE THE RATIONALE FOR A LIMITED CHOICE RULE

Some of the social-contract theories attempt to legitimise a Constitution of Liberty without introducing a normative premiss. Let us make the contractarian argument as strong as possible in order to criticise it. Social-contract theory aims to lend legitimacy to a set of rules by which society might be governed by pointing to the fact that the rules have been agreed to – just as in ordinary contract theory – before the rise of doctrines of substantive unconscionability.[9] Thus, legitimacy is not rooted in the content of the rules, but in the fact that they have been agreed to. Since they cannot point to an actual, *bona fide* consent, a connection between consent and content is established by the following counterfactual claim. Non-normative social-contract theory asserts that there is a contract such that no 'sane' person *would* have good reason to reject it, that is, the terms of the contract *would* be chosen by rational agents[10] because they overcome the Prisoners' Dilemma, they provide access to a Pareto-superior state of affairs. The rationality assumed is means–ends rationality, that is, that each person prefers access above non-access to certain goods. In other words, they assert that a rational agent would, after a cost–benefit analysis, come to the conclusion that the expected benefit outweighs the expected costs. *The statement that there is such a rule is not falsifiable.* Hence, the method of ascertaining whether or not a particular rule could qualify is again stated in the form of a contrary-to-fact conditional: the ideal communication community would, in the long run, unanimously agree to the rule.

There are two difficulties with this procedure: first, the contrary-to-fact conditional cannot provide a regulative principle; second, a contrary-to-fact conditional can only be deduced from a nomological, and the nomological that would be needed cannot exist because it would centre on human action, and the concept of action entails the idea that the agent could have acted otherwise. The statement that there is such a rule is not falsifiable, but it is verifiable. However, the *onus probandi* is on those who claim that there is such a rule. There are no good reasons for assuming the existence of such a rule, since, because of the subjective evaluation element involved in evaluating the expected outcomes there is no reason to assume that unanimity could ever be reached.

Still more important appears to be the following argument. As we have seen, the contractarian asks: 'Would a reasonable person have a reason to reject that contract?', and he answers: 'No – because access is better than non-access.' *But such a theory cannot produce the rationale for a limited choice rule, for a Constitution of Liberty*. That needs an additional value constraint. You can have a rule, but not a limited rule, hence not a limited constitution. The whole problem consists in how to restrict the contract making to the constitutional rules for rule making. How can it be restricted? Only by a value constraint – which, if held by all, would *eo ipso* solve the problem. But what if people supposed to sign the contract don't accept that value constraint? Hence, the whole approach appears to have an aura of circularity.

Circularity lurks also in another dimension. Any kind of contractarianism presupposes that there already exists a cultural context in order that there be criteria to distinguish between stupid and non-stupid contractarian agreements. This is but a particularisation of Hayek's thesis that all our efforts to improve our institutions must operate within a working whole which we cannot entirely control. Contract theories usually assume that the individuals who are invited to consider a particular contract offered to them already possess some rights, some enforceable, alienable rights, and then they make a contract. The principle of freedom of contract already presupposes property rights. But rights can exist only if there exists a legal framework or at least an implicit recognition of rights and some enforcement or sanctioning mechanisms. Even gift-giving presupposes recognition of property rights. Robinson and Friday can make a contract at least in a formal sense; but it would not be enforceable and it appears pointless. To speak of a 'voluntary contract' is pleonastic, because a contract made under threat is not regarded as a contract at all. It is also relevant to point to the basic difference between (a) voluntarily giving up some of your freedom when you join a club or a church or whatever else and (b) your being born in a state where you are regarded as part of an organic whole, that is, your individuality is denied – that is what 'collectivity', in a politically significant sense, means.

### 3. WHAT DO SOCIAL-CONTRACT THEORIES ACHIEVE?

Social-contract theories assure us that we actually need what we have, that is, the system we call 'the State'.[11] They may concede that the anonymous society and the State, beginning from the commercial city state, is a spontaneous order. But they assure us that it also is rational and morally appealing that mankind lives in states. Thereby they reassure also the constructivists and the statists. Originally they reassured the advocates of the protective state, later on in particular the adherents of the welfare state. In my opinion the social-contract type of theory, even if it is restricted to the constitutional framework, to rules for rule-making, runs a great risk: that by attempting to avoid taking a stand on value issues (like, for example, giving individual freedom priority in the public–political arena) it is likely to fall into the trap of an *'ethics of consensus'* – popular particularly with the Soft Left – according to which good *is* what all, or a majority, or a qualified majority, *regard* as being good.[12] An argument of that form is often labelled the 'naturalistic fallacy'. The ethics of consensus has a strong affinity to contractarianism.

*It is impossible to produce a Constitution of Liberty without explicitly declaring that individual freedom ought to be the central value for the public–potential sphere, that is, without making a genuine, a*

*non-instrumental value judgment.* (A central value must not be
confused with an absolute value; a central value does not
preclude that there may be tradeoffs.) The construction of a
Constitution of Liberty is basically a normative issue. Only
when the above-mentioned value judgment has been introduced can the scientific problem be approached, the problem
of how best – given the existent constraints – to proceed in
order to realise as much individual freedom as possible.

### 4. WHEN WOULD RATIONAL AGENTS, IF GIVEN A CHOICE, OPT FOR A SOCIAL CONTRACT?

A rational agent has to conduct a cost–benefit analysis, and he
will sign the contract only if he has come to the conclusion that,
although this submission to the coercion by the State produces
a cost, that cost is outweighed by the expected benefits.[13] What
sort of benefits could motivate him to sign? Hobbes assumed
that people are so afraid of the hurt they might suffer in
un-coerced chaos that the State appears as a maximin, the
best–worse case: 'external and internal security at a cost'. Here
the protective purpose of the State is the only thing that
matters. Later on came the romantic utopianists (like Rousseau).
They would claim that individuals are interested in the beneficial results of coercion – the '*Volksbeglückungsstaat*' (against
which Kant warned) – the paternalistic state and in modern
times the welfare state. These poeple believed, and still believe,
in the 'Principle of Hope' (E. Bloch) instead of the 'Principle of
Experience' (H. Schelsky). The Founding Fathers knew what
they were about when in the Declaration of Independence they
appealed to universal *option* rights (not to welfare rights). An
option right places an obligation on *all* others not to interfere in
the domain protected by that right, while a so-called welfare
'right' or social 'right' is a demand on unspecified addressees
which does not even take into account whether or not these
addressees are willing or able to meet that demand. It has
nothing to do with rights. Rousseau took up an idea of Plato
that the State should realise 'Virtue' and 'Justice' – the 'notion
of the State as the *obliged* enforcer of an absolutely revealed and
unquestionable Faith and Law'.[14] This notion can only exist in
the context of justificationist philosophy.[15] If certain identifiable

conditions are present, a doctrine of supreme value will with high probability lead to a totalitarian state, independent of whether that doctrine is based on a fundamentalist religion or on a *religion séculaire* like Marxism–Leninism. The Constitution of Liberty has to include the following meta principle: No substantive principle must be 'absolutised' in the sense of being *imposed upon* the citizens – *except* this meta principle.

The topical question is not whether State or no State; rather it is the question of how much of it – how large the domain of collective choice should be, given a particular value position. What functions ought the State to have? In particular, what particular mix of protective and redistributive functions, of positive sum social games and negative sum social games[16] is desirable. More than anything else the form of life possible in a society is determined by the relative size of the sphere of *individual* versus the sphere of *collective* choices. Taxation as a proportion of national income is a rough measure of the domains of collective versus individual sovereignty over material resources.

## 5. JAMES A. BUCHANAN'S APPROACH TO SOCIAL-CONTRACT THEORY

Buchanan, the most prominent among the proponents of contractarianism and the key figure in constitutional economics, starts from the correct assumption that the individual is self-interested in the sense that 'he is much more deeply interested in what immediately concerns himself, than in what concerns any other man,'[17] that he is more interested than anybody else to bring about a state of affairs that best fits his concrete aims in life'. He then goes on to assume that it is possible to construct a Constitution of Liberty *without* having recourse to a value judgment (that is, without giving priority to individual freedom) if only the constitution is the result of the unanimous consensus of the people who are 'affected' by that system of rules for rule-making. (I disregard here the problems associated with defining the set of people 'affected' by a constitution or some other political structure.)

Three objections immediately come to mind (in addition to the arguments from circularity mentioned in section 3). (1) In practice unanimous consent does not exist. If everybody has veto power, then the decision costs, transaction and negotiation costs will be insurmountable – some of the holders of veto power may demand compensations for not making use of their veto power that are too costly. If you grant this fact of life and also take the cynosure of contractarianism, to be a contract that every 'sane' person would consent to, then the set is empty. Hence, unanimous consensus cannot provide a facile solution of the practical problem of allocating decision rights. In practice, one would have to work with a subset of the population. (2) The underlying assumption that the individuals wishing to make a constitutional contract possess the knowledge that would be necessary to foresee the consequences of the various stipulations is untenable. Rational ignorance in large-scale societies also concerns constitutional problems. (3) Most important of all: if – *per impossibile* – a constitutional contract would have been arrived at by unanimous consensus, *why* should this guarantee that it constitutes or approximates a Constitution of Liberty? Buchanan is fully aware of the possibility that even slave contracts might be the result of a consensus.[18]

A rational agent will sign the social contract only if he is convinced that he is getting a good deal, that is, that the expected benefits will outweigh the costs, the pains of coercion he thinks he will suffer at the State's hands, such as taxation (which in states like Sweden may become confiscatory). There is only one extreme – theoretical – borderline case in which there are no costs: if the individual has veto power, if he can rely on the State to will only what he wills. Making this peculiar assumption is tantamount to assuming that the State that has the power of coercion lets itself be controlled by those who have none.[19]

There will always be costs, and the crucial question is whether or not the benefits derived from living under the rule of a particular type of state outweigh the costs of doing so. So long as the individual has a practicable exit option, the more attractive a state is the more it should attract immigrants. At this point the market order can be taken as the model: ideally there should be a free competition among states for human capital and financial capital, and voting with one's feet should not be too costly. 'Attractiveness' has to be defined with reference to the particular concrete individual's *subjective* preferences. For instance, an enterprising and hard-working individual will prefer a state in which there are open markets with free entry based on private property and in which achievements are rewarded so that he may expect to enjoy the fruits of his labour and risk-taking. Somebody who is highly risk-averse (approximating the Rawlsian zombies), or who prefers not to exert himself, or who is interested in keeping the possible consequences of criminal activity, if caught, to a minimum, should rationally be attracted by an extreme welfare state like contemporary Sweden, which makes great efforts (so far with little success) to realise an egalitarian society.

## 6. F.A. HAYEK'S APPROACH

By contrast to Buchanan, Hayek explicitly introduces a value judgement: for the public–political arena individual freedom is given priority. Negatively defined freedom is the unobstructed faculty of the individual to take any option that falls within his given budget of time, money, knowledge, and so on, limited only by securing the same option rights for all other citizens. It will be reflected by the set of spheres of action in which individual decision-making is effectively protected from such interference by others, including the State, that is 'not necessary' to secure the same freedom for all others. Since an option right places an obligation on *all* others not to interfere in the spheres of action protected by that right, freedom requires discipline. Hayek's approach makes a recourse to the idea of the social contract with unanimous or almost unanimous consensus superfluous. However, the problem that has yet to be solved is how to clarify and operationalise the idea of 'not necessary coercion'. Hayek provides some clues. The key principle of his new constitutional settlement is to confine the sovereign rule of law to what he calls 'general rules of just conduct', thereby prohibiting arbitrary and unprincipled legislation and coercion. Obviously, coercion is not always bad, and freedom is not an absolute value, since there are trade-offs. For example, coercion is necessary to enforce a contract into which the individual has entered voluntarily. Otherwise, the tenure of property rights could not be secured and such right could not be implemented at low cost. A delicate problem arises from the fact that, although the State has monopoly of coercion (which is necessary to protect the individual against coercion by others), it must also protect the individual against unjust coercion by the State. Since the introduction of an explicit value premiss is the key feature of Hayek's approach, we should have a closer look at the idea of freedom.

## 7. THE IDEA OF FREEDOM AND THE ETHIC OF PRIVACY

The core meaning of this Western idea is private rights: private sovereignty of everybody's own decision over crucial domains of economic and social life, to be left alone, to pursue what the individual subjectively evaluates as worthy to be desired. It is constituted by the individual's option rights; freedom is a characteristic of his *social* life. The main criterion of the degree of freedom in a society is the location of the frontier between the domain of collective decision and the domain of private decision. In the West, freedom is a popular idea. The best available reason for claiming this (short of having poll evidence) is the fact that all the enemies of freedom want persuasively and deceitfully to redefine the term 'freedom'. The claim that people usually prefer to make their own decisions, in particular to spend their income as they wish, is contested. For example the popular television-economist J.K. Galbraith claims that people would prefer less income for private use in exchange for more free, publicly provided goods and services.

The moral problem of classical liberalism and its modern versions is to produce arguments for such 'natural' rights (rights that are claimed to exist prior to government), for respect for the moral right of every individual to be free to live his or her own life – free from tyranny, free from the majoritarian tyranny. The recognition of this moral right of every individual entails a prescription for limited government. Government should secure the individual's private rights. The more it tries to fulfil other purposes, the more it is bound to violate the individual's option rights. The ideal of government that follows from the idea of freedom is a government that is strong enough to fulfil its protective function, but limited in scope. The danger to freedom from government is by far the greatest in modern times. Government is a necessary evil instituted as a means for securing the individual's rights, not an instrument through which to pursue social goals.

## The instrumental and intrinsic value of freedom

To provide arguments for the instrumental value of freedom is relatively easy. The creation of wealth – be it material wealth or human capital – basically depends upon institutional arrangements, and only those institutions are really wealth-creating which are based on freedom, individual choice with incentives for risk taking and with the individual being accountable for his actions. History supports these theoretical claims: there is a clear tendency for those nations which have been most free to be those which have achieved the greatest economic success.[20]

Arguments for the intrinsic value of freedom have to be based on a particular image of man, on a perception of man that emphasises that every individual is unique, but that there are human traits which are universal, so that only the form of their expression varies with the social context. A descriptive model of man (like the REMM-model mentioned in note 10) cannot entail a non-instrumental value judgement, but it can *suggest* that every individual should be accorded certain inviolable rights, that everybody should have a sphere where he is sovereign. However, when all available good reason arguments have been presented, *the decision in the public–political arena to give freedom priority remains an existential choice*. Someone with a taste for life as a slave will remain unconvinced. The same holds for those with a taste for life as a slave-master – surely members of the Procrustean intelligentsia see themselves as present in future members of the nomenclatura of equalisation.

## Economic freedoms, civil liberties and political freedom

Economic freedoms and civil liberties shade into each other and may, in many cases, be indistinguishable.[21] Yet there is a core meaning of economic freedom. For example, the citizen's right to full freedom of capital movements, to free choice of currencies, the individual's exclusive right to his services (which rules out slavery and involuntary servitude, including conscription for military service in time of peace), the right to sell one's services at any wage an employer finds acceptable – which is a corollary of the freedom of contract. It also entails the right to unrestricted market entry into goods and services markets, the right to low marginal income taxes – and here we already make contact with the political sphere.

The core meaning of 'civil liberties' is the exit option: free movement of human capital. To make this fundamental freedom of practical importance, a certain openness of an international system is necessary. In a relatively open system governments come under the threat of emigration by future-oriented, and hence particularly valuable, human capital – much like enterprises afraid of losing their best customers. However, when speaking of 'civil liberties' people tend to associate this with freedom of speech, freedom of expression, of assembly, and so on. These freedoms are by-products of the State's use of coercion to prevent individuals from using violence against each other.

In everyday speech 'political freedom' usually means a kind of acceptance of a democratic system with majority rule and participation in elections every x-th year. Yet, this concept of participation appears to have little to do with freedom. *The vital distinction is between limited and unlimited government. Compared with it, the distinction between elected and non-elected government is insignificant for freedom.* Limited government and a high degree of freedom is possible under autocracy.[22] Big government and little freedom of choice are compatible with model democracy.[23] There is a continuum of regimes according to the degree of freedom they offer that runs from free to less free to totalitarian slavery, *independent of who rules*: a tyrant, a central committee, the tyranny of the majority in a totalitarian democracy. There is an interesting asymmetry here: a large public sector implies government control over much of the economy and also over much of the citizen's daily life; on the other hand, a capitalistically-oriented economy does not imply control or even influence on government. Even if public spending is small, the government can still control the economy by such means as price and wage regulation or licensing. Thus, political freedom in the sense of participation in collective choice is, at most, of instrumental value to freedom. It is not a necessary condition for a free society.

## 8. THE BENEFITS AND COSTS OF DEMOCRACY

The model of 'economic democracy', the model of voluntary exchange beneficial to both parties that underlies the market order, cannot readily be transposed to the political arena. Whenever issues of redistribution arise – which at least in democratic systems will be the rule and not the exception – the parties face a negative sum social game or at best a zero sum game. Hence, modelling political democracy on economic democracy, however attractive the idea may appear, cannot provide a regulative idea for political philosophy.

Whenever there are matters that are treated (in a particular society) as 'inherently public', there will be a domain of choices that are made *for* the individual and others similarly placed in society by somebody else. If those choices are made by the set of persons 'concerned', we speak of collective choice in the narrow sense. Hence, the question arises as to which method of decision making should be used in the domain of collective choice. The meta-rule that guides collective choice, usually called a 'constitutional rule', has a point only in the case of non-unanimity.[24] The possible constitutional rules can be classified into voting procedures and non-voting procedures. There is a continuum of voting procedures that runs from plutocratic to unlimited democratic method. Jasay shows that in any democratic method of collective decision-making, assuming also behaviour is utility-maximising and all have equal influence over collective choice, gains from a decisive coalition are available by two means: by reducing its size to a minimum, and by widening the domain of collective choice.[25] Hence, the dominant rule for rule making must lead to bare majority rule (50% + 1 vote) and to unrestricted domain. Jasay also points out that under popular sovereignty – what some would call 'totalitarian democracy' – there is never an answer to the question of how to protect the individual's freedom against the supposed guardians of his rights to protection and freedom. The ideologies of *unlimited* democracy have replaced the earlier superstition of the divine rights of kings by the modern superstition of the divine right of '*the* people'. The greatest damage has probably been done by the doctrine of 'the will of *the* people' (linked with Rousseau as opposed to Locke), by pretending that 'the society' – treated as if it was an individual (aggregation fallacy) – needs a common goal. Thus, the fiction of a uniform will (the 'will of the people') is upheld in spite of the fact that in reality there are sharp conflicts over public goods.

Every method of collective choice-making and hence every constitutional rule has a bias in favour of particular identifiable interests, since any rule of collective choice-making has a point only in the case of non-unanimity, and any rule has a probabilistic propensity to produce one type of outcome rather than another.[26] If a 'democratic' constitutional rule is practised only a few times, any outcome is possible. The more such a rule approximates the extreme type of unlimited democracy and the longer the period for which the rule has been obeyed, the more it will tend to enlarge its own domain, that is, *the domain of collective choice will steadily grow* (see below on the dynamics of public goods). Moreover, it will also tend to level out rewards. The more sensitive the rulers are to the wishes of the ruled, the more susceptible they are to the demands of rent-seeking interest groups and their blackmail. That sensitivity will reach a maximum in unlimited democracy. The more the domain of collective choice grows, the more the domain of private choice must shrink and with it freedom.

Public goods and semi-public goods (subsidised) are created as a matter of explicit or implicit social choice and thereby resource allocation is transferred from the private to the public domain and individual freedom reduced. The collective provision of goods and services functions as a gigantic machinery of *covert* redistribution. The greater the share of public goods in the national product, the greater is the part of coercion and the smaller that of personal choice. In the process of the growth of government, that is growth in scope due to the insatiable appetite for public goods, the strength of the government is reduced. Government is progressively weakened by pressure-group action calling on the State to provide more of various 'public goods'. The dynamics of the process[27] is as follows: If one interest group gets more of what it wants (all others paying for it), some other group can only recapture some of the consequent loss it indirectly suffers by insisting on the State providing more of the goods *it* wants (all others paying for it, although they do not really want it). Hence, it is rational for each and every group to behave *as if* they each had an unlimited appetite for various public goods. Eventually, the government is so weakened that it is no longer capable of fulfilling its protective function. The politician (a person who makes a living from being elected) must deliver more and more ambitious expenditure programmes if he wants to be re-elected.

To sum up, the way we practise democracy has led to a system with positive feedbacks in which not only will efficiency gradually be reduced but freedom will progressively shrink. In the long run, capitalist economies and social-democratic political values appear incompatible. Insofar as socialist society (with distribution to each 'according to his "needs"') is successful in making its economy more efficient, it will not remain socialist; if it is not successful, it will remain socialist, but lag more and more behind capitalist countries.[28] The more welfarism is grafted upon capitalist society, the more efficiency and freedom will be reduced.

## 9. THE CONSTITUTION OF LIBERTY

The theoretical problem of drafting a Constitution of Liberty is easy compared with the practical problem of getting that constitution to be respected. The following key elements suggest themselves. (1) Minimise the need for collective choice! This will at the same time reduce the temptation to refer matters to the political process in order to further one's own interest, and thereby reduce the incentives to invest in the political process (the negative sum social game associated with redistribution) rather than in productive activities (the positive sum social game of any political structure).

Even in a free society some goods are treated as 'public goods'; because the costs of excluding other people are evaluated as 'too high'. These costs may include, besides financial and material costs, also immaterial costs and moral costs. Thus, a certain domain of collective choice is unavoidable. (2) In the domain of collective choice, avoid any method of collective choice-making which has a built-in bias that automatically will make the domain of collective choice grow! That means that if some sort of 'democractic' method is used, it must not be based on unqualified franchise, because that would (as argued in section 8) relentlessly lead to an unlimited, totalitarian democracy. It is notoriously difficult to specify qualities that are relevant to various kinds of collective decision-making. However, a general requirement suggests itself: that the voter should have some 'experience of life' which can only be gained from having participated in the positive sum social game characteristic of a society based on division of labour (which also means that he should have experienced being a taxpayer).

(3) Redistribution should be permitted only to those who are in need. A clear distinction should be made between Procrustean politics and a state-maintained welfare flow guaranteeing citizens in need a minimum income (compare section 4). Thereby, 'poverty' should be defined in terms of the absence of certain goods and not in terms of the relative distance to the average income per capita. (4) Redistribution should be permitted only in overt form, not in the covert form of public goods.

In summary, to regain some of the freedom lost during the last 75 or 100 years we need a different state: strong enough to protect private rights and freedom under law and order, but limited in scope. The present democratic system leaves Western civilisation more or less helpless against creeping socialism from within, and it makes it very difficult to mobilise sufficient political support for the defence expenditures necessary to preserve peace.

10. THE PRACTICAL PROBLEM OF THE
EFFECTIVENESS OF A CONSTITUTION

The decisive problem is a practical one: to find the conditions under which a Constitution of Liberty, a domain-restricting constitution, would be likely to be adopted and respected for some foreseeable time. How can we ensure that the people who benefit from safeguarding the Constitution of Liberty are stronger than those who would gain by a change? From the Arrow Theorem the statement can be derived that for any distribution (of wealth, income and so on) there is always a different one for which you get a majority, that is, you can always show that, relative to the existing distribution, the new one would benefit the decisive set, the set that is stronger than the rest of the group. The relationship between the existence of groups in favour of limited government and domain-restricting constitutional devices is much like a chicken-and-egg sequence. If these subgroups are weakened, the limits of government will give way, and vice versa. The more big corporations, small firms, farms and households become dependent on transfers through subsidies or public goods, the more the limits of government will break down. Eventually, the trend to growth of the domain of collective choice (underpinned by an ethic of consensus) will lead to the politicisation of everything and to unlimited, totalitarian democracy. This type of democracy undermines its own base and also economic democracy. This must be so, if, given the constraints, all agents act as pure utility-maximisers.

The only remedy appears to be to introduce among the determinants of collective choice an element that overrides the utility-maximising behaviour, a deontological moral rule that overrules the pure utility calculus.[29] That means that what is needed is that among the reasons for acting as we do are 'costs' that matter affectively, independent of the imagined consequences – a deontological rule that has been internalised. If the rules are not internalised, you need a despotic state to enforce them. The cost of disobeying the rules is a function of the prize of enforcement. The cost of enforcement can be reduced only if the rules are internalised, and the most effective way of doing this is by introducing a suitable deontological rule into the intellectual and emotional climate. Let me illustrate this by pointing to the difference in the problem situation of an upstart dictator (like Napoleon, Hitler, Mao) and that of an established dynasty (like the House of Habsburg or the Royal Dynasty of England). The main problem of any dictator is to keep in power. To do this, he has to eliminate all potential rivals (Hitler and Stalin murdered them, while Mao used the 'cultural revolution' to eliminate potentially powerful groups and made his generals circulate so that they could not establish a power base of their own.) There would have been no corresponding risk of a military coup for an established dynasty. For instance, the House of Habsburg would have had nothing to fear from a field marshal like Radetzky, nor would the Hohenzollens have had anything to fear from their generals. Apart from the impossibility that a military coup could succeed, there was also a deontological rule, a taboo: it was simply unthinkable that the supreme commander would dream of becoming the emperor himself.

Without a commitment to a deontological rule which, in the public arena, gives priority to freedom and hence involves accepting risk-taking and accountability for one's actions, there is no way out of creeping socialism and the progressive abolition of freedom that goes with it. That rule must be accepted by a section of the population that is sufficiently strong to defend the Constitution of Liberty. Only such a change of climate could make it possible to reform the way in which we have practised the democratic method. Educating the educable section of the public is part of the task. This involves making explicit the costs of bloated democracy, explaining why the number and importance of interests groups (which use the political process for rent-seeking) increase with the age of a democracy,[30] explaining that the better private rights are protected the less will participation in the political process matter, explaining that in unlimited democracy there is always a decisive coalition that would gain by curtailing a minority right, and so forth. Finally, we should no longer taboo the question of whether it is the way in which we practise democracy or perhaps even the method itself that has been putting us back on the road to serfdom. And we should have the courage to state that in the Western democracies the paternalistic welfare state, by successively eliminating freedom of choice, constitutes the main threat to individual freedom and economic welfare.

## NOTES

I wish to thank Professors Anthony de Jasay, Anthony Flew and Hans-Otto Lenel for constructive criticism of an earlier draft.
    1. As quoted by Boswell, *The Life of Samuel Johnson*, London, 1924, vol. I, p. 351.

2. Boswell, *Johnson*, p. 262.
3. E. Hoppmann, 'Ökonomische Theorie der Verfassung', *Ordo. Jahrbuch für die Ordnung von Wirtschaft und Gesellschaft*, vol. 38, 1987, pp. 31–45.
4. E. Gellner, 'Human Rights and the New Circle of Equity', in F. D'Agostino and I.C. Jarvie, eds, *Freedom and Rationality: Essays in Honour of John Watkins*, Dordrecht, 1989, p. 125.
5. R. Nozick, *Anarchy, State and Utopia*, New York, 1974, Part I.
6. A. de Jasay, 'Pour une Tyrannie Paresseuse'. *Commentaire*, vol. 10, 1987, pp. 317–25, p. 317.
7. For an overview, see, for example, G. Radnitzky, 'An Economic Theory of the Rise of Civilization and its Policy Implications: Hayek's Account Generalised', *Ordo. Jahrbuch für die Ordnung von Wirtschaft und Gesellschaft*, vol. 38. 1987, pp. 47–90.
8. K. Brunner and A.H Meltzer, 'The Uses of Money: Money in the Theory of an Exchange Economy', *American Economic Review*, vol. 61, 1971, pp. 785–805.
9. R. Pilon, 'On Moral and Legal Justification', *Southwestern University Law Review*, vol. 11, 1979, pp. 1327–44, p. 1338.
10. By 'rational agent' I do not mean the model of a man of expected-utility theory, which claims that people behave rationally if they obey certain axioms (established by von Neumann and Morgenstern), the model that is used in general decision-making theory. It is too narrow, and at best it applies to the choice within the possibility set that the agent (subjectively) imagines. It disregards the 'framing' of the situation, what the agent takes to apply to himself, and so forth. The model of man that I am using is the descriptive model of Brunner and Meckling, which is more in tune with the economic approach. (Cf. K. Brunner and W. Meckling, 'Perception of Man and the Conception of Government', *Journal of Money, Credit and Banking*, vol. 9, 1977; and K. Brunner, 'The Perception of Man and the Conception of Society: Two Approaches to Understanding Society', *Economic Inquiry*, vol. 25, 1987.) This model of man: *resourceful-evaluating-maximising man* (known as the REMM model) is a reformulation and elaboration of the image of man used in the Scottish Enlightenment.
11. A. de Jasay, *The State*, Oxford, 1985, ch. 1.
12. A. de Jasay, 'The Ethics and Mechanics of Social Democracy or Having it Both Ways', *Economic Affairs*, vol. 7, 1987; J. Dorn, 'Public Choice and the Constitution: A Madisonian Perspective', in J. Gwartney and R. Wagner, eds, *Public Choice and Constitutional Economics*, Greenwich, CT, 1988, p. 95.
13. Jasay, *The State*, pp. 32, 46.
14. Gellner, 'New Circle', p. 140.
15. W.W. Bartley, III, 'Philosophy of Biology *versus* Philosophy of

Physics', in G. Radnitzky and W.W. Bartley, III, eds, *Evolutionary Epistemology, Theory of Rationality and the Sociology of Knowledge,* La Salle, 1987.

16. K. Brunner, 'The Ambivalence of Political Structure: Illusions and Reality', in K. Brunner and R. Wagner, eds, *The Growth of Government,* Rochester, 1986.

17. Adam Smith, *The Theory of Moral Sentiments,* London, 1759.

18. J.M. Buchanan, *The Limits of Liberty: Between Anarchy and Leviathan,* Chicago, 1975, pp. 10, 59; Hoppmann, "Ökonomische Theorie", (note 3), p. 42.

19. Jasay, *The State,* p. 42.

20. N. Rosenberg and L. Birdzell, *How the West Grew Rich: The Economic Transformation of the Industrial World,* New York, 1986; E. Weede, 'Der Sonderweg des Westens', *Zeitschrift für Soziologie,* vol. 17, 1988.

21. Milton Friedman provides examples, such as those in M.A. Walker, ed., *Freedom, Democracy and Economic Welfare,* Vancouver, 1988, p. 52.

22. Jasay, 'Tyrannie' (cf. note 6), p. 325, and A. de Jasay, 'Is Limited Government Possible?', *Critical Review,* vol. 3, 1989, pp. 283–309, p. 287.

23. Contemporary Sweden provides a good example: it has a super-democratic constitution, a one-chamber system and the powers of the government are practically unrestricted. The economy is an open economy with few regulations, but individual freedom is severely limited, and in practice you have not even a free choice of your doctor or dentist. The situation may be epitomised by the formula 'Enterprises are free, individuals are socialised'.

24. Jasay, 'Limited Government', p. 288.

25. Jasay, 'Limited Government', pp. 301–3.

26. Anthony de Jasay, *Social Contract, Free Ride: A Study of the Public Goods Problem,* Oxford, 1989, pp. 4, 7, 107.

27. Jasay, *Social Contract.*

28. A. de Jasay, 'The Quality of Life in Capitalist and Socialist Economies', Paper for the PWPA Colloquium on 'The Common Heritage and Future of Europe', Dubrovnik, 1–5 October 1987.

29. Jasay, 'Limited Government'; cf. also W.W. Bartley, III, *The Retreat to Commitment,* New York, 1962, 2nd ed., La Salle, 1984.

30. M. Olson, *The Rise and Decline of Nations,* New Haven, 1982.

CHAPTER 15

# Thoughts on liberalisation

## J.G. Merquior

Liberty is generally established with difficulty in the midst
of storms; it is perfected by civil discord; and its benefits
cannot be appreciated until it is already old.

Tocqueville

The nineteen-eighties witnessed a dramatic increase in the pace
of liberalisation across the world. The overall empirical picture is
so complex as to support a conceptual proposal: going beyond
liberalisation in its current, newspaper sense, tantamount to the
adoption or restoration of *political* freedom, we could try to
establish a twofold meaning, covering both the polity and the
economy. Thus conceived, liberalisation would mean *decentralisation* in both spheres: devolution of powers, in the political
realm; and decentralisation of decisions, in the economic system.
Privatisation, which relates to ownership besides the decentralisation of economic decisions, might be considered a special case
of economic liberalisation, since it tends to go along with 'popular capitalism', through the floating of shares in state enterprise.

The global picture also allows one to discern at least three big
trends. First, there is *the return of liberism*, that is to say, of
economic decentralisation, though obviously not in the form of
Victorian laissez-faire. Laissez-faire seems ruled out if only
because so much of modern economy (and technology) is
predicated on huge and costly infrastructure requirements
which the state alone can provide. However, the impossibility
and undesirability of a 'stateless' economy by no means impairs
the advantages of a decentralised structure of decisions concerning production, exchange and research; and its dirigiste
opposite turned out to be dismally inefficient. South Korea is
far from being a laissez-faire economy, yet its strong market
element gives it an overwhelming superiority over its North
Korean counterpart. Die-hard statists like to seize on the fact
that state action was so bold in the fledgling years of East Asian

'Little Dragons' to deny that their astonishing economic performances – like Japan's, for that matter – are instances of liberism. But the denial rests on a fallacy. For state action does not mean overbearing state intervention, planning does not mean working against the market. The long-run path taken by South Korea, Taiwan, Singapore and Hong Kong has been conspicuously divergent from the dirigiste ways of state socialism or the Third World statism of, say, India.

The second liberalising trend (in chronological order) was the near *completion of the Iberian wave of democratisation*. Greece, post-Francoist Spain and Portugal were converted into democracies in the mid seventies (in Portugal, not before the removal of a paracommunist military junta, bravely fought by civil society, especially in the Catholic North, and by left democrats like Mario Soares). But in the 1980s these South European democratisations were joined by several countries in Iberoamerica: Argentina, Uruguay, Bolivia, Brazil, Chile. Peru came out of praetorian rule even earlier, and Paraguay saw the end of Stroessner's tyranny. In 1980, democratic régimes were still the exception in Latin America, and among major countries free politics were long established only in Colombia and Venezuela. In 1990, by contrast, one can count the *authoritarian* residues on the fingers of one hand: Cuba, Haiti, Surinam. Even in Central America, plagued by civil war, democracy set foot in Salvador and Nicaragua. Now taken together, these democratisations amount to the widest democratic wave since the postwar years. Then, Italy, Germany and Japan were restored (or in Japan's case, given) to democracy. But while their democratisation was bound up with defeat and occupation, the contemporary Iberian process culminating in Latin America has been a more endogenous phenomenon. In development terms, for Latin America as a whole, the 1980s may have been a 'lost decade' – yet the decade was hardly lost for Latin American freedom.

Lastly, and most significantly, the eighties closed with the *liberalisation of eastern Europe* – the (quite unexpected) quick crumbling of communist order east of the Elbe. One after the other, Leninist 'politbureaucracies' (if I may use Konrad and Szelenyi's apt label) fell from power, or at least from undivided power, in Poland, Hungary, Czechoslovakia, Bulgaria, East

Germany and Romania. It is too early to tell the fate of the Soviet empire – but in the meantime Moscow's former satellites have parted institutional company with their politico-military master and grow increasingly attracted by a western pull: the gravitational force of liberal Europe and the EEC economy. At the dawn of 1990, the only communisms still hegemonic in East Europe were in Yugoslavia (already stirring) and in the Stalinist relic, Albania. But even Tirana starts to grant a modicum of thaw.

Such a frantic spread of freedom changed dramatically the balance within the typology of liberalisation. Broadly speaking, liberalising processes result either from *conquest* or from *concession*. Conquered liberalisations are imposed by rebel civil societies, often in the wake of military defeat or stalemate abroad, as in Greece, Portugal or Argentina. Liberalisations by concession, on the other hand, are granted by authoritarian governments, as in Spain, Brazil, South Korea, Chile and Gorbachev's Soviet Union. Obviously while up to 1988 most liberalisations, and the ones in the larger countries, were granted rather than conquered, the 'revolution of 1989' tipped the scales in favour of conquest liberalisations, thanks to the democratic stampede in East Europe. As a result, even the *primum movens* of communist liberalisation, Gorbachevian reformism, is no longer a clearcut case of *von oben* apertura. Unlike the post-Stalin Thaw or Kruschev's enlightened despotism, Gorbachev's tactics of glasnost are under growing pressure from civil society, as shown in the Soviet elections of March 1989 and the continuing demands from the non-Russian nationalities.

Economic distress played a significant role either way. If we take post-Francoist Spain, and Brazil in the mid eighties, as archetypes, respectively, of the first and second phases of liberalisation in the Iberian world, then it is easy to see that while Spanish democracy was, as it were, a consequence of prosperity, the Brazilian apertura was intended as a sop for the harsh interruption of the country's *Wirtschaftswunder*. From the softening of repression under President Geisel (1974–79) and full amnesty under Figueiredo (1979–85) to the democratic turnover under Sarney (1985–90), political liberty has been the lightning rod of economic hardship. Once upon a time, in countries like Brazil, inflation was the great means for preventing the escalation of social conflict. The tacit social contract of Latin American liberal populism was a compromise which used to pump income into industry without taxing landowners, by a clever combination of easy credit, overvalued currency and protectionism.[1] Inflation was the inevitable result. Yet by stepping up inflation the whole mechanism eventually became growth-inhibiting: budget imbalances grew overburdened with the service of foreign debts acquired in the 1970s, and 'exploded' – owing to soaring new levels of international interest rates – in the 1980s. Accordingly, the role of inflation as an informal legitimiser was undermined. Tame inflation used to do the job; wild inflation simply cannot. In its stead, another safety valve was found: democracy. Authoritarianism fares rather well in times of growth; but the coincidence of repression with depression is a different matter.

What about the liberalisation in the socialist area? In the (ex)communist bloc, liberalisation came as an upshot of economic reform rather than as a means to cope with the eclipse of growth. To be sure, economic reform itself was dictated by many a shortage and also by the increasingly invidious comparison with the wealth of the West – a West reaping, in 1989, the fruits of seven years of sustained growth and poised to spend the nineties in the cosy embrace of a bounteous economy. How could this fail to impress poverty-stricken, indebted Poland, or even Hungary, where the inability of market socialism to generate stable growth became only too visible? In 1970, 'goulash communism' looked like a nice alternative to Gulag communism. Alas, two decades later goulash communism was still at a clear disadvatage beside capitalism's consumer society.

　　Liberal democracies are probably legitimised less because their masses share the beliefs of their upper classes than because most wage-earners in the West see that they are generally better off than their communist counterparts, and in addition enjoy far greater freedoms. This means that the attitudinal cluster based on 'economism' and pragmatic rather than normative acceptance of capitalism – something long acknowledged by realistic, though far from conservative, socio-logists – naturally unfolds into implicit comparison with the main alternative on offer, namely, the highly unattractive, unfree life under state socialism.[2]

But the point is, this kind of comparison works both ways. Certainly, during the 1980s, on the other side of what used to be the Iron Curtain, there grew the realisation that the welfare and freedom of the Western masses went on unmatched by communism, soft or hard. No wonder it undermined the legitimacy of the party-states, from Berlin to Moscow and from Warsaw to Belgrade. To be sure, one would be hard put to present the economic deprivation of East Europe as the direct, immediate cause of the 1989 uprisings. According to one of the keenest observers of the East European scene, Timothy Garton Ash, while economic discontent was very much there, acute in Poland and Romania and increasing almost everywhere else, it was not consumerist but political and ideological protest that precipitated the revolution – a kind of hunger for truth and freedom, symbolised by the prestige of dissident intellectuals (Havel, Geremek, Mazowiecki, Berlin artists, Budapest philos-ophers) and by the activities of civic forums rather than trade unions, Solidarity excepted.[3] In this reading, 1989 was, like 1848, a 'revolution of the intellectuals', in Namier's famous label. But no one would dream of denying the importance, as a general detonator of popular animus, of the comparison between eastern penury and western affluence.

Still, for all the daring economic reforms scheduled, notably by Polish and Hungarian leaders, there is no gainsaying that the East European revolution of 1989 would hardly have happened without the permissive new climate – perestroika weather – in Moscow. Nowhere was this more evident than in East Germany, for the GDR was both a strategic linchpin and a bastion of orthodoxy. If the Kremlin was not prepared to employ the Red Army to keep Honecker in power, or at least a more conciliatory yet loyal communist leader like Egon Krenz, then it became quite obvious it would not use force anywhere else. Thus the perestroika mood at the red metropolis was naturally perceived as a green light for liberalisation through-out eastern Europe.

But why the perestroika in the first place? Again, the root of

Gorbachev's own liberalisation was international comparison. One cannot read his book, *Perestroika*, without acknowledging the USSR's acute sense of inferiority vis-à-vis the West. After all, the Soviet Union is indeed an underdeveloped superpower. Forty million of its citizens are said to live on less than seventy rubles a month. This means that there is an 'African', or 'Latin American' underclass in the motherland of socialism, seven decades after the Revolution. Now Gorbachev and his team know, as well-informed rulers (not for nothing he was once a KGB man), that such shameful lags do incriminate the neostalinist method of putting guns (or missiles) before butter. Hence the original gaols of perestroika:

(a)   modernising, in order to strengthen, the Soviet economy, basically by injecting a modicum of market mechanisms into it and by reducing its current military burden;
(b)   restructuring the party-state to ensure greater responsiveness to social needs and aspirations;
(c)   accommodating as much as possible ethnic claims within the Soviet Union, albeit short of secessions.

Clearly, then, perestroika was meant to be a change within the system, not a system change. Its underlying objective was, not unlike Krushchev's, catching up with the West *without giving up socialism*. Accordingly, Gorbachev began – like Imre Nagy in the early fifties, or Alexander Dubcek in the late sixties – by legitimising his reformism with references to Lenin. Perestroika was to be a repristination of the NEP. True, some measure of ambiguity lingers on from the start. For instance, Lenin's NEP was sheer tactics: but the rehabilitation of Bukharin is there to prove that the current leadership holds a far less instrumental view of the market. While for Lenin, in 1920, with revolution under siege, the market was just a survival kit, for Gorbachev, as for Bukharin, it is essential to a better kind of socialism. Still, as a whole, both strategies clung to socialist premises and goals.

Unfortunately, however, the pragmatic intentions of Gorbachev's neo-Bukharinism did not translate into tangible benefits. In the Spring of 1989, soon after the Polish Pact establishing trade union freedom and political democracy, the Gorbachevian economist, Afanasiev, recognised the practical futility of four years of Soviet reforms. And Gorbachev himself in his

New Year speech, pointed out rather bitterly that for the first
time the USSR had experienced massive work stoppages in
industry. Presumably President Gorbachev was paying tribute
to the memory of his master, Andropov the disciplinarian.
Nevertheless, the problem is very real; and it shows that
perestroika, instead of breaking with inefficiency, has added
disorder to it.

At any rate, since 1987 Gorbachev often sounds as though,
having realised that the system needs a radical overhaul rather
than a mere (however extensive) rectification, he was growing
inclined to break the Leninist mould. He came to define
socialism as something about 'human values', with a focus on
peace, rights and liberties, instead of a call to class struggle and
anti-imperialist strife. Ironically, however, the softer and more
ecumenical his socialism became, the deeper became the social
revolution – away from communism – in Eastern Europe. For a
change big enough to alter both the political formula and the
production system of several societies, replacing the ruling class
in the process, is nothing less than a social revolution.

Why did Gorbachev, the darling of the West, allow it? Could
he not see that the East European revolution would dangerously overtake his own unsuccessful reformism? Here two
remarks seem in order. First, success itself. If there is one area
where Gorbachev succeeds, it is the international arena. Perestroika got bogged down, but diplomatic glasnost goes on
scoring points, from leaving Afghanistan to the arms agreements and from Yalta-to-Malta turning point. Actually, what
convinced Western opinion of Gorbachev's sincerity has been
precisely his attitude of benign neglect towards the overthrow
of communism among the Soviet Union's vassal neighbours.
On the other hand, maybe he simply couldn't help it. A politics
of repression, re-enacting the Brezhnev doctrine, would play
into the hands of his enemies at home, jeopardising glasnost
and perestroika. So the only way left was a *fuite en avant*.

In East Europe, in any event, the issue seems settled: the
overall trend is a thorough westernisation. But in the Soviet
Union things are not so clear; and the main trouble is that, by
graciously yielding to liberalisation *à outrance* westwards, Gorbachev seems to be initiating serious storms inside his border.
Alain Besançon has suggested that Gorbachev's 'surrender' of

the communist bloc is a kind of Brest-Litovsk manoeuvre: by giving up the East European countries, Moscow would help keep her territory safe under a communist regime (however softened), forcing the West to leave the Baltic peoples, the Ukrainians and Caucasians in their Soviet bondage.[4] In fact, however, Gorbachev seems to have had even less room for manoeuvre than Lenin at Brest-Litovsk. If, as indicated, opposing decommunisation in Eastern Europe would have undermined his own position in both party and country, how could he avoid writing off his allies in Europe, the Honeckers, Husaks and Zhikovs, refusing to support them in the face of popular revolt?

On the other hand, having started a liberalisation which quickly turned, west of the USSR, into a sudden emancipation from the Soviet *imperium*, Gorbachev unleashed a domino effect which threatens to eventuate in the very heartland of the régime. Beset by the nationalities problem, the Soviet Union may well emerge as the last domino dislodged by the winds of freedom. Hence Gorbachev's caution towards the Baltic states or his Southern subjects – let alone the Ukraine, the Soviet Union's granary and chief mineral reserve (his visit to the Pope was, among other things, an attempt to get the Holy See's help in quelling Ukrainian budding secessionism by the recognition of Uniatism, a church ruthlessly suppressed by Stalin).

A provocative article in *Daedalus*[5] has recently mused over the stark dilemmas ahead of perestroika. With or beyond Gorbachev, the Soviet Union may go either the Polish–Hungarian way, plunging into market and democracy, or the Chinese way (the market minus democracy) – but either way risking landing, because of two decades of economic decay followed by the dislocations brought about by perestroika itself, in the worst of outcomes: neither recovery nor freedom. Such a predicament might be said to vindicate liberist claims. Perestroika, as an effort at humanising communism, was hoist with its own petard because up to now it has only been a poor half-hearted remake of market socialism. But in the modern world, either you go capitalist or you go bust: *tertium non datur*. There is – pace Ota Sik, the Prague Spring economist – no 'Third Way'. Trying to stage yet another centrist path, perestroika, meant as the reconstruction of socialism, turned out to be just the destruction of the long-ailing Soviet economy. The lesson is clear: get rid of socialism, enhance the role of the market, and things will become much better.

The difficulties of perestroika are obviously compounded by the fact that the nature of the party-state is so inimical to the devolution of decision-making – something quite necessary, on a large scale, if the passage from market socialism to a full-blooded supersession of the command economy is to take place. But in the Soviet Union the communist party, besides being (unlike most of its East European peers) a national institution, ensures almost alone the vertebration of authority in a country bereft of a civil society both in the modern Western and in the traditional sense. Take away the party's hegemony and you can end up with a Hobbesian chaos, not the vigorous, largely self-ordering civil societies most East European countries seem able to deploy. Consequently the withering away of the party-state – the bracing political horizon of Eastern Europe – is a moot issue on the Soviet Union. This very point was made by Ernest Gellner, in his direct observation of the Soviet process in 1988: he contrasted the situation of, say, 1968 Czechoslovakia, where a strong remainder of civil society faced a discredited CP, with Gorbachev's USSR, where communist authority remained strong, with most civil society components weakened or erased since the Bolshevik revolution.[6]

Last but not least, Gorbachev's first presidential appointment in 1990 elevated Professor Nikolai Petrakov, the leading Soviet expert on price reform to serve as his personal economic adviser. It might well be that Mikhail Gorbachev, an inventive statesman if ever there was one, has decided to respond to the breakdown of the Soviet empire by deepening perestroika into a bold global departure from the command economy, saving the party in the process. He may, that is, preserve a key role for the party while giving up much – but by no means all – of the party rule. James Billington, the historian of Russian culture (*The Axe and the Icon*), has recently suggested in the *Washington Post* that by decollectivising agriculture Gorbachev might give a new lease of life to economic reform and stop the slide in living standards while creating a new, sustaining constituency for perestroika. For the moment, however, as the occupation of

Baku proceeds, perestroika is on hold – and the anxiety grows over Gorbachev's ability to survive without surrendering reformism. As Billington says, no one knows whether Gorbachev will end up like Peter the Great (with the Old Believers crushed) or like Alexander II (the reformist eliminated by the radical nemesis of bold reform, followed by a reactionary backlash).

Let us now cast a glance at social theory, as it conceptualises liberalisations. I shall focus on the explanation of *socialist* liberalising. There are at least four candidates for the role of a theoretical explanation of processes like the Prague Spring or the ongoing East European 'Autumn of the Peoples'. The first, favoured by the left, assigns the major causal factor to a drive towards democratic socialism. The second sees such uprisings chiefly as anti-Soviet movements – it is a 'nationalist' theory, as distinct from the socialist one. The third theory is the liberal one. It focuses on economic frustration as the mainspring of popular revolt against communist power.

Finally, a fourth theory, in a more sociological idiom, sees the cause of the will to liberalise in the characteristics of the stage in which the socialist countries find themselves. In Ernest Gellner's words:

an advanced industrial society requires a large scientific, technical, administrative, educational stratum, with genuine competence based on prolonged training. In other words, it cannot rely on rigid ideologies and servile classes alone. It is reasonable to assume that this kind of educated middle class ... capable of distinguishing reality and thought from verbiage and incantation, will develop ... a need for security ... a regard for efficiency and integrity ... a recognition of the fact that errors in good faith are not morally culpable but part of the normal healthy working of institutions and call for no witch-hunts ... At the same time, this class is large enough and indispensable enough not to be lightly or pointlessly thwarted. It can exercise a sustained, quiet, pervasive pressure. It may infiltrate high places. Overt dissidents are its miniscule, heroic, probably indispensable, yet expendable advance guards; but the real battle may be won by the incomparably larger, cautious, compromising but pervasive and persistent main body, which advances like an insidious sand dune, rather than by dramatic self-immolation. This class is large, and it cannot be penalised effectively without a cost to the economy which may no longer be acceptable.[7]

How are we to assess each of these theories of liberalisation given the events and trends making up the 1989 revolution? The democratic socialism theory is flawed from the start, since it hardly chimes with the liberalisers' actual motivations. Those who voiced their hostility to incumbent rulers in the Polish ballot box, or in the streets of Leipzig, Prague and Bucharest, were not asking for socialism of another kind – they were not asking for socialism at all. This may be bad news for many Western intellectuals, for whom socialism in various guises has long been The Creed. But the fact is that the clamour in East European towns in 1989 was not a demand for socialism but for freedom – political, economic and ideological. As noticed by Garton Ash,

The hope of a third way, of 'socialism with a human face', has faded throughout East Central Europe (and even, arguably, in the Soviet Union). It has faded above all, it seems to me, because of the failure to produce any convincing economic alternative to capitalism. Poland and Hungary are off in search of Ludwig Erhard's 'social market economy', not a *socialist* market economy.[8]

That is why, by the way, Vaclav Havel, and not Alexander Dubcek, was morally chosen by the Czechs as their new leader. Dubcek is treated with great respect; but the Prague Spring no longer sets the ideological tone. 'Socialism with a human face' is not enough – it is at most a transitional stage on the long road to freedom, as Gorbachev himself, its current standard-bearer, is painfully realising.

As for the nationalist and liberal theories, they are closer to empirical reality. But, if taken in isolation, they are only partially true. Seething economic frustration was no doubt a significant factor in the popular uprisings. All the same, national resentment, directed against Russian power, has long been active in the minds of many dissidents. Poland is famously a case in point; but so is East Germany, where the problem of communism was precisely that it had a state, yet no nation, for an underpinning. To be sure, the national card did not contribute much emotional fuel in the overthrow of Ceaucescu, because the dictator himself had been playing it for twenty years. But one felt its strong presence in Hungary and Czecho-slovakia as much as among Poles and East Germans.

Moreover, that nationalism should act as a vehicle of democratic passions was unsurprising since (a) the ruling stratum associated with foreign power exercised an authoritarian kind of rule and (b) historically national movements in these countries have long been bound up with democratic traditions. Warsaw, Budapest and Prague mixed nationalist with liberal aspirations throughout the last century, and this very mix was rekindled when Poland, Hungary and Czechoslovakia became independent after World War One. The one-time appropriation of nationalism by the authoritarian Right in interwar Poland or Hungary did not deprive democratic nationalism of its titles in their culture and their heritage of nation-building, and of course four decades of 'Red Army communism' did still less so.[9]

What about the fourth, sociological theory – explaining the liberalising drive in terms of technocratic pressure for, at once, more liberty and more efficiency? Does it tally with the shared attributes of the 1989 East European upheaval? Yes and no. Gellner's thesis – that an advanced industrial society requires a technocratic middle class whose own needs for security and efficiency induces them to demand liberalisation from polit-bureaucracies, or, in short, that technocracy is, in the long run, an enemy of ideocracy – was actually spelt out as a rejoinder to Raymond Aron's demurrals about Gellner's 1976 suggestion that, as a social myth, almost in the Sorelian sense, liberalisation was replacing revolution.[10]

While warning that liberalisation occurs in 'a variety of dramatically contrasted contexts',[11] Gellner had surmised the prospect of its extension to Eastern Europe. Aron disagreed. In a coda to his book, *Plaidoyer pour l'Europe décadente* (1977), he asserted that the well-armed centralist bureaucracies of the communist world did represent 'one of history's most lasting and most stable political forms so long as the ruling clan kept its coherence and the masses were aware of their impotence.[12] Therefore, there was little in common between the South European liberalisations of the mid 1970s – Greece, Portugal, Spain – and the Prague Spring, so quickly repressed. It was in reply to this pessimistic statement of the limits of liberalisation that Gellner elaborated on his first essay, fleshing out his from-revolution-to-liberalisation theme, eastwards, with a sketch of a sociology of industrialism. That was done by anchoring liberalising drives in social structure. The claim was that the very characteristics of the large technological stratum indispensable to high industrialism would in time necessitate the liberalisation of state socialism.

Today, one senses that Gellner was right, in his general prophecy, against Aron's cold war pessimism. Yet Aron himself underscored a proviso: for ideocracies to retain their control, the masses ought to be conscious of their own weakness. Indeed, Aron's phrasing – 'la conscience de son impuissance' – was a masterpiece of dialectical ambiguity, since it made the impotence of 'la masse' contingent on mass consciousness, and hence on the possibility of a revolutionary mood. Curiously enough, and although Aron is well-known in Anglo-Saxon countries as one of the main theorists of industrial society, it was Gellner, rather than Aron, who upheld an industrial society perspective connoting an 'end of ideology' outcome: high industrialism breeds a generalised concern with efficiency and security, eventually incompatible with authoritarian ideology, that is, ideocracy.

At the same time, Gellner's position looks like a variant of infrastructuralism. In his well-known theory of nationalism, he points out that the division of labour in industrial society calls for a homogeneous literate culture, since workers' skills tend to be generic, as opposed to the know-how of craftsmen in traditional society. There is therefore a stress on broad types of production techniques and the kind of personnel required to man them. The theoretical focus falls on the economic infrastructure, though not, as in classical Marxism, on *relations* of production. Now the same stress on infrastructure is the main conceptual prop of Gellner's theory of liberalisation. As in the case of nationalism, there is a basis – advanced, technological industrialism – prompting a certain kind of social structure: a meritocratic middle class, based on cognitive and technological skills.[13] Compared to this, Aron sounds more like a 'power materialist' of the Weberian sort, emphasising politico-military resources rather than technoeconomic infrastructures.

But how right was Gellner in his *analysis*, as distinct from his prophecy? After all, the East European liberalisations did not come as the gradual result of cautious pressures from the technocracy. It was the masses, not the technical middle class, that did it, suddenly and noisily. Here one of the open-ended questions asked by Gellner at the close of 'From the Revolution to Liberalisation' – is it to be favoured by economic success or by failure?[14] – seems decisive. The target of the East European revolutions appears to be first and foremost an illiberal élite that does not deliver the goods. In other words, dismal economic failure undermined ideocracy, just as in Latin America, when the end of the growth years prompted the sly withdrawal (Brazil) or the shameful fall (Argentina) of the men in uniform.

A quarter of a century ago, in that remarkable book, *Thought and Change*, Gellner proffered a Weberian account of Marxism. Far from bringing about, as its self-image assumed, the overcoming of the ills of industrialism, the actual historical role of Marxism was to work as the Protestant ethic did in its time: it provided a strong ideological incentive for élites bent on capital accumulation and cultural modernisation, and as such a doctrine fit for *promoting*, instead of overcoming, the industrial order.[15] Nowadays, however, what has to be stressed is that what once, in some specific contexts, made Marxism act as a breakthrough, exploding traditional societies with an inert economy, normally becomes, later on, a bottleneck: for now Marxist pieties become a break, a dirigiste obstacle to the very different, centrifugal dynamics of high, intensive rather than extensive, industrialism. Or to put it another way, communism can be a good way to industrialisation; but it is surely inadequate as a way to run advanced industrialism, with its attendant prospect of mass consumption and welfare. This realisation dawned upon the Czech middle classes twenty years ago – thus confirming Gellner's idea of a rift between technocracy and ideocracy. But two decades of economic decay later, it ended up spreading throughout the masses of socialist countries, well beyond the cautious gradualism of their technical bourgeoisies.

There is, then, a Paretian approach to the 1989 revolutions. The East European gerontocracies suffered from a problem of élite circulation. Dismantling the command economy was the only way to ensure civil freedom. Liberism was the entrance ticket to liberty. But this in turn implied dropping the 'leading role' of the CP, enshrined in all communist constitutions. In practice, disestablishing the CP meant moving from a power monopoly to a polyarchy – a polity built on a decentralised power structure, with only occasional but no systematic overlaps between its loci of authority, and an élite composed of several largely independent groups and spheres. Blowing up communist hegemony let the CP survive, though obviously no longer as a party-state with a totalitarian jurisdiction. Ironically, up to now (January 1990), the only country close to outlawing the CP, instead of merely circumventing and demoting it, is Romania, precisely where the decommunisation process is being least liberal. Elsewhere, communists retain the option to turn social democrat – or perish. In any event, the demise of the party-state makes room for a much wider circulation of élites.

Gellner's liberalisation essay, together with its contra Aron elaboration, was the launching pad of the sociology of liberalisation. When the liberalising wave was just at its beginning, Gellner grasped the exhaustion of the revolution myth and its replacement by a general preference for liberalisation. The messianic politics of redemption so typical of socialist revolutionism was giving way to another generic phenomenon – a 'central preoccupation' with liberalising politics. This in turn was not just 'one reform amongst others' but 'a profound change'. In Gellner's description, liberalisation was a true watershed. Yet it was also a skilful strategy of patience and compromise operating through peaceful transitions rather than by violent *tabulae rasae*.[16]

But Gellner's scenario for the liberalisation of communism – episodic dissident challenge plus continuous technocratic pressure and infiltration – missed both the rhythm and the actual agents of the current upheaval. In this, he was far from alone. Indeed, nobody properly foresaw 1989. Even those who dealt most perceptively with the decline of the Soviet empire, by speaking – like Timothy Garton Ash – of its likely 'Ottomanisation', predicted a long war of attrition rather than the quick domino crumbling of 1989. Also, almost everyone was prepared to conceive of red liberalisations as of the granted, *concession* (and therefore controlled) type, not as the direct result of massive street demonstrations or the outbreak of popular wrath. All the same, Gellner's forecast can be found wanting in one element – the depth of popular feeling for economic change. Gellner's liberalisation theory tells us of the technological bourgeoisie's instrumental need for freedom, to an extent normally denied by ideocratic interference; but it does not focus on the common man's distress amid dearth of goods and poor services, nor on the general apprehension, through travelling and the media, of Western wealth and welfare (the existence of Western poverty, though certainly real, was never so widespread as to alter this perception).

Now I suspect that the failure to give this aspect its true weight stems to a large measure from Gellner's indifference to liberism, something which did not go unnoticed by his ablest interpreter, John A. Hall.[17] In his collections, *Contemporary Thought and Politics* (1974), *Spectacles and Predicaments* (1979) and *Culture, Identity and Politics* (1987), containing his most important diagnoses of recent social trends, one finds little support for economic, as distinct from political, liberalism. More often than not, his references to liberism are curt dismissals, and do not distinguish sufficiently economic freedom from Victorian-like laissez-faire. The most sustained discussion dating from 1975, has a Polanyian air about it. It claims that the separation of the economic and the political spheres in classical capitalism was an institutional trait 'highly eccentric, historically and sociologically speaking'.[18] *Modern* capitalism, with its huge, costly technological infrastructure, makes a mockery of the laissez-fairist notion that 'individuals combine factors of production and then exchange the results'. Under such conditions the independent market is but an illusion, and 'inordinate profits' become unacceptable. Since the state, representing the collectivity, is now *obliged to pervade economic activity*, economic activity is no longer perceived as the fruit of private efforts, entitled to big rewards.

The trouble with this unwillingness to accept the relevance of liberism, even when laissez-faire capitalism no longer obtains, is that it averts the sociological eye from the crucial problem of *economic decision*. The state as provider of a technical and educational infrastructure to modern industrialism is indeed necessary; yet this fact by no means detracts from another fact, namely, that the state as direct producer and dirigiste master of a command economy has generally been an appalling disaster, especially in the age of modern, that is advanced, hi-tech industrialism, on which modern affluence is predicated. That those combining factors of production be private owners or not is of little importance. What is significant is that the decisions concerning such combinations remain decentralised – otherwise the whole system becomes cumbersome and inefficient. In the last analysis, capitalists, *stricto sensu*, could be dispensed with – but *capitalism* (including profit) cannot, if wealth and innovation are to be attained and sustained. The penury of much of their societies seems to have convinced East Europeans, a contrario, that this is indeed so. As Alec Nove puts it,

the essential problem is the impossible *scale* of centralised micro-economic planning, the fact that subordinate units adjust their actions to the plan targets laid down from above, and not to the needs of other enterprises or to the revealed preferences of the citizens.[19]

But if this is so, then economic liberalism *has* a case which cannot be overlooked or minimised in a sociology of liberalisation.

To be sure, Gellner is perfectly aware of the economic superiority of the West. From his early essays he has granted that probably social and economic pluralism cannot survive without economic pluralism, nor the latter 'be genuine without the legal institution of private property'.[20] Moreover in his own remarkable discussion of modern legitimacy he stresses the interplay between economic performance and the validation or revalidation of rulership in the modern world. Not only has legitimacy become a multidimensional affair, since 'in our world, it is not merely rulers and régimes, but also *types of ownership, production*, education, association, expression, thought, art and research which can have, or fail to have, legitimacy in the eyes of beholders and practitioners', but also, and crucially, there are now many rulers and régimes, most notably in the developing world, whose validation depends on passing the test of economic success.[21] Still, unlike Aron, Gellner shows little inclination to substantiate a preference for capitalism within their common 'industrial society' approach (which in Gellner becomes the theory of transition). In a significant essay from 1967 'Democracy and Industrialisation', he even suggested that the division of societies into industrial and non-industrial ones is 'far more important' than the capitalist/non-capitalist dichotomy.[22]

This sounds rather like Aron around 1960, in the famous Sorbonne course begun with the *Eighteen Lectures on Industrial Society*. The realisation that the gap between industrial and non-industrial nations was much wider than the differences within industrialism led Aron to stress that the real divergence was to be found, Tocqueville-wise, at the *political* level: industrialism cum pluralism and constitutionalism in the West; industrialism under ideocratic dictatorship in the communist world. Since then, however, there has been a major shift in the international differentiation, and therefore the ranking, among countries. With all the main countries now being industrial societies, the larger or smaller presence of capitalist institutions is of undeniable moment when it comes to assessing growth performances and the speed in the achievement of affluence. Thus the *Wirtschaftswunder* of the Four Little Dragons in East Asia put them patently ahead of the shabby-looking economies of East Europe; but by general consensus the difference has much to do with embracing or rejecting capitalism (though emphatically not laissez-faire) as a system of production and exchange.

Furthermore, there are political implications. In 1967, Gellner expatiated on the second paradox of democracy (the first, noticed by Popper, being its ability to commit suicide, as in Weimar Germany). Bearing in mind the ghastly dilemmas of Transition, Gellner focused on a key issue: whether the preconditions of democracy (roughly, the culture of modernity) are not such that they can hardly be secured through democracy.[23] But once Transition is over, or nearly so, at least on its basic industrialising level, then those societies apparently best equipped to adopt democracy, even as a gift from *von oben* liberalisations, *are precisely those enjoying high rates of growth and widespread wealth*. South Korea has distinctly less of a national democratic tradition than impoverished countries like Poland or Argentina; but its chances of enhancing and consolidating democracy are no smaller. Again, the decisive variable seems to be the presence or absence of a vigorous capitalist economy.

As far as I can see, the root of Gellner's reluctance to

incorporate the capitalist factor into his rich theoretical framework lies in the Russellian side of his thought. Like Bertrand Russell, the hero of his philosophical youth, Gellner is no believer in socialist utopias and resists Marxism on cognitive as well as ethical grounds. Nevertheless, like Russell, he also dislikes capitalist society, chiefly for egalitarian reasons. This much showed even in his response to the Prague Spring. A good deal of his liberalisation theory, notably in the nuclear technocracy-versus-ideocracy theme, was inspired by the work of the dissident Czech sociologist, Pavel Machonin, on the connection between intensive industrial growth, techno-meritocratic stratification and political liberalisation. But Gellner actually *deplored* Machonin's lukewarmness toward egalitarianism.[24] Actually Gellner holds a peculiar ideological stance. He sheds no tears at the decline of the 'Keynesian' state, and can be sarcastic about gauchiste excitement of the May 1968 ilk. But somehow his old socialist flame keeps creeping back, preventing him from fully recognising the need for the liberist revival and crippling his comments on the market with a bit of genetic fallacy (even if the breakthrough of the market economy was the creature of laissez-faire, this proves nothing against its functional role today). It is true, however, that in the mid 1970s the lack of conceptual room for the liberist drive in liberalisation surges was not an ugly sin, for none of the pro-market trends – the Thatcherite, the Dengian or the Hungarian – was yet under way.

Finally, there is a further reason, apart from possible socialist Sehnsucht, for Gellner's reticence about the will to capitalism – a reason best explained in his thought-provoking work, *Plough, Sword and Book*, a crisp study on the 'structure of human history'. There the idea is entertained that the present state of mankind opens up the possibility of standing Malthus on his head. We are invited to envisage a society 'where output grows markedly faster than population'. In such a society adds Gellner, the post-scarcity one, it may well be that the expansion of output matters less than the maintenance of order.[25] Granting that 'liberal societies' tend to do much better, in productive terms, than 'over-centralised ones', he suggests that nonetheless output growth may become irrelevant after the general attainment of a certain level of technological mastery. Moreover in this post-security era 'status-consumerism' may throw wealth differentials into relative unimportance. Just as the emergence of the market economy on a wide scale made wealth, for the first time in history, conceivable without power, the transition to a post-scarcity world can make position attainable without wealth. Henceforth, four options offer themselves: (1) a kind of 'perpetual potlatch' society, based on useless, compulsive and competitive consumption for status-keeping or status-seeping purposes; (2) a universal counterculture, breaking with consumerism altogether; (3) a re-ritualisation of society, diverting leisure time from private use into communal symbolic rites; and (4) a Soviet-like system, in which a unified, authoritarian élite confers both power and perks.[26]

As Gellner noted in passing (in 1987), communism was conspicuously failing at rekindling its utopian faith. 'The Communist Counter-reformation' in Eastern Europe (presumably the Brezhnev reign) proved far less successful than its Jesuit-led predecessor in the seventeenth century.[27] One feels therefore tempted to say that, a decade after writing his seminal liberalisation essays, Gellner was fairly alert to the prospect of a withering away of the party-state – a political animal to whose sad predicament, in terms of economic and ethnic strains, he was a privileged witness during his residence in Russia for much of the academic year 1988–89, on leave from his Cambridge chair. Still, the very last page of *Plough, Sword and Book* stresses the ongoing need for state coercion in an affluent economy requiring an immense and indivisible infrastructure – the same argument he used to deride neoliberal slogans in praise of the market.

In Gellner's own tale the slow transition from Agraria into Industria put producers on a par with predators, besides giving birth to the 'cognitive growth' revolution. In both cases, the consequences were as a whole as clearly beneficial to freedom as they were to the welfare of mankind. But as the next transition approaches, he sees no compelling reason – quite the contrary – for the growth of liberty, or the need for economic freedom. Significantly, none of the four paths open to a post-scarcity society sets much store by economic rationality. All in all, Gellnerian liberalisation can be no more than a minor aggiornamento of some laggard industrial societies, with more breathing space negotiated by technical strata. Fortunately, however, the promise of recent events is not that meagre – and we can only expect the sharp, nimble mind of Ernest Gellner to probe into their meaning.

We seem to have entered a new epoch, which – provided one avoids wishful-thinking idealising – well deserves the label of the Age of Liberalisation, political, economic and cultural. There are, of course, drawbacks and backlashes. It is after all possible, perhaps even probable, that the decomposition of communism, chiefly imposed by economic discontent and/or ethnic strife, produces a deep, dangerous social dislocation where groping for the market and dabbling with democracy could remain very far from their 'Western', stable institutionalisation. Capitalism without its complex institutional underpinning, democracy without its constitutional anchorage could be a highly immature – and highly volatile – post-communist situation. As Jon Elster has aptly put it, 'when sclerotic communism dissolves, the result might be savage capitalism'.[28] And in savage capitalism the liberist drive works less as an engine of economic strength than as an enzyme of social disintegration: a catalyst, that is, of anarchy and anomie. Meanwhile, democracy, too, can have the wrong dosage and unintended effects. If unchannelled into proper institutional grooves, at both the state and the societal levels, democracy may flare up as a mere blaze of democratism. Indiscriminate participation can then block the consistency of policies for the sake of blind decision-sharing – once again to the detriment of efficient, well-balanced liberalism.

Clearly, then, liberalisation as an abstract recipe is no panacea. Both liberism and liberalism require a grounding in a modicum of political and legal culture, as well as of the right economic motivation, still largely unavailable in countries like Romania or Bulgaria or, for that matter, Russia. Take private property, for instance. It kept some significant roots in Eastern Europe, for example in the GDR's trade sector, in Polish agriculture, in Hungary's small industries; but it leads a puny existence in the Soviet Union. The existence of a sizable entrepreneurial stratum cannot be dismissed in East Europe, but is sadly missing from the Russian social landscape. Moreover, even within countries such differences can count: thus in Czechoslovakia Bohemia was certainly better nurtured in precommunist capitalism than Slovakia; and so is, in Yugoslavia, Croatia rather than Serbia. Similarly, a country may have a modern past familiar – up to a point – with pluralist democracy, yet not so much with modern capitalism, like pre-war Poland; or with neither, like pre-war Romania.

Each of these configurations of background carries a great deal of weight on the threshold of postcommunism – not always to the advantage of the 'Westernising' of the economy and the polity. Little wonder if there are remarkable differences, along the liberalisation spectrum both in the pace and in the path of reforms. Hungary, which has managed to attract General Electric, General Motors and Pirelli, treads rather easily the road of stock exchange growth, joint ventures and further stakes in the world market. In Prague, where the economic ministers form a troika of outspoken free marketeers, a 1990 reform package should open the country to foreign capital, roll back dirigiste planning and allow free enterprise and private ownership. But in Poland – the first socialist country to intro-duce, early in 1990, overall economic liberalisation, just as it was the first to hold pluralist elections – wages are expected to fall by 20 per cent and prices to rise by 50 per cent. It is an ominous beginning for economic freedom.

Most East European countries are by now industrial societies which yearn for Western standards and a close relationship with the West. Yet as noticed by Susan Strange,[29] much of their industry is undercapitalised, obsolete, overstaffed and suffer-ing from low productivity. So it can hardly compete in the international arena. All it can do is to process or assemble goods designed and traded by the West – a slow track aggravated by the lack of proper roots for capitalism and democracy. What is more, the age of timid tinkering seems well over. The twenty years of Hungarian attempts at adopting limited markets provide evidence enough that the incremental approach leads to failure, and that shock therapy is the only way open to lasting economic recovery.

Thus liberalisation in ex-communist countries faces two sets of problems. One is how to handle the thorny issues of the transition towards democracy and the market. The other set of problems refers to the greater or smaller fitness of their respective national backgrounds for the market economy and liberal democracy. As already indicated, the sheer economic burden of the transition to capitalism can prove enormous. A Latin American spectre – hyperinflation, foreign debt, social inequality – haunts Eastern Europe. On the political side, for the time being transition looks no brighter. In the institutional limbo created by the fall of state socialism, most rulers 'possess neither the former power of state communism nor yet the mandate of their people expressed in free elections'.[30]

Above all, as everyone agrees, the Soviet transition can prove a gigantic challenge. Twenty years ago the doyen of comparative economic history, Alexander Gerschenkron, acknowledging that in the USSR the communist régime was 'an obstacle . . . to the utilisation of the fruits of growth by the population', singled out the *differentia specifica* of Stalinist industrialisation as follows:

It was a distinguishing feature of European industrialisation in the nineteenth century that, whatever the degree of backwardness of the country concerned, they allowed a smooth transition from the great spurts of growth to the post-spurt periods. It is a peculiarity of Soviet industrialisation that the political regime of the country must be considered as the main obstacle to such a transition.

Now, after almost forty years of post-Stalinism, that transition continues to look very problematic – and certainly no smooth affair. Educated guesses about even the near future tend to degrade into mere hunches, mostly pessimistic. Yet as long as the two colossi of communism, the Soviet Union and China, one industrial and the other semi-industrialised, do not liberalise, liberalisation as a world phenomenon is robbed, if not of its undeniable strength as a general trend, at least of its finality as an epochal watershed.

Moreover, whatever the global outcome, we know that the hardships of transition are often aggravated by the lack of proper roots for capitalism and democracy. As we saw, while some countries, like Hungary, East Germany or Czechoslovakia, seem readily convertible into market economies, this might prove harder to achieve, or at the very least initially very painful, in Poland or the Soviet Union. Instant markets do pop up almost everywhere; but of course they do not add up that quickly to capitalism as a true system, a whole network of ingrained markets. The big mistake of command economies was to act as though wealth and production could be summoned into existence by administrative fiat. Now, after the noisy burial of the communist power monolith, the socialist countries are beginning to realise that the market cannot be created by decree either, for all its being closer to popular aspirations and spontaneous social intercourse. Like democracy, the market needs many rules in order to function – and rule-compliance presupposes in turn a vast capital of acculturation into norms, customs and institutions. If it is to succeed, quite beyond the natural dangerous difficulties of transition, liberalisation needs *grounding* – and the grounding is the easier the stronger the 'bourgeois' heritage of each country involved.

Neoliberal enthusing over the Age of Liberalisation often overlooks the problem of grounding, which boils down, on a theoretical level, to a sense of context. Hence the obvious relevance, to the ongoing liberalising processes, of two classics, Montesquieu and Tocqueville. For while Tocqueville saw that raising expectations through reformism can sometimes precipitate, instead of preempting, revolution and an illiberal outcome, Montesquieu may be deemed the founder of contextualist political sociology, stressing both the structure and the spirit of régimes within a framework of *moeurs* as well as of physical and social preconditions.

Gellner's striking contributions to the analysis of nationalism and liberalisation are well attuned with this sociological wisdom. In fact his work, so powerfully shaped by anthropological research, normally has a highly contextualist flavour. But he differs from mainstream anthropology in that his own brand of contextualism gets rid of functionalist pieties by tending to concentrate on conflict situations and disruptive factors. Neither the former nor the latter seems likely to be absent from the current physiognomy of liberalising East Europe. In more than one place the Age of Liberalisation could be best described as the agony of liberalisation.

NOTES

1. For a brief comment on this point, see J.G. Merquior, 'Power and Identity: Politics and Ideology in Latin America', *Government and Opposition*, vol. 19, 1984.

2. For good sociological analyses on these lines see Michael Mann, *Consciousness and Action Among the Western Working Class*, London, 1973, and Frank Parkin, *Marxism and Class Theory – a Bourgeois Critique*, London, 1979.

3. Timothy Garton Ash, 'Eastern Europe: The Year of Truth', *New York Review of Books*, 15 February 1990.

4. Alain Besançon, 'Gorbatchev: une mystification?'. *Le Figaro*, 26 Décembre 1989.

5. From an article in *Daedalus*, vol. 119, 1990, signed by 'Z', on the Soviets' terminal crisis. A shortened version was published in the *New York Times*, at the end of 1989.

6. Philip Peters (alias Ernest Gellner), 'Moscow Notes', *Times Literary Supplement*, 9 December 1988; see also Gellner, 'Perestroika Observed', *Government and Opposition*, vol. 25, 1990.

7. E. Gellner, *Spectacles and Predicaments*, Cambridge, 1979, (henceforth SP), p. 339.

8. Timothy Garton Ash, 'The German Revolution', *New York Review of Books*, 21 December 1989.

9. René Girault, 'L'Automne des peuples', *Le Monde*, 4 Janvier 1990.

10. E. Gellner, 'From the Revolution to Liberalisation', *Government and Opposition*, vol. 11, 1976, now ch. 16 in SP (see note 7 above).

11. Gellner, SP, p. 330.

12. Raymond Aron, *Plaidoyer pour l'Europe décadente*, Paris, 1977, p. 472. (Aron's emphasis, my translation.)

13. Cf. E. Gellner, *Nations and Nationalism*, Oxford, 1983.

14. Gellner, SP, p. 333.

15. E. Gellner, *Thought and Change*, London, 1964, pp. 136–39. The same basic view (minus the Weberian parallel) has been presented by Aron in 'Social Structure and Ruling Class', a lecture series delivered at the London School of Economics in 1949 (cf. *British Journal of Sociology*, vol. 1, 1950). Moreover the interpretation of Marxism as essentially an authoritarian industrialising ideology has been brilliantly put forward by Alexander Gerschenkron (*Economic Backwardness in Historical Perspective*, Cambridge, Mass., 1962), for whom, in European history, the more one goes eastwards, the greater the role of the state (thus England > Germany > Russia). In Hegel's philosophy of history, it is well known, liberty is *heliodromic*: its course, like the sun's runs westwards. One feels tempted to say that Gerschenkron translated Hegel into economic history – most illuminatingly.

16. Gellner, SP, p. 331.
17. John A. Hall, *Diagnosis of Our Time, Six Views of Our Social Condition*, London, 1981, pp. 227, 230.
18. Gellner, SP, pp. 285–91, from 'A Social Contract in Search of an Idiom', first published in *The Political Quarterly*, 1975; my emphasis.
19. Alec Nove, 'The Soviet Economy: Problems and Prospects', *New Left Review*, 119, Jan/Feb 1980, p. 14.
20. E. Gellner, *Contemporary Thought and Politics* (henceforth CTP), London, 1974, p. 40 (from a 1967 essay on 'Democracy and Industrialization').
21. E. Gellner, *Legitimation of Belief*, Cambridge, 1974, pp. 24–26 (emphasis added).
22. Gellner, CTP, pp. 39–40.
23. Gellner, CTP, ch. 3. I have commented on this point in 'The Politics of Transition: On the Work of Ernest Gellner', *Government and Opposition*, vol. 16, 1981.
24. See E. Gellner, 'The Pluralist Anti-Levellers of Prague' (1972) reprinted as ch. 12 of CTP.
25. E. Gellner, *Plough, Sword and Book: The Structure of Human History*, London, 1988, pp. 224 and 238.
26. Gellner, *Plough*, pp. 230–31
27. Gellner, *Plough*, pp. 235–36.
28. Jon Elster, 'When Communism Dissolves', *London Review of Books*, 25 January 1990.
29. Susan Strange, 'Helping Eastern Europe: A Piecemeal Approach Won't Work', *International Herald Tribune*, 24 January 1990.
30. John Lloyd, 'East Europe in Ferment', *Financial Times*, special report, 24 January 1990.
31. Alexander Gerschenkron, *Europe in the Russian Mirror: Four Lectures in Economic History*, Cambridge, 1970, pp. 120–21.

CHAPTER 16

# *Peace, peace at last?*

## *John A. Hall*

If the extraordinary range of Ernest Gellner's writings over the last two decades makes it clear that his intellectual project is nothing less than that of characterising the spirit of modernity, his most striking statement about the principles of social organisation suited to the modern era remains that offered in *Thought and Change*. Legitimacy in the modern world, he asserted, does depend and ought to depend upon obeisance to two, and only two, principles: nationalism and industrialism.[1] On reflection, the latter of these two principles should be considered the more important for Gellner, given his insistence on explaining nationalism as a corollary of industrialism – or, more precisely, as an unintended consequence of the uneven diffusion of industrialism around the globe. Although a consideration of the prospects of peace requires some consideration of nationalism, the privileged position Gellner lends to industrialism in his thought is taken as justification for a similar concentration in this essay. My intention here is to flesh out one aspect of the industrial society thesis, namely its attitude towards geopolitical conflict. In summary terms, the industrial society theorists expected that their new world would bring peace. Gellner puts the matter like this:

On any moderately realistic estimate of human nature, as long as the price of decent behaviour was, in effect, total self-sacrifice (which was the case in the conditions of scarcity which characterised pre-industrial society), the prospects of decent behaviour were negligible. But thanks to the cognitive and technical effectiveness of industrial society, the *possibility*, though no more, is now present.[2]

This is cautious and sensible, but it is also rather vague. To what extent can we rest our hopes for a liberal political order upon the workings of the industrial order? What changes in

343

world politics would allow those hopes to increase? All in all, is modernity a stage which we have not yet reached, and if so will all then be sweetness and light?

The issues to be discussed can be highlighted by admitting that my own earlier work led to suspicion of Gellner's position. To presume that the transition between Agraria and Industria changes all social life is virtually an obstacle to understanding Western history.[3] The characteristic social pattern of European civilisation was already in place well before the industrial revolution: states existed and had to swim within the larger societies of international state competition and of the international market, relations between which were extremely complex. This formulation analytically privileges capitalism and state competition, but it is not thereby blind to the sea change in human history that the industrial revolution represents. To the contrary, the dynamism of the European pattern, about which Gellner has written so discerningly, proved to be catastrophic shortly after industry was applied to war.[4] But was the Pelopponesian war of the twentieth century the last throw of an old order or merely history as normal?[5] What shape will the continuing interactions of the autonomous but interrelated realms of industry, capitalism and state competition – that is roughly speaking, science, the profit motive within the marketplace and the search for security – give to modern world politics? Somewhat to my surprise, this paper does note pacific tendencies in contemporary world politics that make major war less likely. Tendencies are one thing, however, and realities another. In consequence, this paper inquires as to whether the political intelligence needed to make the best of beneficent tendencies is likely to be available.

## THEORY: OPTIMISTS VS PESSIMISTS

More important than the hope that affluence would make war less than rational has been the insistence that the growth of commerce would make war less feasible in direct proportion to any increase in economic interdependence. This theory is by no means new – not surprisingly, given that capitalism predates the industrial revolution. Perhaps the most striking of early formulations is Benjamin Constant's *The Spirit of Conquest and*

*Usurpation*, which appeared in Hanover in 1814. Constant had distanced himself from Napoleon's drive for imperial glory, and used the occasion of his impending downfall to sit in judgement on the very idea of the acquisition of wealth via territorial aggrandisement. In his discussion of 'the character of modern nations in relation to war', he asserted bluntly that:

War then comes before commerce. The former is all savage impulse, the latter civilised calculation. It is clear that the more the commercial tendency prevails, the weaker must the tendency to war become.[6]

In addition, Constant insists that territorial conquest has now become self-defeating: it leads to a 'universal horror' that defeats the purpose of the enterprise.[7] That this was so delighted Constant: the more powerful the warrior ethic, the less likely was it that constitutionalism, which he admired and endorsed, would be safe, let alone have the capacity to spread.[8] Constant is an exceptionally subtle thinker who added much to what he learnt whilst a student in Edinburgh, and his hopes were accordingly by no means unqualified. The rational calculation brought by commerce was not, Constant feared, sufficiently strong to overcome Paris's capacity to create excessive ambition; as importantly, the privatisation of social life characteristic of commercial society might lead a passive populace to gain vicarious pleasure from conquest.

In contrast, few doubts as to the peace-inducing consequences of the spread of commerce were entertained by the Manchester School, perhaps because their experience was of *industrial* capitalism. The views of this school were marvellously captured by Cobden in his parliamentary speech during the Don Pacifico affair in 1850:

The progress of freedom depends more upon the maintenance of peace, the spread of commerce, and the diffusion of education, than upon the labours of cabinets and foreign offices . . . [There should be] as little intercourse as possible between Governments; as much connexion as possible between the nations of the world.[9]

This prescriptive view turned into a descriptive account of reality by 1909 in Normal Angell's *The Last Illusion*: the intercourse of capitalists was held to be so extensive that war was impossible.[10] It is important, both in the abstract and for the purposes of this essay, to remember that other important liberal voices could not accept that a harmony of interests would be brought about naturally and spontaneously. Such thinkers favoured social engineering so that basic liberal values and institutions could be put in place. The market mechanism, upon whose beneficent workings so much depended, had to be put in place by an act of will.[11] Equally, most liberals allowed some room for intervention so as to help the fight of nations struggling to throw off the oppression of foreign rulers, although the extent of such intervention was very much a matter of debate.[12] Similarly, where Cobden was prepared to leave the abolition of slavery to the workings of the market, John Stuart Mill insisted that the West African Squadron of the Royal Navy be kept in place so as to establish basic workings of civilised society – within which, of course, market principles might then work.[13] Interestingly, Mill's views on this point angered his friend Tocqueville, who saw the Navy's actions in terms of the interests of Britain rather than those of humanity. This type of reaction proved to be much more general, and it is at the back of an entirely different way in which the spread of commerce was conceptualised.

Alexander Hamilton made an early contribution to the alternative approach when insisting, in his 1791 'Report on Manufactures', that the young United States needed to protect its infant industries against Britain's commercial might. An open world economy was very much in the interest of a nation which had an established economic lead; it was advisable, in Hamilton's view for latecomers to reject the terms of the leading power so as to ensure their own development.[14] What was at issue here was simple: the fact that capitalism had no single centre meant that the pure laws of the market were not accepted by developing nations. The need for special practices to overcome economic backwardness was most clearly articulated by German thinkers, most notably by Fichte's *The Closed Commercial State* (1808) and by List's *The National System of Political Economy* (1841); it is generally familiar today in the form of dependency theory.[15]

The fact that capitalism was divided by nation, in time led other theorists to a much more pessimistic view. Karl Polanyi remains the most considerable of all the pessimists. His rich and subtle *The Great Transformation* was a sustained reflection on the social origins of those wars that began in Europe and which then engulfed the world.[16] Polanyi argued that capitalism depends upon constant changes, a never-ending story of the destruction of settled social and economic practices. This circumstance naturally creates a demand for the protection of society against impersonal forces. The desire to protect society often entailed a search for full economic security only realisable through conquest. The spread of capitalism, in other words, caused war.

The key insight of Polanyi's account has been formalised and developed by modern American thinkers, particularly by those who posit a 'theory of hegemonic stability'.[17] The most obvious claim of this school is that capitalism works best when a hegemonic power is capable of providing certain services or public goods – most notably, a top currency, capital for export, absorption of excess world product and an insistence on free trade throughout the larger society. Both Britain in the nineteenth century and the United States after 1945 are held to have served as such hegemons. If this first claim tends to tautology, a second claim makes entirely concrete predictions. Problems for world political order are caused by the uneven development of capitalism: more particularly, there is a complex interaction between the hegemon and its rivals, the former seeking to retain its lead in adverse circumstances and the latter all the more driven to grab at world power in consequence. The justification for this claim is to be found in its rather idiosyncratic interpretation of modern world history. Peace reigned whilst Britain was hegemon but war followed thereafter, because of both Germany's challenge and the United States's unwillingness, during the interwar years, to take on the mantle of leadership which its actual power would have allowed it to bear. Similarly, peace reigned while the United States was supreme, but the undermining of its position is again likely to lead to some sort of war of all against all.[18]

This is a very striking theory indeed, but it is also quite vague at key junctures. Its principal theorists are realists, prone to see the actions involved as having been taken by state leaders for reasons of national interest. But the theory is open to more economistic readings. Thus the demand for openness to or protection from international economic forces can be interpreted as being occasioned by special interest groups pressing their point of view upon state leaders. Insofar as there is any

truth to this later position, it opens the way to the classic charge
against realism, namely that insufficient attention is paid to the
character and workings of the states upon whose external
manoeuvrings the theory concentrates. If the pressure of
special interest is often seen as a source of constraint upon a
state, that factor is itself often more or less strong as the result
of the actual political regime in place. It is at this point that a
second theory can be distinguished which allows us to entertain
optimistic thoughts about the possibility of peace within the
world polity. The classic statement of this position was produced in 1795 by Immanuel Kant in his *Perpetual Peace*.[19]

Kant shared hopes that the spread of trade would increase
peace's chances naturally and spontaneously, but his own
contribution was to offer a list of changes that had to be made
in political institutions in order to give peace a decent chance.
His arguments are hard-headed in suggesting why states might
find it in their self-interest to adopt liberal practices – albeit,
one cannot but help think that the reasons are likely to appeal
most to states which are somehow liberal-spirited in the first
place. Above all, it was necessary, Kant argued, for governments to be republican – that is, to have political processes
sufficiently open that the views of the people, so often the
cannon fodder of militaristic élites, could be heard. It can be
said immediately that the historical record is, precisely, schi-
zophrenic as the extent to which the participation of the people
limits war. On the one hand, the birth of modern citizenship
during the French revolution made militarism popular and
aggressive, thereby giving rise to an interpretation of this
variable as pessimistic as was that of Polanyi and the hegemonic
stability theory of the economic variable discussed above.[20] But
equally, on the other hand, popular pressure, especially in the
history of the United States, has made it sensible – at times,
pessimists have claimed, regrettably so[21] – to accept Tocqueville's insistence that a democratic people is slow to anger.[22]
And this is not the end of the matter. Kant's demand that
liberal states respect each other seems, as Michael Doyle has
noted, to be borne out historically by the fact that no two liberal
states have ever waged war on each other.[23] But here too there
is a darker, pessimistic side to the equation. If liberal states have
respected each other, the wars they have waged against their

enemies have tended to be remorseless: such enemies are seen not just as threats to security but as ideological opponents of the proper moral life.[24]

No general theory of the opportunity costs of liberalism in the conduct of foreign affairs has yet been produced, and perhaps none is available. Nonetheless, the evidence to which we can now turn does justify the contention that authoritarian regimes of the modern age are likely to cause war. To say this is, of course, to argue against Gellner, to insist that liberal political arrangements ought to be a principle of legitimacy, despite the solid structural reasons limiting their actual salience.[25] Something more is involved here than a prescription, which Gellner would in any case probably share. The presence or absence of liberalism has affected the actual shaping of foreign affairs, and a consideration of this needs to enter our social philosophy. Whether such polities have to be created by will or whether their genesis might be helped by beneficent workings of industrialism or capitalism concerns us below. What is not at issue is the fact that such politics have an autonomous impact on the course of events. The interactions that must concern us here are nothing less than those between industry, capital, nation and regime.

## AN ASSESSMENT OF THE HISTORICAL AND SOCIOLOGICAL RECORD

A first look at the evidence makes it seem that the pessimists' position is so superior as to render redundant any continuing debate in the whole matter. If nineteenth-century history can be interpreted in terms of the triumph of capitalism – of free trade, retrenchment and reform, as Gladstone had it – the first half of twentieth-century history, in contrast, was driven by geopolitical conflict of the most savage sort. This fact famously makes sociological theory, whether derived from liberal or Marxist roots, of little use for any general understanding of historical development: that theory was created in the long peace between 1815 and 1914, and its concepts, with few exceptions, reflected that fact in seeing the coming of industry as of greater importance than war.[26] Awareness of these considerations led Raymond Aron to consider, with characteristic brilliance, the relations between war and industrial

society.[27] Aron was extremely critical of the view that industrial
society would automatically bring peace – not surprisingly, for
what greater refutation could that theory have had than two
world wars! Accordingly, he accepted classical realism *tout court*.
Nonetheless, Aron continued to hope that the industrial era
might be peaceful. He sought to position himself between, say,
Thucydides and Kant – although the exact way in which
liberalism and realism were to be combined was never clearly
spelt out. For reasons to be noted, there is much to be said for
standing between Thucydides and Kant *at all times*. But the
question remains as to whether changes in the contemporary
world might make peace more likely. Aron never gave us his
final opinion on these matters: his work on industrial society
remained largely separate from that on international relations,
and he was generally reluctant to write openly about his own
liberal hopes. This essay tries to fill this gap.

It is certainly true that the first three-quarters of the nineteenth century witnessed both the spread of free trade, in theory
and in practice, and an increase, partly in consequence, of actual
world trade. Was this happy situation the result of conscious
British determination to spread the doctrines in which it
believed and which were to its advantage? There seems little
evidence to support the theory of hegemonic stability at this
point. Britain was not especially aggressive in seeking to break
down tariff barriers.[28] That such barriers did come down in
Europe between the 1850s and the 1870s was essentially because
the nations concerned found such a policy in their immediate
interest. Britain had found in the 1840s that a rationalisation of
tariff barriers actually increased state revenue. Prior to 1846
over 1200 items had been subject to various levels of tariff, even
though by far the greatest proportion of revenue derived from a
mere nine items. The taking of hundreds of items off the books
hurt smugglers badly and made it possible to police the remaining items in such a way that enhanced revenues were assured,
even at lower tariff rates, whilst costs of collection were dramatically slashed. Not surprisingly, other countries followed
suit.[29] That Britain played no positive hegemonic role does not,
however, distract from the fact that the nineteenth century saw
the spread of free trade and an increase in economic growth.
Why then was this possible? Mercantilist policies in the century

between 1713 and 1815 had been massively encouraged by the visceral conflict between France and Britain, especially in the War of the Atlantic. With the ending of those hostilities, together with the entry of both Germany and Russia onto the scene, basic European order could be maintained by the traditional means of a balance of power between the leading states. Differently put, Britain was at no time in the nineteenth century a genuinely hegemonic power. It had certain advantages – an economic lead and the Royal Navy – but it was continually faced with continental powers whose armed forces were greater than its own. It was never in a position to dictate to genuine geopolitical rivals.

At the end of the nineteenth century, tariffs were set up in continental Europe, and all hopes of the reign of peace were dashed by the onset of a general European war in 1914. To what extent can these events be seen within the terms of hegemonic stability theory? When concentrating on the role of Germany, as is necessary given the consensus of contemporary historians that that state was responsible for the onset of war, it is necessary to make many distinctions. There was to begin with, no automatic link between the imposition of tariffs and the onset of war. If there was an indirect link, it was that states were forced to re-impose tariffs in order to finance the military revolution of the late nineteenth century;[30] but if this increased international trade rivalries, it did not directly translate into war. War between Britain and Germany in fact became likely in 1897 when the decision to build a fleet underlined the creation of a genuine *Weltpolitik*. It is important to insist that this decision was not forced on Germany for reasons of economic necessity – that there was, to utilise the title of a book by Werner Sombart, a genuine choice between an heroic and a trading strategy.[31] The German economy was dynamic and expansionary, and a few years would have ensured its lead within Europe; furthermore the British Empire remained open to trade, although few German goods actually went there. Of course, it is always possible to say that what matters in economics is not the facts, but what social actors believe to be the facts. This will help us to understand some elements in the German situation, just as it must form part of any explanation of why Britain acquired and maintained an empire that, by and large, never paid.[32] But other more important points need to be made. What needs to be explained is why Germany went to war in 1914 on two fronts. This is exactly what Bismarck had always warned against and successfully avoided by means of defensive alliances which allowed Germany to increase its preponderance on the continent.

Germany's actions can best be explained by considering the nature of its state. War on two fronts was guaranteed by Germany having two expansionary policies at one and the same time. The army and the Junkers favoured a traditional Eastern policy whilst the Navy, some of heavy industry and the Social Democrats (who feared the possibilities of an army for purposes of internal repression) favoured a *Weltpolitik*. What is really striking, especially in comparison with the subtle calculations of Bismarck, is the way in which it proved not to be possible, despite some significant efforts, to assign priorities so as not to offend most of the great powers at the same time. Perhaps the fundamental reason for this failure is the fact that Imperial Germany was effectively a court society in which the personal rule of the Kaiser was of great significance. The continuity and consistency lent to policy by Bismarck could not be recaptured by his successors.[33] If nineteenth-century German politics had always involved 'divide and rule' tactics, a constant process of log-rolling between special interests, the task of later chancellors was made much harder by the entry of the people into the political stage. Both left and right mobilised support, and the ability to gain some autonomy for the state by constantly changing alliances accordingly decreased. The move to war was in consequence far more the result, in Walter Lippman's phrase, of drift than of mastery. After the famous meeting of 1912 that envisaged war, no thought was given to matters of general strategy. Furthermore, there is no evidence of much thought being devoted to economic affairs at all:

to most members of Wilhelm's entourage, economic expansion and even world power were first and foremost means to maintain the domestic status quo. Their intrinsic advantages were secondary. They were meant to provide somehow enough prosperity and/or nationalist prestige to quell the pressure for reform at home. How they managed this did not matter. MittelAfrika, MittelEuropa, it was all the same so long as the victory was large enough to sustain the power of the

Junkers and their Kaiser. The means thus stood only in oblique relationship to the end, making it all the harder to fashion a consistent policy. The usual ways to measure success, economic growth, acquisition of territory, increase of influence, could not be used under such a system because the question was not 'have we expanded' but 'have we expanded enough' (to reach the greater goal).[34]

This is not to say that there were not some people who thought in terms of economic interest – even though their views as to that interest were probably far removed from reality. Such 'Fleet Professors' as Max Weber had an altogether excessive view of the need for imperial possessions, and it mattered enormously in 1914 that Bethman-Hollweg was sympathetic to their views. Nonetheless what remains most striking about Germany's action is the extent to which no agreed notion of national interest had been hammered out. This failure led precisely to the encirclement that German leaders feared. When nationalist passions in the Balkans presented an opportunity, Germany risked war in an attempt to break out of a situation largely of its own making.

What has been said needs summarising. There is no especial reason to accept the pessimistic view that the development of capitalism entails war between nations. Neither economic nor realist considerations entailed war, and the onset of war is best explained in rather different terms. War was created by a half-modern authoritarian state, that is an authoritarian state with a democratic facade, paralysed by its internal contradictions and accordingly extremely unstable. Liberal hopes for an extension of space within the world polity need not, in other words, be completely abandoned. Authoritarian old regimes create instability, not least by politicising their working classes.[35] The evidence suggests a simple generalisation: established liberal democracies diffuse social conflict, whilst mobilised authoritarian systems enhance them.[36]

But if liberalism can be 'saved' in this manner, some other ways in which its legacies did not help the cause of peace have to be noted. A clearer warning to Imperial Germany in June 1914 that the invasion of Belgium would entail a British declaration of war might have prevented war.[37] Whatever the fact of the matter, it is certain that Sir Edward Grey could not have issued such a declaration for fear of the radical liberals in both the Liberal party and the cabinet. And there was a similar lack of realism in the liberalism of the interwar years. Woodrow Wilson's Gladstonian redrawing of the map of Europe created new nations, but left many of them without any real capacity to ensure their own security – and this in a situation in which two major powers, the Soviet Union and Germany, felt aggrieved by the nature of the post-war settlement. Peace in such circumstances could only have been ensured if the victorious powers had been prepared to place their power firmly behind their principles. It was precisely this that did not happen. No determined attempt was made to help Weimar. The United States withdrew into an isolation that very effectively constrained even Roosevelt, whilst both Britain and France, after the collapse of Weimar, were torn between a naive liberalism, hoping that appeasement would work, and an awareness of the electoral punishment likely to follow any move towards war.[38] The slowness to respond that Tocqueville felt to be characteristic of democracy played some part in the origins of the Second World War.

The generation of American leaders who came to power during the Second World War was determined that these mistakes should not be made again. Many of this generation had been trained in the Kiplingesque surroundings of Groton, and they jumped with delight at the opportunity of having the leading say in the running of world politics, although certain of its members, most notably Acheson and Kennan, were embarrassed by the fact that an end to isolation was only made possible by drawing upon a generalised crusading anti-communism. This new cohort of the American political élite embraced something like hegemonic stability theory as its guiding ideology; American culture was seen at work in these leaders in their view that the ending of free trade in the interwar years had partly occasioned war. The American system thus had a geopolitical and an economic component, both of which must be examined if we are to explain the successful way in which this war ended; and to see both of these components is essential to understanding the extent to which the Pax Americana has been, precisely, a system.

The most obvious reasons for the success of the postwar settlement are geopolitical. The terms of the settlement reflected the realities of power in the bluntest possible way.[39] Thus nationalism mattered so little that both Korea and Germany were divided. The realities of power, moreover, made this a simple system to operate. The fact that this system was effectively bipolar from the start and definitively so with the advent of nuclear weapons made it easy for 'enemy partners' to respect each others' spheres of influence. In addition, the fact that the opposition was between different and competing principles of civilisation also induced the type of clarity of thought that had been so missing in the interwar period.[40] It may well be that some of the complete freezing of history was overdone; but there can be no doubt but that it led to stability. Certainly the situation as a whole commended itself to Europeans who actively sought to tie America to Europe. This was in very large part an empire by invitation.[41]

The other side to the post war system was the allegiance given to liberal values. A huge debate has, of course, raged as to whether the United States sought to establish a free world or a world free for market forces, and no completely unshaded answer is in order. Some key economic actors, whose transactions were increasingly international, did favour involvement in the world for immediate economic reasons.[42] On the other hand, and rather more importantly, various economic policies, in particular the Marshall Plan, were created and accepted in order to shore up the geopolitical situation.[43] Whatever the case, there can again be no doubt about the success of the system established.[44] Political liberalism was imposed upon Japan and Germany, and they made the transition to a trading rather than a geopolitical strategy for national ascendancy. A historic class compromise that ruled out both extreme right and extreme left was extended, at American bidding, throughout the advanced nations of capitalist society.[45] The economic and social settlement as a whole was not, however, simply the result of the imposition of American might. Just as the Europeans had pulled the United States into NATO, so too were they able to dilute the initial full-blooded nature of American economic demands, particularly in matters of social welfare. The system that emerged was one of 'embedded liberalism' in which some national autonomy was allowed to facilitate adjustment – that is, to help with the political problems identified by Polanyi – to the international economic forces whose importance was stressed quite as much in the founding of liberal regimes such as GATT, the IMF and the World Bank.[46]

Even if the settlement was in part the result of the pressure and suggestion of allied powers, there can be no doubting the fact that the United States has been a leader of the world political economy in a sense that always eluded Britain at its moment of greatest strength. The hegemony of the United States results from its being dominant in every source of power that affects world politics – monetary, military and economic.[47] This can be most clearly seen in the workings of the American system over time. Alone amongst the nations within capitalist society, the United States has run a deficit, obviously, in the last years, of huge proportions, in its current account with the rest of the world. The deficit has in effect been paid for by loans to the United States by Germany, Saudi Arabia and Japan. Such loans represent a type of informal military rent: the United States is paid by allies without secure defences for the military services it provides.

All that has been said to this point about the post-1945 situation can be summarised simply by saying that there is much justification for the claim of hegemonic stability theory that the leading position of a liberal United States has stabilised world capitalist society. Things are more complex when we turn to the key question as to whether the demise of the American system will lead to renewed geopolitical struggle. Generalised caution should be directed to this claim for the simple reason that this is a unique historical situation, largely because America's position has indeed been that of a hegemon. So before turning to four developmental factors whose salience raises the chances of peace, it is necessary to question the extent to which the American system has in fact disintegrated.[48]

Several considerations suggest that the American system is still alive, albeit in somewhat altered form. First, hegemony is now exercised in a predatory rather than a benign manner. This was always an analytic possibility: for why should not the largest power seeks to extract rather than to spend resources? Thus the United States does not export capital to the rest of the world for development; instead it sucks it in rather than raise its own taxes. Such behaviour causes considerable difficulties to some American allies. Japan's low interest rates in the 1980s helped export capital to the United States, something that Japan wanted, both to prevent the emergence of protectionism in the United States and as informal payment for American defence; but these policies eventually led to a slump in Japanese markets which had risen to excessive levels as the result of those same low interest rates. This ability to pull in the world's capital is an extraordinary demonstration of muscle. Differently put, the emergence of economic rivals within capitalist society does not really disturb world order because the United States can still control by threats to withdraw defence or to protect its huge market. An important and related point is that the rivals within capitalist society are not rushing, as did Imperial Germany, to replace the United States in both economic and geopolitical terms. To the contrary, both Germany and Japan seemed firmly wedded to trading strategies, whilst there is a generalised appreciation amongst the liberal democracies that nuclear strategy is easiest to conduct on a bipolar basis. The position of the United States has, of course, received a spectacular boost from both the ending of the socialist promise and the massive weakening of the Soviet Union's economy. The prospects for continuing world order are, moreover, enhanced by the precise way in which Soviet power diminished:

Unlike Napoleonic France or Nazi Germany, the Soviet challenger to the established order has not been crushed but contained until its revolutionary dynamism has been exhausted. And this, too, may be a reason for believing that the future holds greater promise than the past. For then the world's immediate security problem was solved through war, which tends to create new resentments and insecurities.[49]

Secondly, the weaknesses of the United States tend anyway to be exaggerated. Decline is partly a statistical artefact of measuring America's contemporary position against the extraordinary dominance it had in 1945, when large parts of industrial society lay in ruins. If different measurements are used, America's decline seems less precipitous; and its decline – from nearly 50 per cent to roughly 25 per cent of world product – had taken place by the early 1970s, without much alteration over the last fifteen years.[50] Furthermore, one important reason – that the lesson of Vietnam has been learnt so that America's empire now tends to largely costless

non-territorial dominance – suggests that any decline the
United States does experience is likely to be less precipitous
than that formerly experienced by Britain. Thirdly, the power
of the United States extends well beyond political, military and
economic matters. The ideology of American – or perhaps
Anglo-Saxon – popular and consumerist culture has an extraordinary reach throughout the whole world. Finally, there is
something to be said for the argument, made most forcefully by
Robert Keohane, that the liberal system established by the
United States has considerable resilience.[51] Nations with leading economies are constrained by international institutions to
continue to talk to each other. This factor helps explain why
bargaining rather than trade war has characterised the world
political economy in the years since 1971, when the United
State's decision to close the gold window seemed to give
warning of its loss of hegemony. In any case, it is extremely
doubtful that a genuinely protectionist policy can any longer be
successfully operated. How can America be protected against
Japanese goods given Japan's ability to shift production centres
offshore, say to Thailand and to Korea, and then to route
goods via Mexico?[52]

If the cohesion of capitalist society was guaranteed in part by
the unique situation in which one power defended the whole,
the removal of an effective challenge from socialism may for
the first time lead to fissiparous tendencies, particularly on the
part of Germany and perhaps of Japan. All this is to say that no
general consensus as to the situation of the United States within
the world political economy is likely to be forthcoming in the
near future. Nonetheless, four novel developmental tendencies, some of which are interrelated and mutually supportive,
may yet mitigate the pessimists' fears of renewed geopolitical
conflict. These can be outlined immediately before then entertaining some necessary qualifications.

1. Overwhelmingly the most important novelty is the presence of
nuclear weapons, together with new technologies of surveillance that
diminish the uncertainties of armed adversaries.[53] Human beings
often become rational, capable of accurately assessing their self-
interest, only when the stakes are high. The possibility of destruction
seems to have made the political élites of both superpowers averse to
risk.

2. In recent years, the recognition given to nationalism as a principle of world politics has increased. There is a very positive side to this development which much recent commentary has ignored. Militarily, expansion no longer brings security since nuclear missiles ignore the size of any empire or buffer-zone in the possession of a leading state. If this is now apparent to the Soviet Union, so too has that state recognised an economic side to the question. If possession of territory increased power and wealth in the agrarian era, it no longer has that role, for two reasons. Negatively, nationalist movements, on whose character since 1945 Gellner is an excellent guide, have the capacity to make the retention of imperial possessions prohibitively expensive. Positively, economic success seems ever more dependent on the creation of human capital capable of allowing one's economy to move up the product cycle; one way of helping such movement is participation in advanced markets rather than through trading with secure colonial markets – whose capacity to absorb one's product, given their poverty, was anyway often exaggerated. Europe was made to realise this largely within the two decades after 1945; current Soviet behaviour suggests that the principle is now commonly understood.[54]

3. Marx famously remarked that re-enacted historical events have an air of farce about them; this can indeed be so. But sometimes historical events can catch up with theories which have preceded them, and there are good reasons for believing that this is true of the hope that interdependence would limit geopolitical conflict. One important change since 1945 has been the creation, for the first time, of a genuinely international division of labour. The demand for free trade now begins to have domestic political roots given that employment often depends upon companies whose very being depends upon world trade; both votes and campaign funds are now available to those who resist protectionism.[55] Some indication of what is involved can be gained by noting that perhaps a third of world trade is now intra-firm in character – something which makes nonsense of any simple view of national accounts. More important than this, however, is the fact that economic success depends, as noted, upon participation in the market. The history of the world economy in recent years has seen that nations which protect their industries for any length of time after their initial nurturing condemn their societies to increasing poverty. Argentina is the prime example of the false trail of protectionism, but the Latin American practice of import-substitution-industrialisation makes the general point equally well, especially when compared to the export-led growth of the East Asian Newly Industrialising Countries.[56] The basic underlying structural fact explaining this seems to be that the speed of technological change is now so fast that *not* to be involved in it invites inefficiency.

If this set of considerations if not fully understood – that is, if this is a tendency whose force may not yet be fully realised – the extent to which it has already been acted upon does seem to me remarkable. The political élite in Mexico, for example, is risking its political base largely because it is convinced of these truths.

4. One of Gellner's most considerable achievements has been his work in the area of liberalisation, not least because it sensitised us to potential changes in Eastern Europe – which is not to say, of course, that it predicted the exact manner let alone the speed of the collapse of that whole social world.[57] It is now possible, however, to distinguish between the difficulties facing societies making a double transition to the market and to democracy and those which simply seek to soften or to democratise authoritarian capitalist rule. Despite the greater difficulties facing the former societies, it may well be, as we shall see, that geopolitical considerations will ensure the success of at least some of them.

Societies which are heavily involved in world trade and which seek to move up the product cycle are likely to generate pressures for liberalisation. Economic success in these circumstances depends ever more upon the willing participation of educated labour – that is, of people whose jobs depend upon freedom of movement and information. If this goose is to lay a golden egg, it is imperative that rigidly authoritarian and ideocratic regimes loosen their hold. And if that hold is not loosened demands will be made, especially by students, for liberalisation from below.

The pressure generated by this segment is of more significance than that generated by European working classes at the end of the nineteenth century.[58] Every time such pressure is successful, the chances of authoritarian rule occasioning war are reduced.

The diverse considerations offered – that is, the critical comments on hegemonic stability theory as well as the four factors just identified – can now be drawn together. Our situation is made entirely novel both by the new geopolitical balance and by the developmental tendencies that played their part in creating this new situation. If we cannot return to old certainties, we must now consider not just how to preserve the world but rather how to change it.[59] Some maxims whose character helps reveal the presuppositions of the argument, may help us in our new situation.

It remains vital to respect the world of Thucydides whilst hoping for that of Kant. An end to war has been expected before, with disastrous consequences:

Recurring optimism is a vital prelude to war. Anything which increases that optimism is a cause of war. Anything which dampens that optimism is a cause of peace.[60]

Accordingly, sense dictates absolute caution. We can hope more strongly than before, but must remember that the largest reason for the long peace since 1945 has been preparation for absolute war. The reasons of states must continue to dominate our thought. The hope inherent in this essay will only be proved right if we remain hard-headed.[61]

Equally clearly, our hopes should not blind us to difficult realities. In every sense, we are in a situation of opportunity/ costs. This is most strikingly true of the re-emergence of nationalist forces in East and Central Europe.[62] Many nations within this world, moreover, inhabit the uneasy and unstable world between a previous authoritarianism and a liberal democracy where conflicts can be diffused through society. Moreover, the Soviet state itself may become far less stable. Totalitarianism gave the political élite genuine autonomy in the conduct of foreign policy and made it a particularly cautious actor on the world stage: unfettered sectoral pressures may make things far more difficult. Equally some attention has already been given to the difficulties attendant on the happy fact that Japan and Germany have so successfully followed trading strategies. In this connection it is worth stressing that a larger obstacle than Japanese barriers, formal or informal, to multilateral norms is the behaviour of the United States. A genuine resurgence of the United States in economic terms would seem to depend upon abandoning certain Anglo-Saxon practices, from the excessive role given to equity markets to the inability to create human capital through education. Many of the changes needed depend upon raising taxes, still a virtual impossibility for domestic political reasons; if this means that excess world capital continues to pour into the leading nation in capitalist society, that will disastrously affect the chances for debt-ridden Latin America to maintain the more liberal political regimes achieved in the last decade. In general, the United States may prefer to continue to seek to use its weight to change the rules of the game to its advantage rather than seek to put its own house in order; it remains at least half addicted to an heroic rather than to a trading strategy.

If we should recognise the worst it is only in order to try to prepare for the best. The room for creative policy is exciting, but it is so immense that a single instance must stand as exemplar. The uneasy situation in East and Central Europe might well be ameliorated by skill on the part of the Common Market. Just as the hope of gaining entry helped Spain's transition to democracy, so a joint policy on the part of the Community – insisting on the spread of democracy and holding out the promise of membership if it is achieved – might so shift the internal balance of forces as to increase the chances of a successful transition to democracy.[63]

## CONCLUDING WITH A MAJOR CAVEAT

The focus of this essay has been on the diminished likelihood of major war, that is, war between highly developed societies capable of generating disaster. The optimism entertained in this regard must, for moral and practical reasons be complemented with some concluding comments about the situation in the Third World, about 'them' rather than 'us'. A large and sobering dose of pessimism cannot and should not be avoided when contemplating the fate of the vast majority of the members of mankind.

War has continued to plague much of the Third World. If it is the classical engagements – between India and Pakistan, Iran and Iraq and Vietnam and China – that spring to mind most quickly, an altered reality nonetheless deserves attention. Since 1945 astonishingly few state boundaries have been changed. Agreement on the norms of sovereignty and of non-intervention has been very wide, including for most of the time not just the superpowers, but most Third World countries as well. But this new facet of the world polity should not be allowed to hide the very large number of civil wars that have taken place or look likely to take place within Third World countries. Two points deserve to be made in this connection. On the one hand, such wars are, given the character of modern weapons, massively and repulsively destructive. On the other hand, Third World states are not forced to organise and mobilise their societies as European states had done beforehand. This absence may well have overall negative effects for both political and economic development. Third World states have the capacity to remain top heavy, that is, possessed of significant arms designed to oppress their own people.

Any consideration of the economic situation facing the Third World engenders further pessimism. Something of an apogee to this whole situation can be seen in the debt crisis facing Latin America: large sections of the populations of most Latin American countries have had their living standards cut for the last several years so that capital can be exported to the advanced world. The analytic point that must be made as the result of these considerations is simple. The development of most East Asian NICs required highly idiosyncratic gifts, most notably traditions of bureaucracy, high levels of literacy, favoured geopolitical treatment, and land reform pushed through by the Japanese. Most countries do not have such advantages and do not look at all likely to develop successfully. There may be no more – or at least few more – NICs.[64]

All that has been said to this point accentuates the misery under which the many live. This is offensive to liberal values, but at first sight it does not matter in terms of traditional *Realpolitik*. Are these countries not weak and helpless? Is it not the case that most of them scarcely matter economically, as is so clearly shown by trade and investment figures? Such a position seems to me as blind as it is cruel. I have always feared that nuclear weapons may fall into the hands of leaders of mobilised and ideocratic societies who feel, justly or unjustly, aggrieved at the advanced world; the behaviour of Saddam Hussein, already possesssor of terrifying chemical weapons and reputedly close to the nuclear threshhold, has turned private nightmare into public horror. A great deal more political intelligence needs to be shown by both élites and people of the advanced world if the world is to survive, let alone to make the most of developmental trends that otherwise promise so much.

## NOTES

1. E. Gellner, *Thought and Change*, London, 1964, pp. 3–4.
2. E. Gellner, *The Concept of Kinship*, Oxford, 1987, ch. 4, 'The New Idealism – Cause and Meaning in the Social Sciences', p. 72.
3. J.A. Hall, *Powers and Liberties*, Oxford, 1985.
4. E. Gellner, *Plough, Sword and Book*, London, 1988.
5. Cf. R. Aron, *The Century of Total War*, London, 1954.
6. B. Constant, *Political Writings*, ed. B. Fontana, Cambridge, 1988, 'The Spirit of Conquest and of Usurpation', ch. 2, 'The Character of Modern Nations in Relation to War', p. 53.

7. Constant, 'The Spirit of Conquest and of Usurpation', p. 79.
8. On Constant's liberalism as a whole, see S. Holmes, *Benjamin Constant and the Making of Modern Liberalism*, New Haven, 1984.
9. R. Cobden, *Political Writings*, vol. 2, p. 377, cited in A.J.P. Taylor, *The Troublemakers*, London, 1969, p. 49.
10. N. Angell, *The Last Illusion*, London, 1909. Both M. Howard, *War and the Liberal Conscience*, London, 1978, and Taylor, *The Troublemakers* have excellent discussions of his views; see also J. Joll, *The Origins of the First World War*. London, 1984, p. 137 and passim.
11. The basic distinction between a natural and an engineered harmony of interests derives, of course, from E. Halévy, *The Growth of Philosophical Radicalism*, London, 1928. Cf. S. Collini, J. Burrow and D. Winch, *That noble science of politics*, Cambridge, 1983, especially ch. 4, and W.I. Thomas, *The Philosophical Radicals*, Oxford, 1979.
12. Howard, *War and the Liberal Conscience*, especially ch. 2.
13. This story is told in B. Semmel's excellent and important *Liberalism and Naval Strategy*, Winchester, Mass., 1986.
14. A. Hamilton, *Papers on Public Credit, Commerce and Finance*, New York, 1934, 'Report on Manufactures'.
15. A superlative discussion of this whole approach can be found in R. Szporluk, *Communism and Nationalism*, New York, 1988.
16. K. Polanyi, *The Great Transformation*, Boston, 1957.
17. The earliest statement of this thesis was C. Kindleberger, *The World in Depression 1919–1933*, Berkeley, 1973. The fullest working out of the thesis is R. Gilpin, *War and Change in World Politics*, Cambridge, 1981.
18. A third claim is often implicit in the theory, namely that hegemonic leadership is necessarily self-liquidating given the 'unfair' burdens that fall on the shoulders of the leader. For a sceptical assessment of that claim, see J.A. Hall, 'Will the United States decline as did Britain?', in M. Mann, ed., *The Rise and Decline of the Nation State*, Oxford, 1990.
19. I. Kant, *Political Writings*, ed. H. Reiss, Cambridge, 1970, 'Perpetual Peace: a Philosophical Sketch'.
20. Howard, *War and the Liberal Conscience*, ch.2.
21. G. Kennan, *American Diplomacy*, Chicago, 1951.
22. A. de Tocqueville, *Democracy in America*, New York, 1969. Part Three, ch. 26, 'Some Considerations Concerning War in Democratic Societies'.
23. M. Doyle, 'Kant, Liberal Legacies and Foreign Affairs', *Philosophy and Public Affairs*, vol. 12, nos. 3 and 4, 1983.
24. Doyle, 'Kant, Liberal Legacies and Foreign Affairs'. Cf. Tocqueville, 'Some Considerations Concerning War in Democratic Societies'.

25. E. Gellner, 'Democracy and Industrialisation', *European Journal of Sociology*, vol. 8, 1967. For an alternative view, see A. Kohli, 'Democracy and Development', in J.P. Lewis and V. Kallab, eds, *Development Strategies Reconsidered*, Washington, 1987.

26. M. Mann, *War, States and Capitalism*, Oxford, 1988, chaps 4–6.

27. R. Aron, *War and Industrial Society*, London, 1958 and 'War and Industrial Society: A Reappraisal', *Millennium*. vol. 7, 1978.

28. T. McKeown, 'Hegemonic Stability Theory and nineteenth century tariff levels in Europe', *International Organisation*, vol. 37, 1983.

29. I am drawing here and for the rest of this paragraph on P. O'Brien, 'Free Trade, British Hegemony and the International Economic Order in the Nineteenth Century' in J. Hobson and M. Mann, eds, *States and International Markets*, forthcoming.

30. I am indebted here to various unpublished papers on nineteenth century tariffs by John Hobson. For some conception of his important findings, see his 'The Autonomous Powers of the State: Economic Development under the Tsarist Regime', in Hobson and Mann, *States and International Markets*.

31. W. Sombart, *Handler und Helden*, Leipzig, 1915.

32. L. Davis and R. Huttenback, *Mammon and the Pursuit of Empire*, Cambridge, 1987; P. O'Brien, 'The Costs and Benefits of British Imperialism 1846–1914', *Past and Present*, No. 120, 1988.

33. There is a huge literature on this point, and it is well surveyed in J.M. Mann, 'From Market to Territory: German Economic Development up to World War I', in Hobson and Mann, *States and International Markets*. Cf. S. Van Evera's much cited 'The Cult of the Offensive and the Origins of the First World War', *International Security*, vol. 9, 1984.

34. I. Hull, *The Entourage of Kaiser Wilhelm II, 1888–1918*, Cambridge, 1983, p. 253.

35. There is now a substantial literature on this point; see, inter alia: C. Waisman, *Modernisation and the Working Class*, Austin, 1982; T. McDaniel, *Autocracy, Capitalism and Revolution in Russia*, Berkeley, 1987; I. Katznelson and A. Zolberg, eds, *Working Class Formation*, Princeton, 1987; J.M. Mann, 'Citizenship and Ruling Class Strategies', *Sociology*, vol. 21, 1987.

36. S.P Huntington, *Political Order in Changing Societies*, New Haven, 1968. Much is made of Huntingdon's work in an impressive essay from which I have learnt a great deal: J. Snyder, 'Averting Anarchy in the New Europe', *International Security*, vol. 14, 1990.

37. C.Nicolson, 'Edwardian England and the Coming of the First World War' in A. O'Day, ed., *The Edwardian Age: Conflict and Stability, 1900–1914*, London, 1979.

38. The classic account of the naivety of the majority of liberals in these years remains E.H. Carr, *The Twenty Years Crisis, 1919–1939*, London, 1951.

39. J.L. Gaddis, *The Long Peace: Inquiries into the History of the Cold War*, New York, 1987, ch. 8, 'The Long Peace: Elements of Stability in the Postwar International System', p. 220 and passim.

40. Gaddis, 'The Long Peace', pp. 233–7.

41. G. Lundestad, 'Empire by Invitation? The United States and Western Europe, 1945–52', *Journal of Peace Research*, vol. 23, 1986.

42. W. Domhoff, 'Defining the National Interest' and 'The Ruling Class Does Rule', unpublished papers; J. Frieden, 'Sectoral Conflict and US Foreign Economic Policy 1914–40', *International Organisation*, vol. 41, 1988.

43. R. Pollard, *Economic Security and the Origins of the Cold War*, 1945–50, New York, 1985.

44. One opponent of this view is A. Milward in *The Reconstruction of Western Europe, 1945–51*, London, 1984. He suggests that Europe's recovery was very much its own achievement, not least because the role of the capital provided by the Marshall Plan has been exaggerated. But the large amounts of European investment capital were forthcoming at least in part because of the climate of security that America's geopolitical commitment represented.

45. C. Maier, 'The Two Postwar Eras and the Conditions for Stability in Twentieth Century Europe', *American Historical Review*, vol. 86, 1981. There is much to be learnt from consulting two books by Maier: *Recasting Bourgeois Europe*, Princeton, 1975 and *In Search of Stability*, Cambridge, 1987.

46. J.G. Ruggie, 'International Regimes, Transactions and Change: Embedded Liberalism in the Postwar Economic Order', *International Organisation*, vol. 36, 1982.

47. Hall, 'Will the United States Decline as Did Britain?' Cf. J. Nye, *Bound to Lead*, New York, 1990.

48. Important early contributions to a necessary scepticism about the extent of America's decline are: B. Russett, 'The Mysterious Case of Vanishing Hegemony, or, Is Mark Twain Really Dead?', *International Organisation*, vol. 39, 1985; S. Strange, *Casino Capitalism*, Oxford, 1986 and 'The Persistent Myth of Lost Hegemony', *International Organisation*, vol. 41, 1987.

49. C.W. Maynes, 'America without the Cold War', *Foregn Policy*, vol. 77, 1990, p. 4.

50. Nye, *Bound to Lead*, introduction.

51. R. Keohane, *After Hegemony*, Princeton, 1984.

52. I.M. Destler and J. Odell, *Anti-Protection: Changing Forces in United States Trade Politics*, Washington, 1987; H. Milner, 'Resisting the Protectionist Temptation: Industry and the Making of Trade Policy in the United States during the 1970s', *International Organisation*, vol. 41, 1987.

53. Two particularly helpful accounts on which I have relied are R. Jervis, *The Meaning of the Nuclear Revolution: Statecraft and the Prospect of Armageddon*, Ithaca, 1989; McGeorge Bundy, *Danger and Survival: Choices about the Bomb in the First Fifty Years*, New York, 1988.

54. C. Kaysen, 'Is War Obsolete?', *International Security*, vol. 14, 1990.

55. Destler and Odell, *Anti-Protection*; Milner, 'Resisting the Protectionist Temptation'.

56. I draw here principally on C. Waisman, *Reversal of Development in Argentina*, Princeton, 1987; F.C. Deyo, ed., *The Political Economy of the New Asian Industrialism*, Ithaca, 1987; and N. Mouzelis, *Politics in the Semi-Periphery*, London, 1986.

57. E. Gellner, 'From the Revolution to Liberalisation', *Government and Opposition*, vol. 11, 1976. See also the marvellous exchange with Aron occasioned by this article: R. Aron, 'On Liberalisation' and E. Gellner, 'Plaidoyer pour une libéralisation manquée', *Government and Opposition*, vol. 14, 1979.

58. J.A. Hall, 'Classes and Elites, Wars and Social Evolution', *Sociology*, vol. 22, 1988.

59. M. Howard, 'Prison that history built comes tumbling down', *Guardian Weekly*, 25 March, 1990, p. 11.

60. G. Blainey, *The Causes of Wars*, London, 1973, p. 53, cited in Gaddis, 'The Long Peace', p. 229.

61. M. Howard, 'A Death Knell for War?', *New York Times Book Review*, 30 April, 1989, p. 14.

62. Z. Brzezinski 'Post-Communist Nationalism', *Foreign Affairs*, vol. 68, 1989; G. Hosking, *The Awakening of the Soviet Union*, London, 1989, especially ch. 5.

63. Snyder, 'Averting Anarchy'.

64. R. Broad and J. Cavanagh, 'No More NICS', *Foreign Policy*, no. 72, 1988.

# Name index

# Subject index

375